LOVELESS

Volume 4

HAMBURG // LONDON // LOS ANGELES // TOKYO

Loveless Volume 4
Created by Yun Kouga

Translation - Ray Yoshimoto
English Adaptation - Christine Boylan
Copy Editor - Stephanie Duchin
Retouch and Lettering - Star Print Brokers
Production Artist - Kimie Kim
Graphic Designer - Al-Insan Lashley

Editor - Lillian Diaz-Przybyl
Digital Imaging Manager - Chris Buford
Pre-Production Supervisor - Erika Terriquez
Art Director - Anne Marie Horne
Production Manager - Elisabeth Brizzi
Managing Editor - Vy Nguyen
VP of Production - Ron Klamert
Editor-in-Chief - Rob Tokar
Publisher - Mike Kiley
President and C.O.O. - John Parker
C.E.O. and Chief Creative Officer - Stuart Levy

A  Manga

TOKYOPOP Inc.
5900 Wilshire Blvd. Suite 2000
Los Angeles, CA 90036

E-mail: info@TOKYOPOP.com
Come visit us online at www.TOKYOPOP.com

LOVELESS Volume 4 © 2004 by Yun Kouga.
All rights reserved. First published in Japan in 2004 by
ICHIJINSHA, Tokyo. English translation rights in the United
States of America and Canada arranged with ICHIJINSHA
through Tuttle-Mori Agency, Inc., Tokyo
English text copyright © 2007 TOKYOPOP Inc.

ISBN: 978-1-59816-224-0

First TOKYOPOP printing: February 2007
10 9 8 7 6 5 4 3 2 1
Printed in the USA

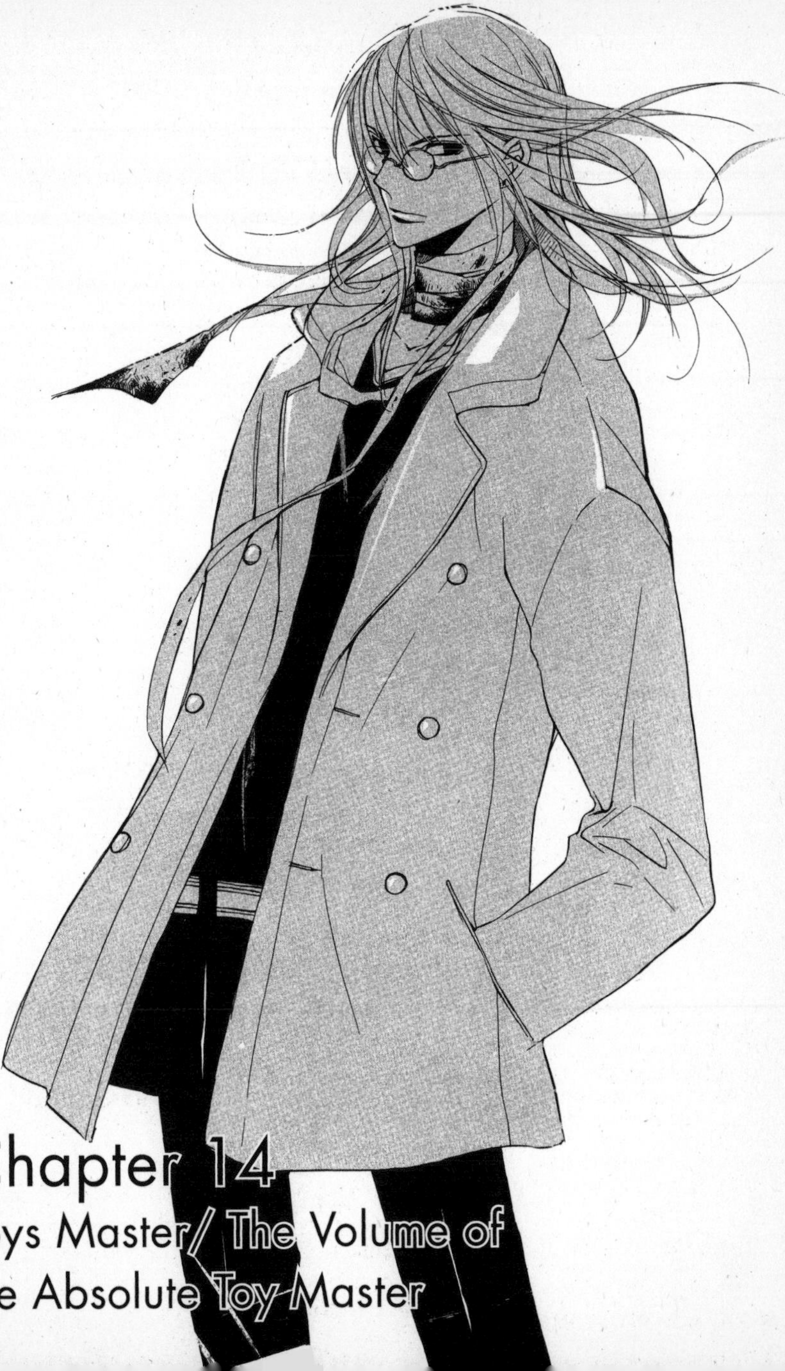

Chapter 14

Toys Master/ The Volume of the Absolute Toy Master

The time for games is over.
If you want to set the world ablaze...

...lay down your weapons.

There is nothing to fear.

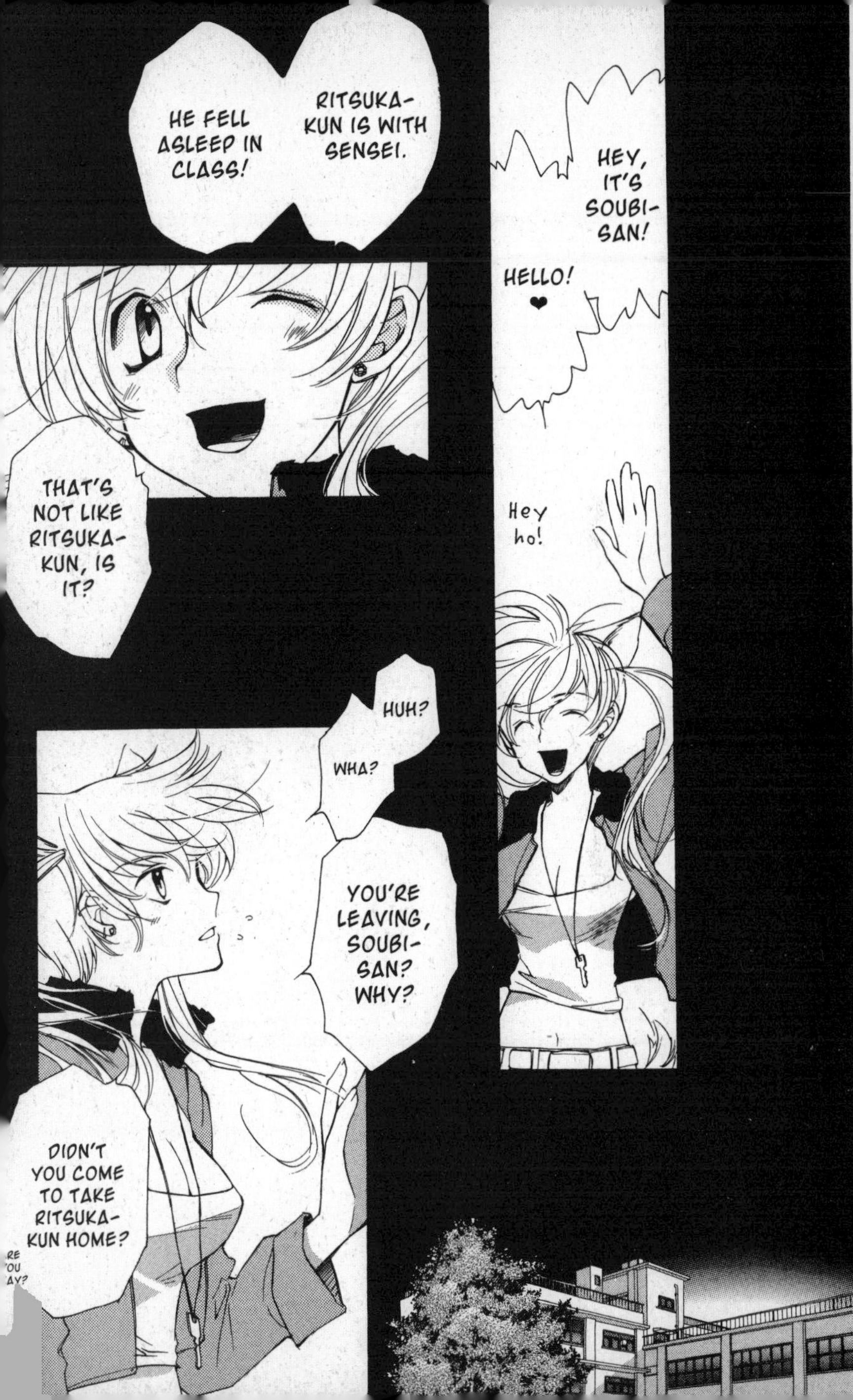
HEY, IT'S SOUBI-SAN!
HELLO! ❤
Hey ho!
RITSUKA-KUN IS WITH SENSEI.
HE FELL ASLEEP IN CLASS!
THAT'S NOT LIKE RITSUKA-KUN, IS IT?
HUH?
WHA?
YOU'RE LEAVING, SOUBI-SAN? WHY?
DIDN'T YOU COME TO TAKE RITSUKA-KUN HOME?

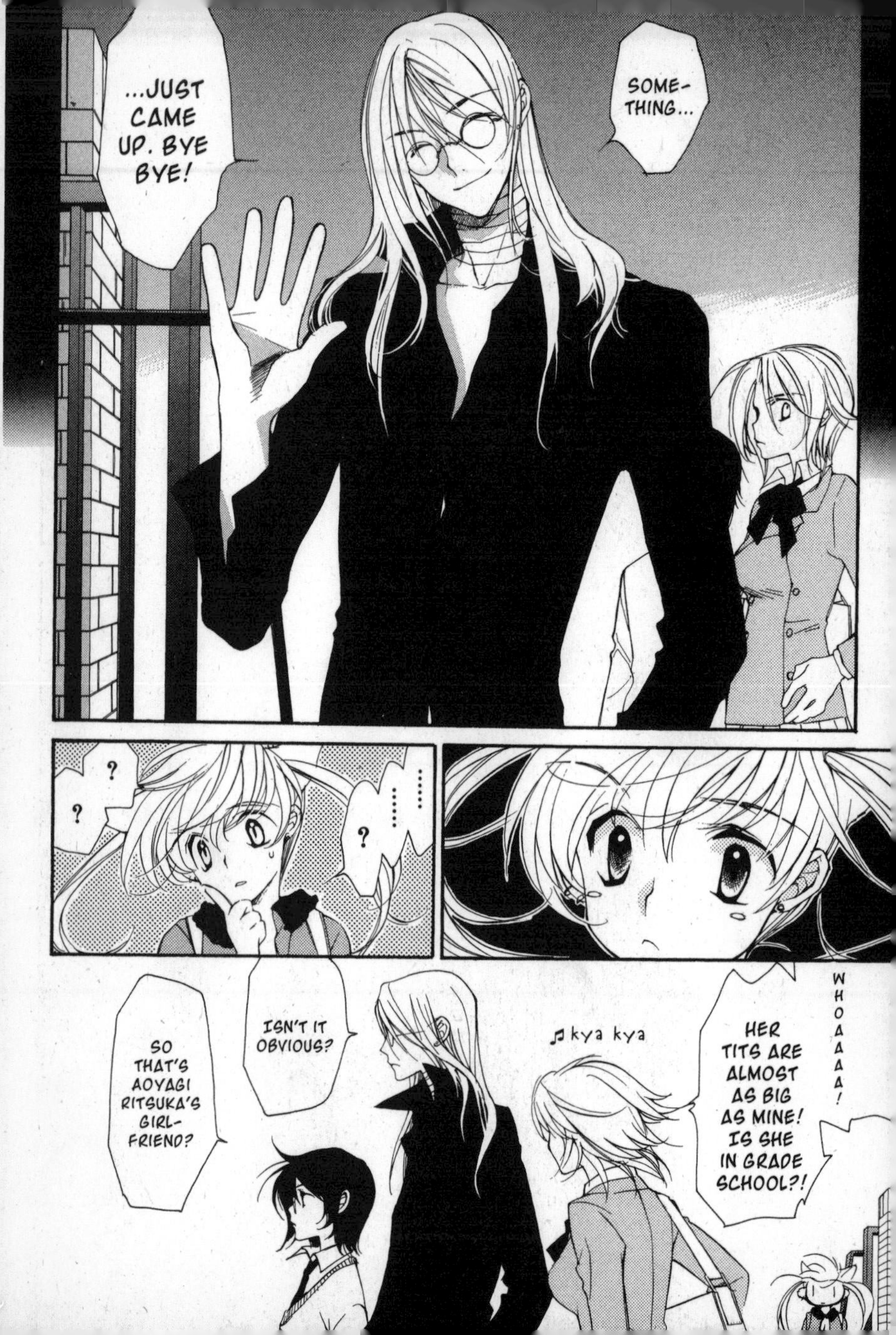
SOME-THING...
...JUST CAME UP. BYE BYE!
?
?
?
......
WHOAAAAA!
HER TITS ARE ALMOST AS BIG AS MINE! IS SHE IN GRADE SCHOOL?!
♫kya kya
ISN'T IT OBVIOUS?
SO THAT'S AOYAGI RITSUKA'S GIRL-FRIEND?

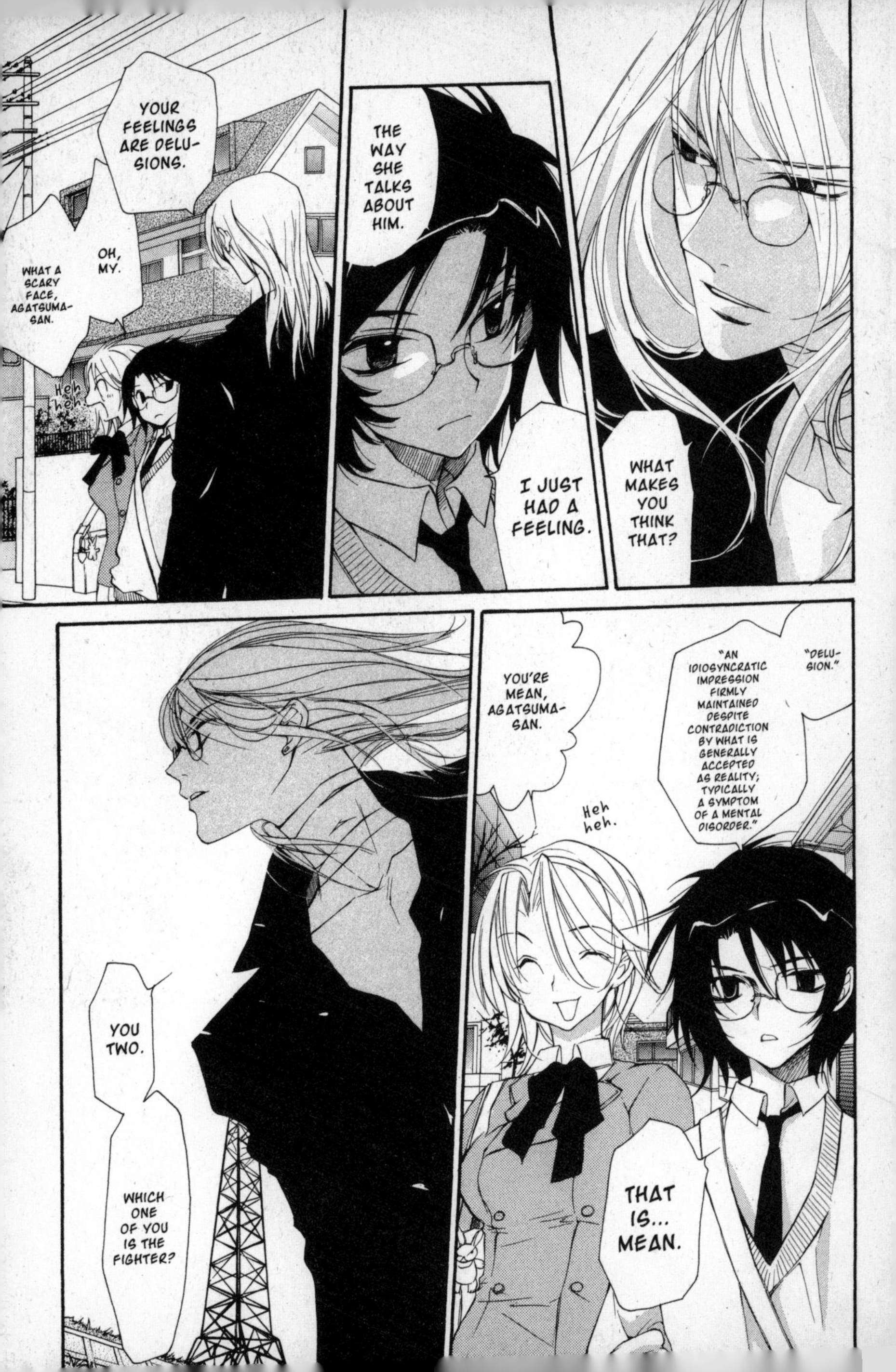
WHAT MAKES YOU THINK THAT?
I JUST HAD A FEELING.
THE WAY SHE TALKS ABOUT HIM.
YOUR FEELINGS ARE DELUSIONS.
OH, MY.
WHAT A SCARY FACE, AGATSUMA-SAN.
Heh heh.
"DELUSION."
"AN IDIOSYNCRATIC IMPRESSION FIRMLY MAINTAINED DESPITE CONTRADICTION BY WHAT IS GENERALLY ACCEPTED AS REALITY; TYPICALLY A SYMPTOM OF A MENTAL DISORDER."
YOU'RE MEAN, AGATSUMA-SAN.
Heh heh.
THAT IS... MEAN.
YOU TWO.
WHICH ONE OF YOU IS THE FIGHTER?

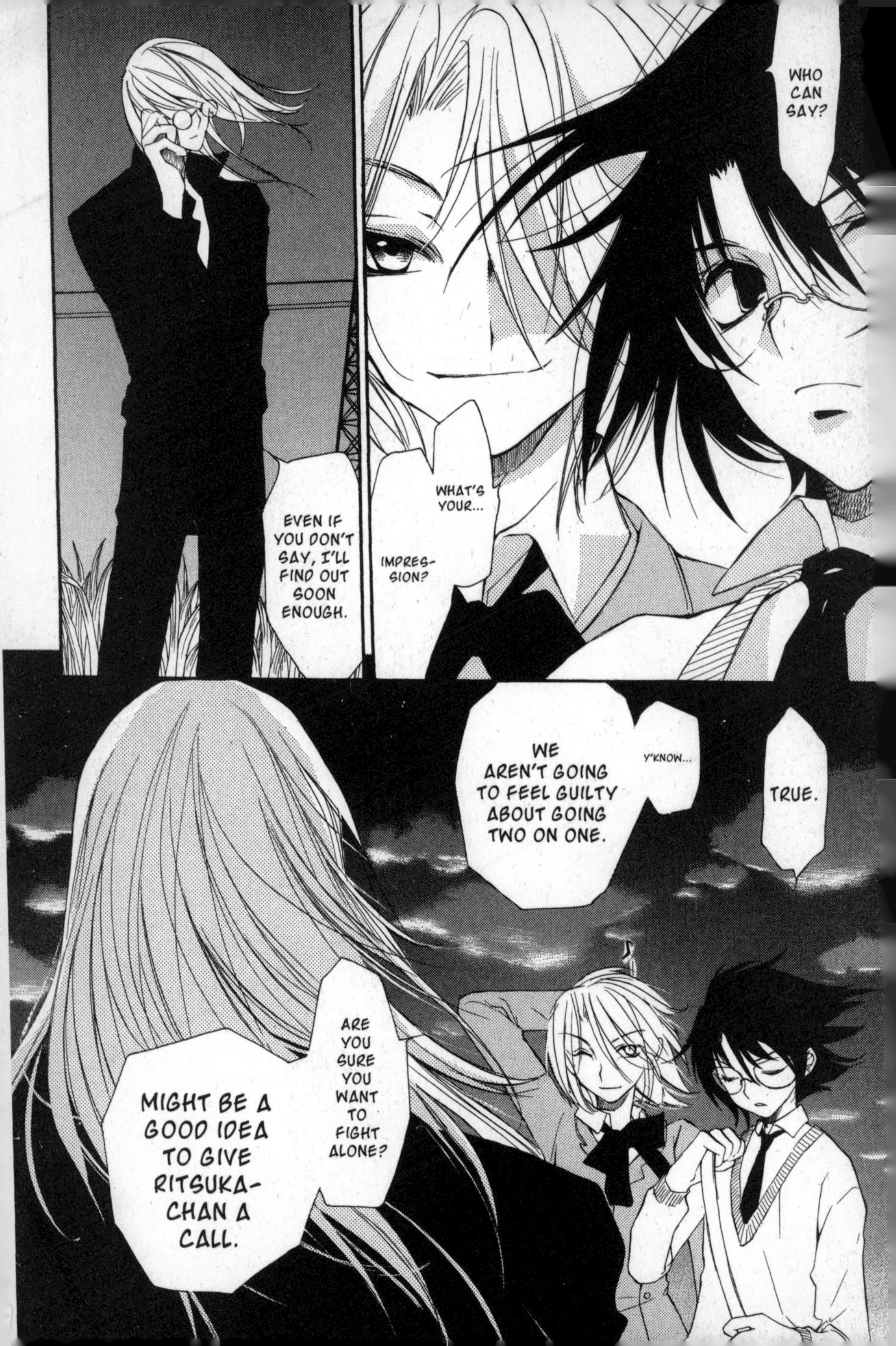
WHO CAN SAY?
WHAT'S YOUR...
IMPRESSION?
EVEN IF YOU DON'T SAY, I'LL FIND OUT SOON ENOUGH.
TRUE.
Y'KNOW...
WE AREN'T GOING TO FEEL GUILTY ABOUT GOING TWO ON ONE.
ARE YOU SURE YOU WANT TO FIGHT ALONE?
MIGHT BE A GOOD IDEA TO GIVE RITSUKA-CHAN A CALL.

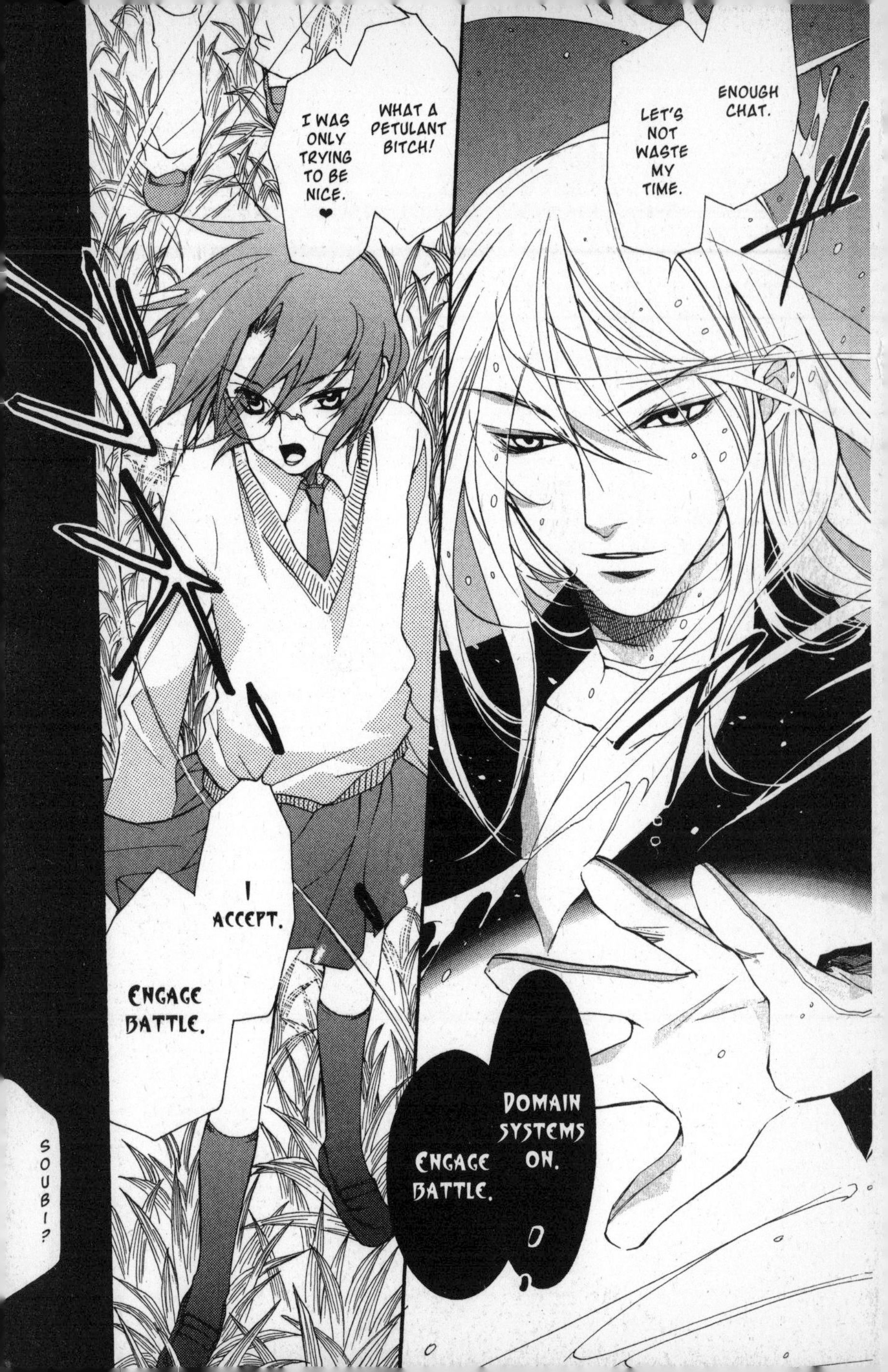
ENOUGH CHAT.
LET'S NOT WASTE MY TIME.
DOMAIN SYSTEMS ON.
ENGAGE BATTLE.
WHAT A PETULANT BITCH!
I WAS ONLY TRYING TO BE NICE. ❤
I ACCEPT.
ENGAGE BATTLE.
SOUBI?

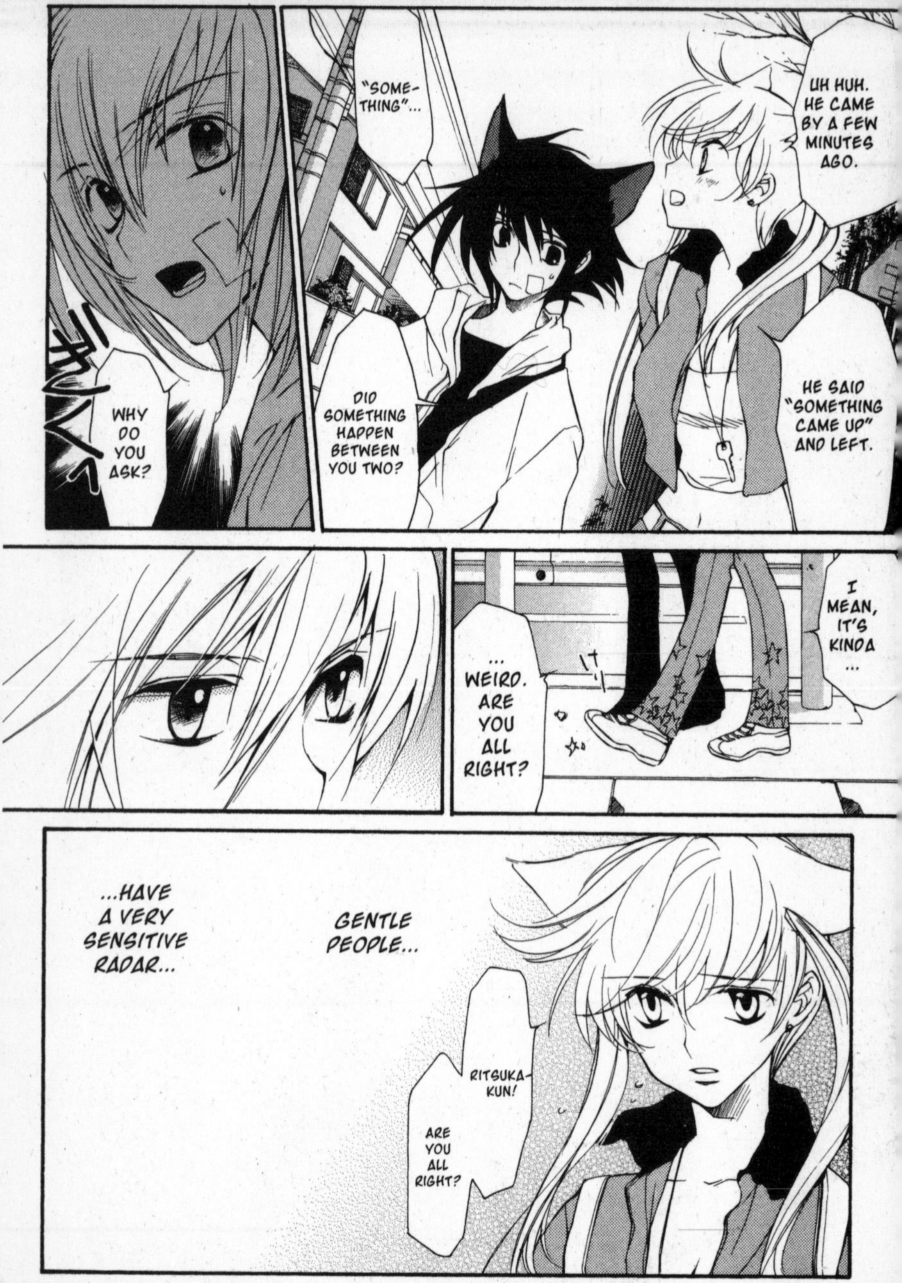
UH HUH. HE CAME BY A FEW MINUTES AGO.
HE SAID "SOMETHING CAME UP" AND LEFT.
"SOME-THING"...
DID SOMETHING HAPPEN BETWEEN YOU TWO?
WHY DO YOU ASK?
I MEAN, IT'S KINDA ...
... WEIRD. ARE YOU ALL RIGHT?
GENTLE PEOPLE...
...HAVE A VERY SENSITIVE RADAR...
RITSUKA-KUN!
ARE YOU ALL RIGHT?

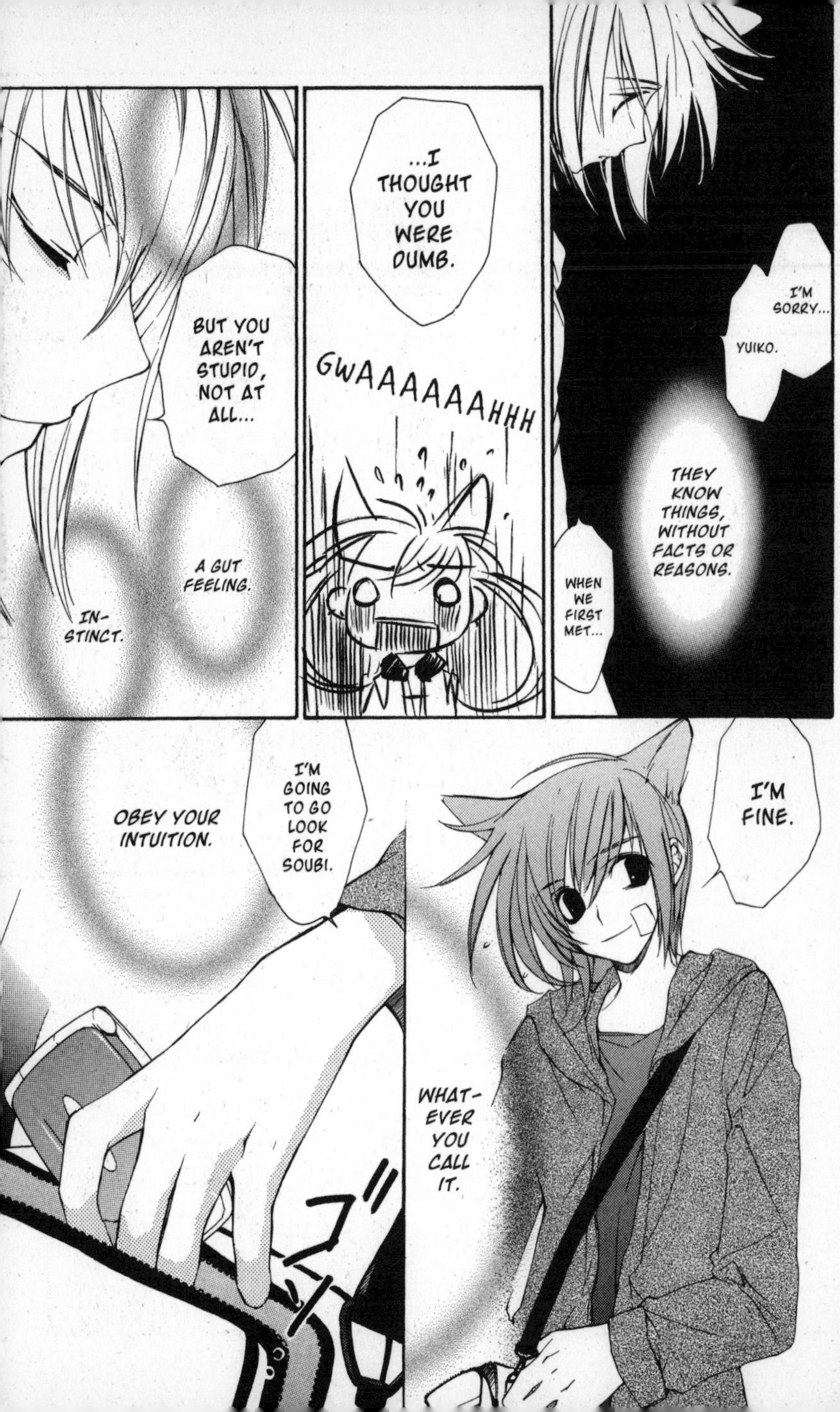
I'M SORRY...
YUIKO.
THEY KNOW THINGS, WITHOUT FACTS OR REASONS.
WHEN WE FIRST MET...
...I THOUGHT YOU WERE DUMB.
GWAAAAAAAHHH
BUT YOU AREN'T STUPID, NOT AT ALL...
A GUT FEELING.
IN-STINCT.
I'M FINE.
WHAT-EVER YOU CALL IT.
I'M GOING TO GO LOOK FOR SOUBI.
OBEY YOUR INTUITION.

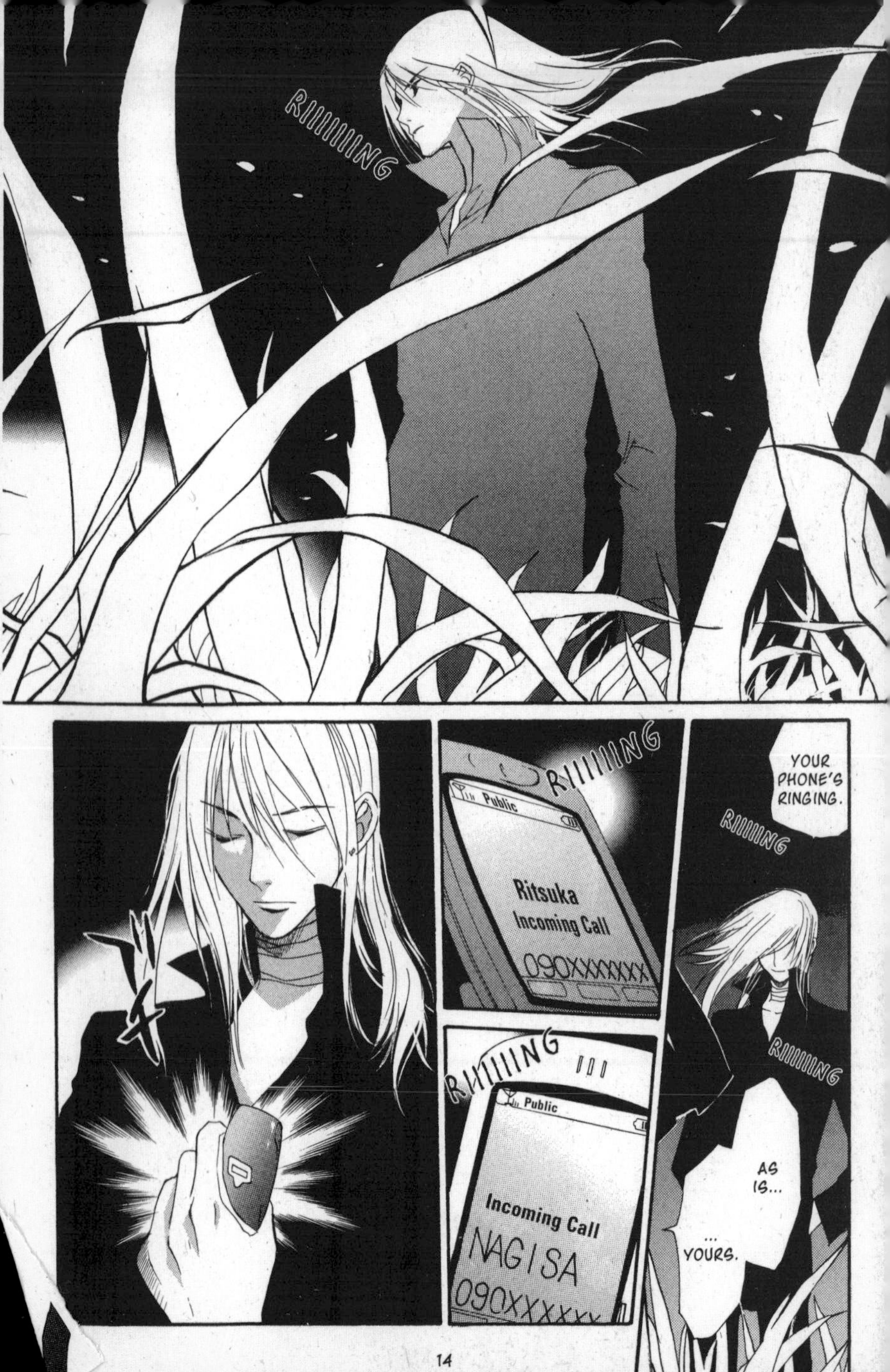
RIIIIIIIING
YOUR PHONE'S RINGING.
RIIIIING
RIIIIIING
AS IS...
... YOURS.
RIIIIIIING
Public
Ritsuka
Incoming Call
090XXXXXXX
RIIIIIING
Public
Incoming Call
NAGISA
090XXXXX

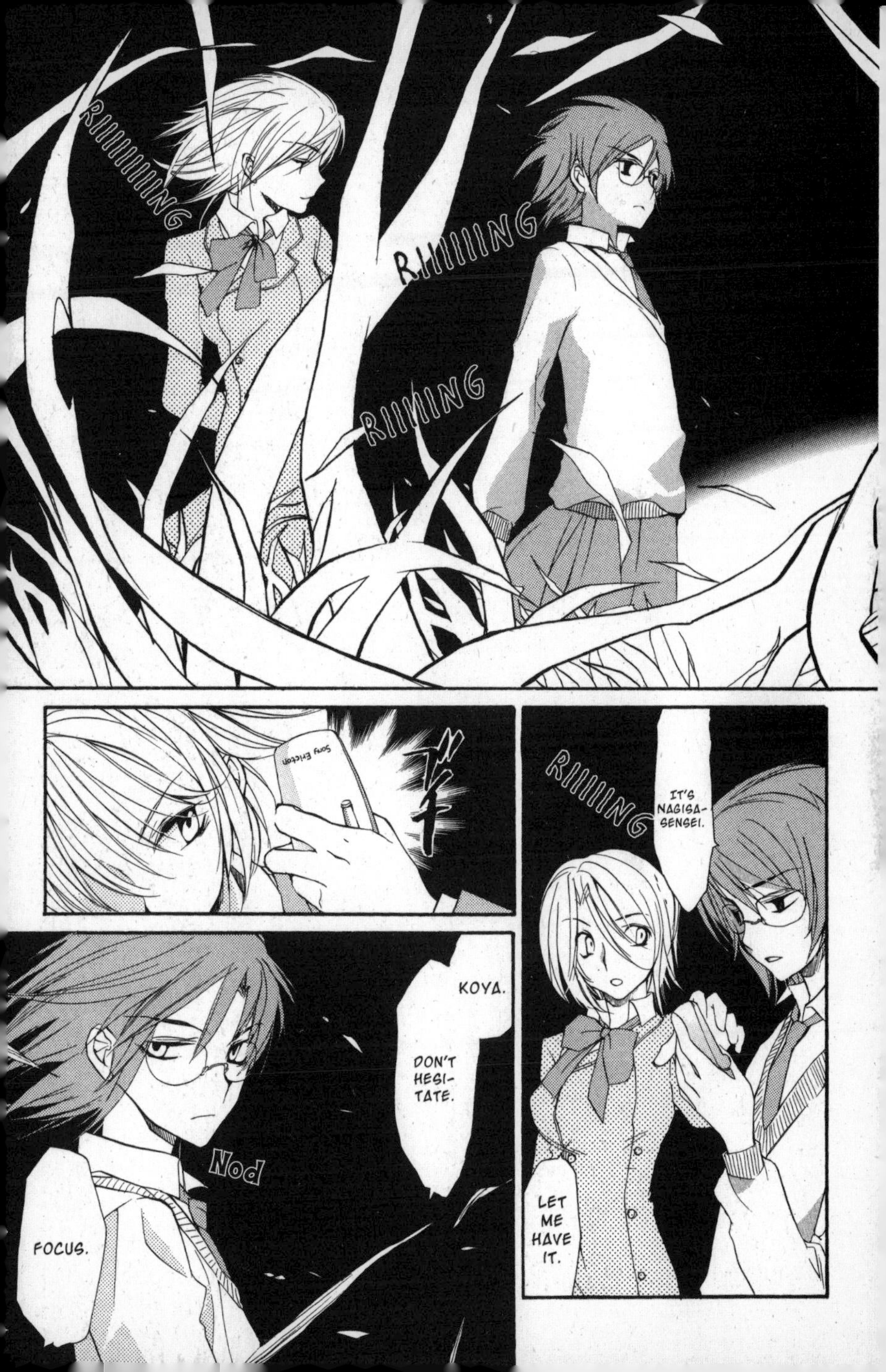

RIIIIIING
RIIIIING
RIIIIIIIIING
RIIIIING
IT'S NAGISA-SENSEI.
LET ME HAVE IT.
KOYA.
DON'T HESI-TATE.
Nod
FOCUS.

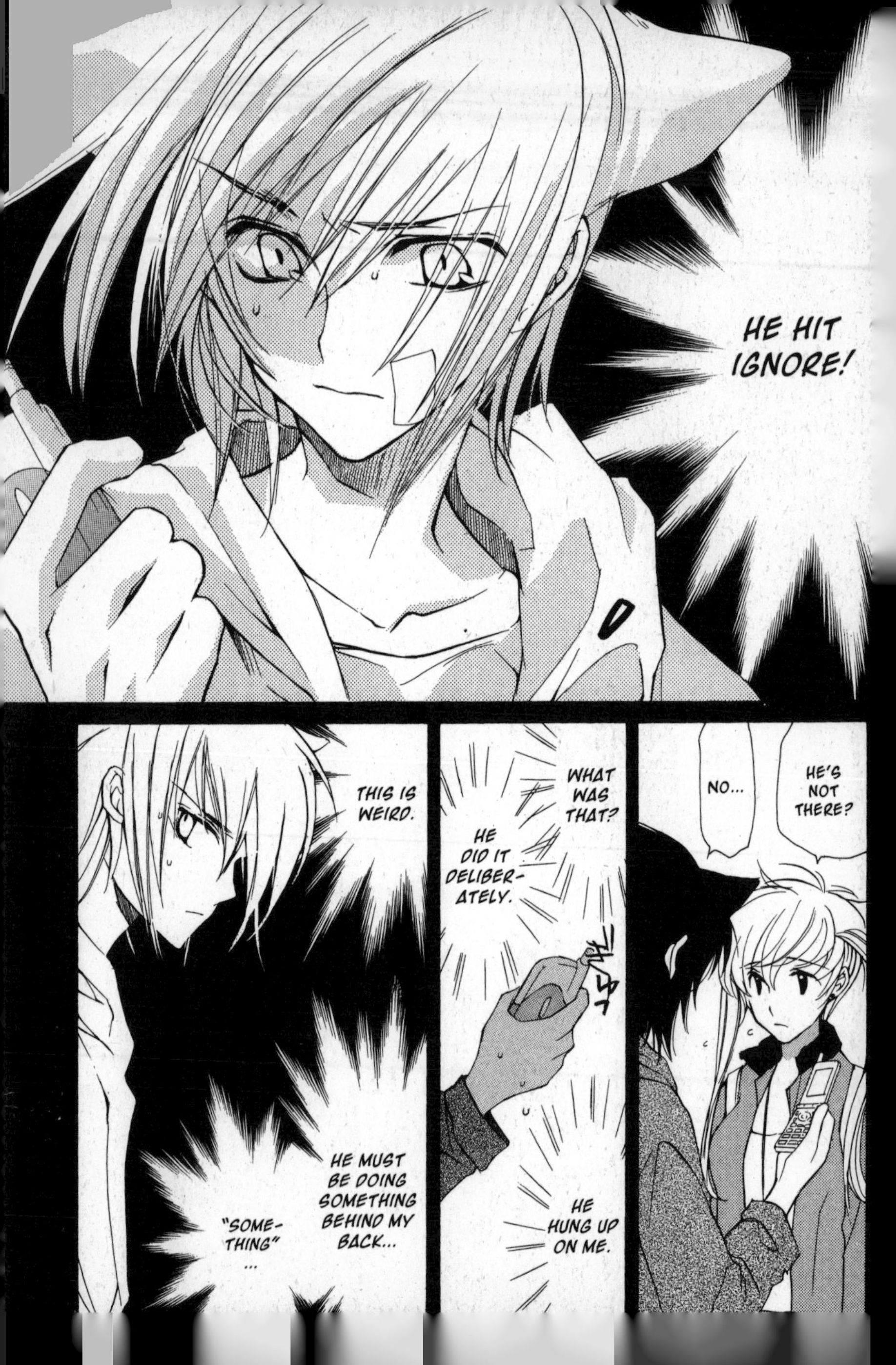
HE HIT IGNORE!
HE'S NOT THERE?
NO...
WHAT WAS THAT?
HE DID IT DELIBERATELY.
HE HUNG UP ON ME.
THIS IS WEIRD.
HE MUST BE DOING SOMETHING BEHIND MY BACK...
"SOME-THING"...

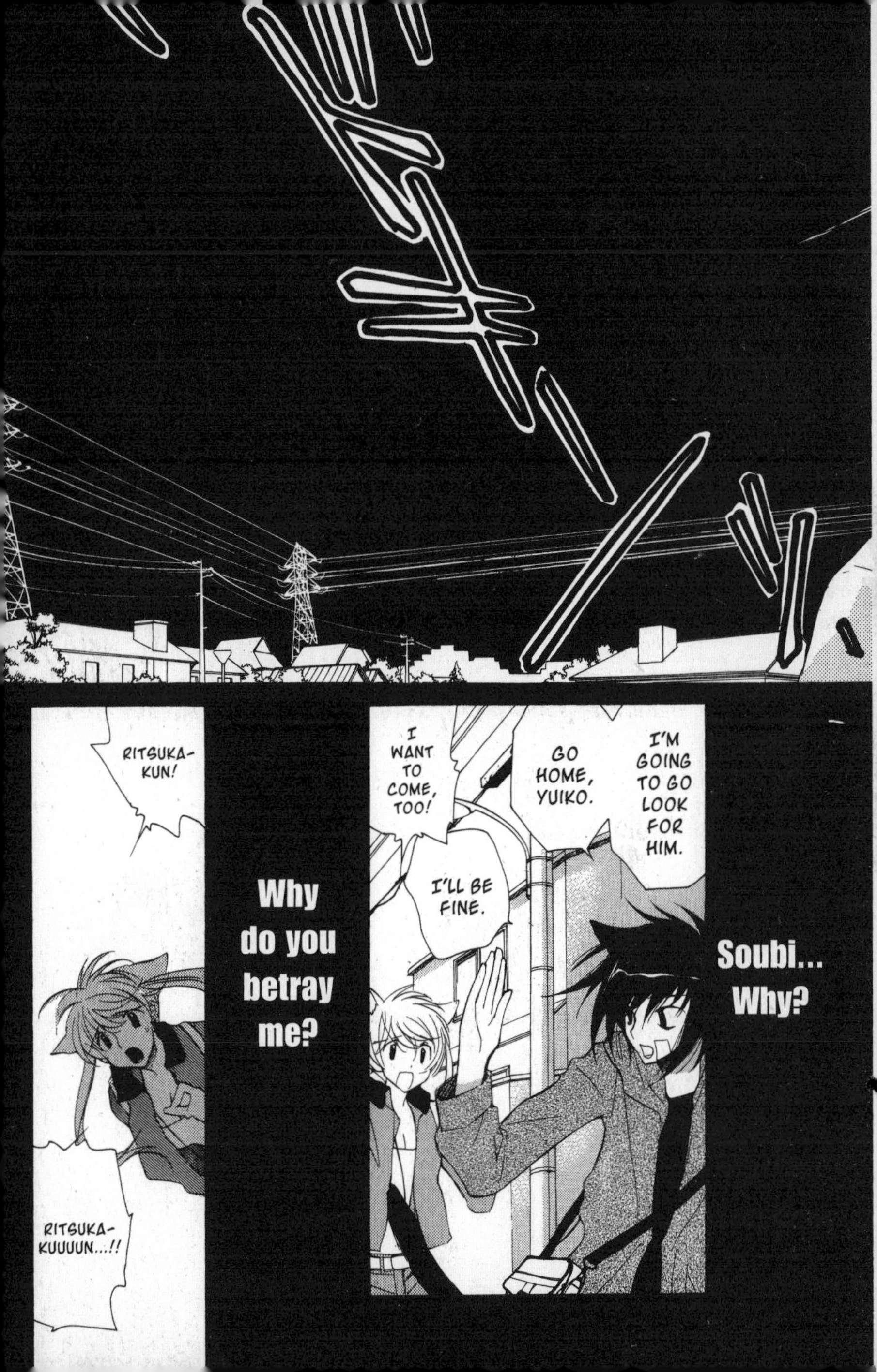
Soubi... Why?
I'M GOING TO GO LOOK FOR HIM.
GO HOME, YUIKO.
I WANT TO COME, TOO!
I'LL BE FINE.
Why do you betray me?
RITSUKA-KUN!
RITSUKA-KUUUUN...!!

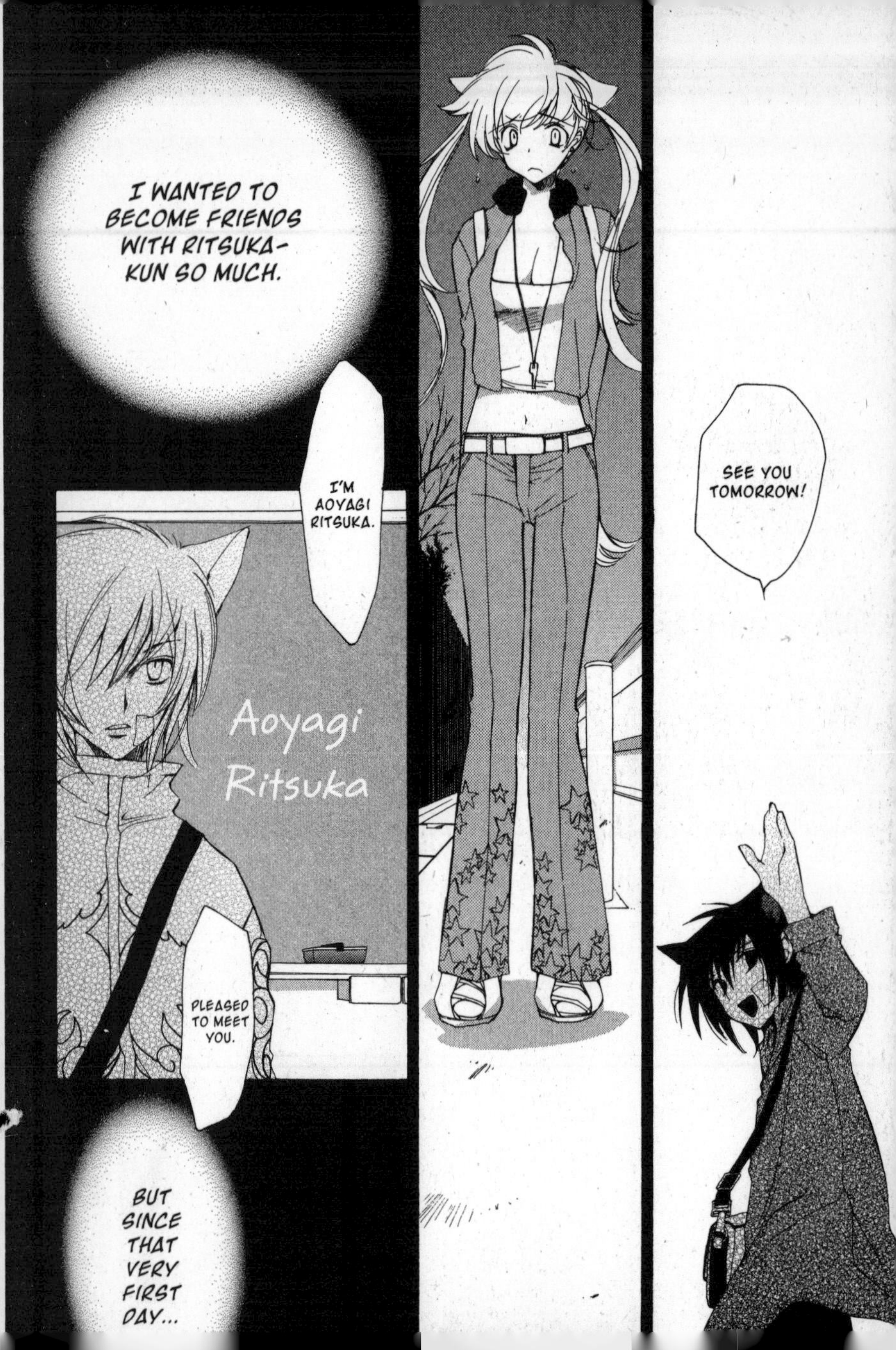
SEE YOU TOMORROW!
I WANTED TO BECOME FRIENDS WITH RITSUKA-KUN SO MUCH.
I'M AOYAGI RITSUKA.
Aoyagi Ritsuka
PLEASED TO MEET YOU.
BUT SINCE THAT VERY FIRST DAY...

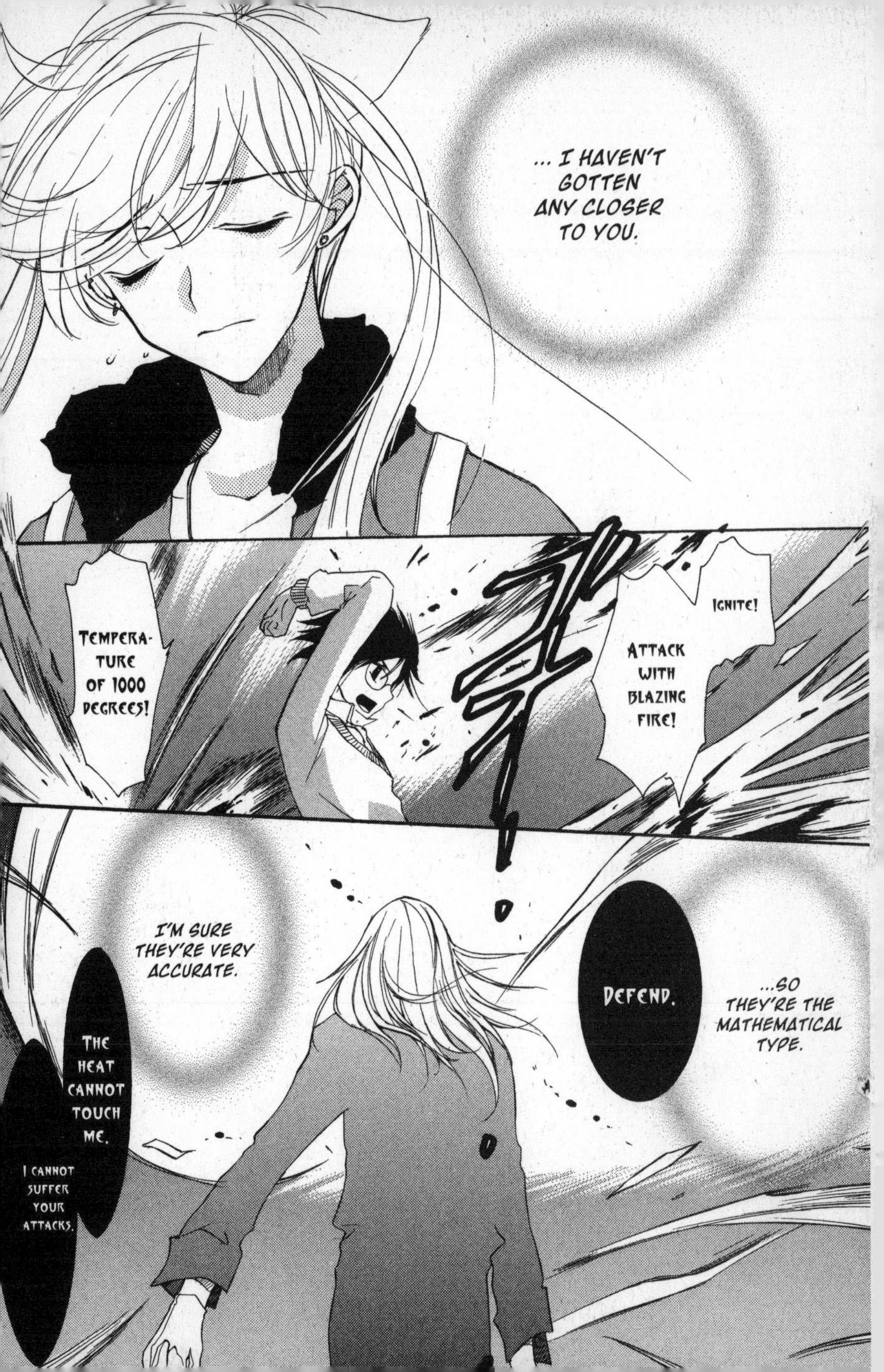

... I HAVEN'T GOTTEN ANY CLOSER TO YOU.
IGNITE!
ATTACK WITH BLAZING FIRE!
TEMPERA-TURE OF 1000 DEGREES!
...SO THEY'RE THE MATHEMATICAL TYPE.
DEFEND.
I'M SURE THEY'RE VERY ACCURATE.
THE HEAT CANNOT TOUCH ME.
I CANNOT SUFFER YOUR ATTACKS.

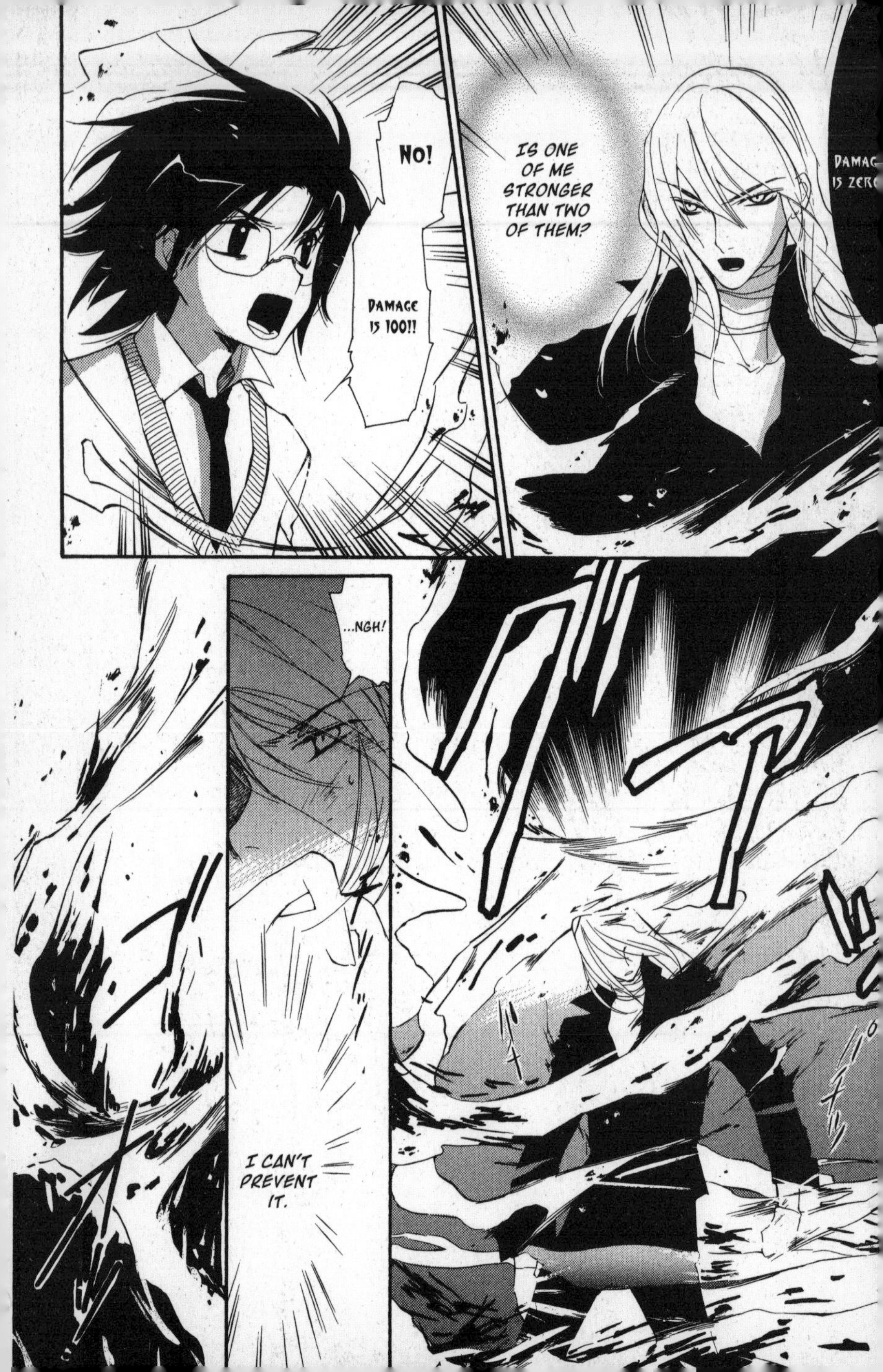
DAMAG IS ZER
IS ONE OF ME STRONGER THAN TWO OF THEM?
NO!
DAMAGE IS 100!!
...NGH!
I CAN'T PREVENT IT.

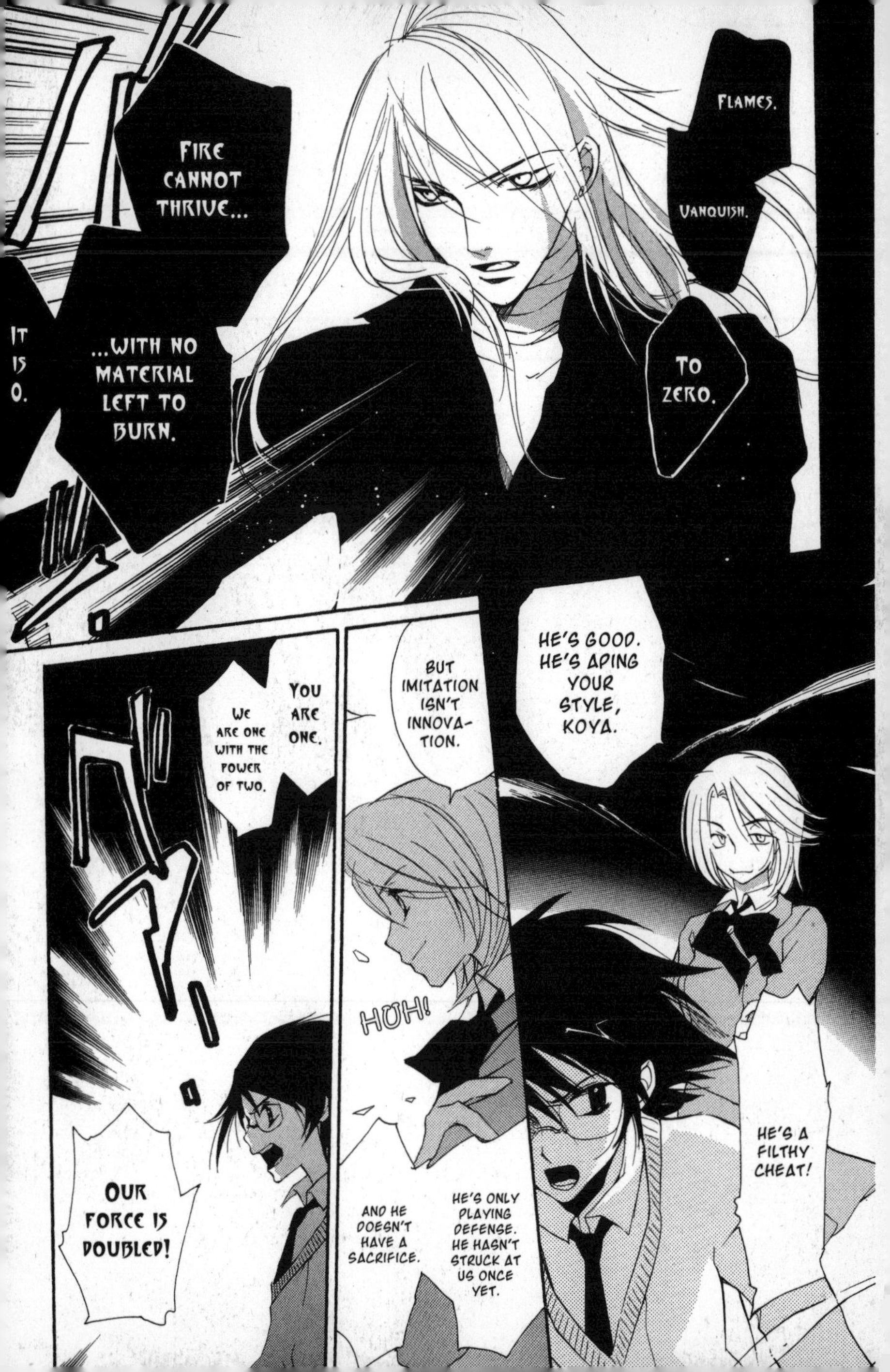
Flames.
Vanquish.
To zero.
Fire cannot thrive...
...with no material left to burn.
It is 0.
He's good. He's aping your style, Koya.
He's a filthy cheat!
But imitation isn't innovation.
Huh!
He's only playing defense. He hasn't struck at us once yet.
And he doesn't have a sacrifice.
You are one.
We are one with the power of two.
Our force is doubled!

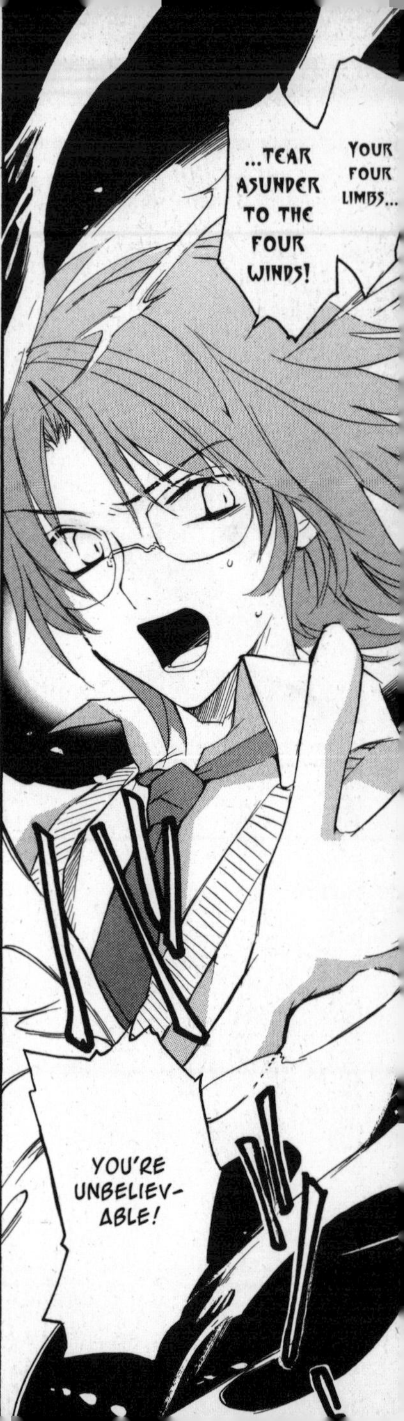
YOUR FOUR LIMBS...
...TEAR ASUNDER TO THE FOUR WINDS!
YOU'RE UNBELIEV-ABLE!

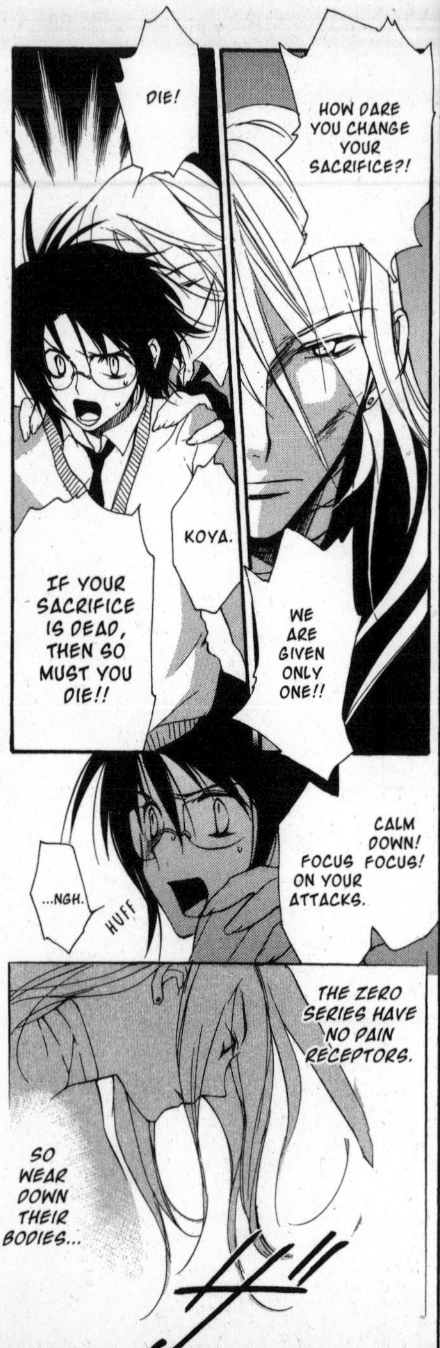
HOW DARE YOU CHANGE YOUR SACRIFICE?!
KOYA.
WE ARE GIVEN ONLY ONE!!
DIE!
IF YOUR SACRIFICE IS DEAD, THEN SO MUST YOU DIE!!
CALM DOWN! FOCUS!
FOCUS ON YOUR ATTACKS.
HUFF
...NGH.
THE ZERO SERIES HAVE NO PAIN RECEPTORS.
SO WEAR DOWN THEIR BODIES...

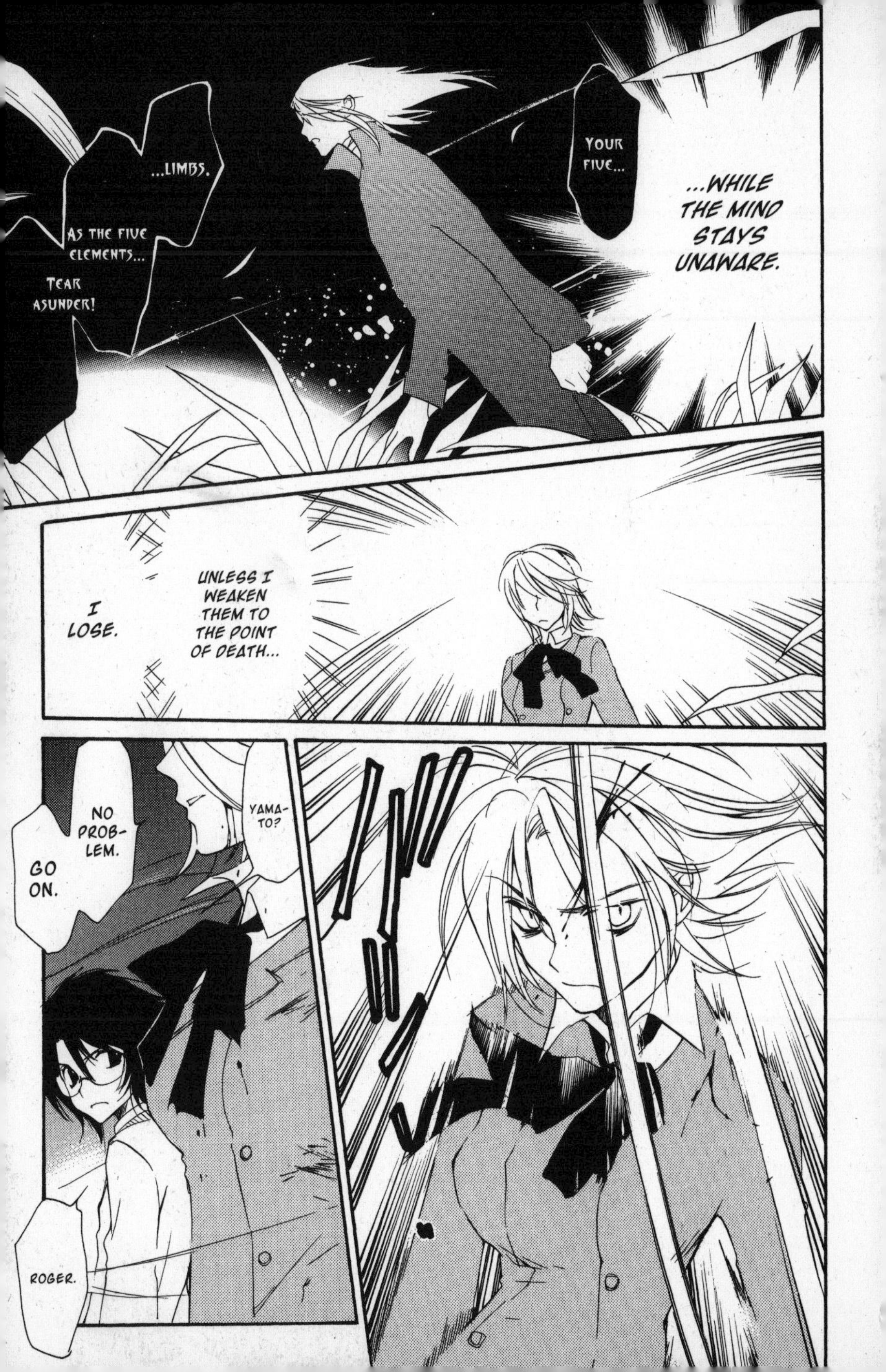
...WHILE THE MIND STAYS UNAWARE.
YOUR FIVE...
...LIMBS.
AS THE FIVE ELEMENTS...
TEAR ASUNDER!
UNLESS I WEAKEN THEM TO THE POINT OF DEATH...
I LOSE.
YAMA-TO?
NO PROB-LEM.
GO ON.
ROGER.

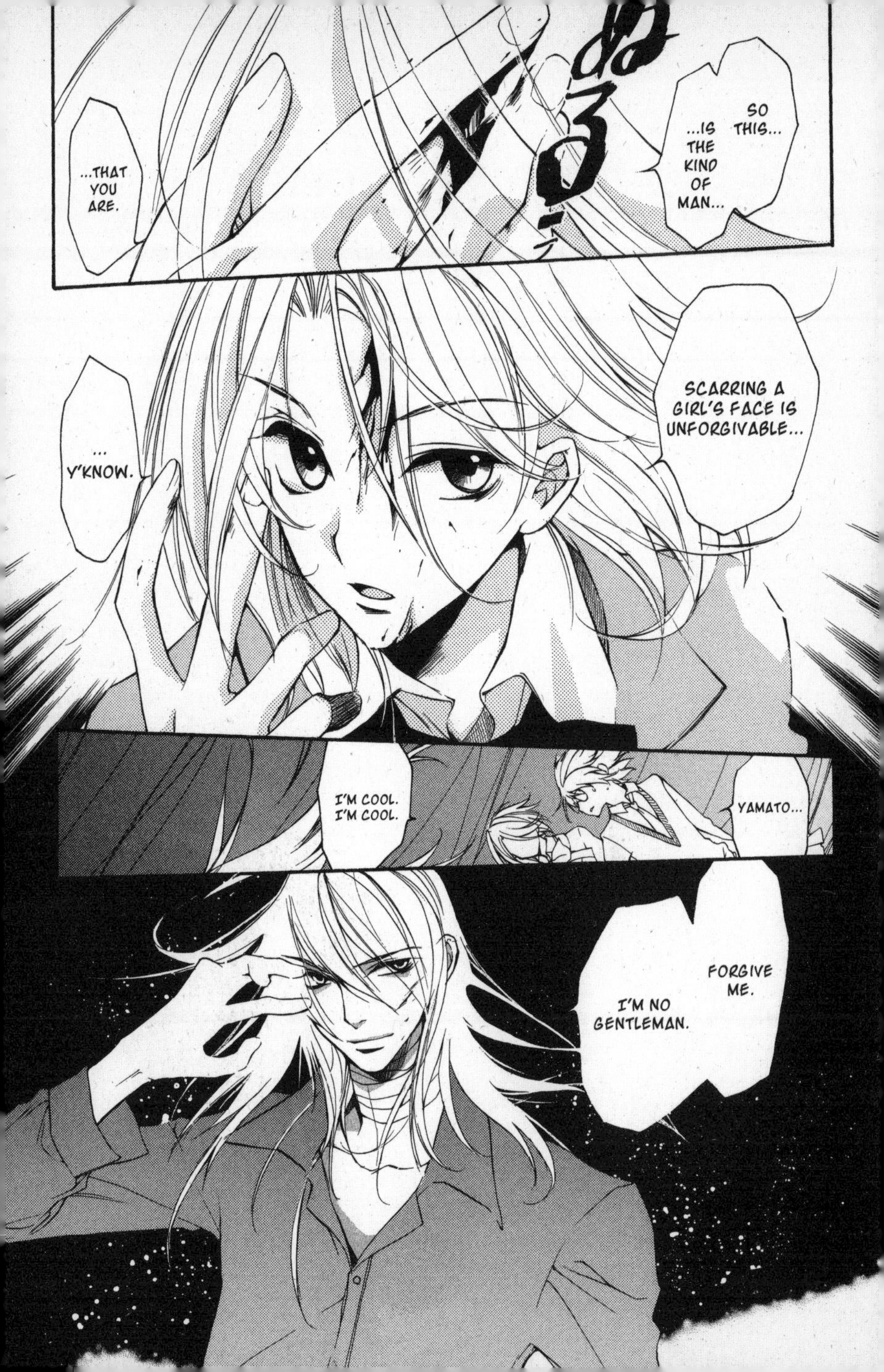
SO THIS...
...IS THE KIND OF MAN...
...THAT YOU ARE.
SCARRING A GIRL'S FACE IS UNFORGIVABLE...
... Y'KNOW.
YAMATO...
I'M COOL. I'M COOL.
FORGIVE ME.
I'M NO GENTLEMAN.

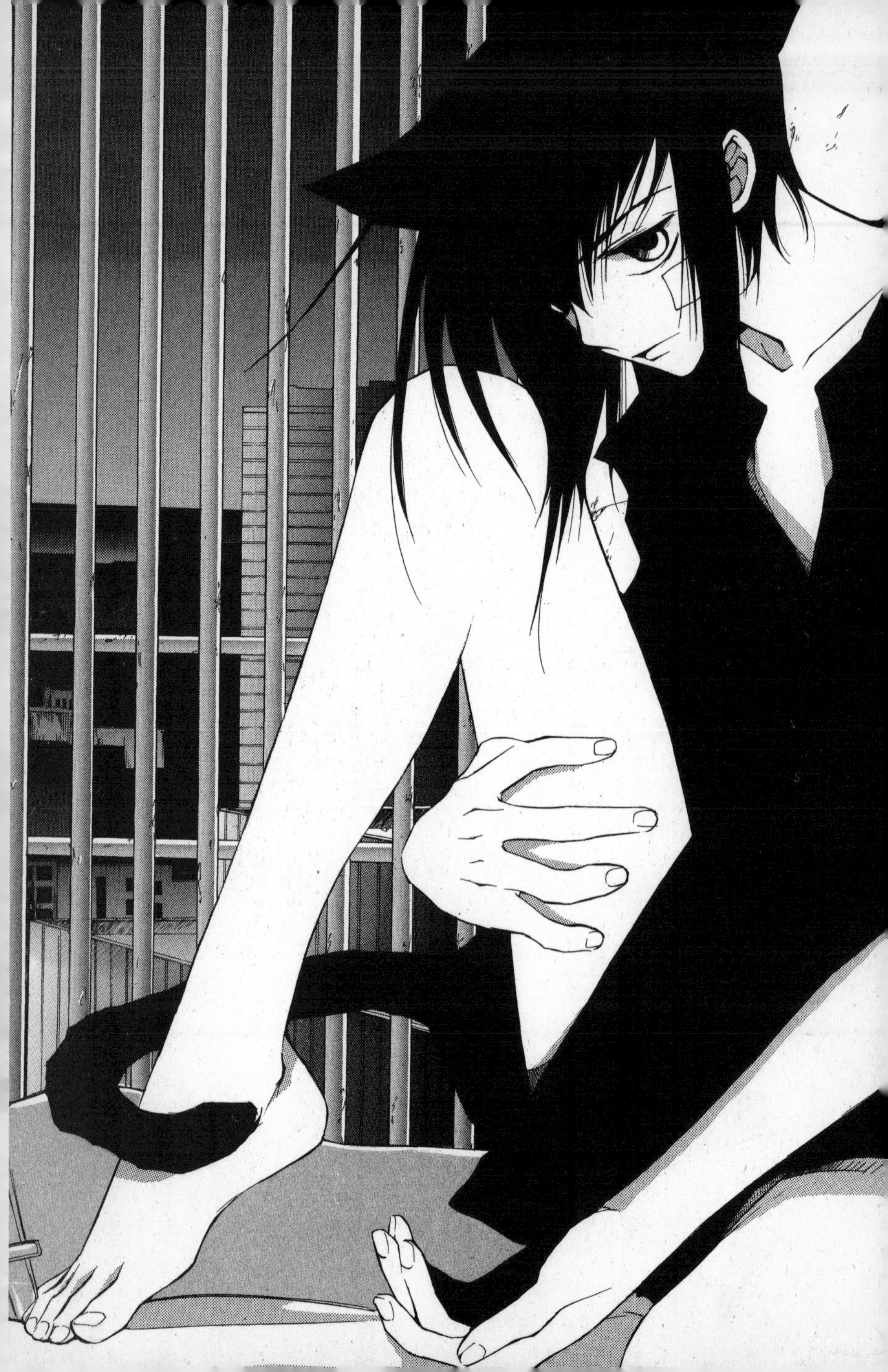

Chapter 15

Toys Master / The Volume of the Absolute Toy Master

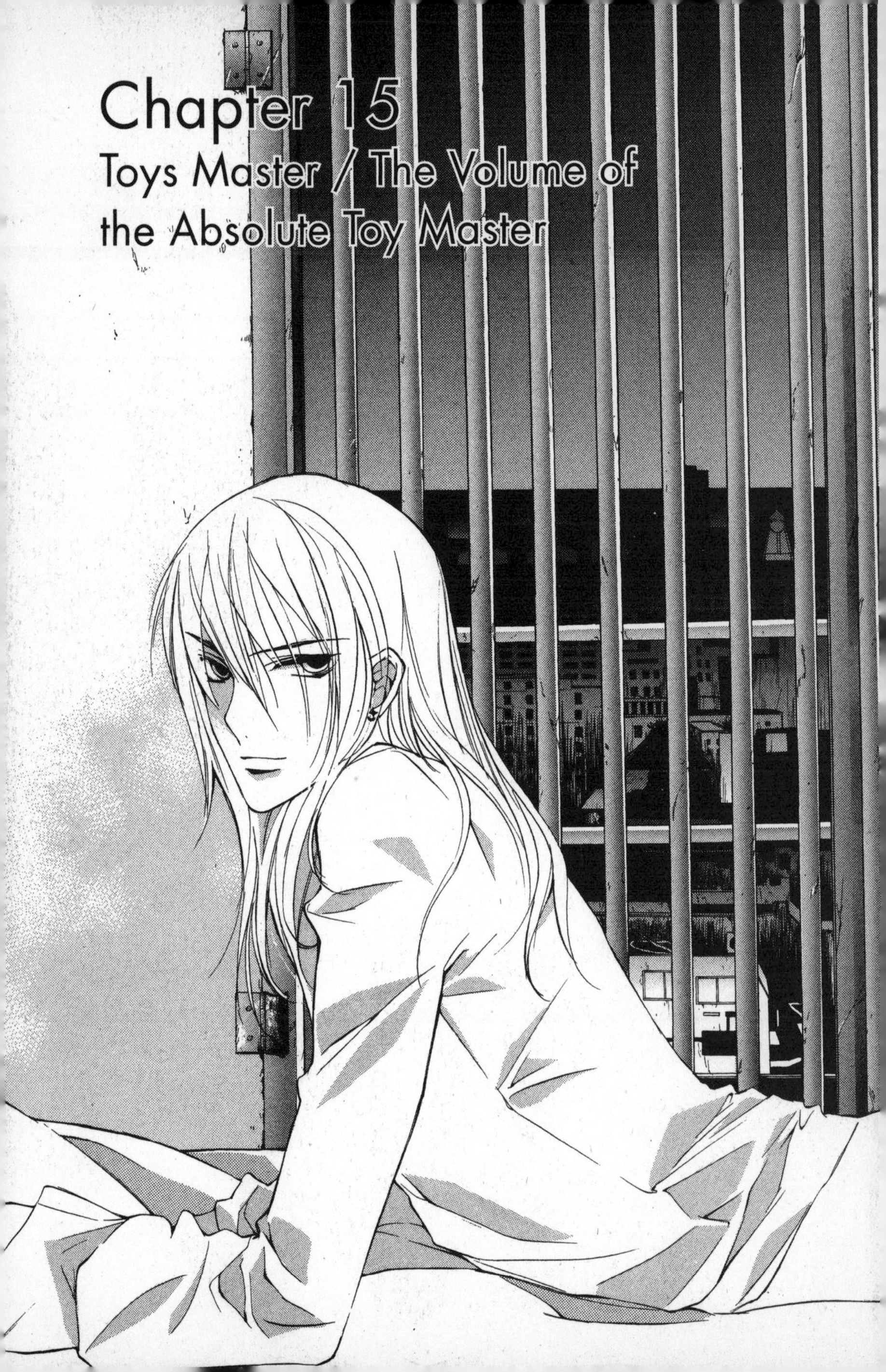

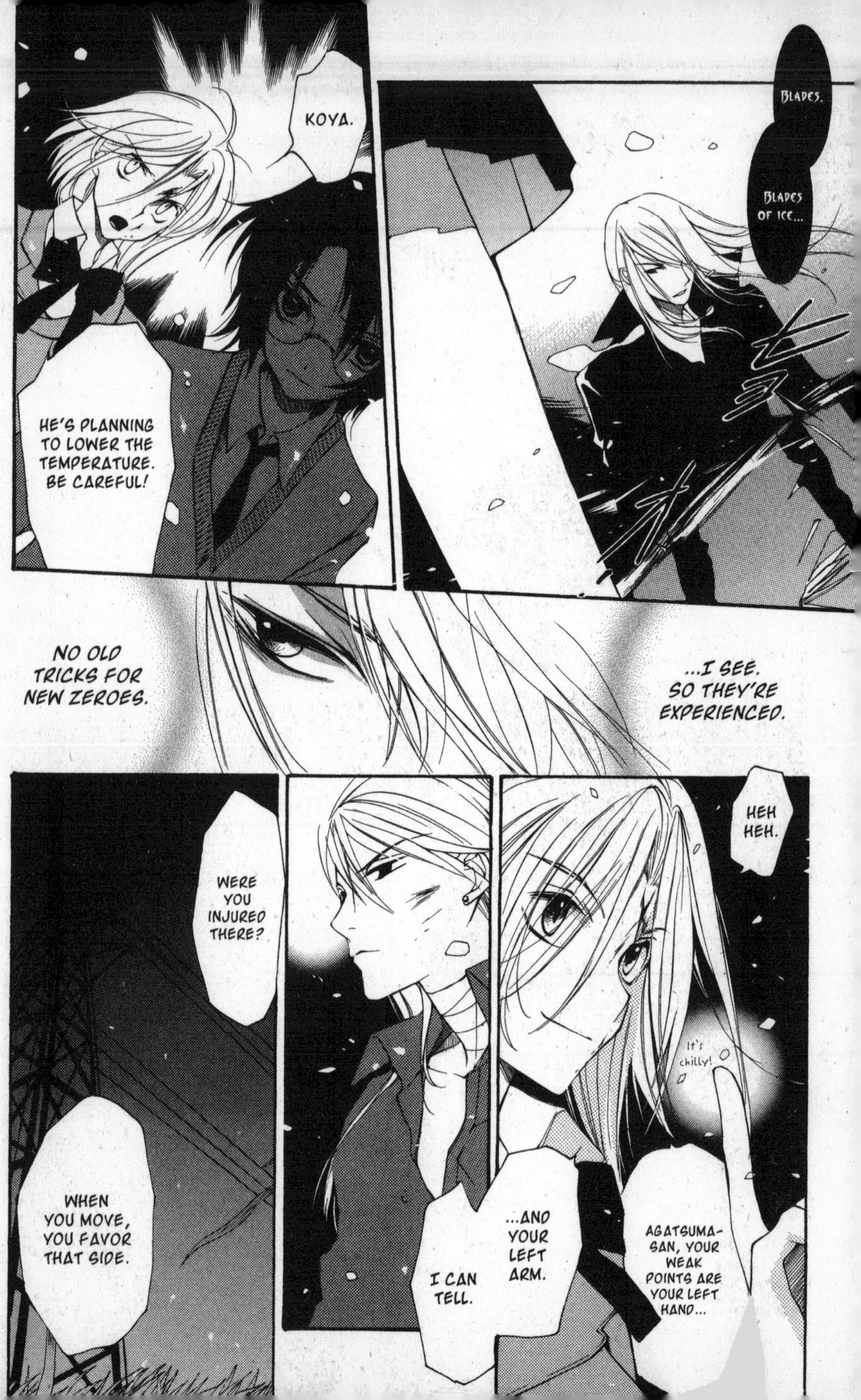
Blades.
Blades of ice...
Koya.
He's planning to lower the temperature. Be careful!
...I see. So they're experienced.
No old tricks for new zeroes.
Heh heh.
It's chilly!
Agatsuma-san, your weak points are your left hand...
...and your left arm.
I can tell.
Were you injured there?
When you move, you favor that side.

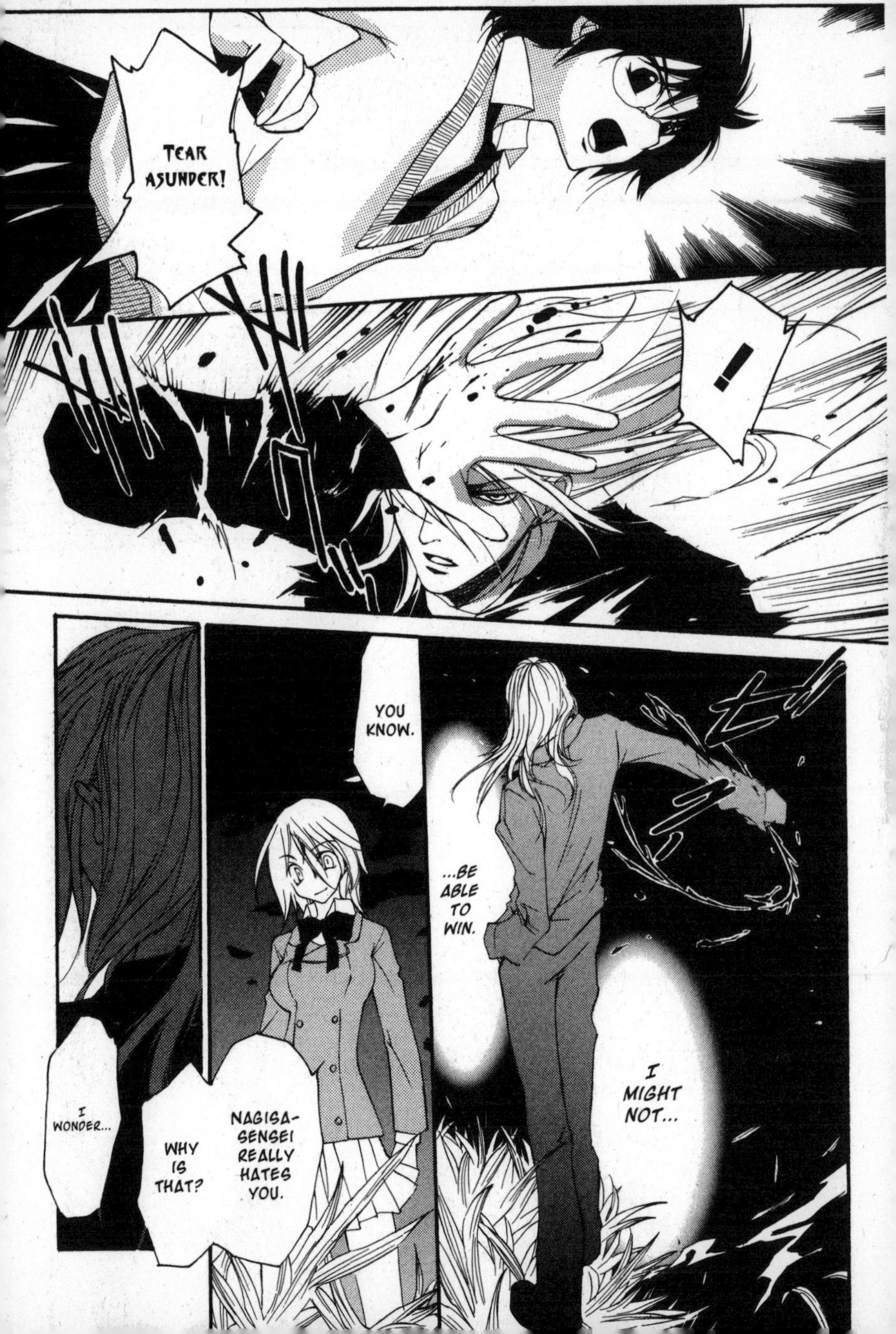
TEAR ASUNDER!
!
I MIGHT NOT...
...BE ABLE TO WIN.
YOU KNOW.
NAGISA-SENSEI REALLY HATES YOU.
WHY IS THAT?
I WONDER...

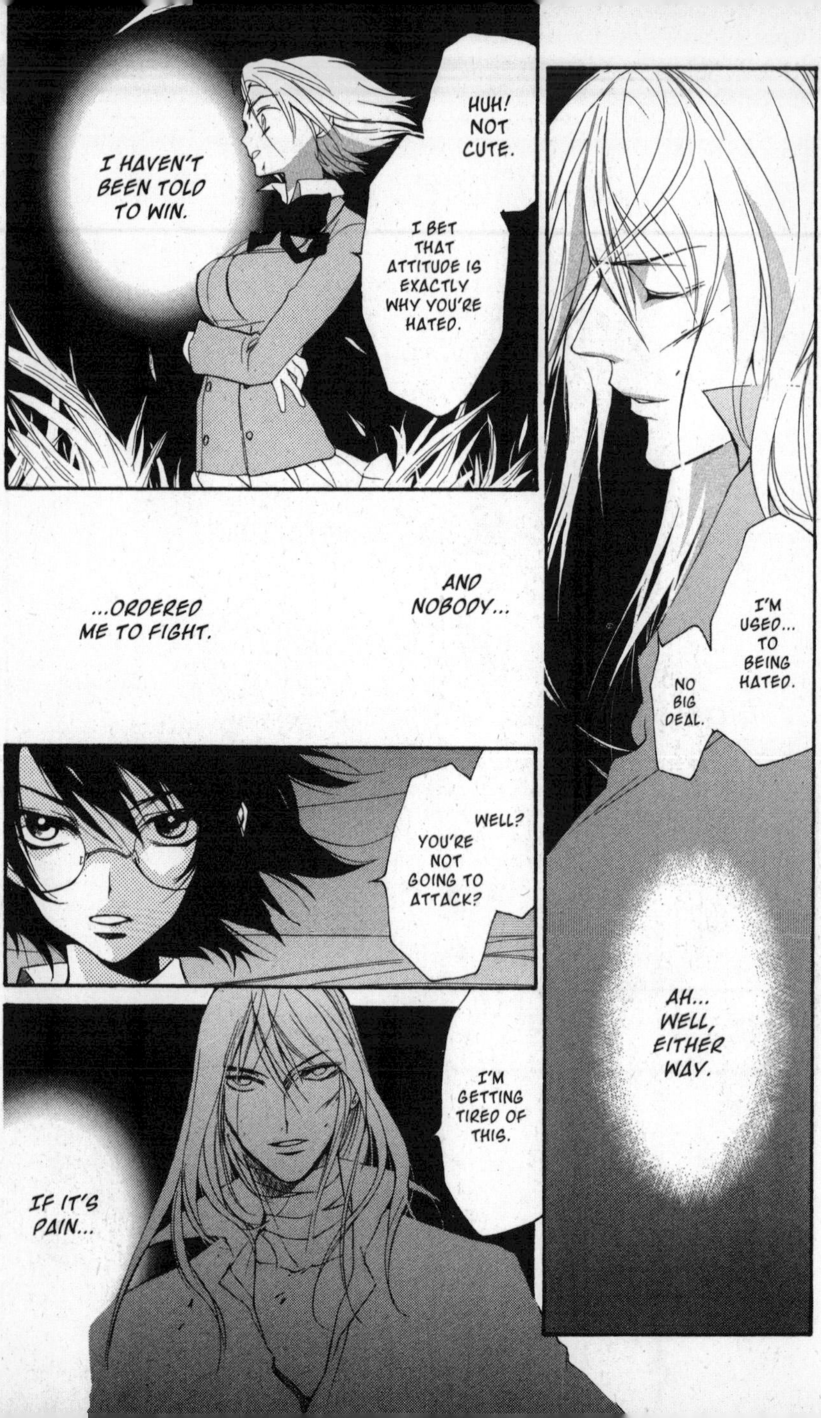
HUH! NOT CUTE.
I BET THAT ATTITUDE IS EXACTLY WHY YOU'RE HATED.
I HAVEN'T BEEN TOLD TO WIN.
I'M USED... TO BEING HATED.
NO BIG DEAL.
AND NOBODY...
...ORDERED ME TO FIGHT.
WELL? YOU'RE NOT GOING TO ATTACK?
AH... WELL, EITHER WAY.
I'M GETTING TIRED OF THIS.
IF IT'S PAIN...

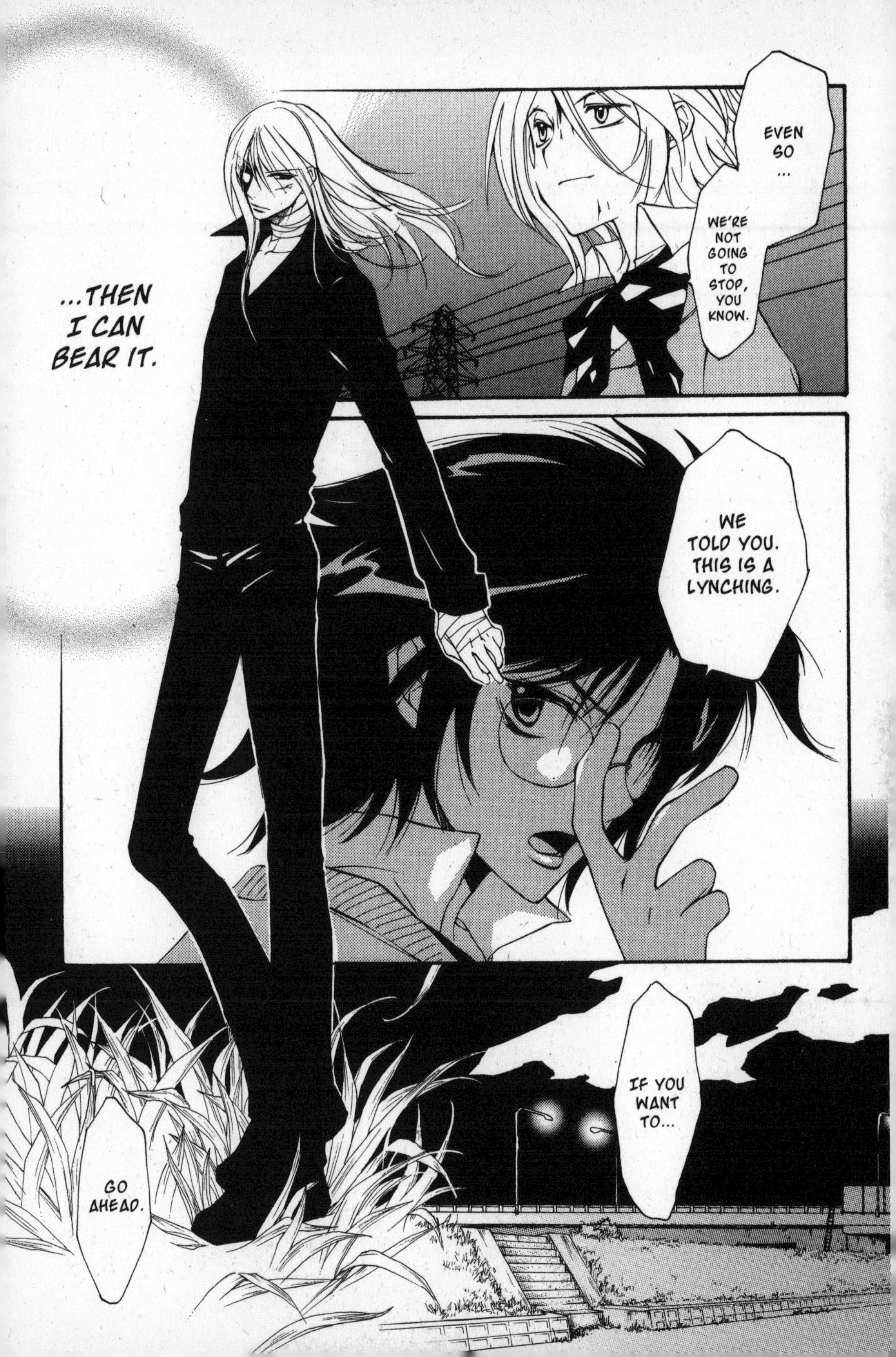
EVEN SO ...
WE'RE NOT GOING TO STOP, YOU KNOW.
...THEN I CAN BEAR IT.
WE TOLD YOU. THIS IS A LYNCHING.
IF YOU WANT TO...
GO AHEAD.

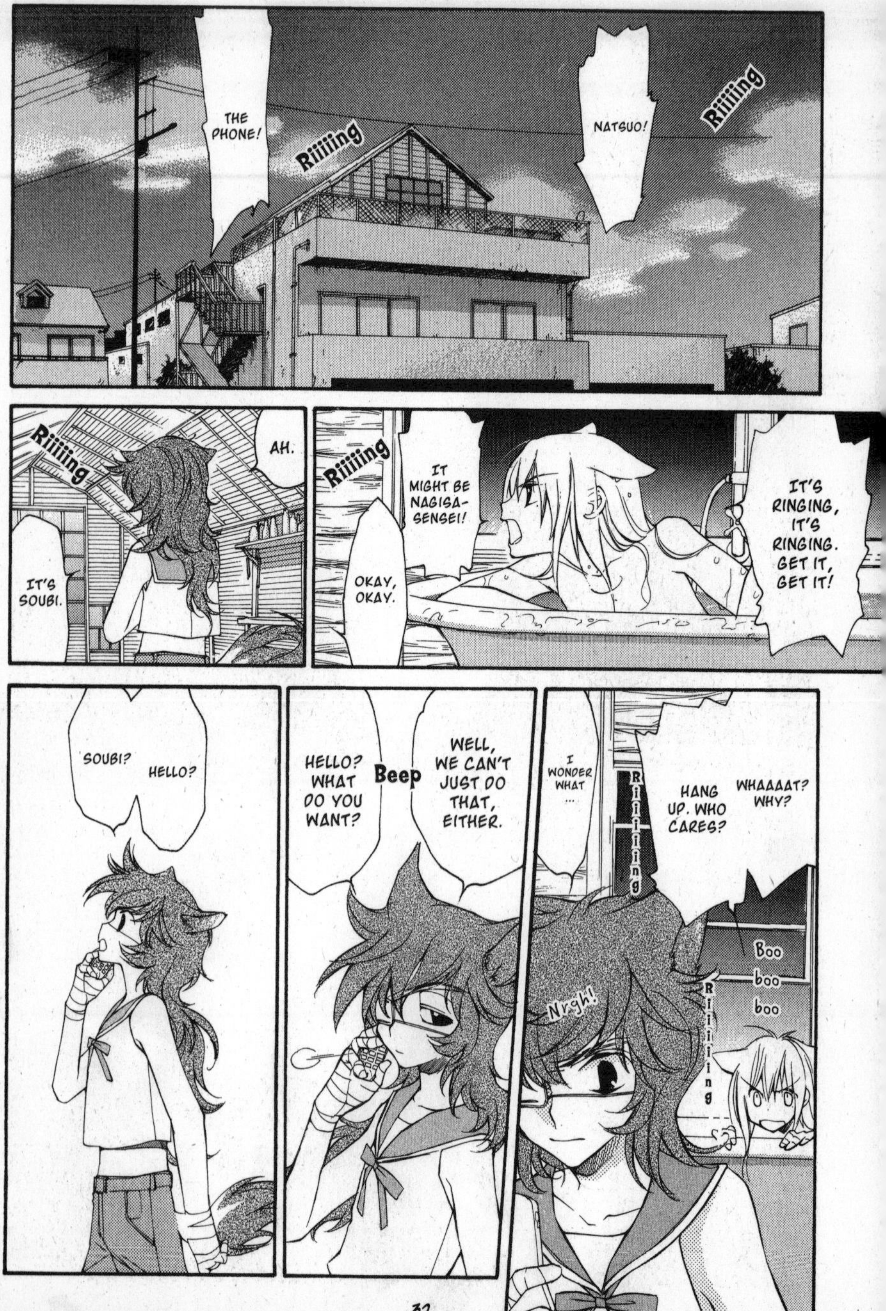
Riiiiing
NATSUO!
Riiiiing
THE PHONE!
IT'S RINGING, IT'S RINGING. GET IT, GET IT!
IT MIGHT BE NAGISA-SENSEI!
Riiiiing
OKAY, OKAY.
AH.
Riiiiing
IT'S SOUBI.
WHAAAAT? WHY?
HANG UP. WHO CARES?
Riiiiing
I WONDER WHAT ...
Nrgh!
Boo boo boo
Riiiiing
WELL, WE CAN'T JUST DO THAT, EITHER.
Beep
HELLO? WHAT DO YOU WANT?
HELLO?
SOUBI?

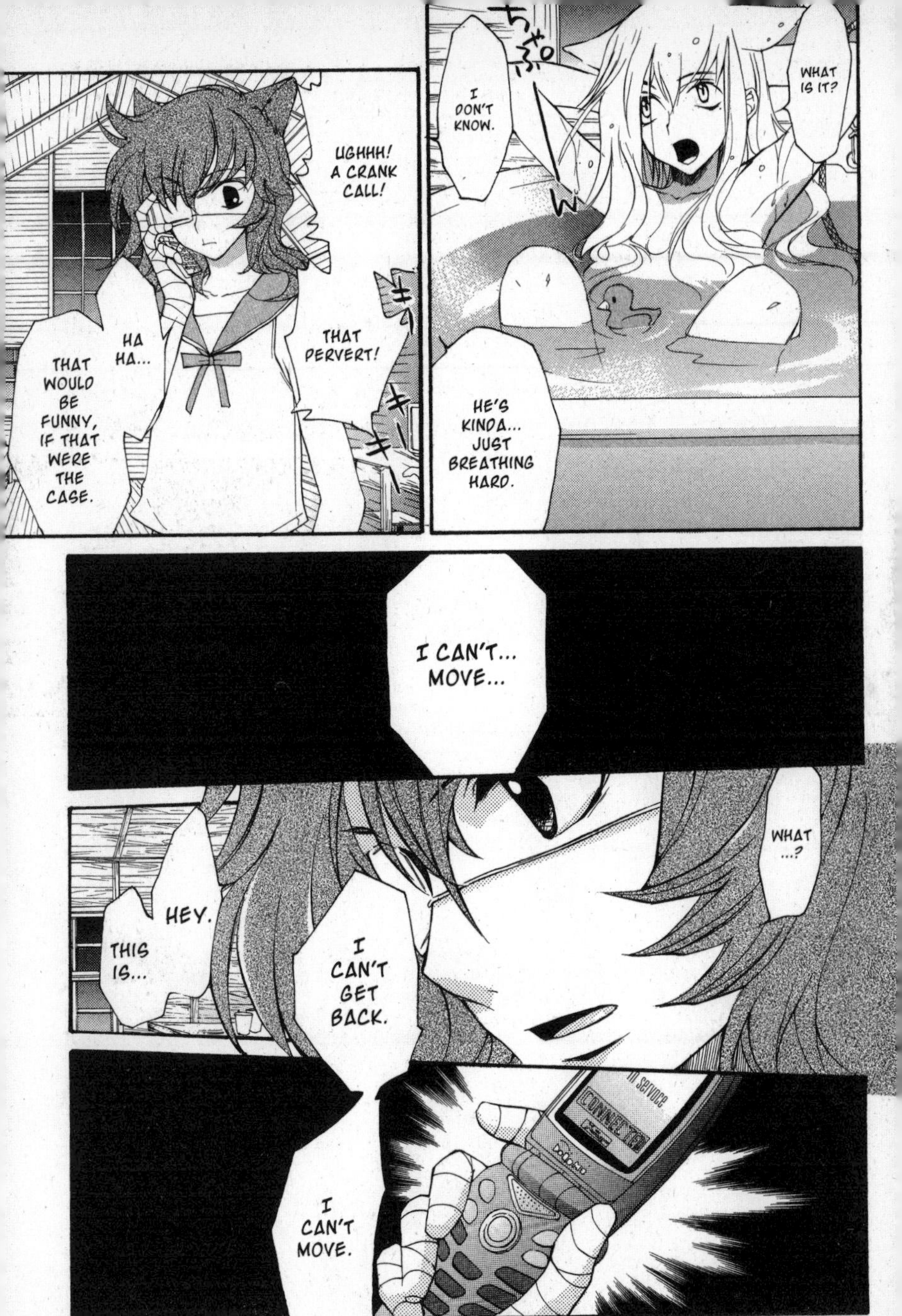
WHAT IS IT?
I DON'T KNOW.
HE'S KINDA... JUST BREATHING HARD.
UGHHH! A CRANK CALL!
THAT PERVERT!
HA HA...
THAT WOULD BE FUNNY, IF THAT WERE THE CASE.
I CAN'T... MOVE...
WHAT ...?
I CAN'T GET BACK.
HEY.
THIS IS...
I CAN'T MOVE.

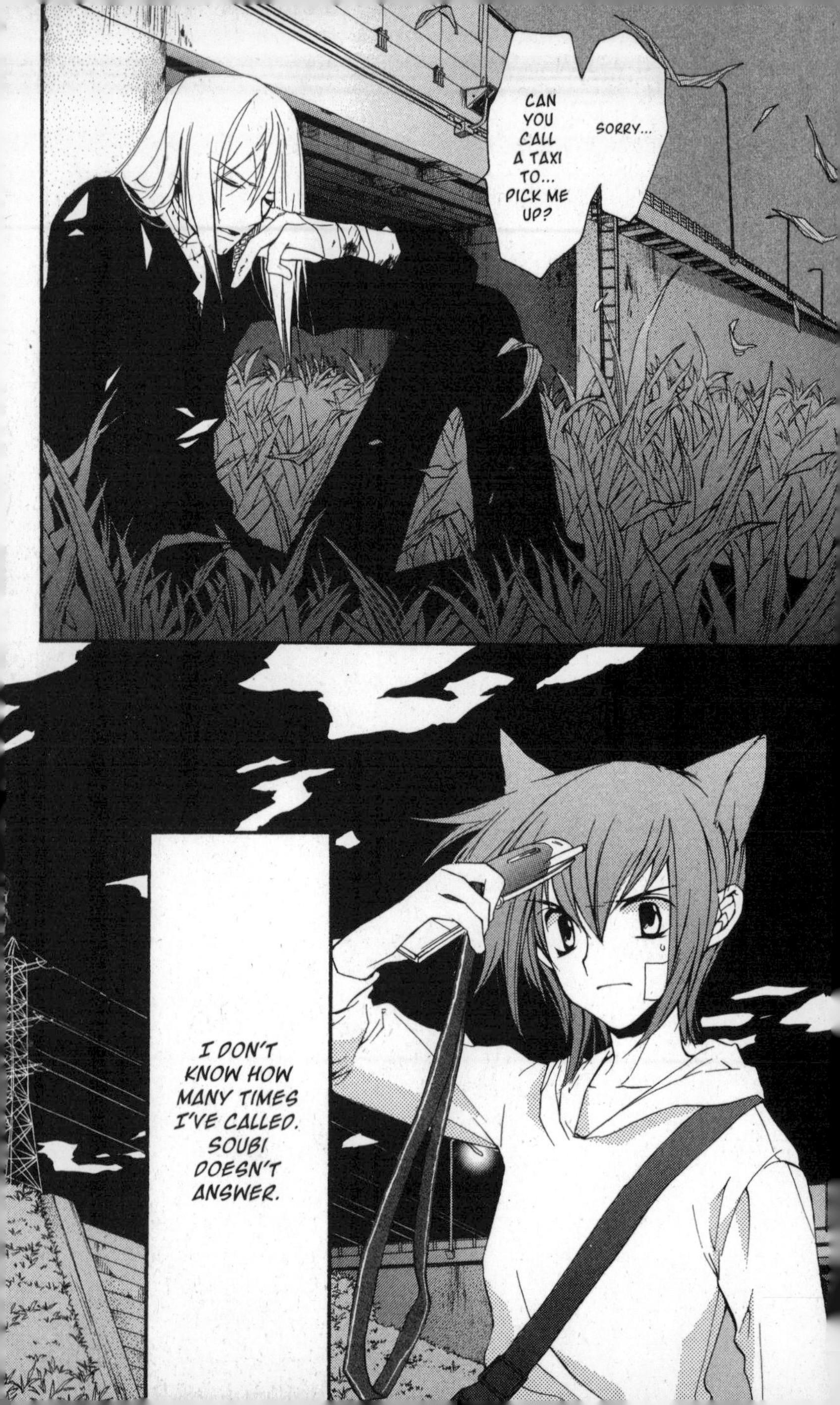
SORRY...
CAN YOU CALL A TAXI TO... PICK ME UP?
I DON'T KNOW HOW MANY TIMES I'VE CALLED. SOUBI DOESN'T ANSWER.

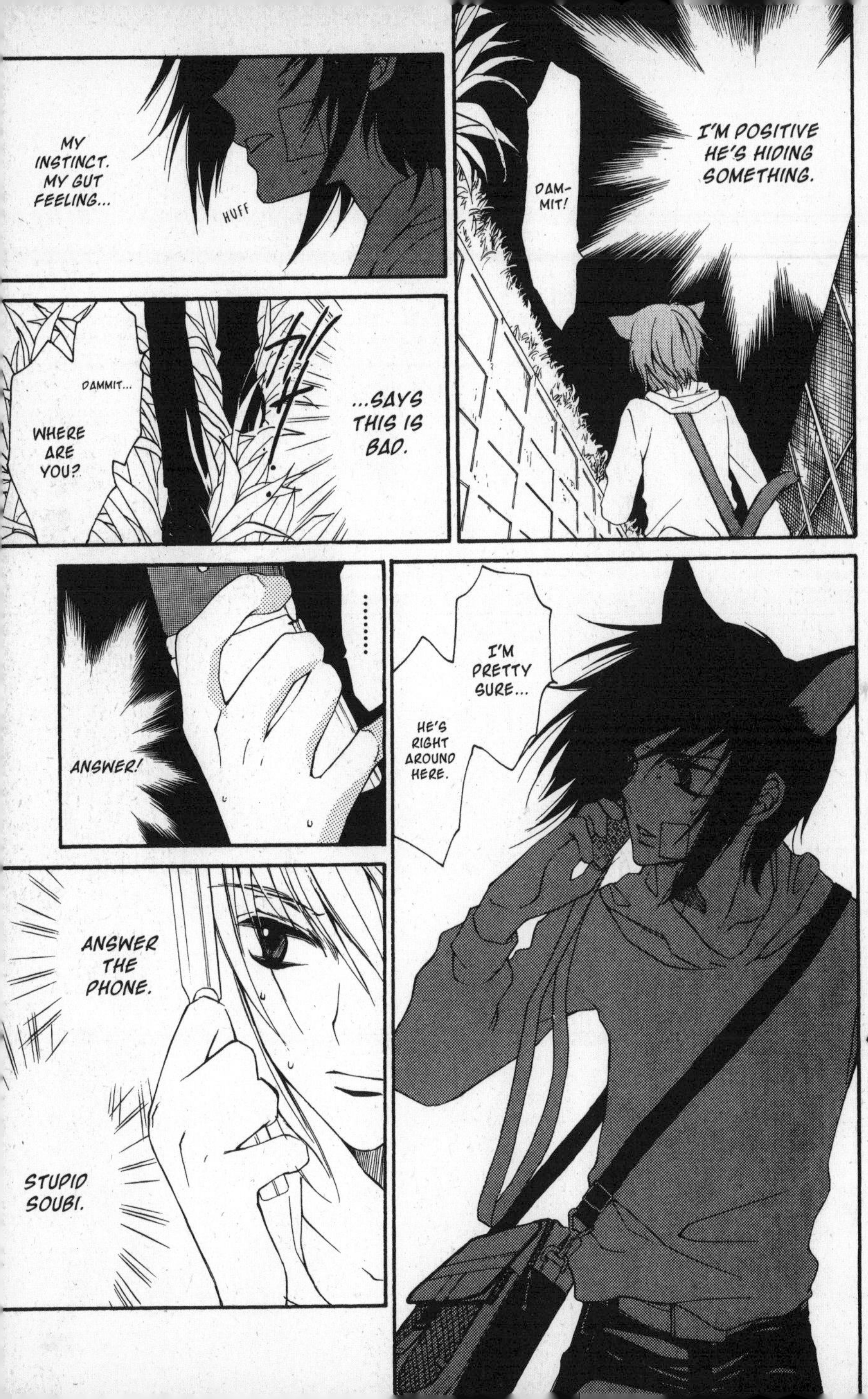
I'M POSITIVE HE'S HIDING SOMETHING.
DAM-MIT!
MY INSTINCT. MY GUT FEELING...
HUFF
...SAYS THIS IS BAD.
DAMMIT...
WHERE ARE YOU?
I'M PRETTY SURE...
HE'S RIGHT AROUND HERE.
......
ANSWER!
ANSWER THE PHONE.
STUPID SOUBI.

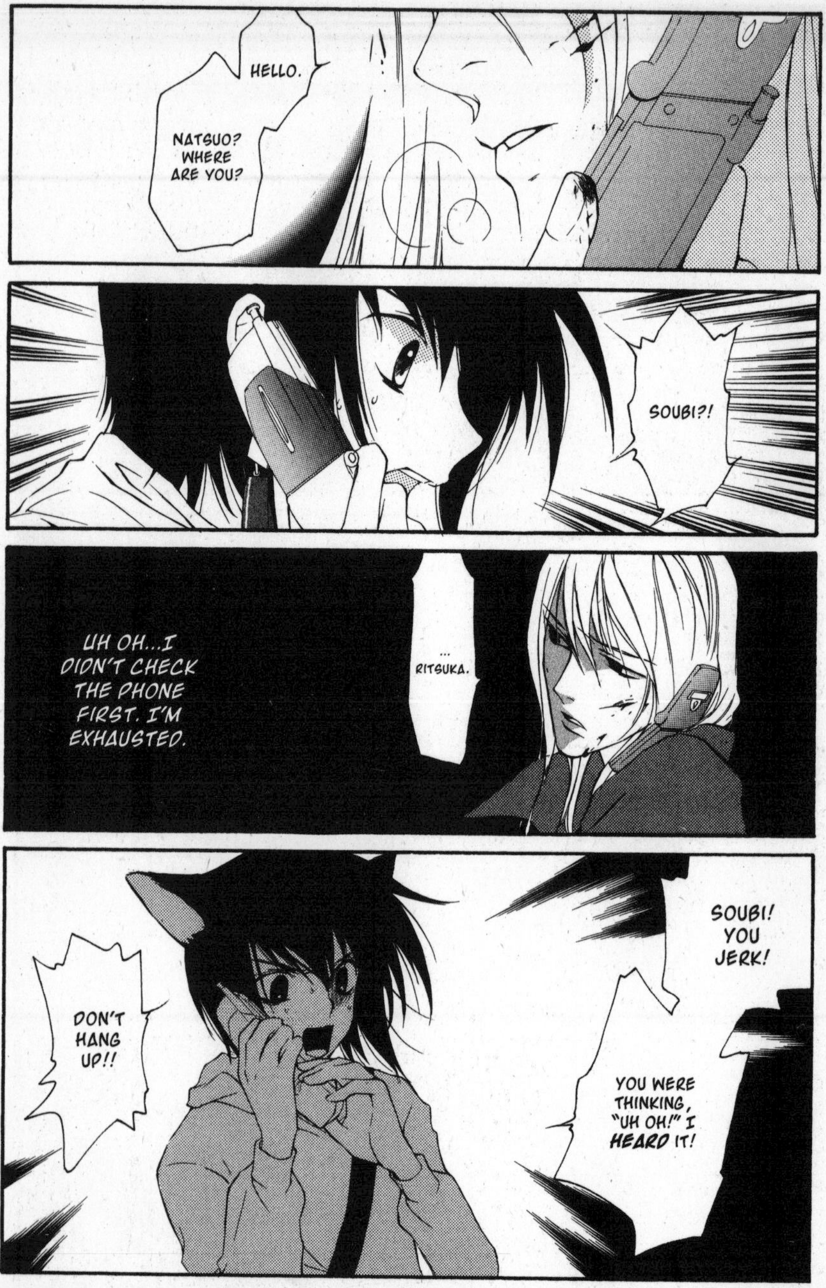
HELLO.
NATSUO? WHERE ARE YOU?
SOUBI?!
... RITSUKA.
UH OH...I DIDN'T CHECK THE PHONE FIRST. I'M EXHAUSTED.
SOUBI! YOU JERK!
YOU WERE THINKING, "UH OH!" I HEARD IT!
DON'T HANG UP!!

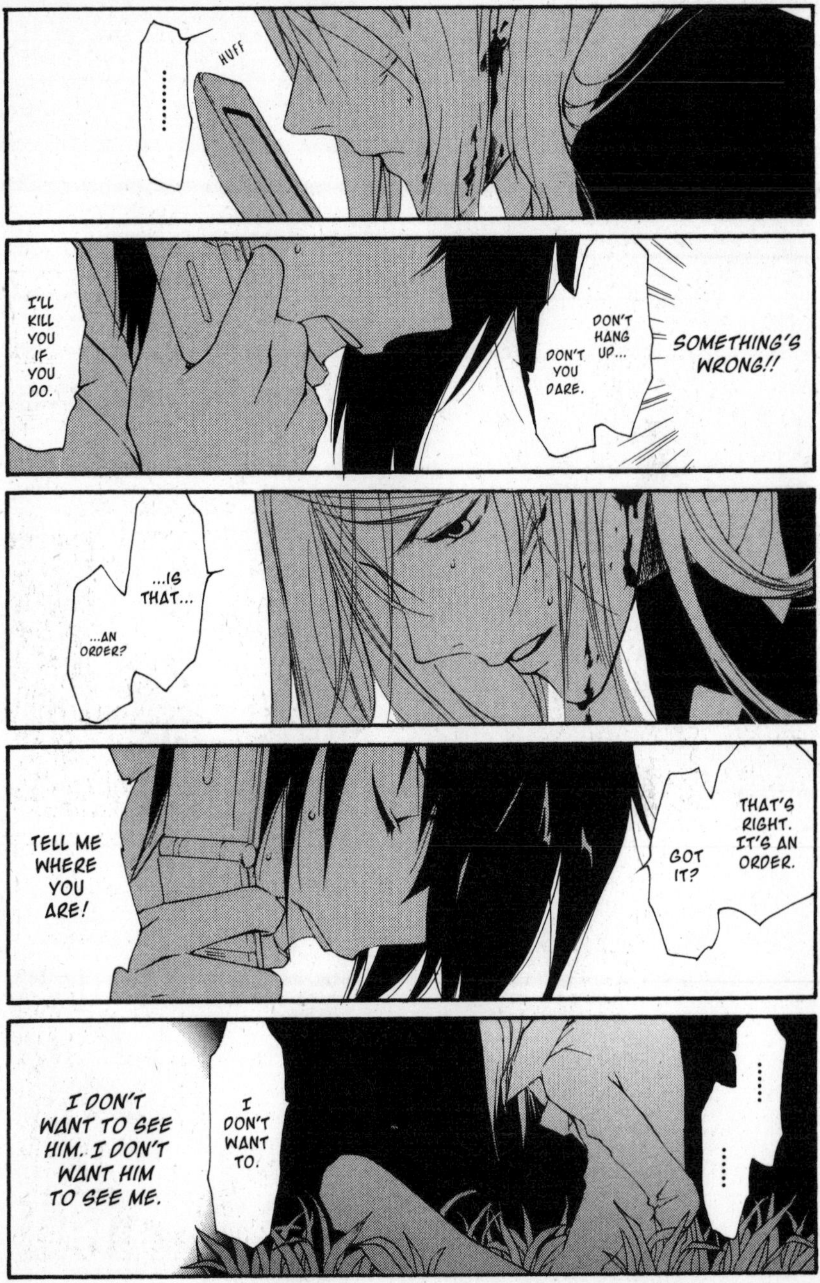
HUFF
......
SOMETHING'S WRONG!!
DON'T HANG UP... DON'T YOU DARE.
I'LL KILL YOU IF YOU DO.
...IS THAT... ...AN ORDER?
THAT'S RIGHT. IT'S AN ORDER. GOT IT?
TELL ME WHERE YOU ARE!
......
......
I DON'T WANT TO.
I DON'T WANT TO SEE HIM. I DON'T WANT HIM TO SEE ME.

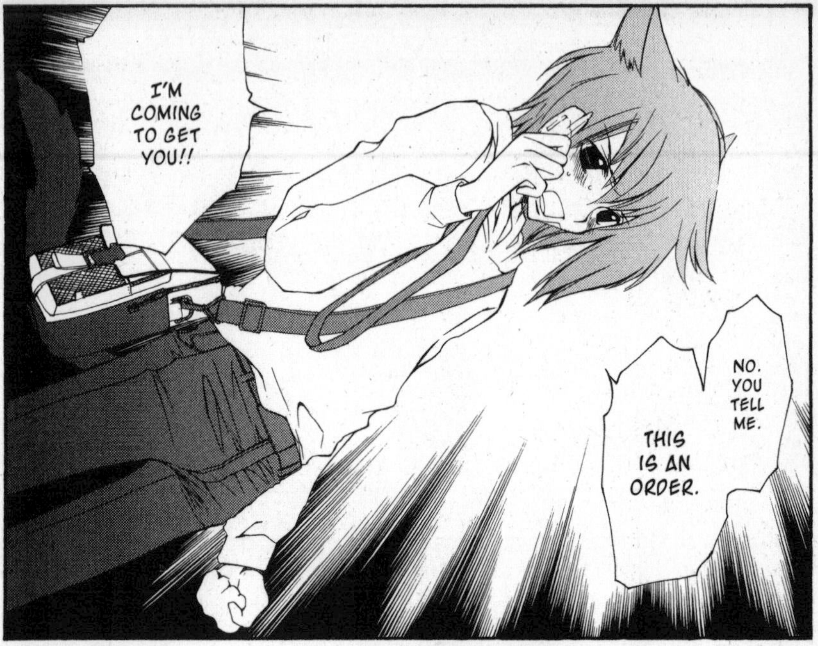
NO. YOU TELL ME.
THIS IS AN ORDER.
I'M COMING TO GET YOU!!

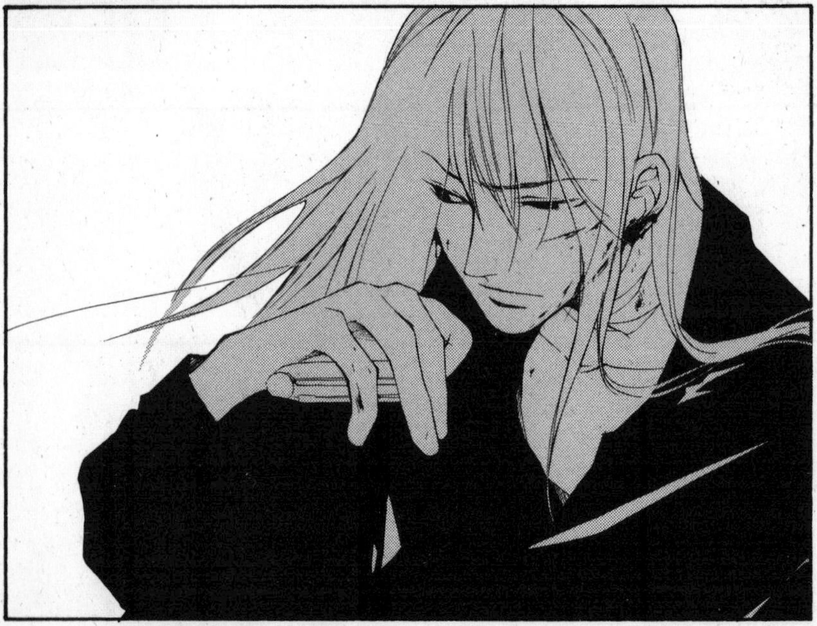

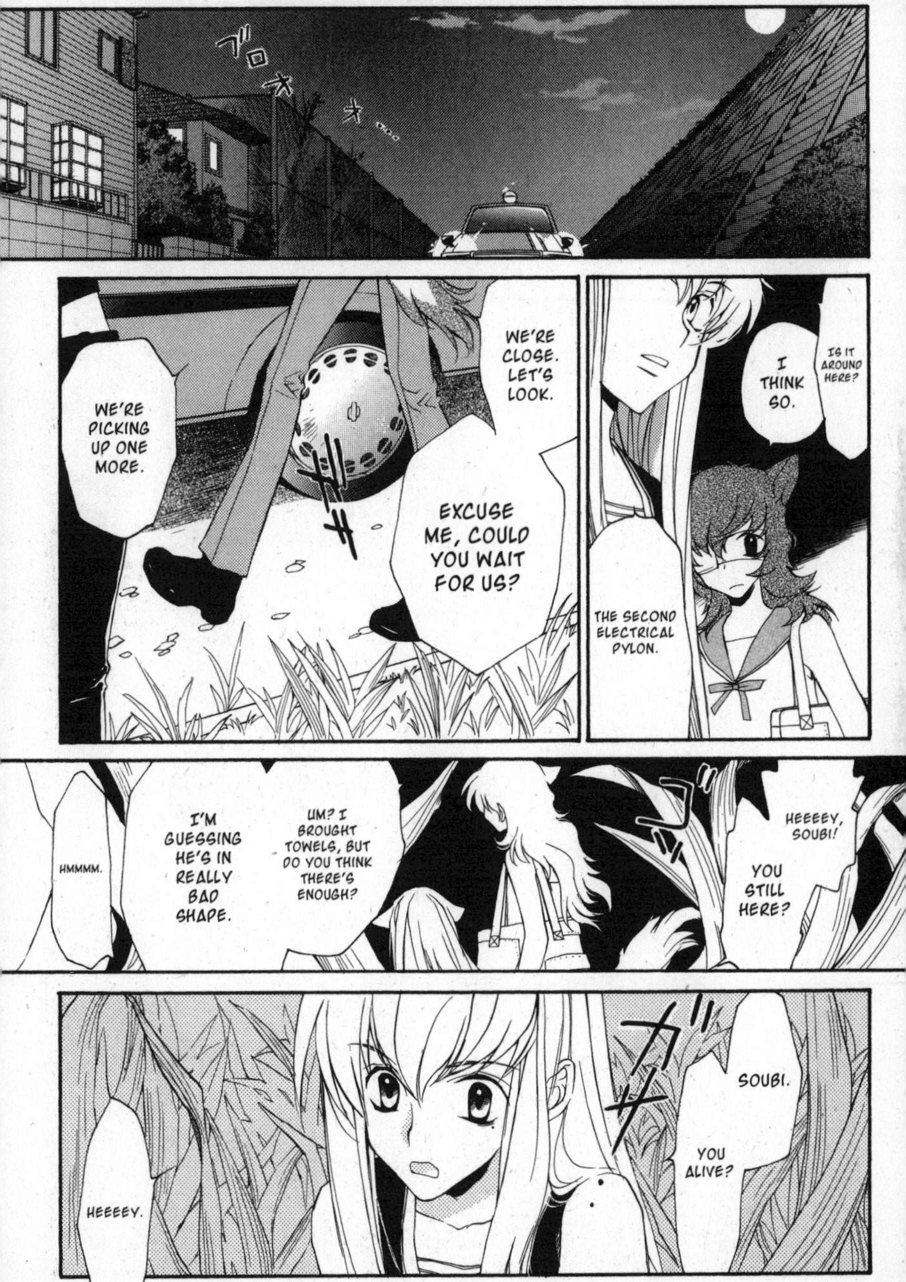
IS IT AROUND HERE?
I THINK SO.
THE SECOND ELECTRICAL PYLON.
WE'RE CLOSE. LET'S LOOK.
WE'RE PICKING UP ONE MORE.
EXCUSE ME, COULD YOU WAIT FOR US?
HEEEEY, SOUBI!
YOU STILL HERE?
UM? I BROUGHT TOWELS, BUT DO YOU THINK THERE'S ENOUGH?
I'M GUESSING HE'S IN REALLY BAD SHAPE.
HMMMM.
SOUBI.
YOU ALIVE?
HEEEEY.

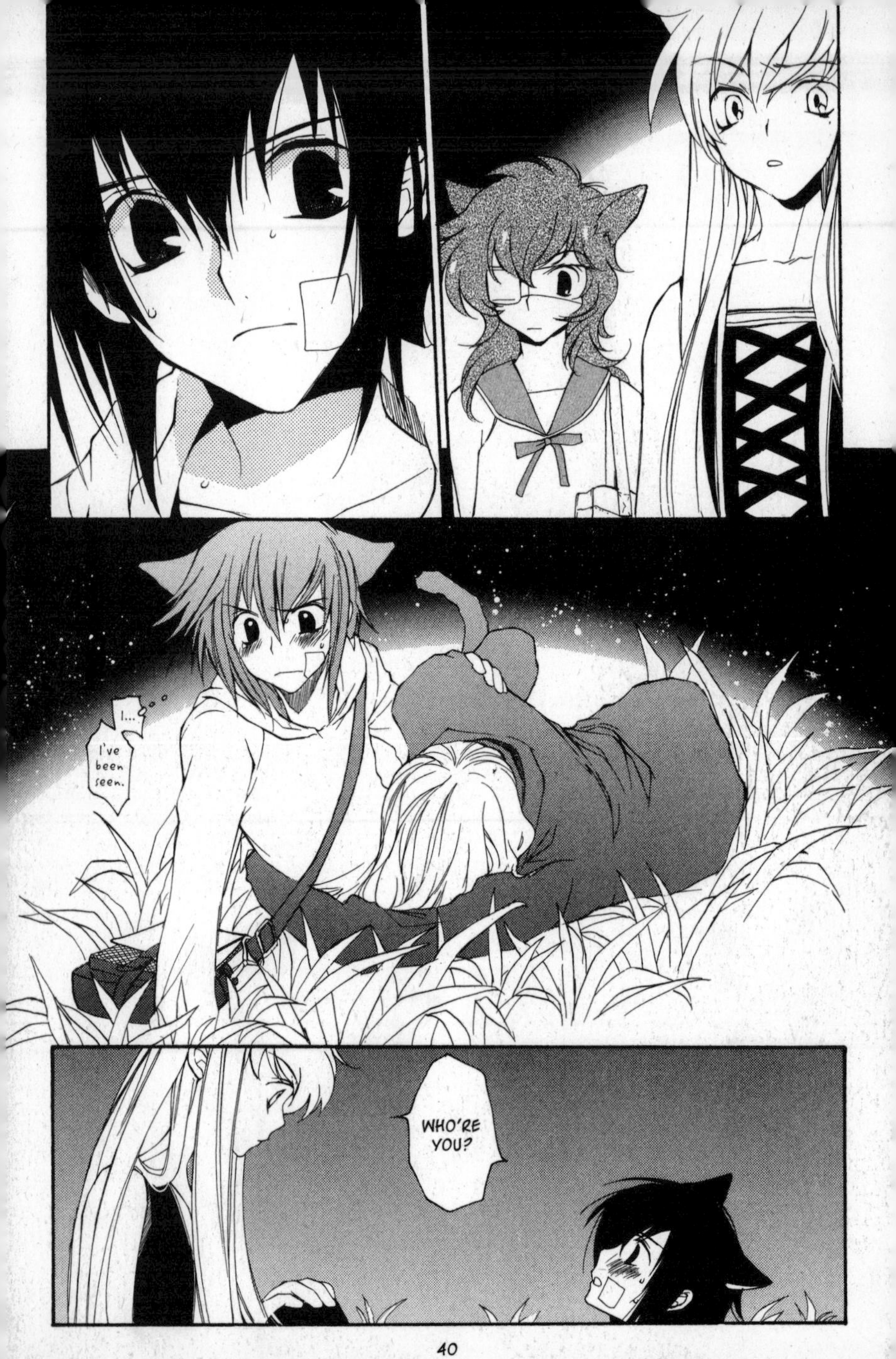
I...
I've been seen.
WHO'RE YOU?

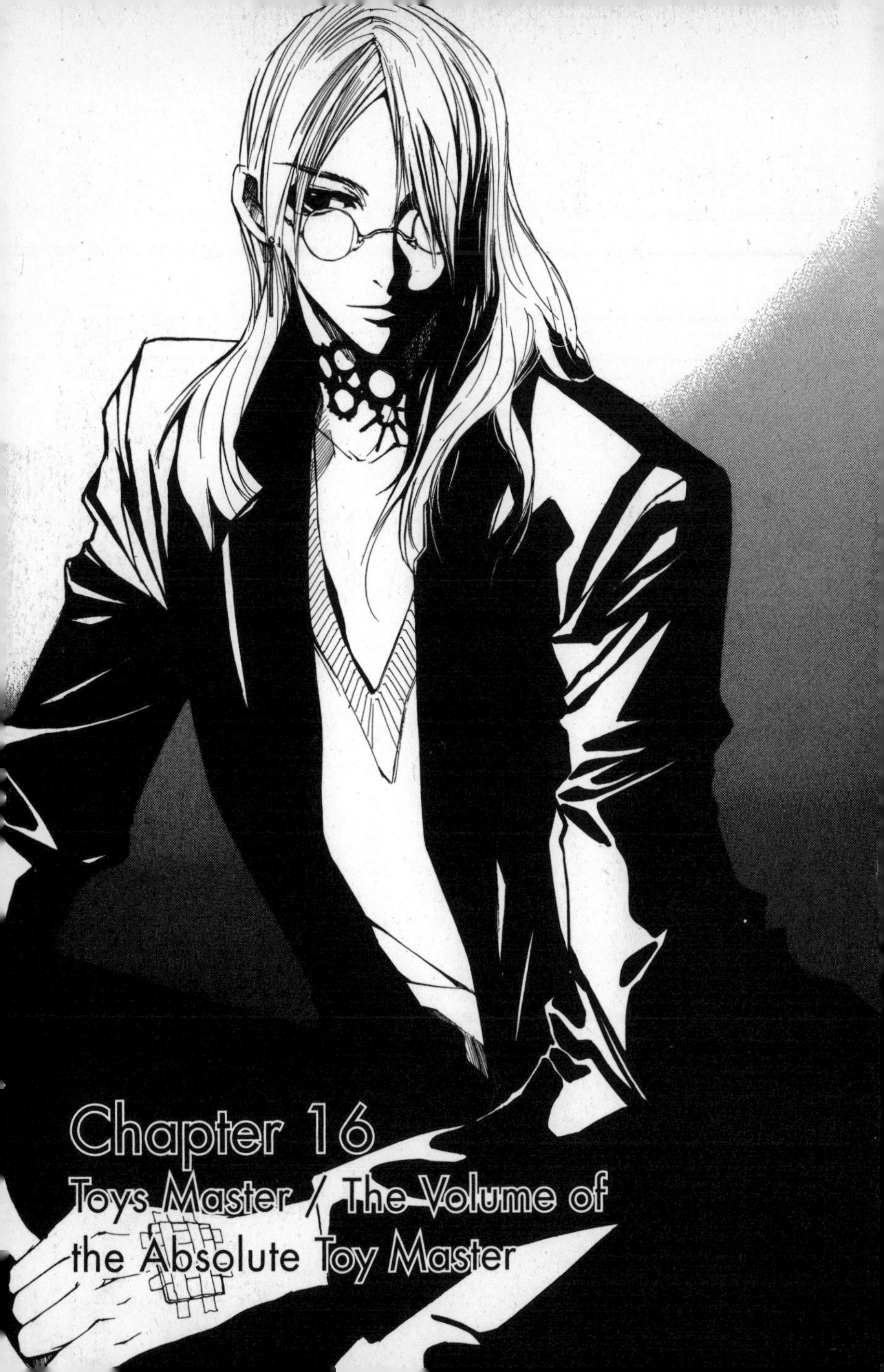

Chapter 16

Toys Master / The Volume of the Absolute Toy Master

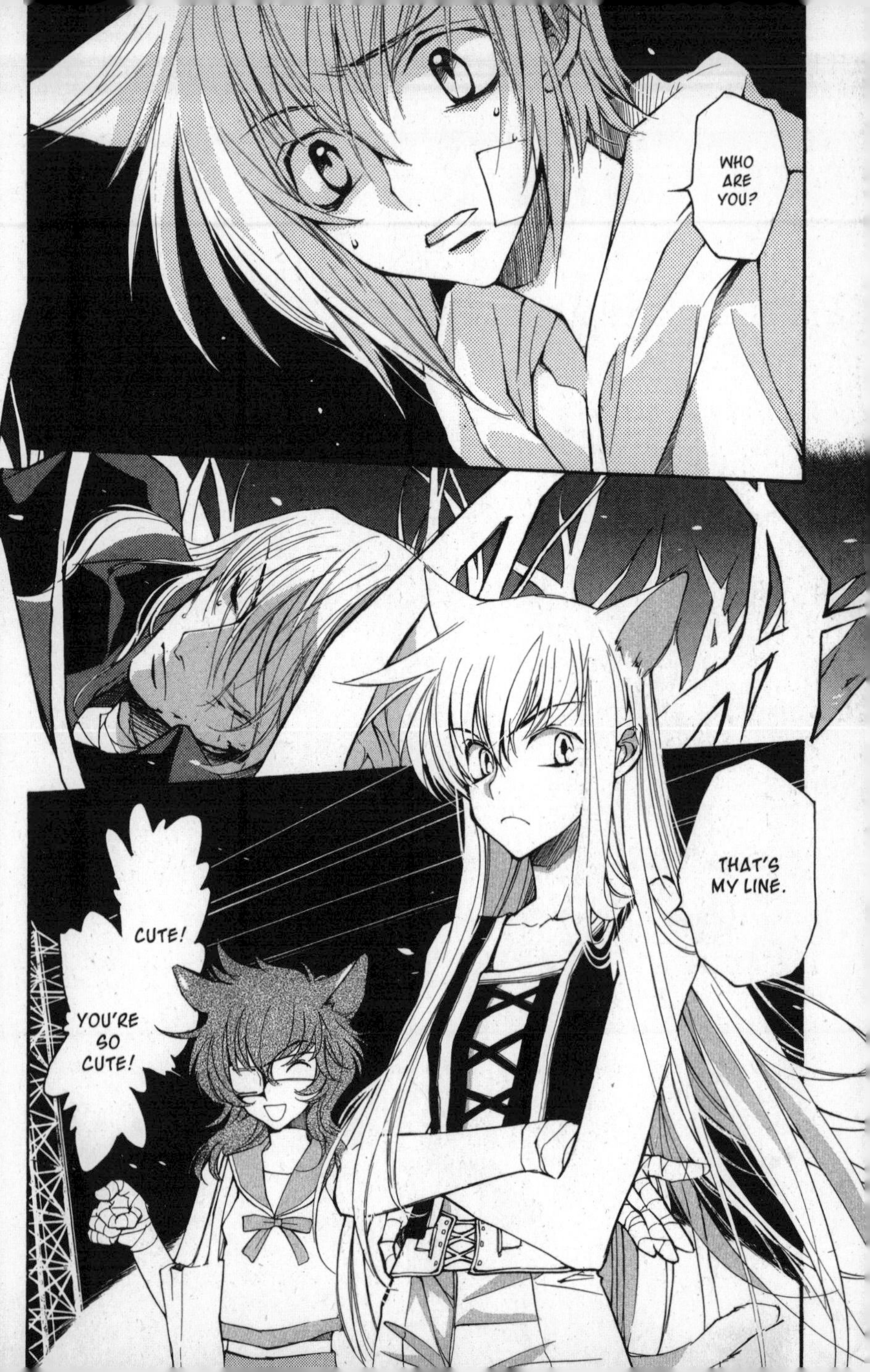
WHO ARE YOU?
THAT'S MY LINE.
CUTE!
YOU'RE SO CUTE!

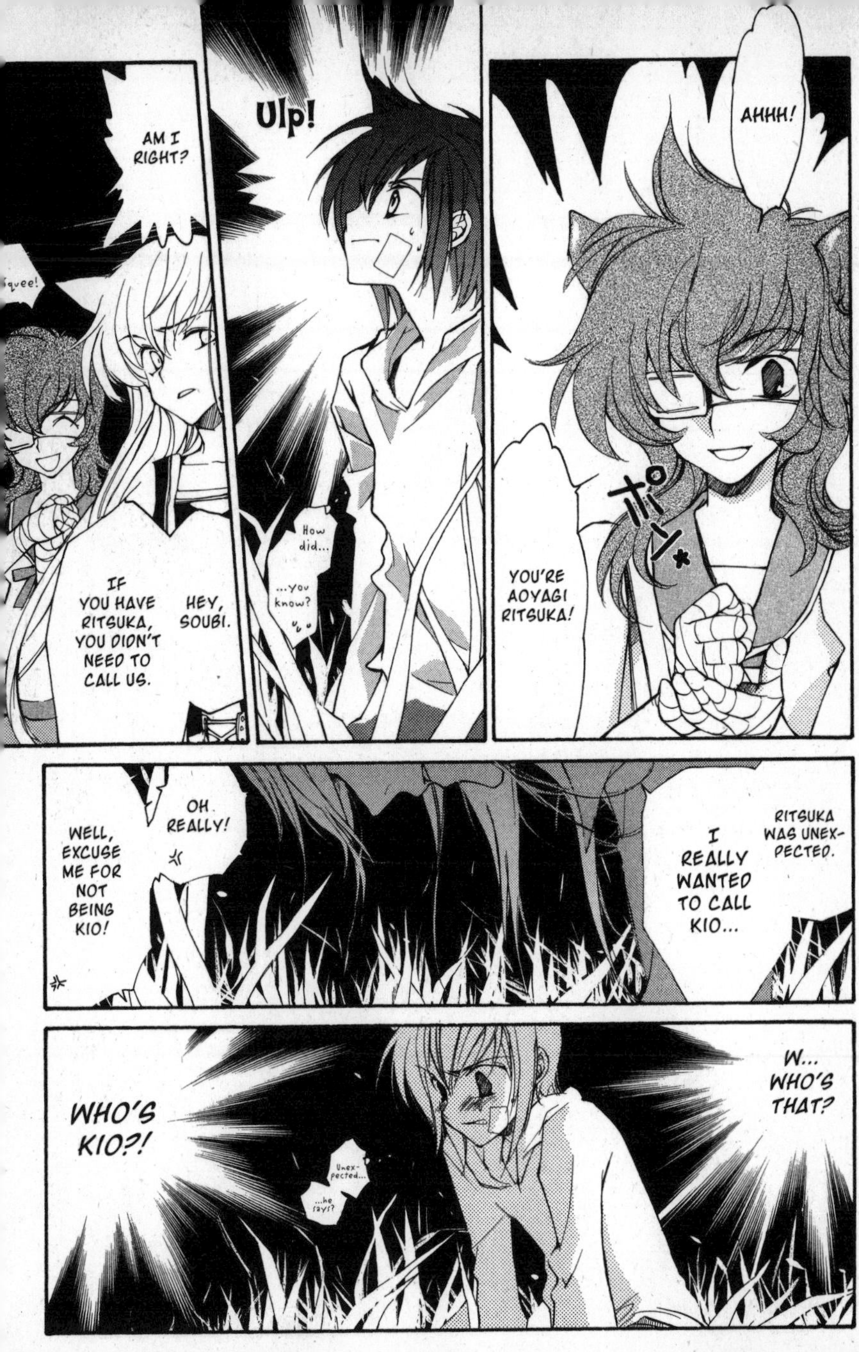
AHHH!
YOU'RE AOYAGI RITSUKA!
Ulp!
How did...
...you know?
AM I RIGHT?
quee!
HEY, SOUBI.
IF YOU HAVE RITSUKA, YOU DIDN'T NEED TO CALL US.
RITSUKA WAS UNEXPECTED.
I REALLY WANTED TO CALL KIO...
OH REALLY!
WELL, EXCUSE ME FOR NOT BEING KIO!
W... WHO'S THAT?
Unexpected...
...he says?
WHO'S KIO?!

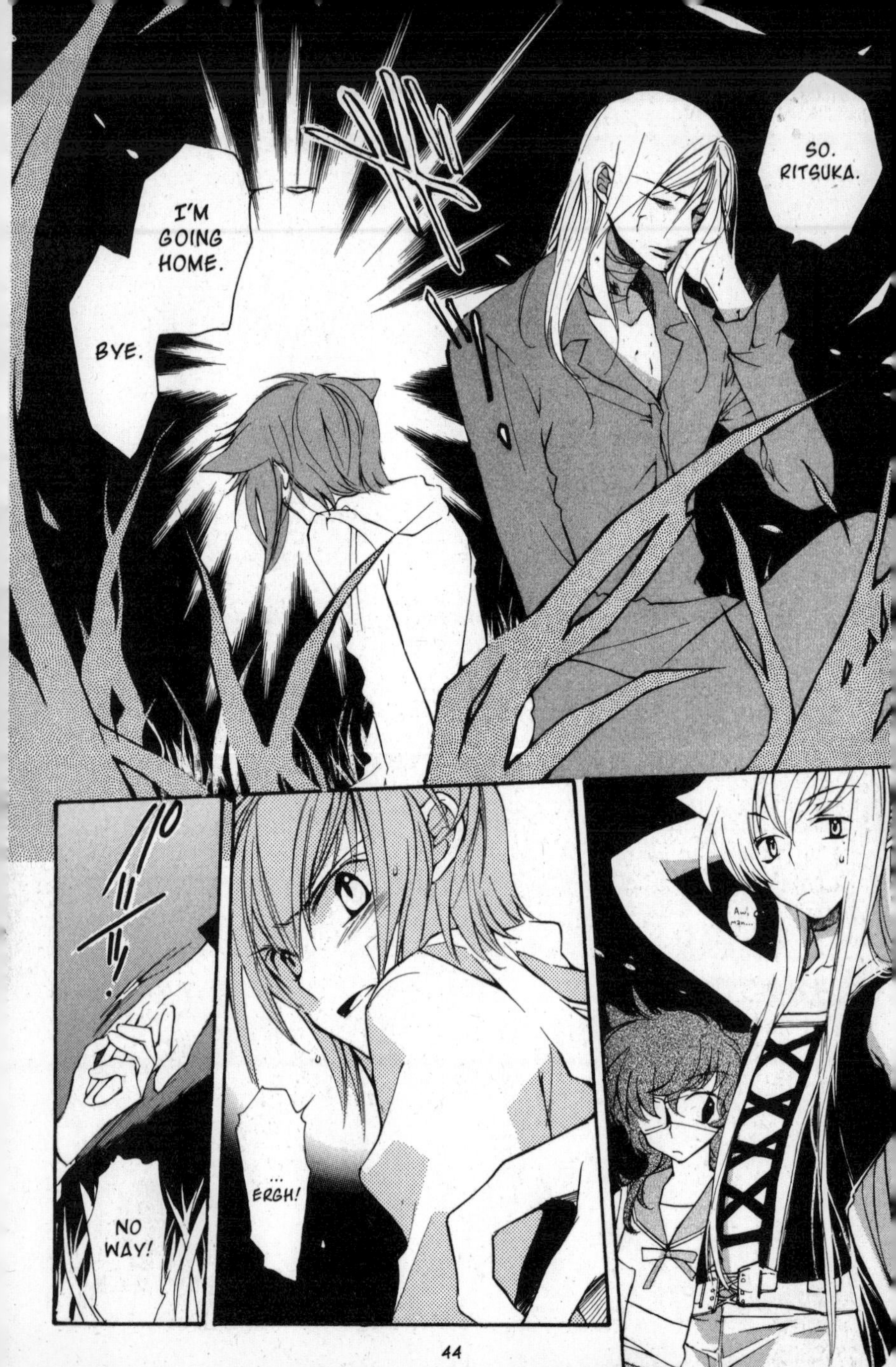
SO. RITSUKA.
I'M GOING HOME.
BYE.
Aw, man...
... ERGH!
NO WAY!

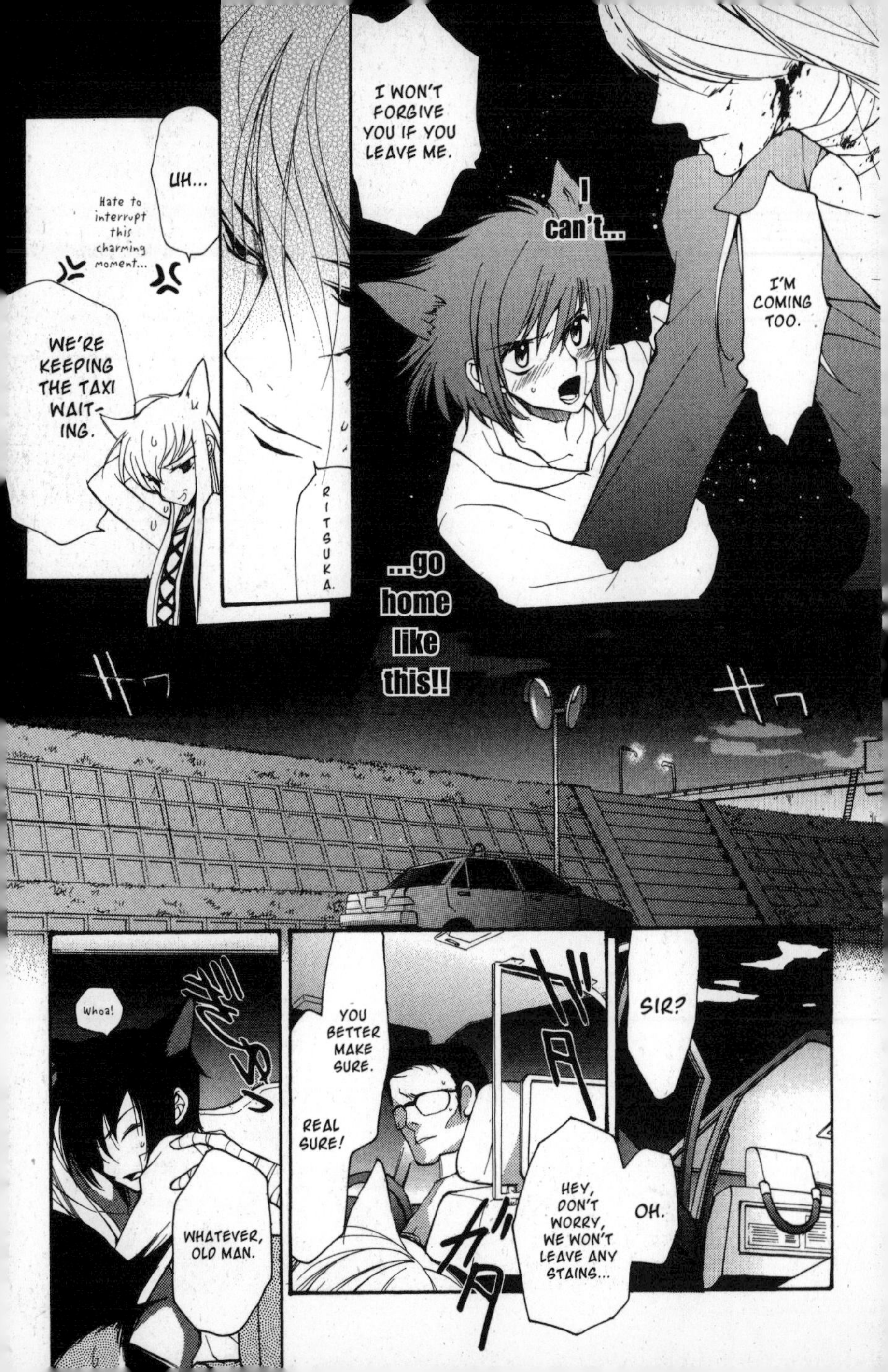
I'M COMING TOO.
I can't...
...go home like this!!
I WON'T FORGIVE YOU IF YOU LEAVE ME.
RITSUKA.
UH...
Hate to interrupt this charming moment...
WE'RE KEEPING THE TAXI WAITING.
SIR?
OH.
HEY, DON'T WORRY, WE WON'T LEAVE ANY STAINS...
YOU BETTER MAKE SURE.
REAL SURE!
Whoa!
WHATEVER, OLD MAN.

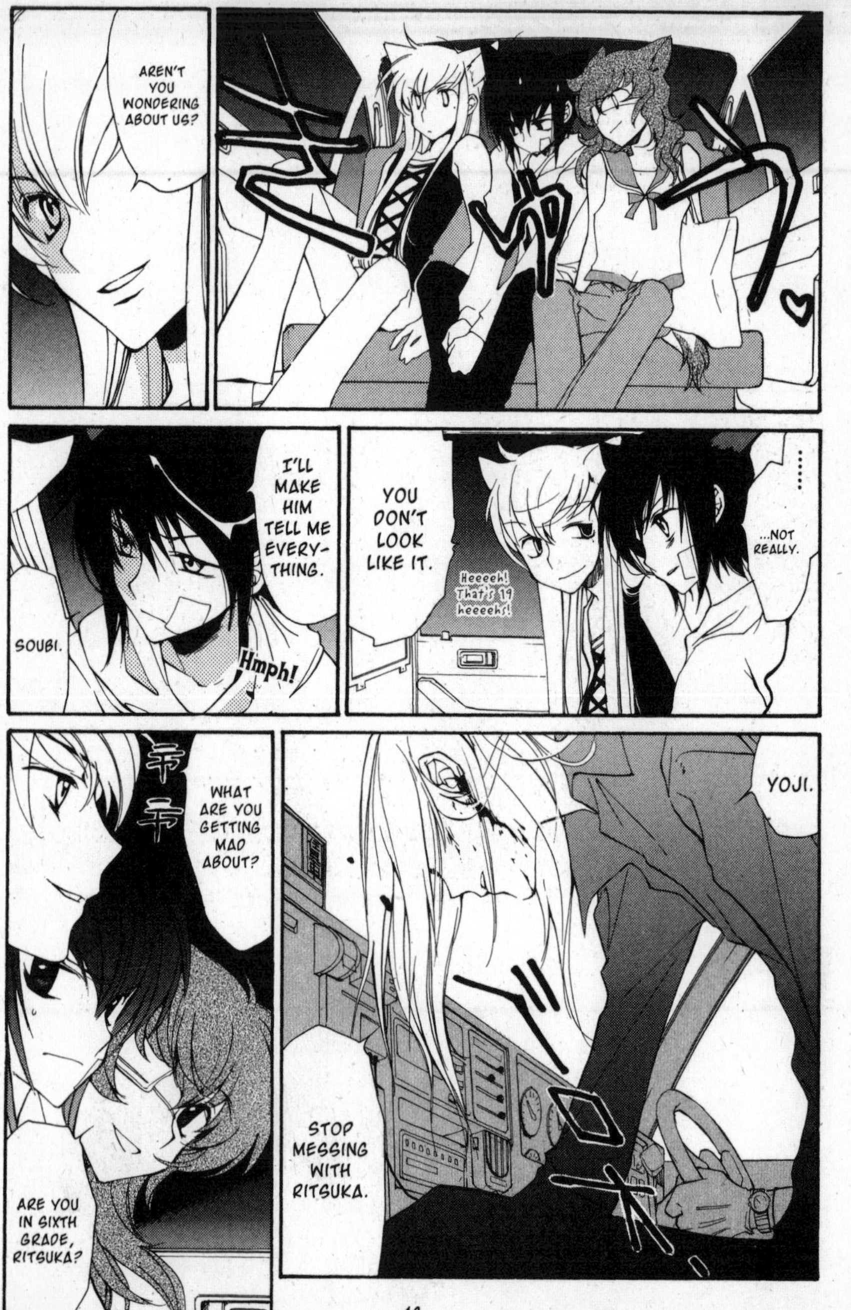
AREN'T YOU WONDERING ABOUT US?
......
...NOT REALLY.
YOU DON'T LOOK LIKE IT.
Heeeeh! That's 19 heeeeehs!
I'LL MAKE HIM TELL ME EVERY-THING.
SOUBI.
Hmph!
YOJI.
STOP MESSING WITH RITSUKA.
WHAT ARE YOU GETTING MAD ABOUT?
ARE YOU IN SIXTH GRADE, RITSUKA?

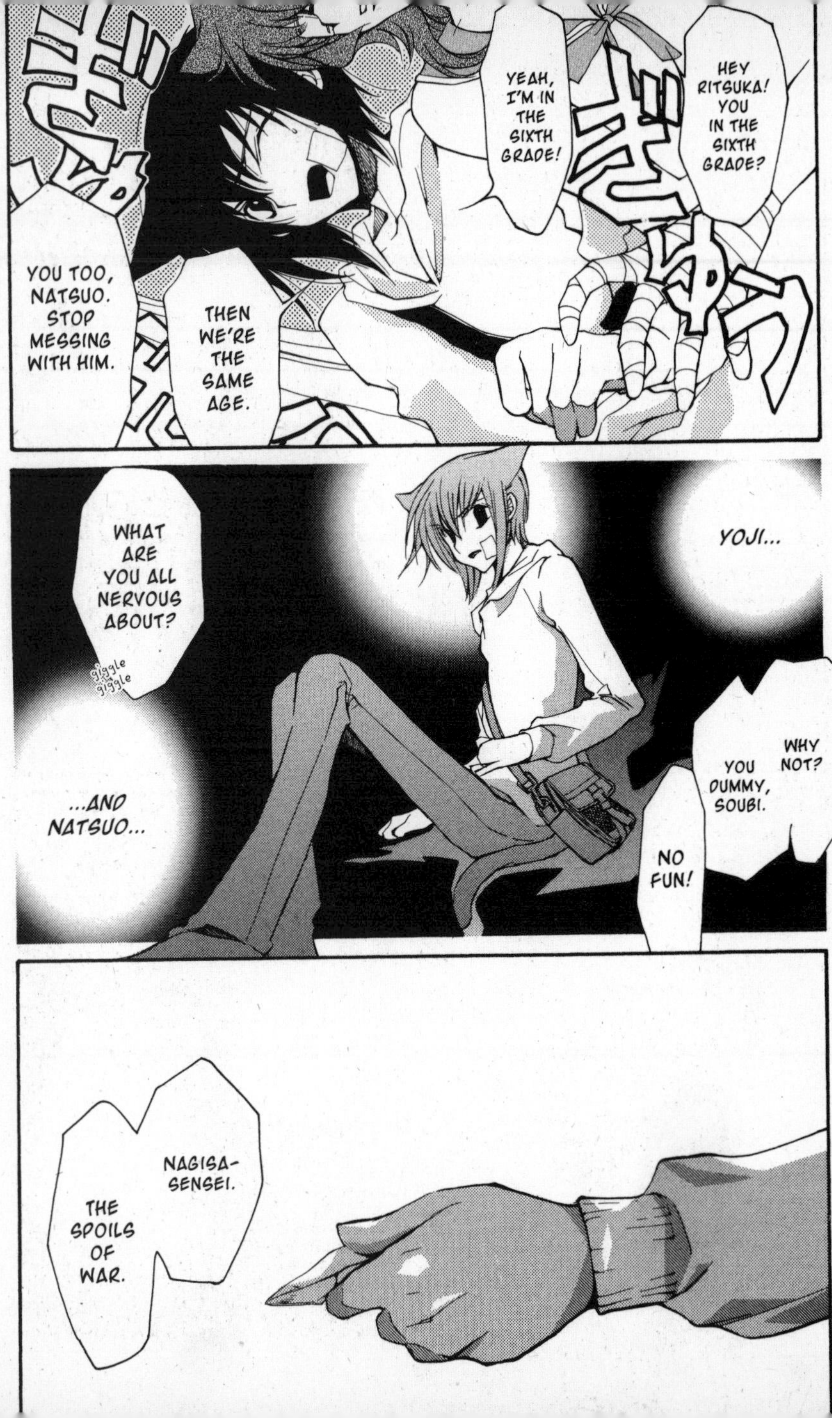
HEY RITSUKA! YOU IN THE SIXTH GRADE?
YEAH, I'M IN THE SIXTH GRADE!
THEN WE'RE THE SAME AGE.
YOU TOO, NATSUO. STOP MESSING WITH HIM.
YOJI...
WHAT ARE YOU ALL NERVOUS ABOUT?
WHY NOT?
YOU DUMMY, SOUBI.
NO FUN!
giggle giggle
...AND NATSUO...
NAGISA-SENSEI.
THE SPOILS OF WAR.

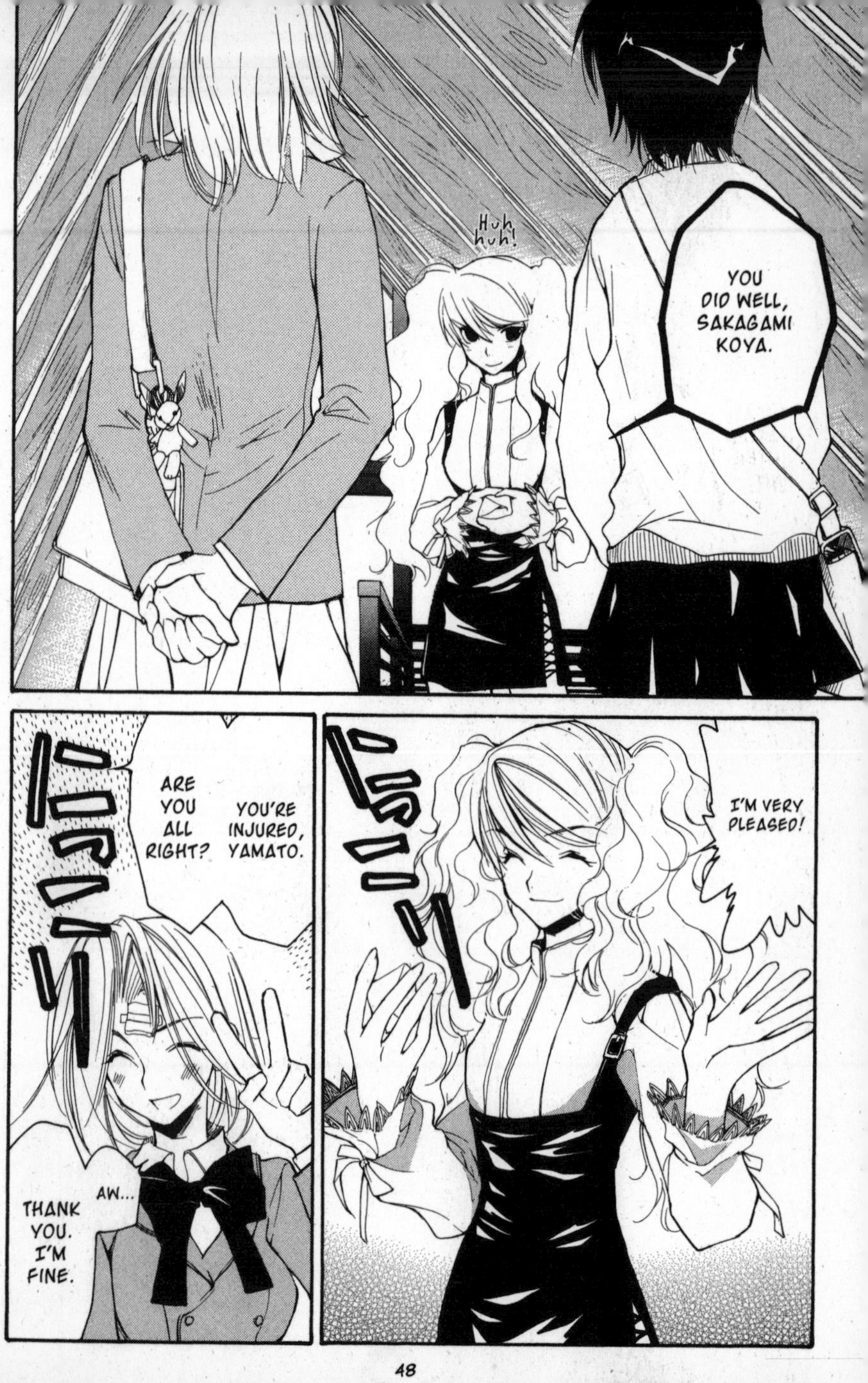
YOU DID WELL, SAKAGAMI KOYA.
Huh huh!
I'M VERY PLEASED!
YOU'RE INJURED, YAMATO.
ARE YOU ALL RIGHT?
AW...
THANK YOU. I'M FINE.

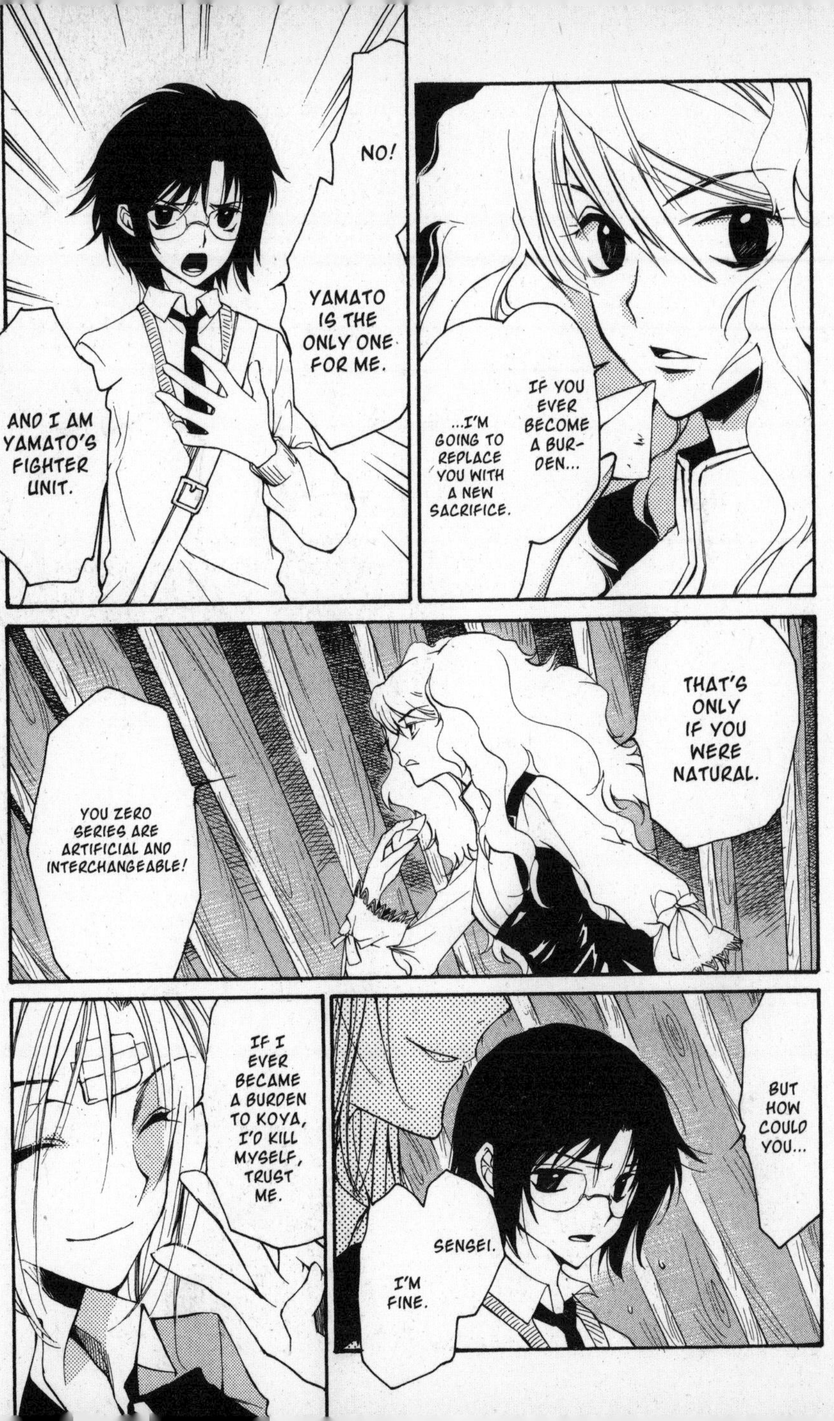
IF YOU EVER BECOME A BURDEN...
...I'M GOING TO REPLACE YOU WITH A NEW SACRIFICE.
NO!
YAMATO IS THE ONLY ONE FOR ME.
AND I AM YAMATO'S FIGHTER UNIT.
THAT'S ONLY IF YOU WERE NATURAL.
YOU ZERO SERIES ARE ARTIFICIAL AND INTERCHANGEABLE!
BUT HOW COULD YOU...
SENSEI.
I'M FINE.
IF I EVER BECAME A BURDEN TO KOYA, I'D KILL MYSELF, TRUST ME.

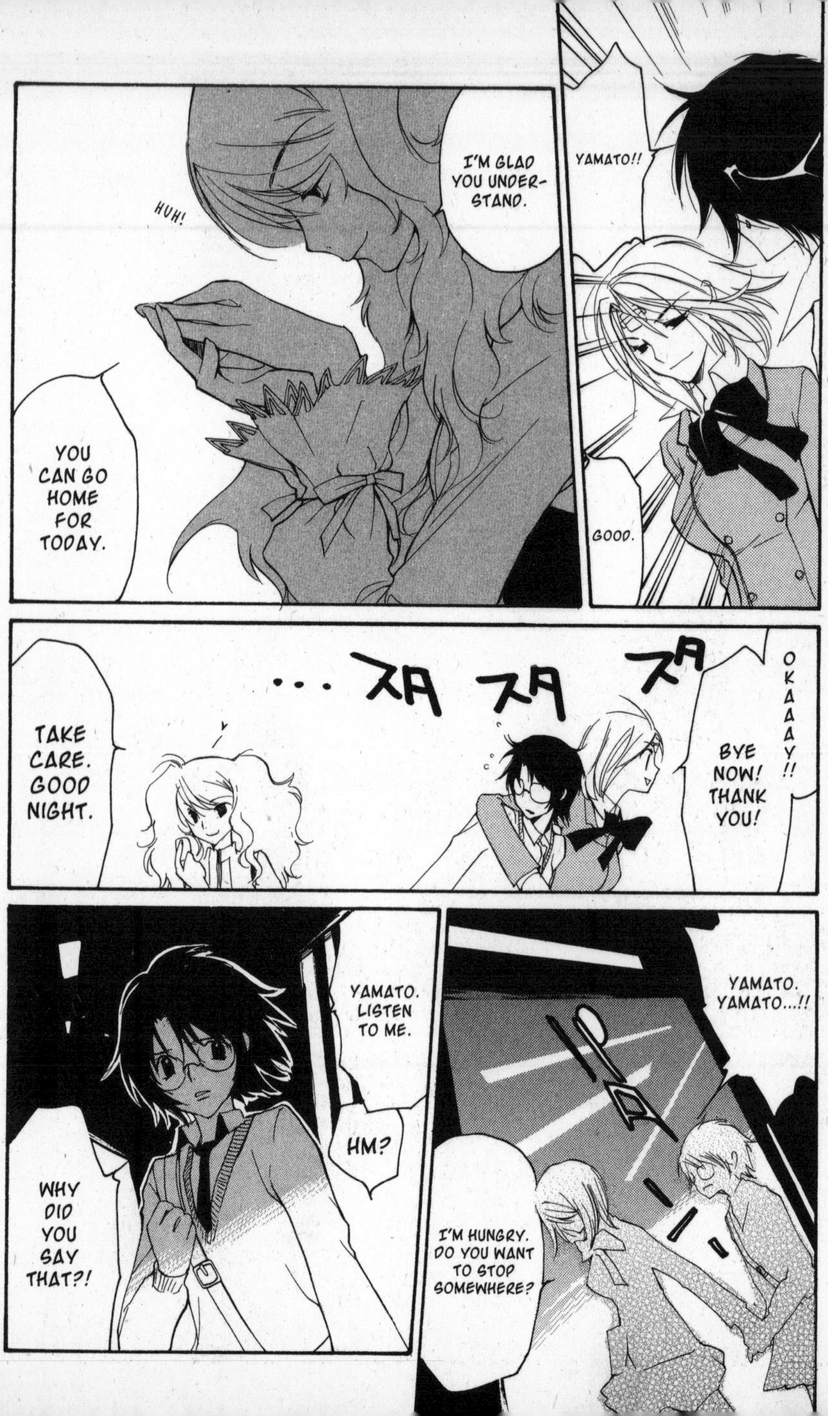
YAMATO!!
GOOD.
I'M GLAD YOU UNDER-STAND.
HUH!
YOU CAN GO HOME FOR TODAY.
OKAAAAY!!
BYE NOW! THANK YOU!
スタ スタ スタ
...
TAKE CARE. GOOD NIGHT.
YAMATO. YAMATO...!!
I'M HUNGRY. DO YOU WANT TO STOP SOMEWHERE?
YAMATO. LISTEN TO ME.
HM?
WHY DID YOU SAY THAT?!

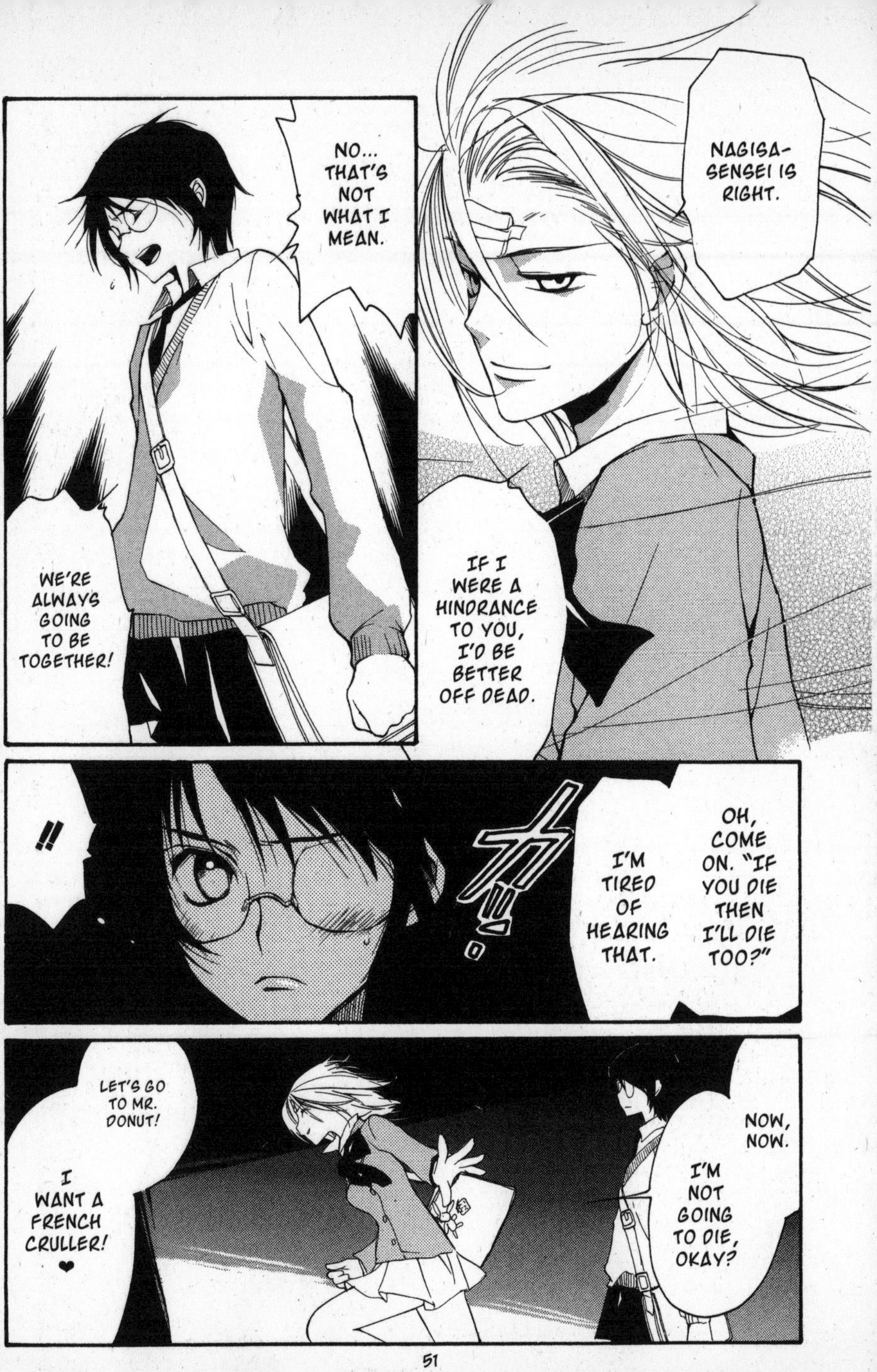
NAGISA-SENSEI IS RIGHT.
IF I WERE A HINDRANCE TO YOU, I'D BE BETTER OFF DEAD.
NO... THAT'S NOT WHAT I MEAN.
WE'RE ALWAYS GOING TO BE TOGETHER!
OH, COME ON. "IF YOU DIE THEN I'LL DIE TOO?"
I'M TIRED OF HEARING THAT.
!!
NOW, NOW.
I'M NOT GOING TO DIE, OKAY?
LET'S GO TO MR. DONUT!
I WANT A FRENCH CRULLER! ❤

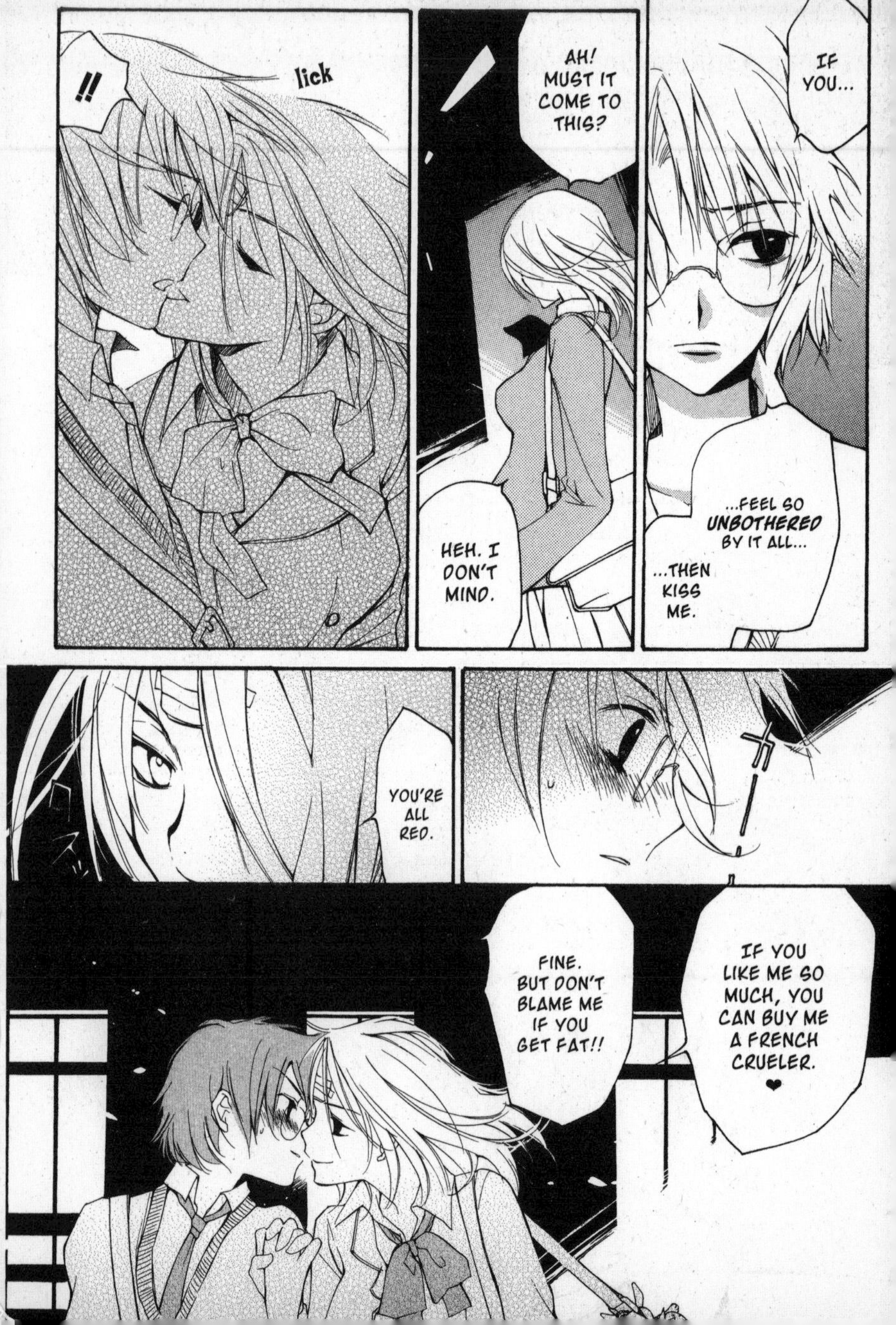
IF YOU...
...FEEL SO UNBOTHERED BY IT ALL...
...THEN KISS ME.
AH! MUST IT COME TO THIS?
HEH. I DON'T MIND.
!!
lick
YOU'RE ALL RED.
IF YOU LIKE ME SO MUCH, YOU CAN BUY ME A FRENCH CRUELER. ❤
FINE. BUT DON'T BLAME ME IF YOU GET FAT!!

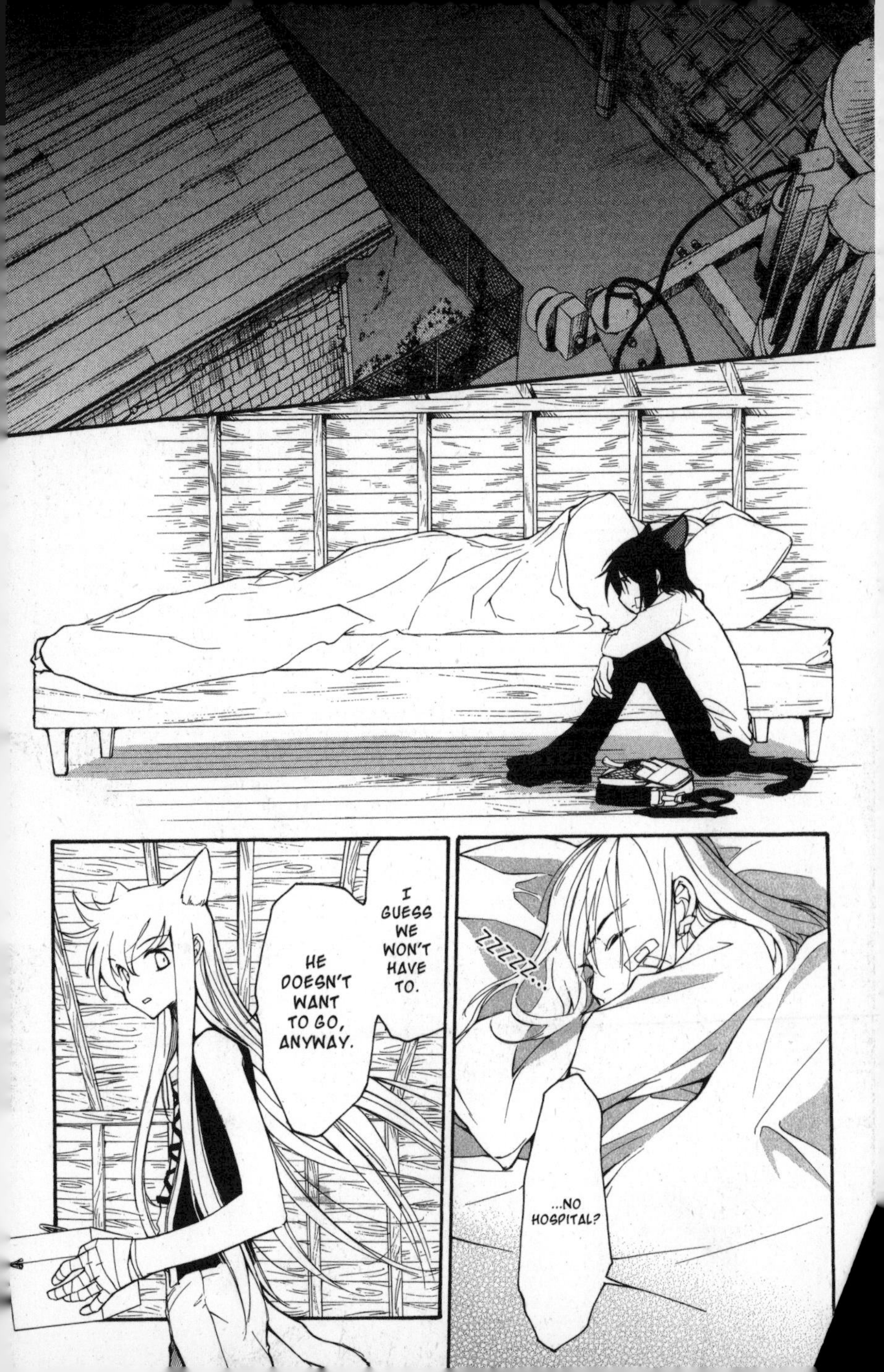
ZZZZZZ...
...NO HOSPITAL?
I GUESS WE WON'T HAVE TO.
HE DOESN'T WANT TO GO, ANYWAY.

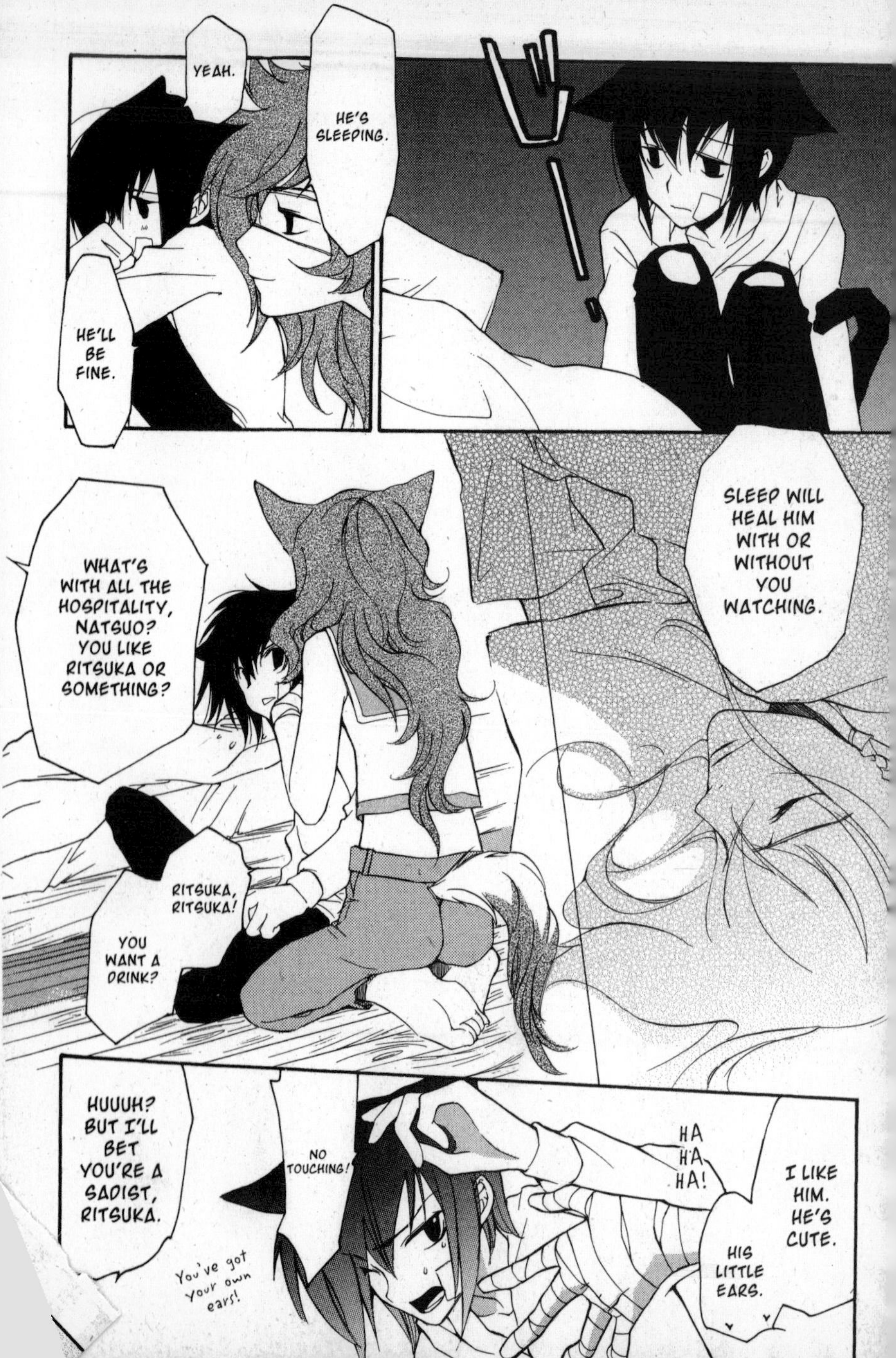
HE'S SLEEPING.
YEAH.
HE'LL BE FINE.
SLEEP WILL HEAL HIM WITH OR WITHOUT YOU WATCHING.
WHAT'S WITH ALL THE HOSPITALITY, NATSUO? YOU LIKE RITSUKA OR SOMETHING?
RITSUKA, RITSUKA!
YOU WANT A DRINK?
I LIKE HIM. HE'S CUTE.
HIS LITTLE EARS.
HA HA HA!
NO TOUCHING!
HUUUH? BUT I'LL BET YOU'RE A SADIST, RITSUKA.
You've got your own ears!

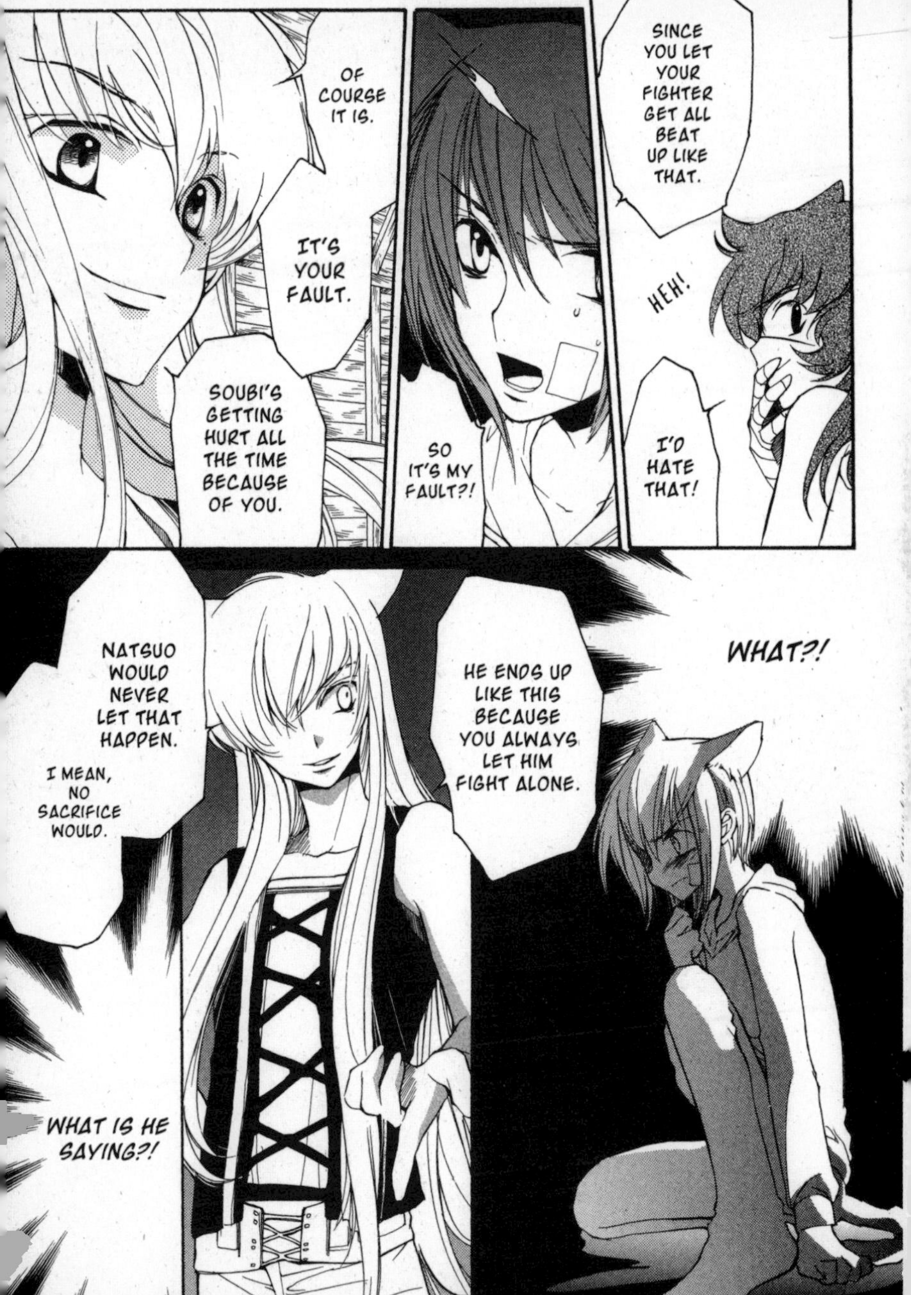
SINCE YOU LET YOUR FIGHTER GET ALL BEAT UP LIKE THAT.
HEH!
I'D HATE THAT!
SO IT'S MY FAULT?!
OF COURSE IT IS.
IT'S YOUR FAULT.
SOUBI'S GETTING HURT ALL THE TIME BECAUSE OF YOU.
HE ENDS UP LIKE THIS BECAUSE YOU ALWAYS LET HIM FIGHT ALONE.
WHAT?!
NATSUO WOULD NEVER LET THAT HAPPEN.
I MEAN, NO SACRIFICE WOULD.
WHAT IS HE SAYING?!

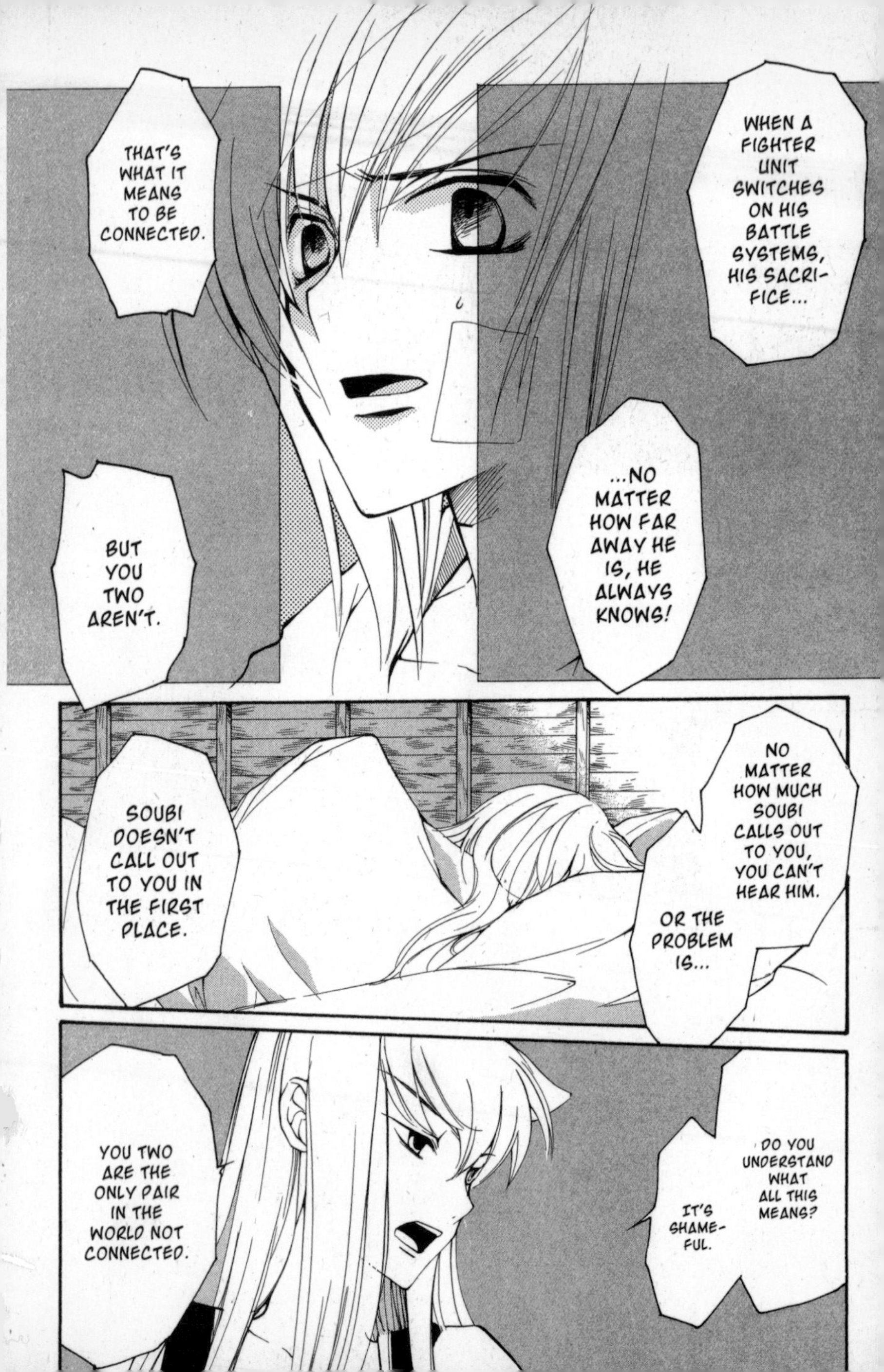
WHEN A FIGHTER UNIT SWITCHES ON HIS BATTLE SYSTEMS, HIS SACRIFICE...
...NO MATTER HOW FAR AWAY HE IS, HE ALWAYS KNOWS!
THAT'S WHAT IT MEANS TO BE CONNECTED.
BUT YOU TWO AREN'T.
NO MATTER HOW MUCH SOUBI CALLS OUT TO YOU, YOU CAN'T HEAR HIM.
OR THE PROBLEM IS...
SOUBI DOESN'T CALL OUT TO YOU IN THE FIRST PLACE.
DO YOU UNDERSTAND WHAT ALL THIS MEANS?
IT'S SHAME-FUL.
YOU TWO ARE THE ONLY PAIR IN THE WORLD NOT CONNECTED.

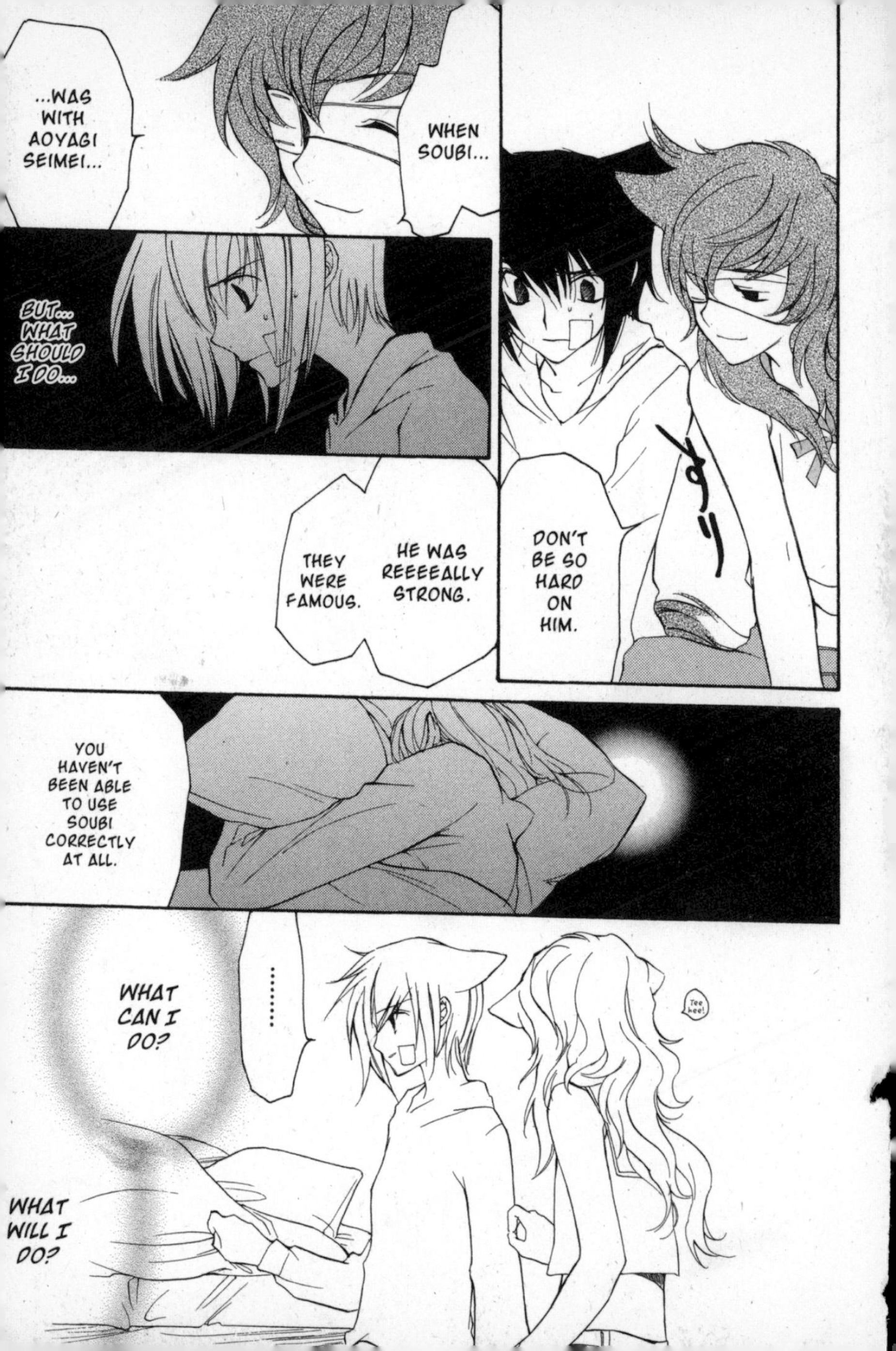

DON'T BE SO HARD ON HIM.
WHEN SOUBI...
...WAS WITH AOYAGI SEIMEI...
BUT... WHAT SHOULD I DO...
HE WAS REEEEALLY STRONG.
THEY WERE FAMOUS.
YOU HAVEN'T BEEN ABLE TO USE SOUBI CORRECTLY AT ALL.
......
Tee hee!
WHAT CAN I DO?
WHAT WILL I DO?

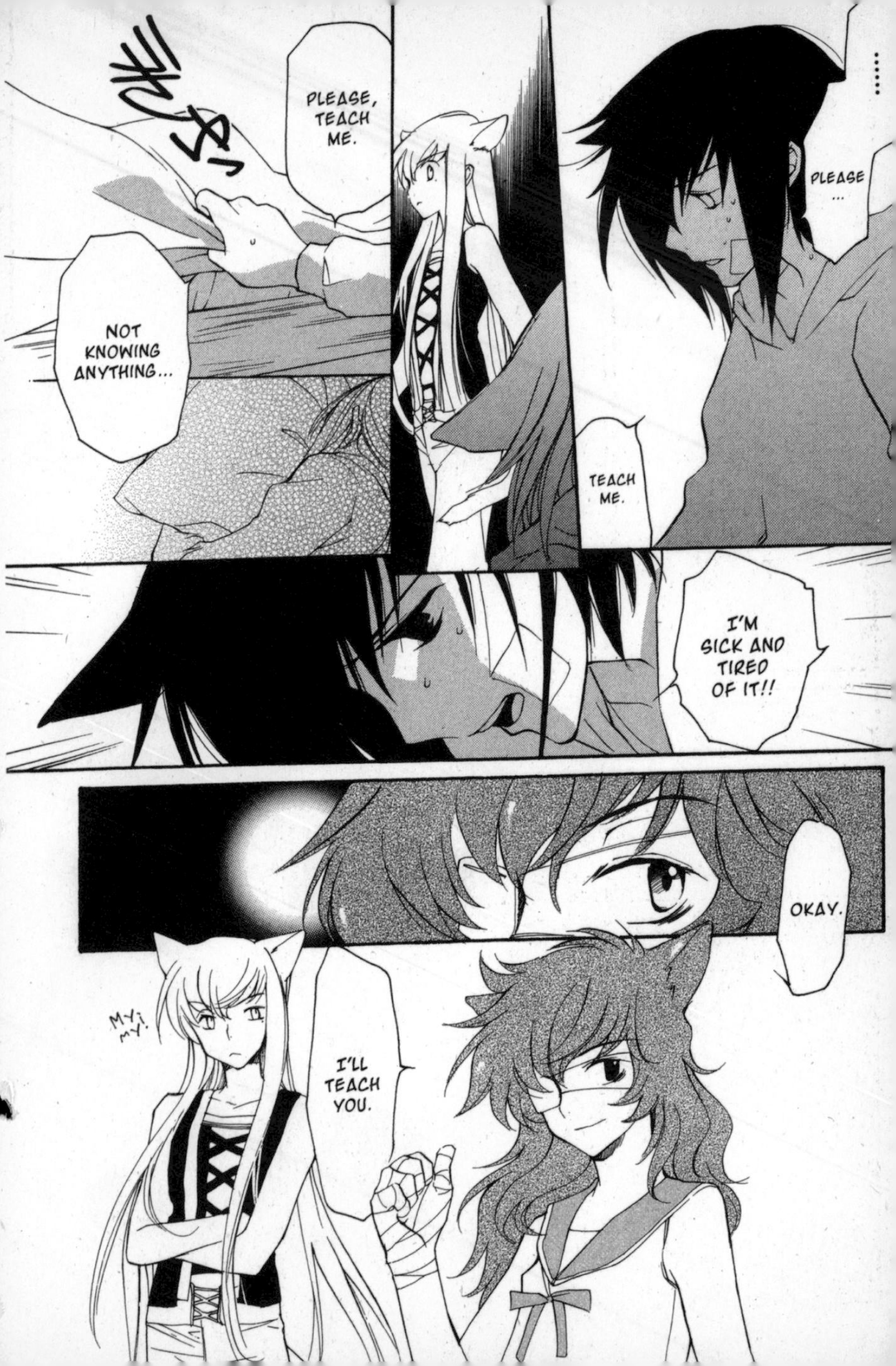
PLEASE ...
TEACH ME.
PLEASE, TEACH ME.
NOT KNOWING ANYTHING...
I'M SICK AND TIRED OF IT!!
OKAY.
I'LL TEACH YOU.
MY, MY.

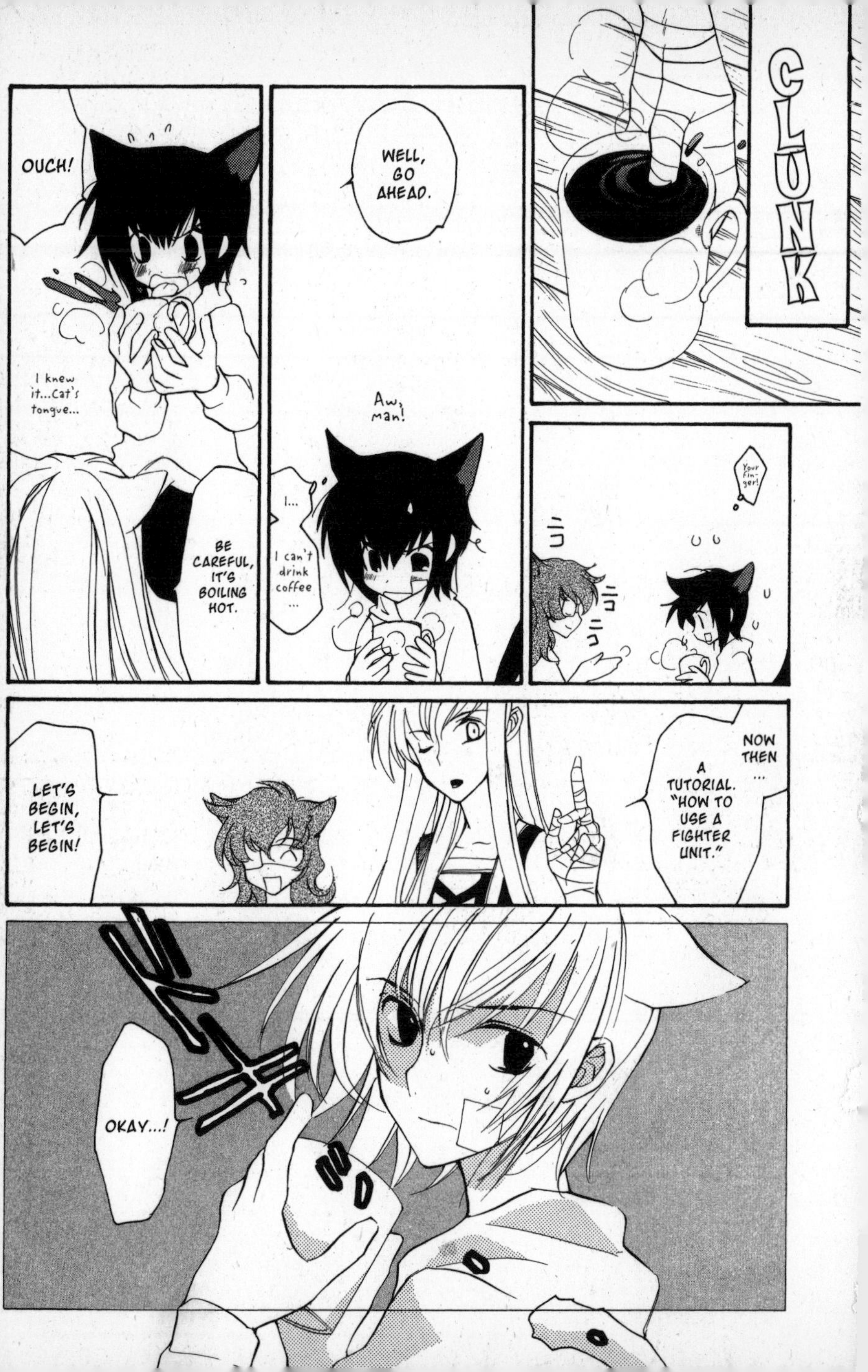
CLUNK
Your fin-ger!
WELL, GO AHEAD.
Aw, man!
I...
I can't drink coffee ...
OUCH!
I knew it...Cat's tongue...
BE CAREFUL, IT'S BOILING HOT.
NOW THEN ...
A TUTORIAL. "HOW TO USE A FIGHTER UNIT."
LET'S BEGIN, LET'S BEGIN!
OKAY...!

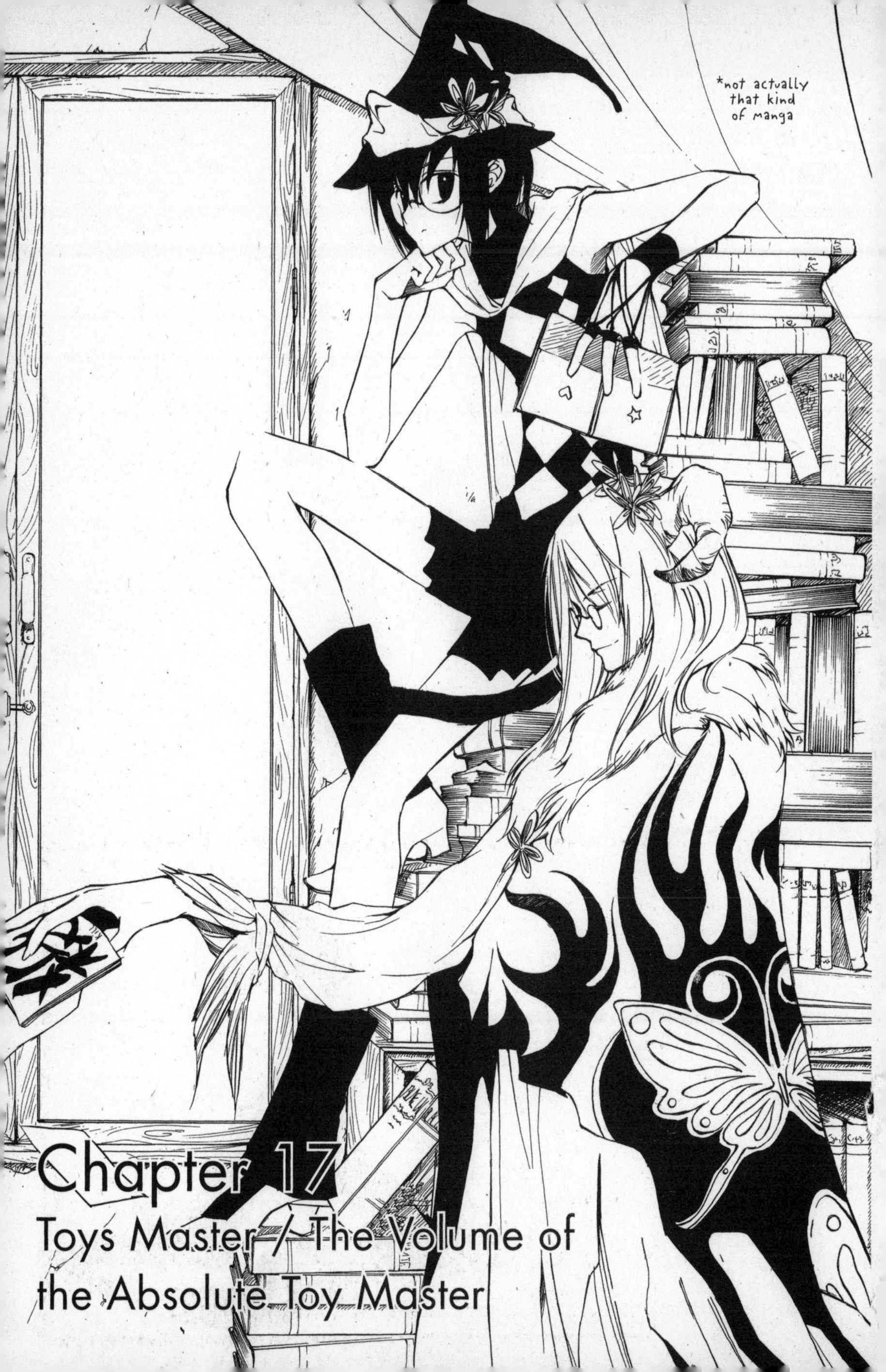
*not actually that kind of manga

Chapter 17
Toys Master / The Volume of the Absolute Toy Master

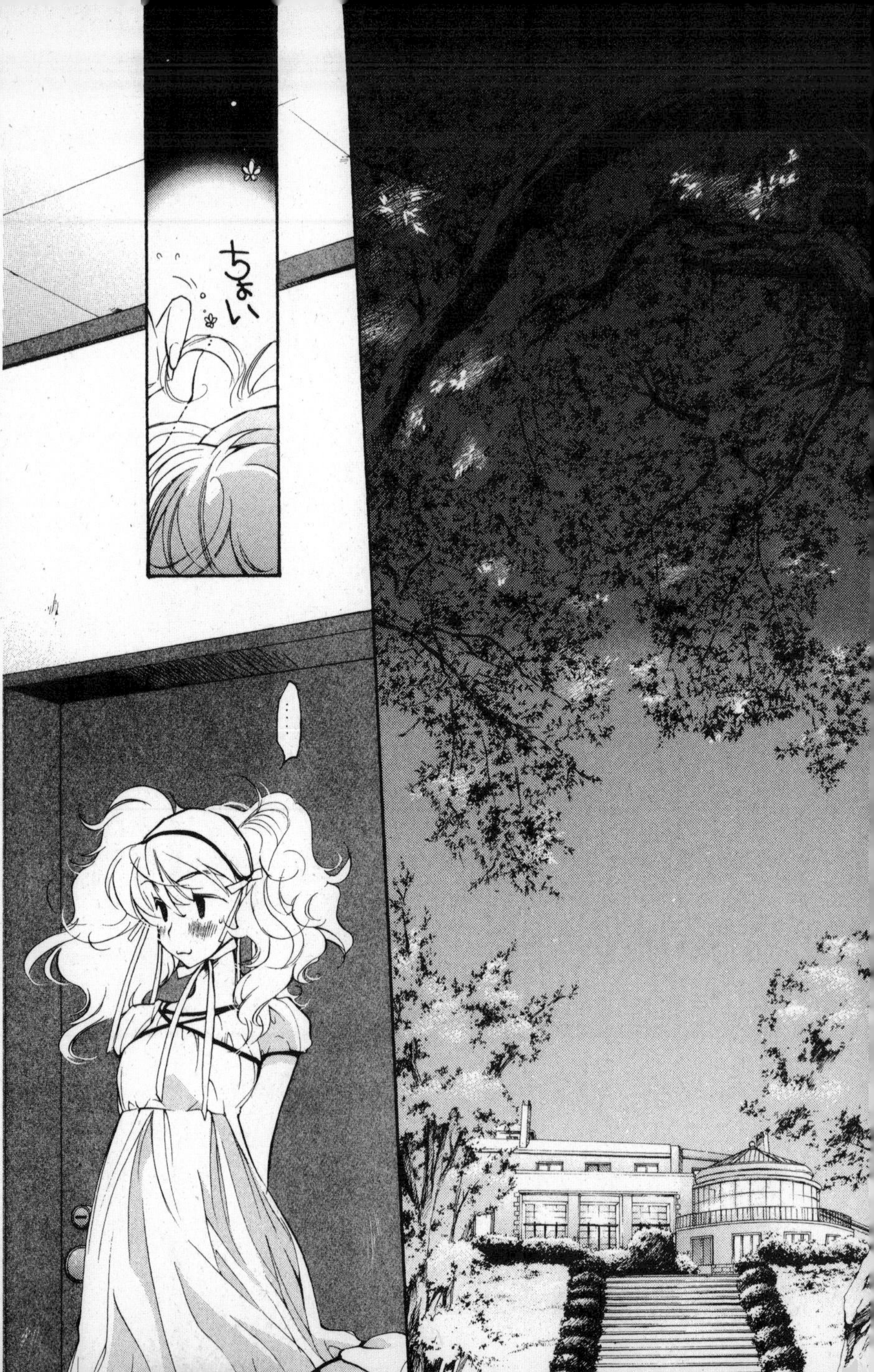
ちょい
……

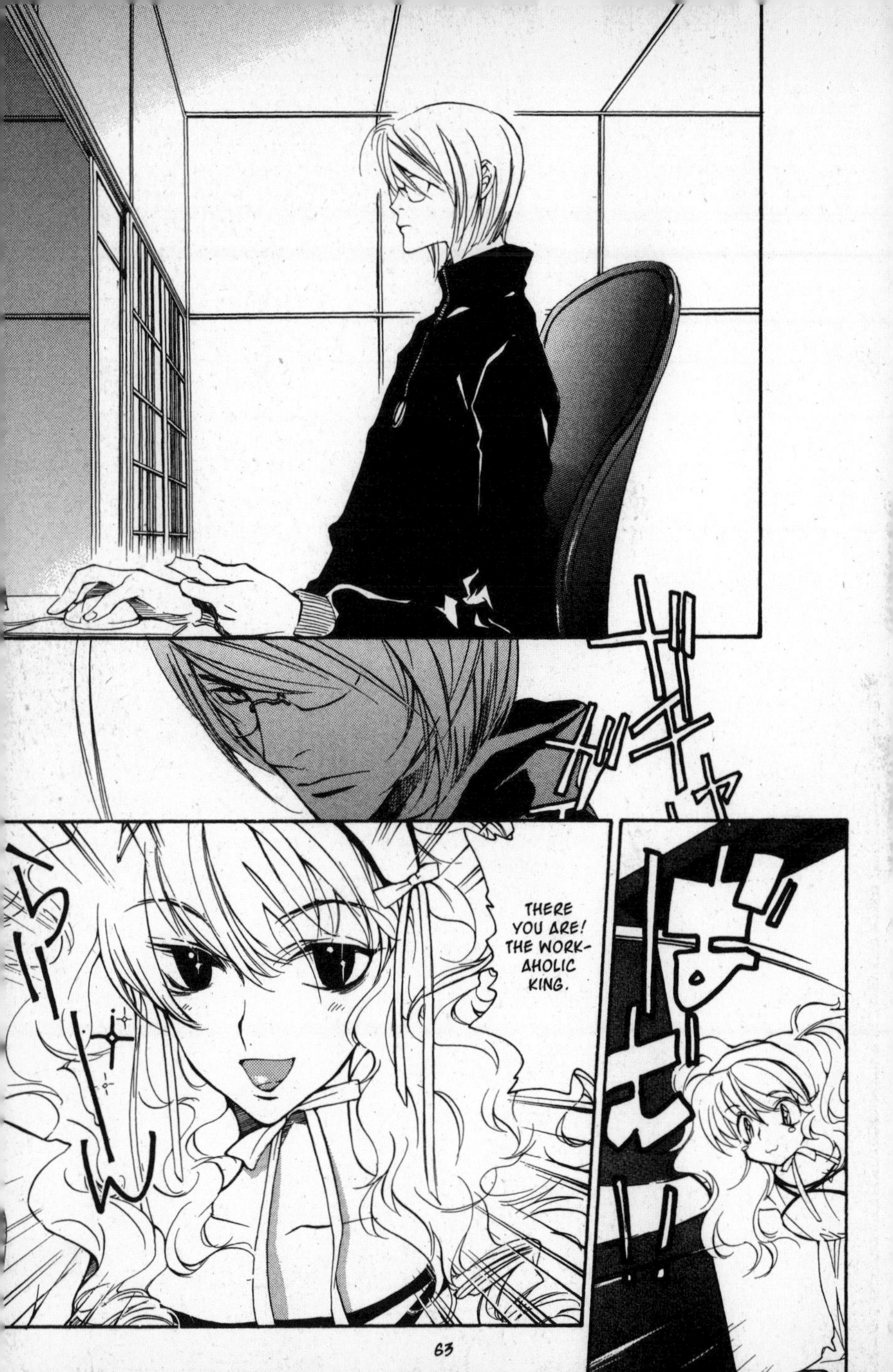
THERE YOU ARE! THE WORK-AHOLIC KING.

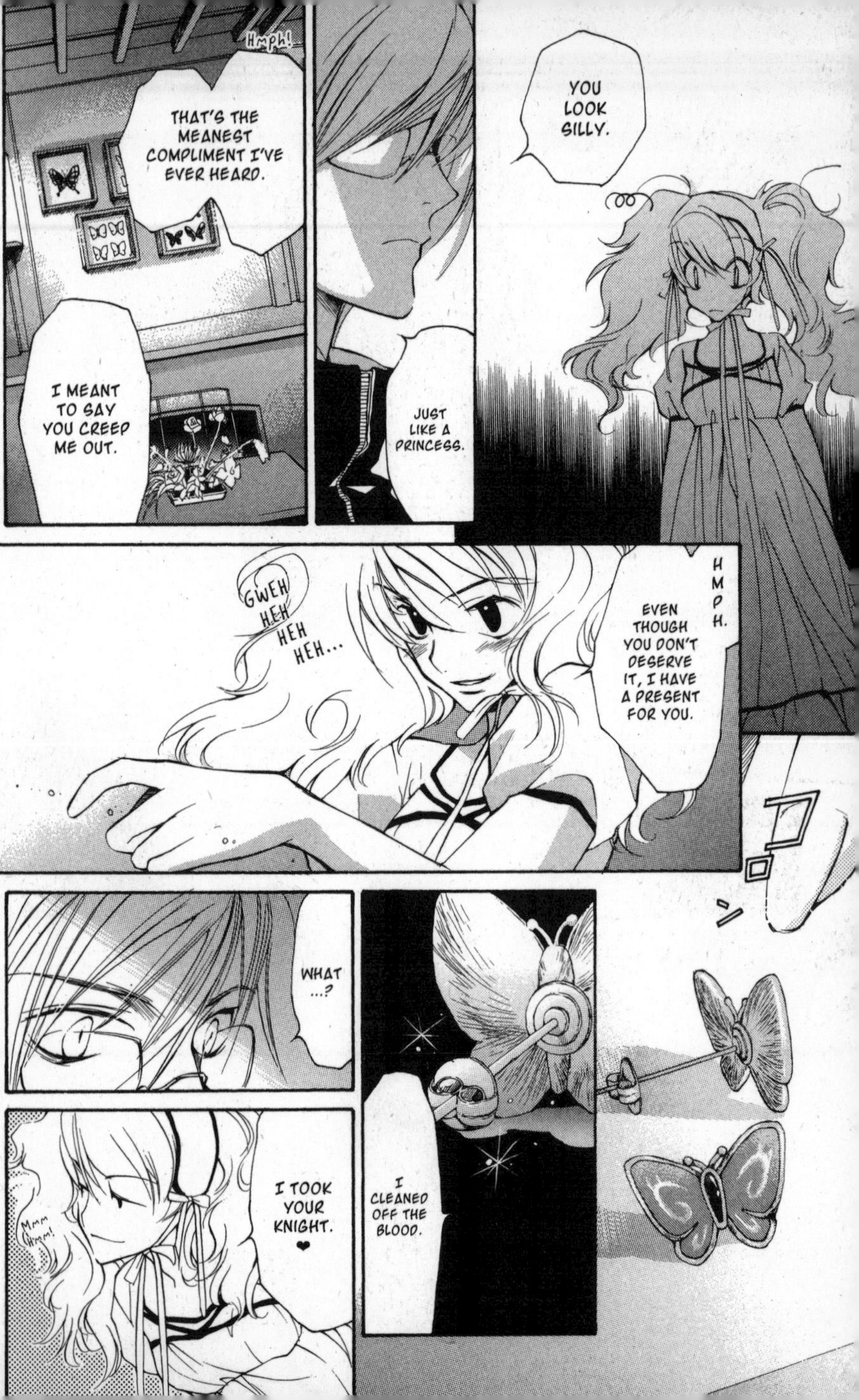
YOU LOOK SILLY.
JUST LIKE A PRINCESS.
Hmph!
THAT'S THE MEANEST COMPLIMENT I'VE EVER HEARD.
I MEANT TO SAY YOU CREEP ME OUT.
HMPH.
EVEN THOUGH YOU DON'T DESERVE IT, I HAVE A PRESENT FOR YOU.
GWEH HEH HEH HEH...
I CLEANED OFF THE BLOOD.
WHAT ...?
I TOOK YOUR KNIGHT. ❤
Mmm Hmm!

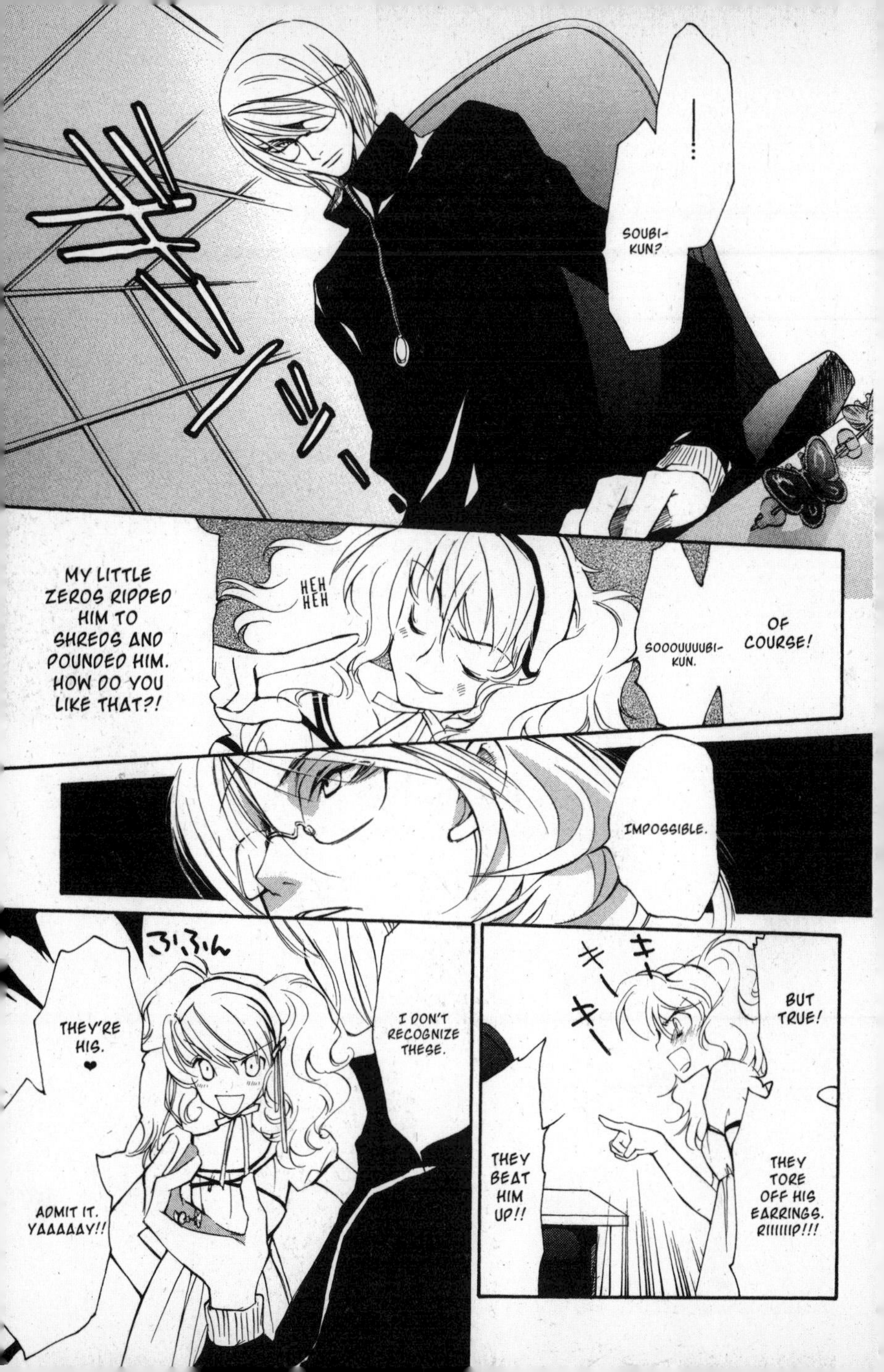
...
SOUBI-KUN?
OF COURSE!
SOOOUUUUBI-KUN.
HEH HEH
MY LITTLE ZEROS RIPPED HIM TO SHREDS AND POUNDED HIM. HOW DO YOU LIKE THAT?!
IMPOSSIBLE.
BUT TRUE!
キーキー
THEY TORE OFF HIS EARRINGS. RIIIIIIP!!!
THEY BEAT HIM UP!!
ふふん
I DON'T RECOGNIZE THESE.
THEY'RE HIS. ❤
ADMIT IT. YAAAAAY!!

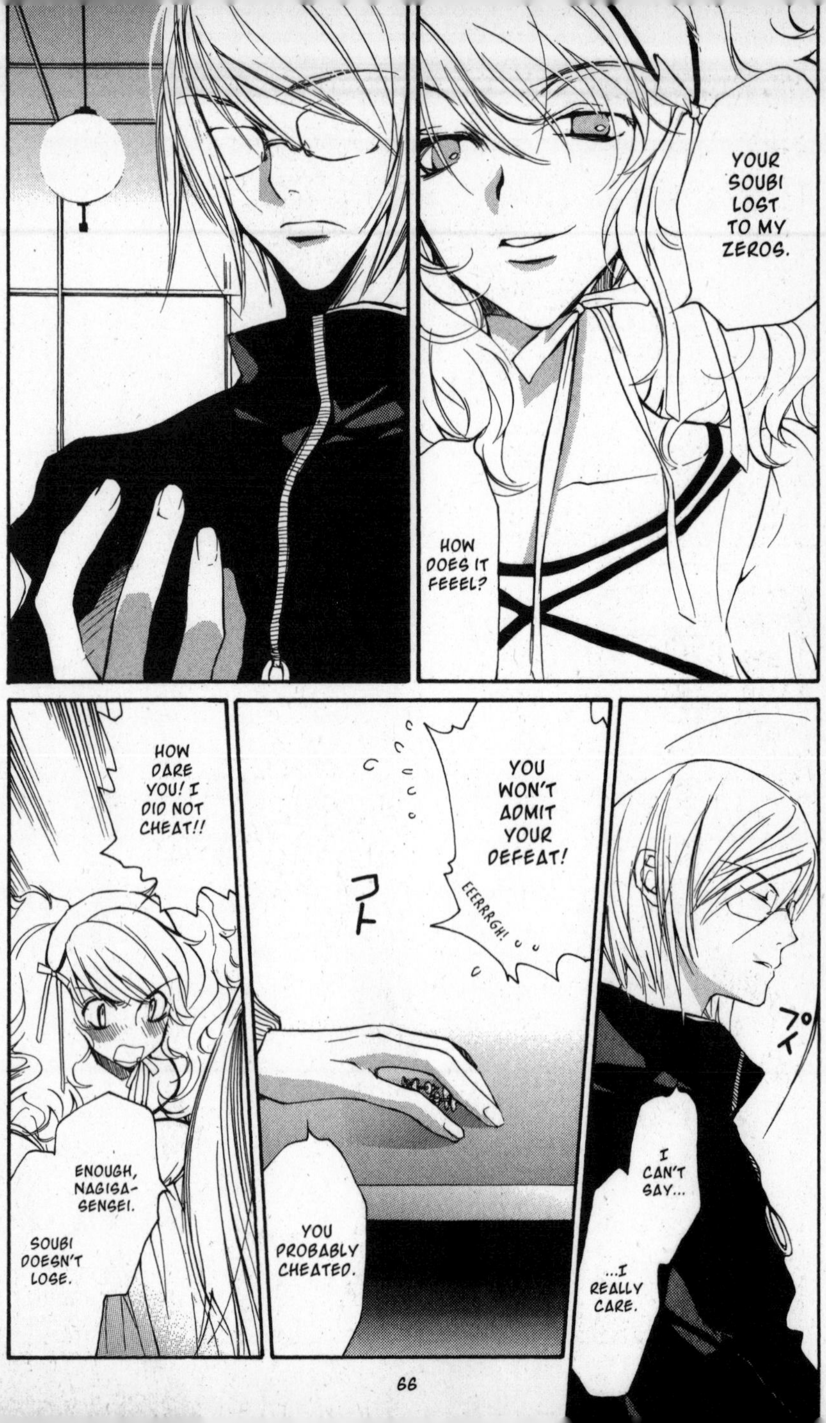
YOUR SOUBI LOST TO MY ZEROS.
HOW DOES IT FEEEL?
プイ
I CAN'T SAY...
...I REALLY CARE.
YOU WON'T ADMIT YOUR DEFEAT!
EEERRRGH!
コト
YOU PROBABLY CHEATED.
HOW DARE YOU! I DID NOT CHEAT!!
ENOUGH, NAGISA-SENSEI.
SOUBI DOESN'T LOSE.

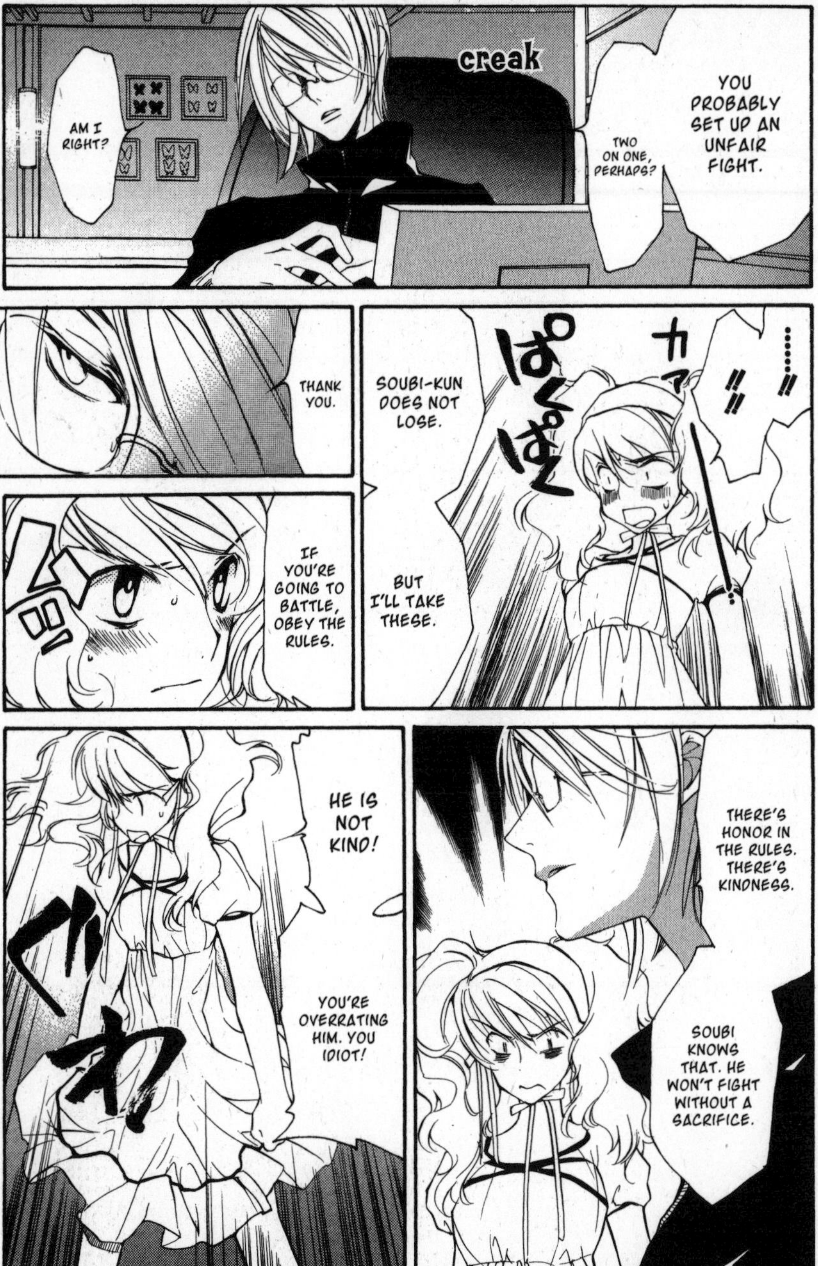
YOU PROBABLY SET UP AN UNFAIR FIGHT.
TWO ON ONE, PERHAPS?
creak
AM I RIGHT?
......!!
カァ
ぱくぱく
SOUBI-KUN DOES NOT LOSE.
BUT I'LL TAKE THESE.
THANK YOU.
IF YOU'RE GOING TO BATTLE, OBEY THE RULES.
THERE'S HONOR IN THE RULES. THERE'S KINDNESS.
SOUBI KNOWS THAT. HE WON'T FIGHT WITHOUT A SACRIFICE.
HE IS NOT KIND!
YOU'RE OVERRATING HIM. YOU IDIOT!

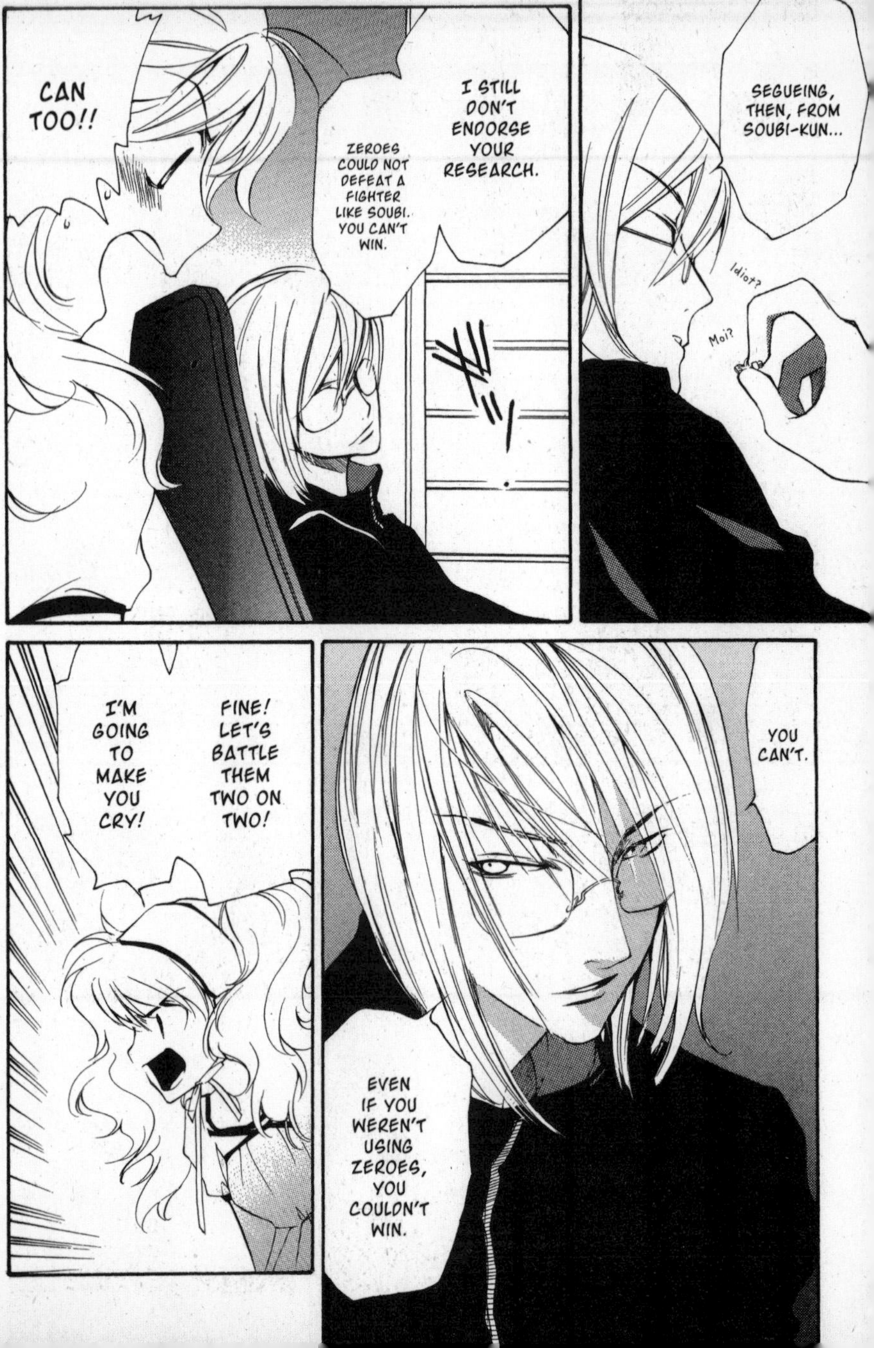
SEGUEING, THEN, FROM SOUBI-KUN...
Idiot?
Moi?
I STILL DON'T ENDORSE YOUR RESEARCH.
ZEROES COULD NOT DEFEAT A FIGHTER LIKE SOUBI. YOU CAN'T WIN.
CAN TOO!!
YOU CAN'T.
EVEN IF YOU WEREN'T USING ZEROES, YOU COULDN'T WIN.
FINE! LET'S BATTLE THEM TWO ON TWO!
I'M GOING TO MAKE YOU CRY!

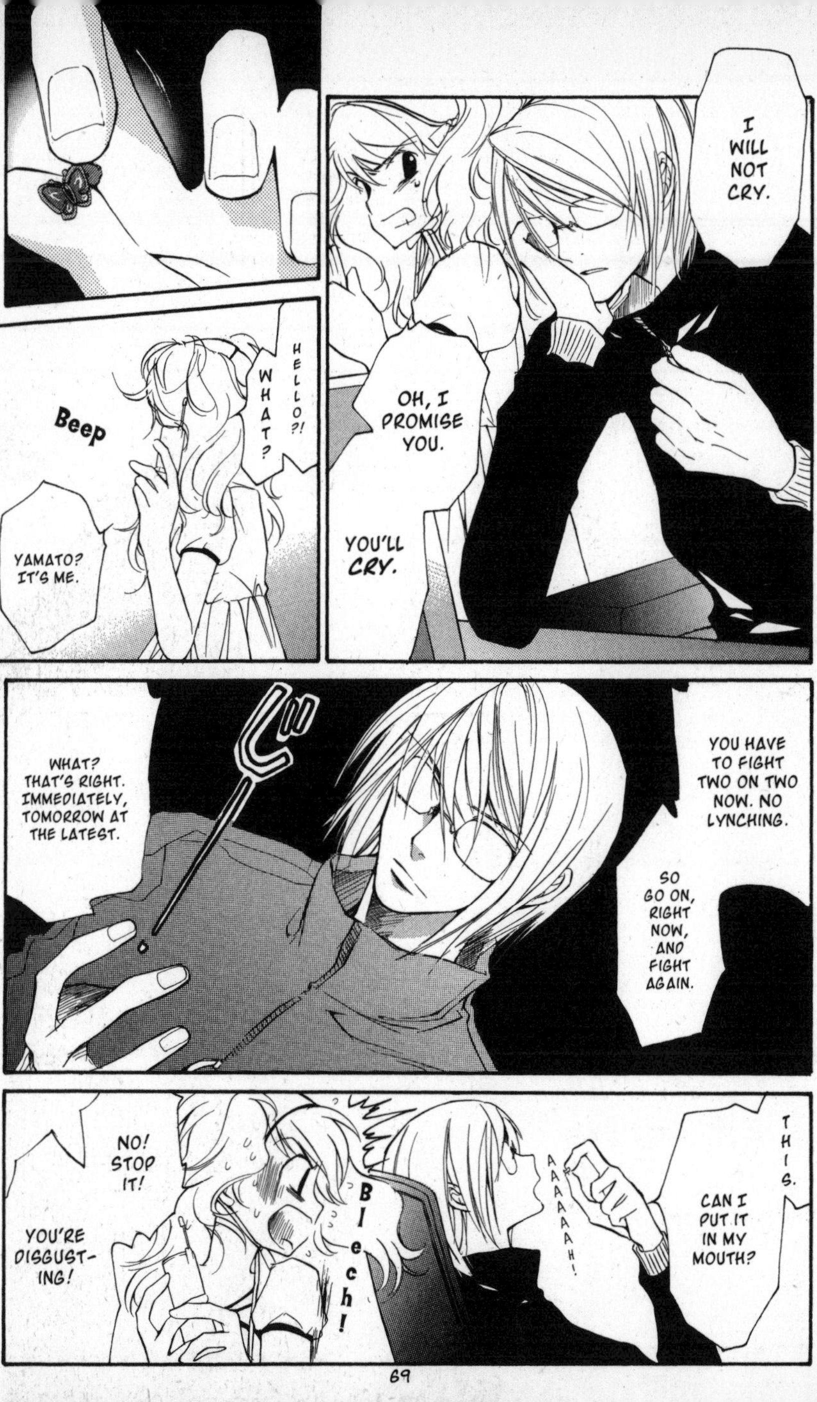
I WILL NOT CRY.
OH, I PROMISE YOU.
YOU'LL CRY.
HELLO?!
WHAT?
Beep
YAMATO? IT'S ME.
YOU HAVE TO FIGHT TWO ON TWO NOW. NO LYNCHING.
SO GO ON, RIGHT NOW, AND FIGHT AGAIN.
WHAT? THAT'S RIGHT. IMMEDIATELY, TOMORROW AT THE LATEST.
THIS.
CAN I PUT IT IN MY MOUTH?
AAAAAAH!
Blech!
NO! STOP IT!
YOU'RE DISGUSTING!

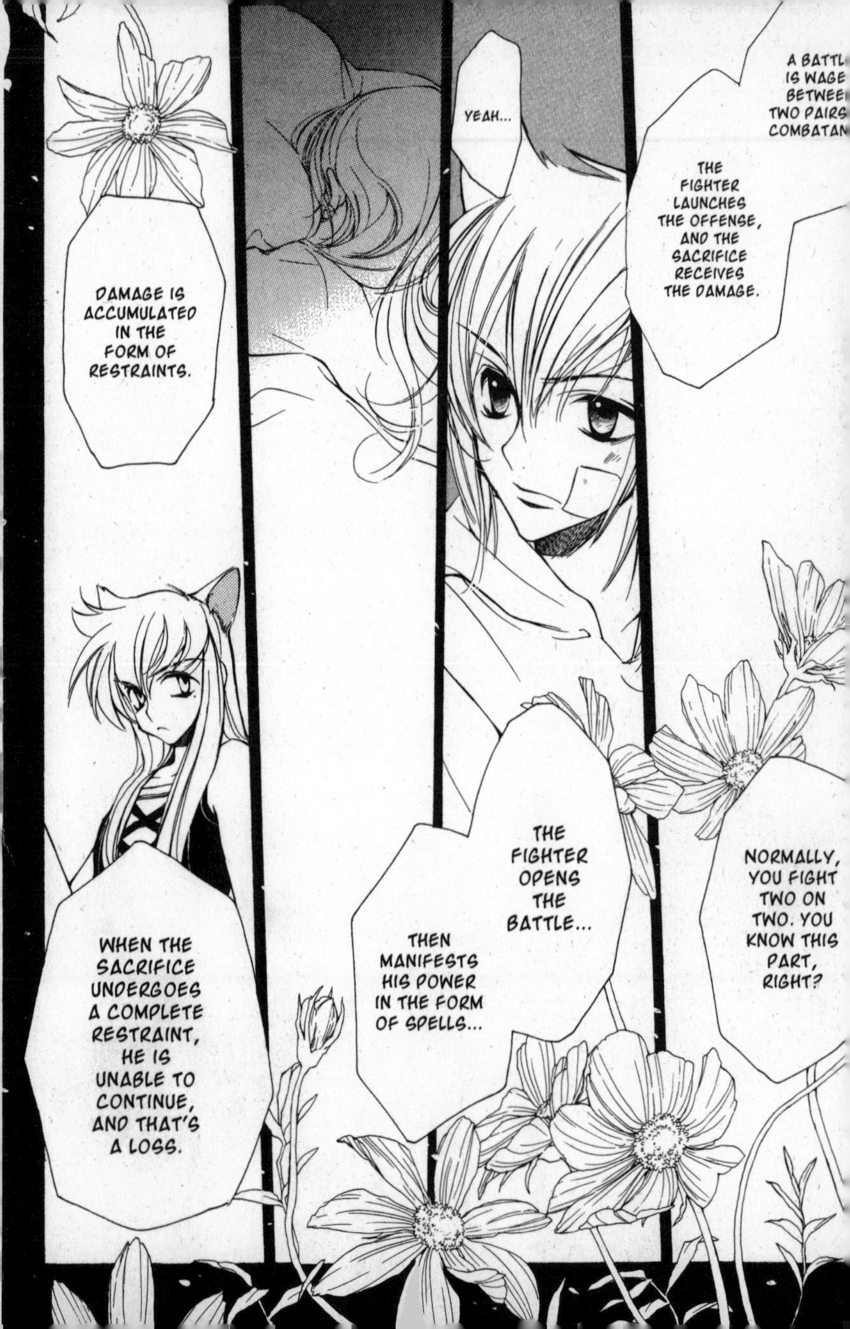
A BATTL IS WAGE BETWEE TWO PAIRS COMBATAN
THE FIGHTER LAUNCHES THE OFFENSE, AND THE SACRIFICE RECEIVES THE DAMAGE.
NORMALLY, YOU FIGHT TWO ON TWO. YOU KNOW THIS PART, RIGHT?
YEAH...
THE FIGHTER OPENS THE BATTLE...
THEN MANIFESTS HIS POWER IN THE FORM OF SPELLS...
DAMAGE IS ACCUMULATED IN THE FORM OF RESTRAINTS.
WHEN THE SACRIFICE UNDERGOES A COMPLETE RESTRAINT, HE IS UNABLE TO CONTINUE, AND THAT'S A LOSS.

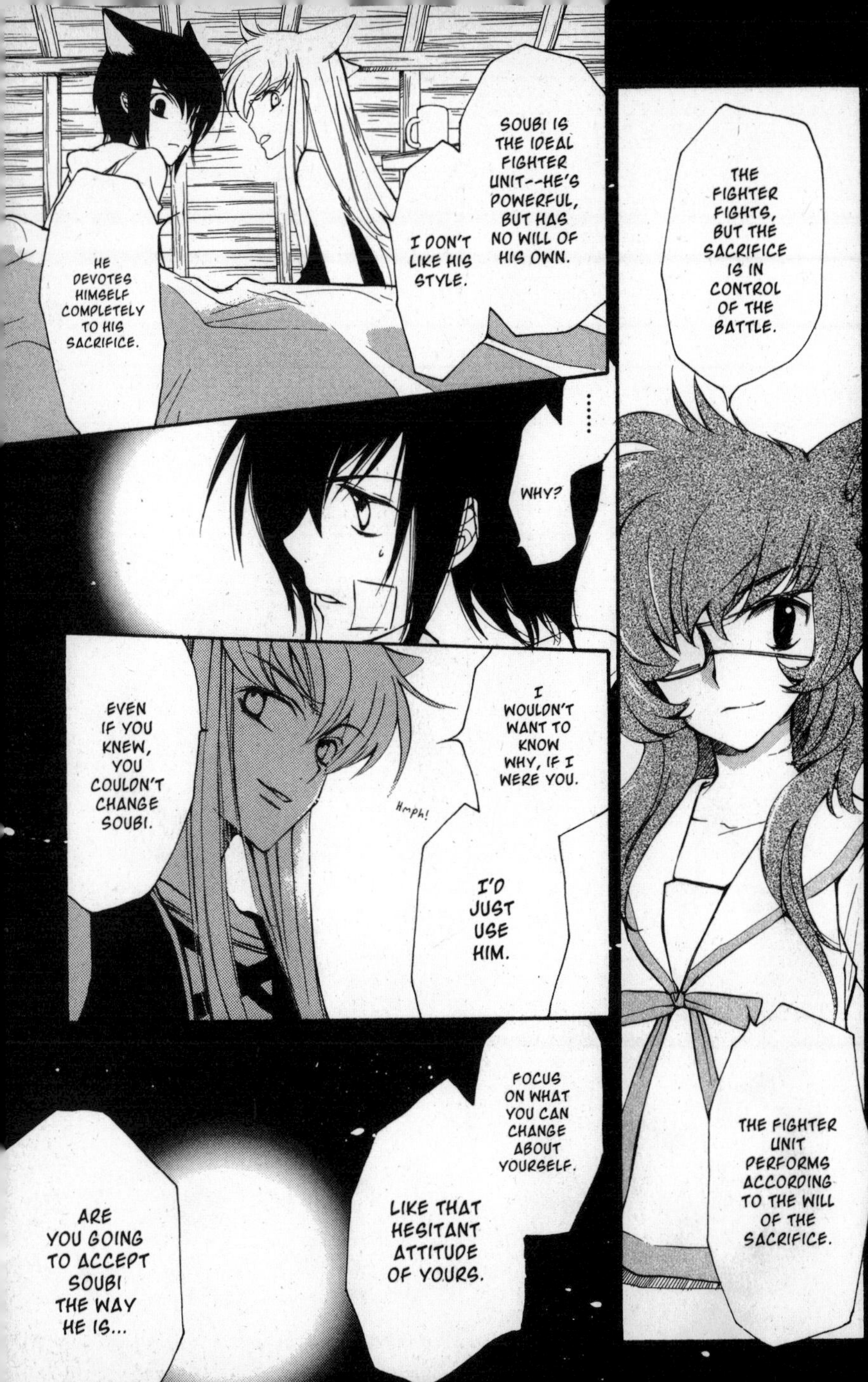
THE FIGHTER FIGHTS, BUT THE SACRIFICE IS IN CONTROL OF THE BATTLE.
THE FIGHTER UNIT PERFORMS ACCORDING TO THE WILL OF THE SACRIFICE.
SOUBI IS THE IDEAL FIGHTER UNIT--HE'S POWERFUL, BUT HAS NO WILL OF HIS OWN.
I DON'T LIKE HIS STYLE.
HE DEVOTES HIMSELF COMPLETELY TO HIS SACRIFICE.
......
WHY?
I WOULDN'T WANT TO KNOW WHY, IF I WERE YOU.
Hmph!
I'D JUST USE HIM.
EVEN IF YOU KNEW, YOU COULDN'T CHANGE SOUBI.
FOCUS ON WHAT YOU CAN CHANGE ABOUT YOURSELF.
LIKE THAT HESITANT ATTITUDE OF YOURS.
ARE YOU GOING TO ACCEPT SOUBI THE WAY HE IS...

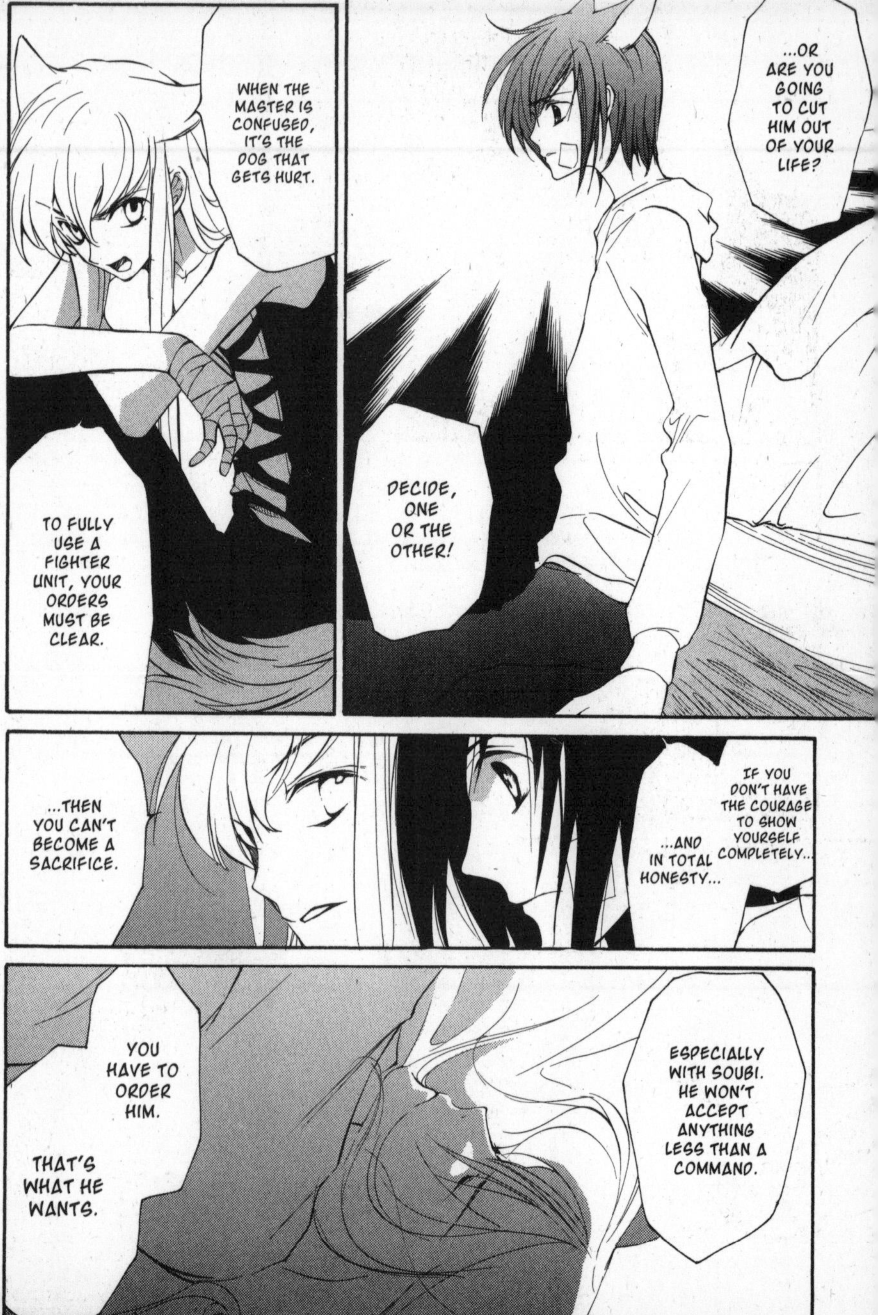
...OR ARE YOU GOING TO CUT HIM OUT OF YOUR LIFE?
DECIDE, ONE OR THE OTHER!
WHEN THE MASTER IS CONFUSED, IT'S THE DOG THAT GETS HURT.
TO FULLY USE A FIGHTER UNIT, YOUR ORDERS MUST BE CLEAR.
IF YOU DON'T HAVE THE COURAGE TO SHOW YOURSELF COMPLETELY...
...AND IN TOTAL HONESTY...
...THEN YOU CAN'T BECOME A SACRIFICE.
ESPECIALLY WITH SOUBI. HE WON'T ACCEPT ANYTHING LESS THAN A COMMAND.
YOU HAVE TO ORDER HIM.
THAT'S WHAT HE WANTS.

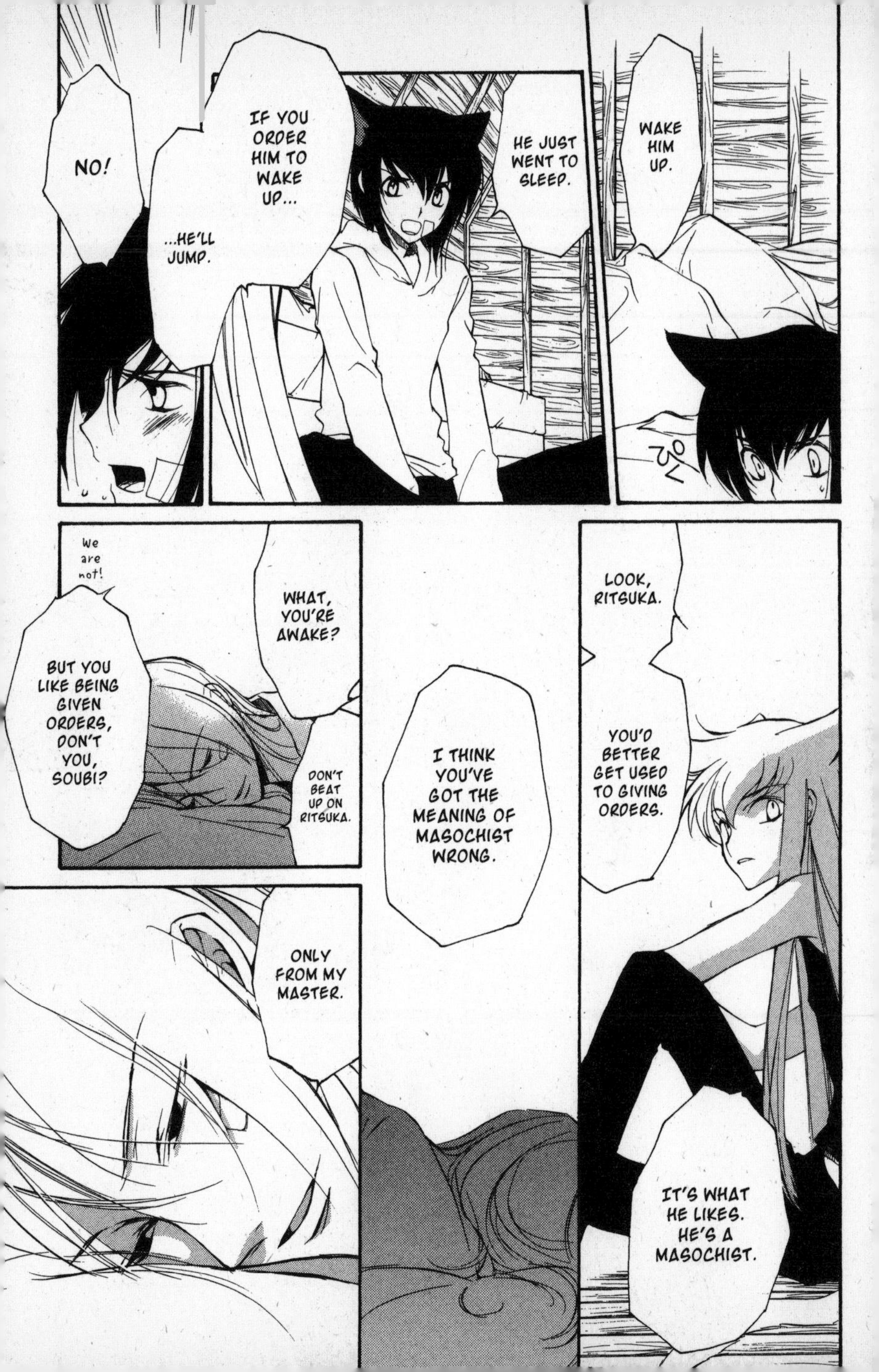
WAKE HIM UP.
HE JUST WENT TO SLEEP.
IF YOU ORDER HIM TO WAKE UP...
...HE'LL JUMP.
NO!
LOOK, RITSUKA.
YOU'D BETTER GET USED TO GIVING ORDERS.
IT'S WHAT HE LIKES. HE'S A MASOCHIST.
I THINK YOU'VE GOT THE MEANING OF MASOCHIST WRONG.
WHAT, YOU'RE AWAKE?
DON'T BEAT UP ON RITSUKA.
BUT YOU LIKE BEING GIVEN ORDERS, DON'T YOU, SOUBI?
We are not!
ONLY FROM MY MASTER.

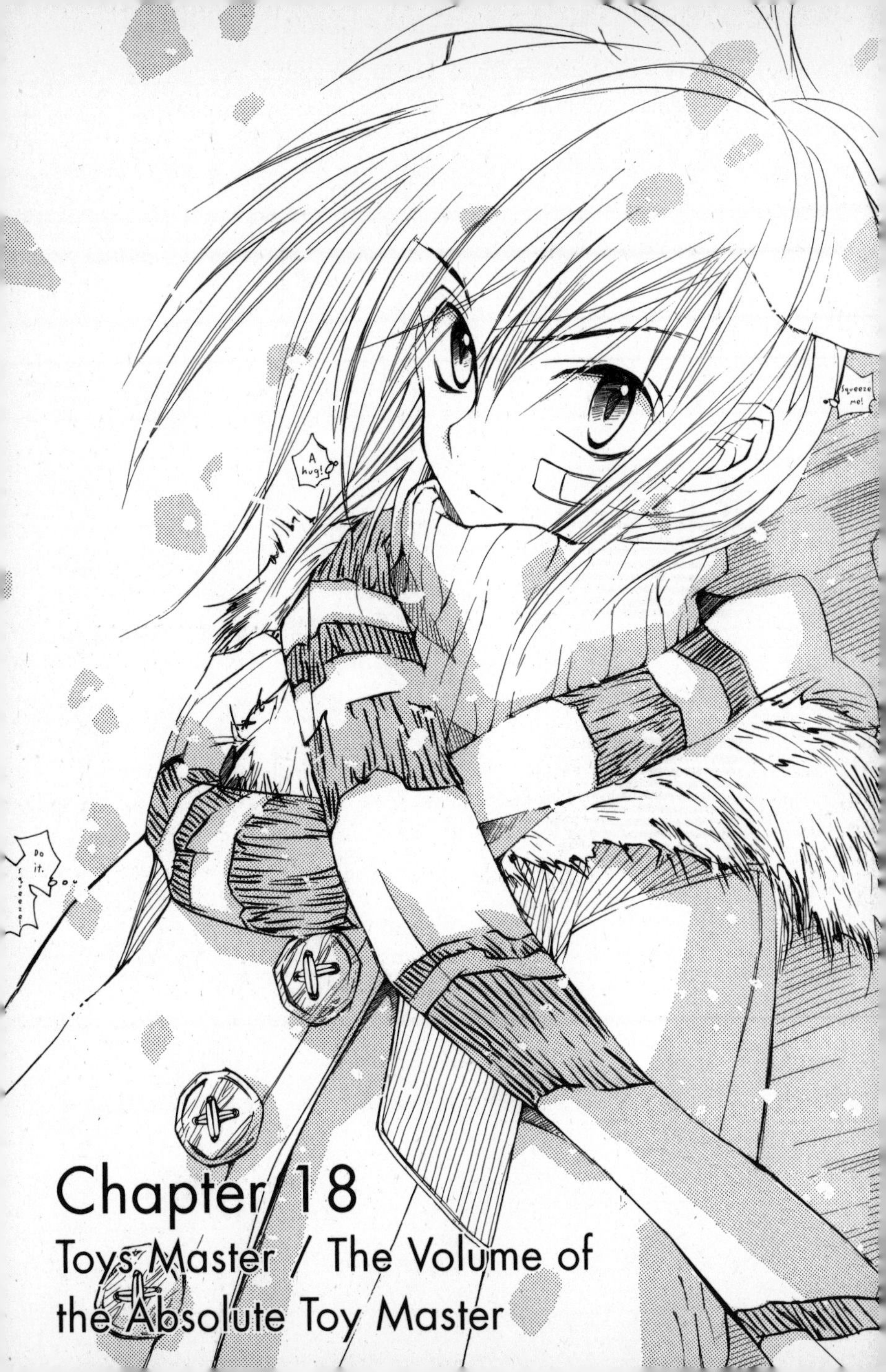
Squeeze me!
A hug!
Do it.
Squeeze!

Chapter 18

Toys Master / The Volume of the Absolute Toy Master

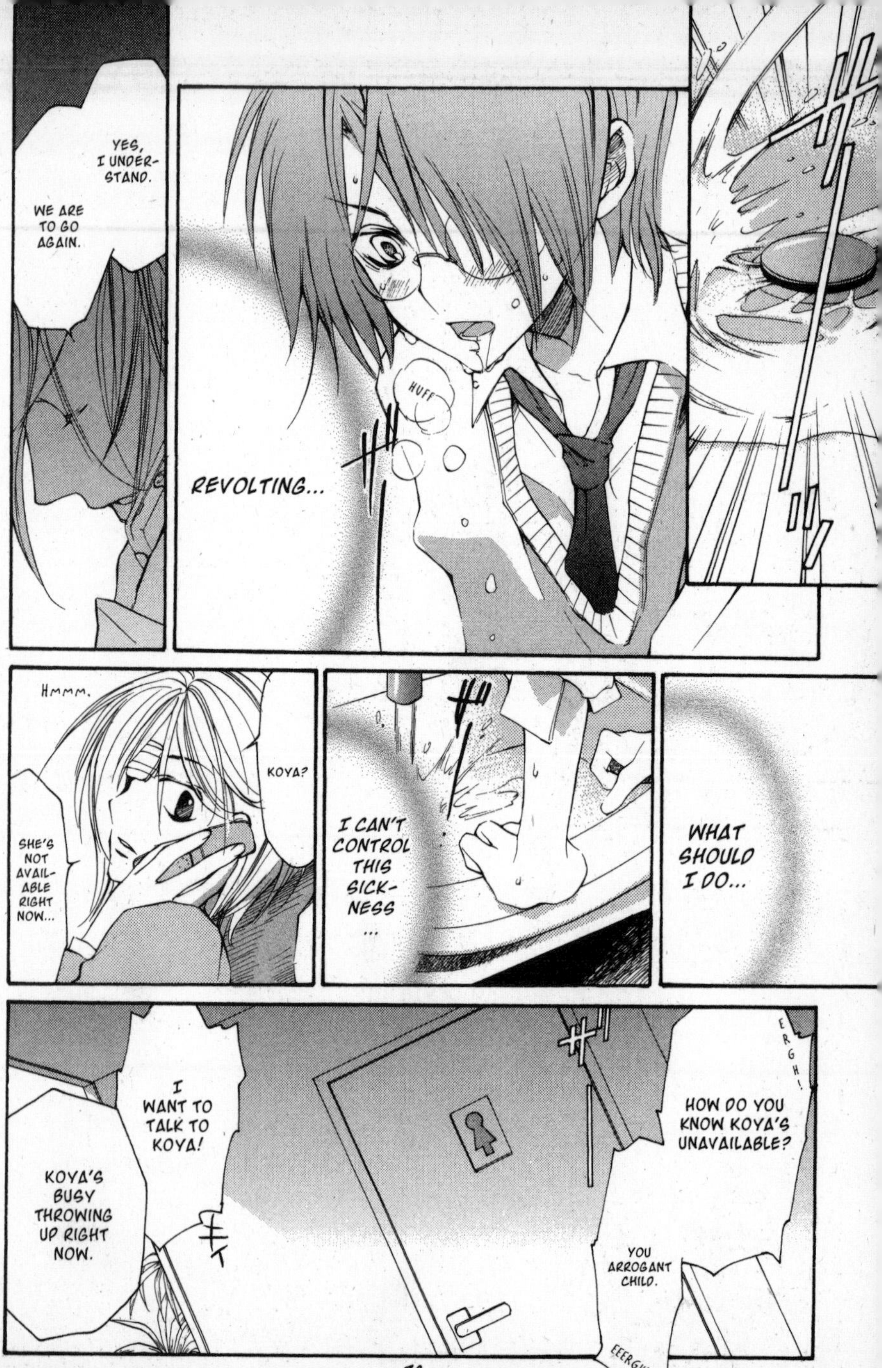
REVOLTING...
HUFF
YES, I UNDER-STAND.
WE ARE TO GO AGAIN.
WHAT SHOULD I DO...
I CAN'T CONTROL THIS SICK-NESS ...
HMMM.
KOYA?
SHE'S NOT AVAIL-ABLE RIGHT NOW...
ERGH!
HOW DO YOU KNOW KOYA'S UNAVAILABLE?
YOU ARROGANT CHILD.
EEERGH!
I WANT TO TALK TO KOYA!
KOYA'S BUSY THROWING UP RIGHT NOW.

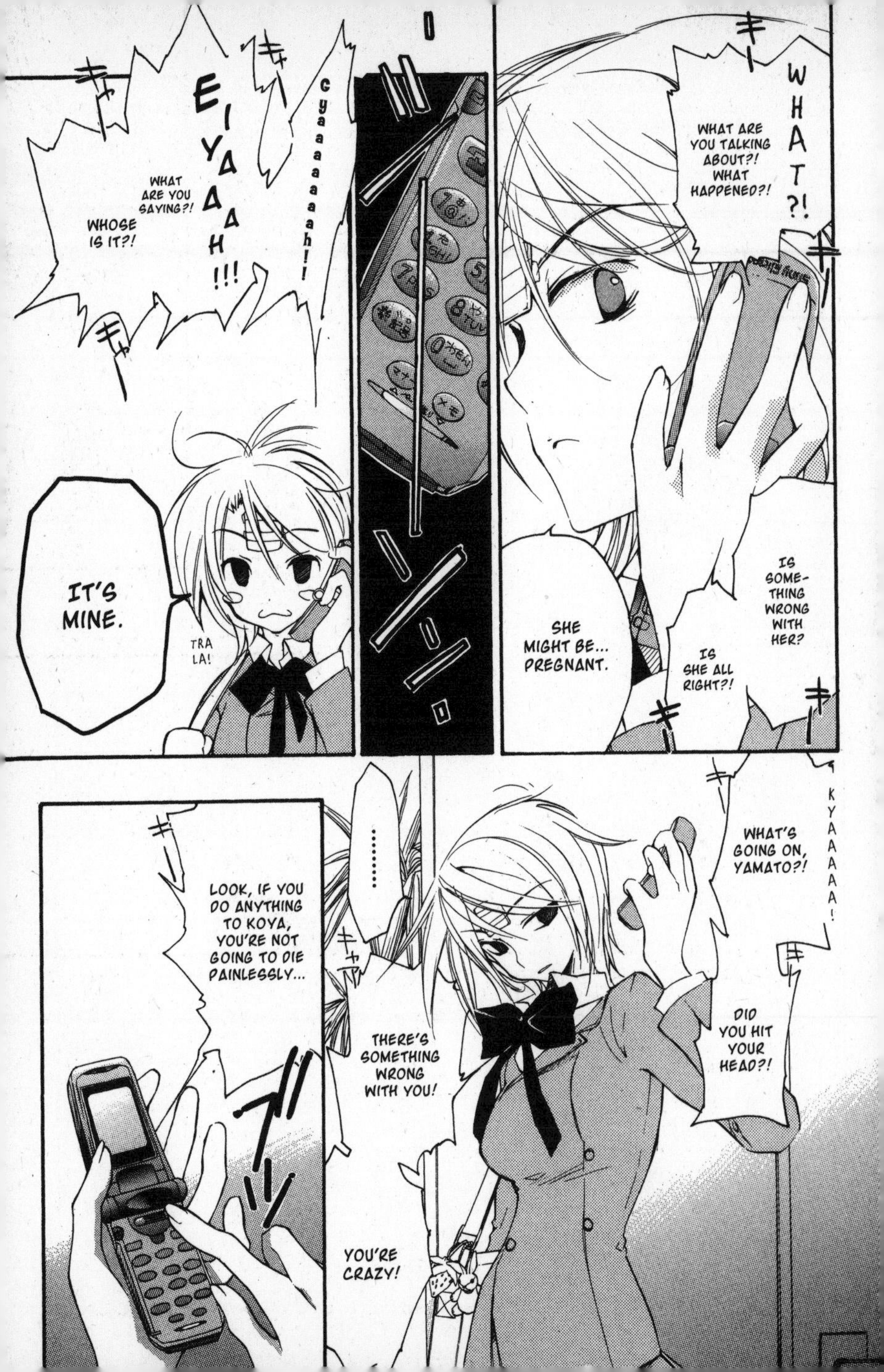
WHAT?!
WHAT ARE YOU TALKING ABOUT?! WHAT HAPPENED?!
IS SOMETHING WRONG WITH HER?
IS SHE ALL RIGHT?!
SHE MIGHT BE... PREGNANT.
Gyaaaaaaaaah!!
EIYAAAH!!!
WHAT ARE YOU SAYING?!
WHOSE IS IT?!
IT'S MINE.
TRA LA!
KYAAAAAA!
WHAT'S GOING ON, YAMATO?!
DID YOU HIT YOUR HEAD?!
......
THERE'S SOMETHING WRONG WITH YOU!
YOU'RE CRAZY!
LOOK, IF YOU DO ANYTHING TO KOYA, YOU'RE NOT GOING TO DIE PAINLESSLY...

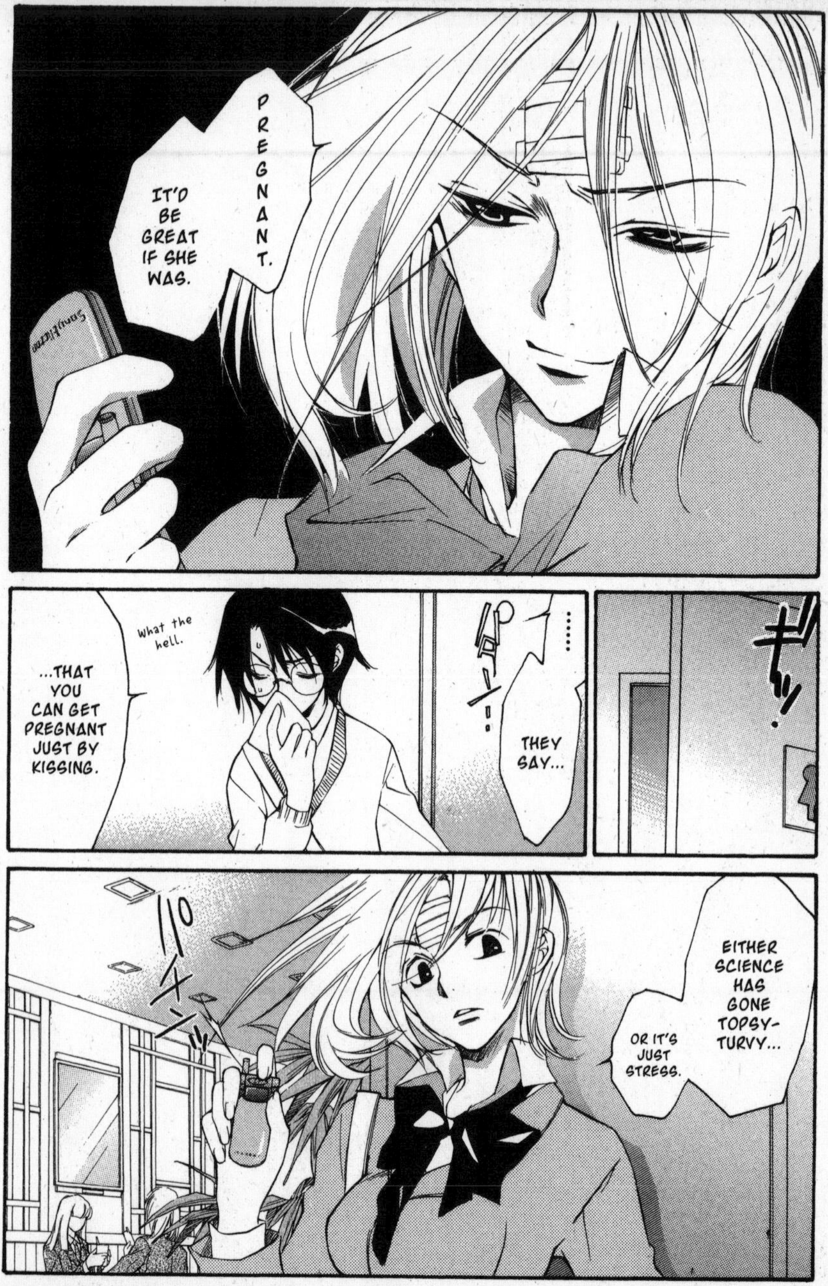
PREGNANT.
IT'D BE GREAT IF SHE WAS.
......
THEY SAY...
...THAT YOU CAN GET PREGNANT JUST BY KISSING.
What the hell.
EITHER SCIENCE HAS GONE TOPSY-TURVY...
OR IT'S JUST STRESS.

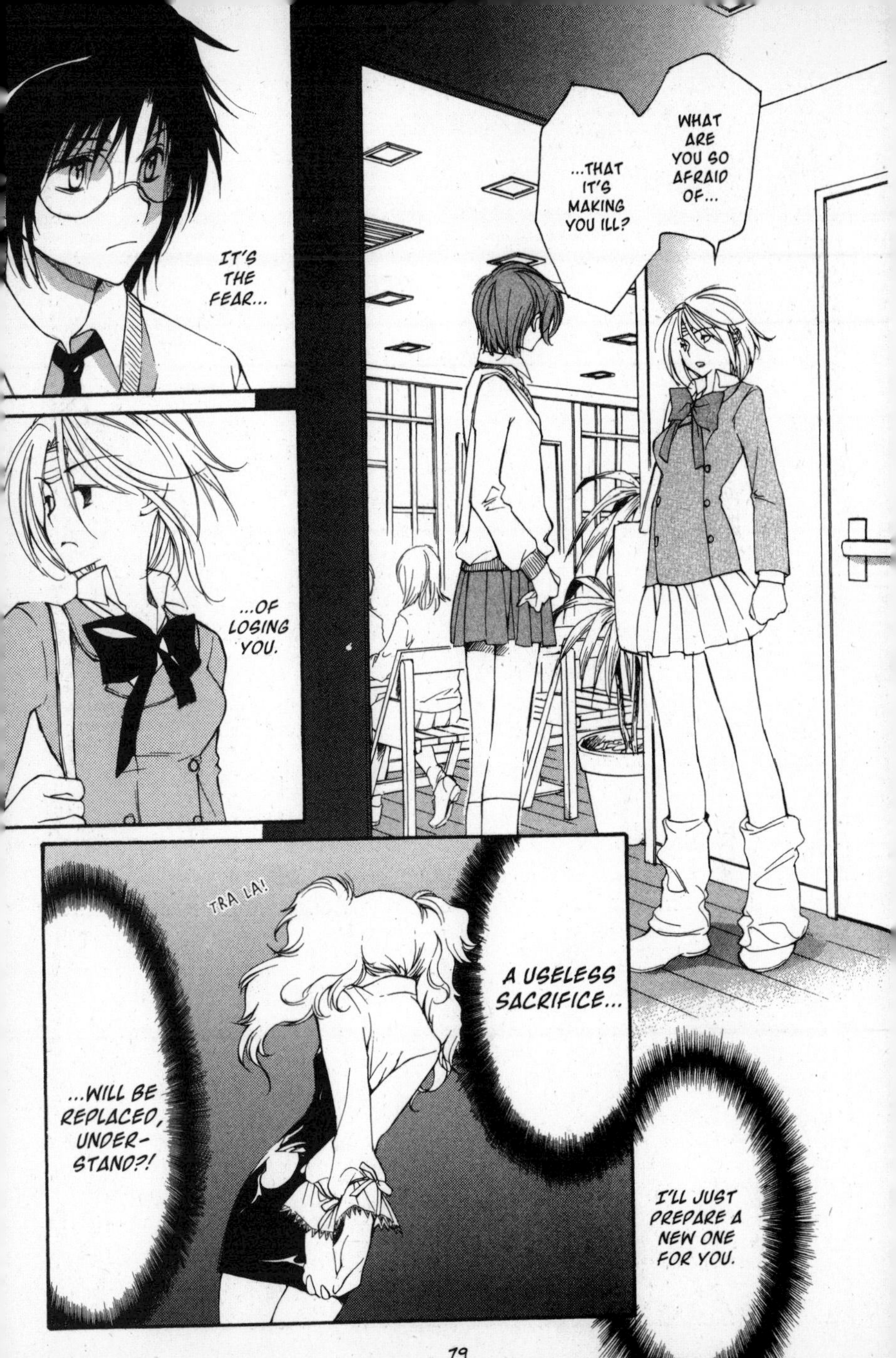
WHAT ARE YOU SO AFRAID OF...
...THAT IT'S MAKING YOU ILL?
IT'S THE FEAR...
...OF LOSING YOU.
TRA LA!
A USELESS SACRIFICE...
...WILL BE REPLACED, UNDER-STAND?!
I'LL JUST PREPARE A NEW ONE FOR YOU.

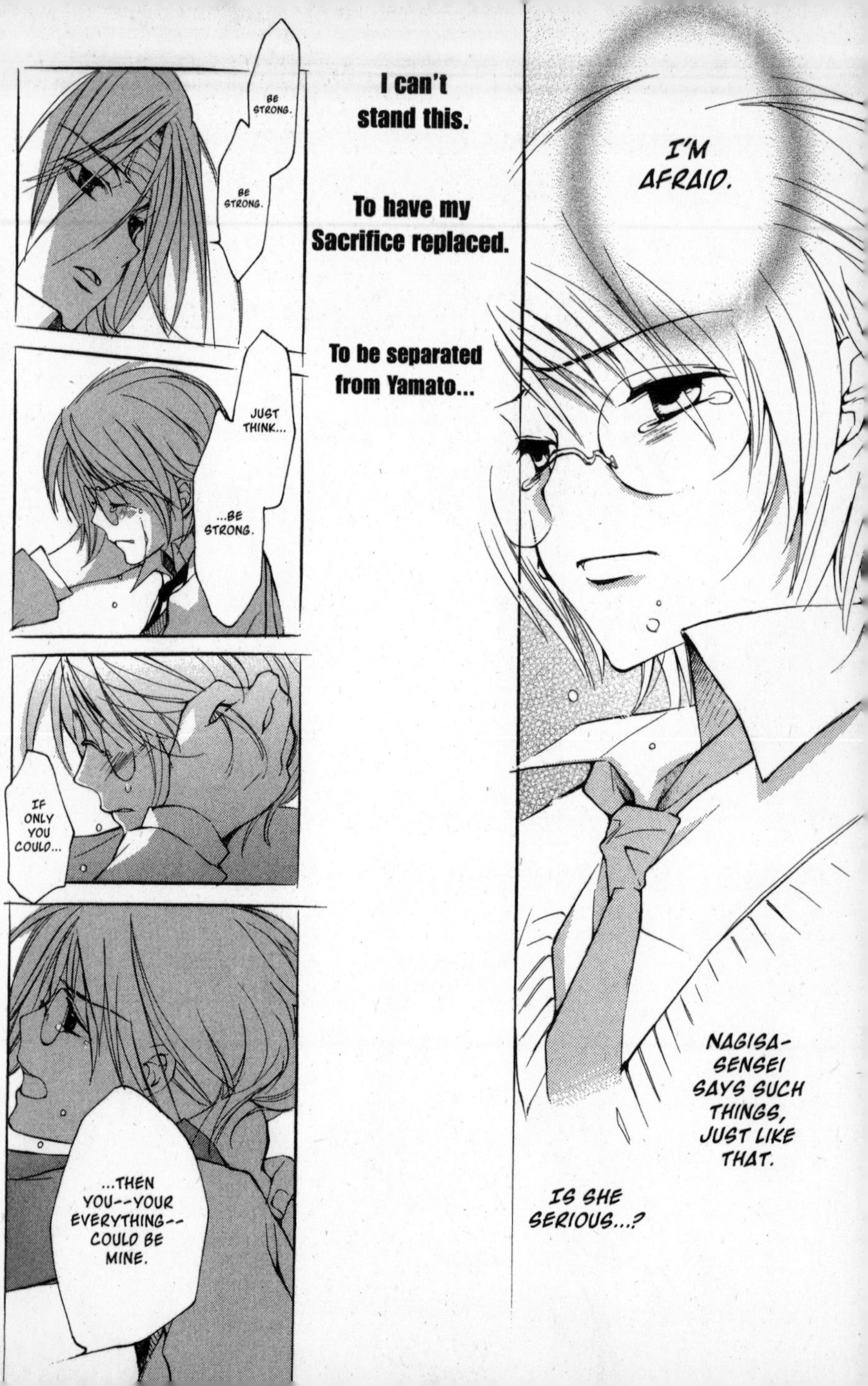
I'M AFRAID.
NAGISA-SENSEI SAYS SUCH THINGS, JUST LIKE THAT.
IS SHE SERIOUS...?
I can't stand this.
To have my Sacrifice replaced.
To be separated from Yamato...
BE STRONG.
BE STRONG.
JUST THINK...
...BE STRONG.
IF ONLY YOU COULD...
...THEN YOU--YOUR EVERYTHING--COULD BE MINE.

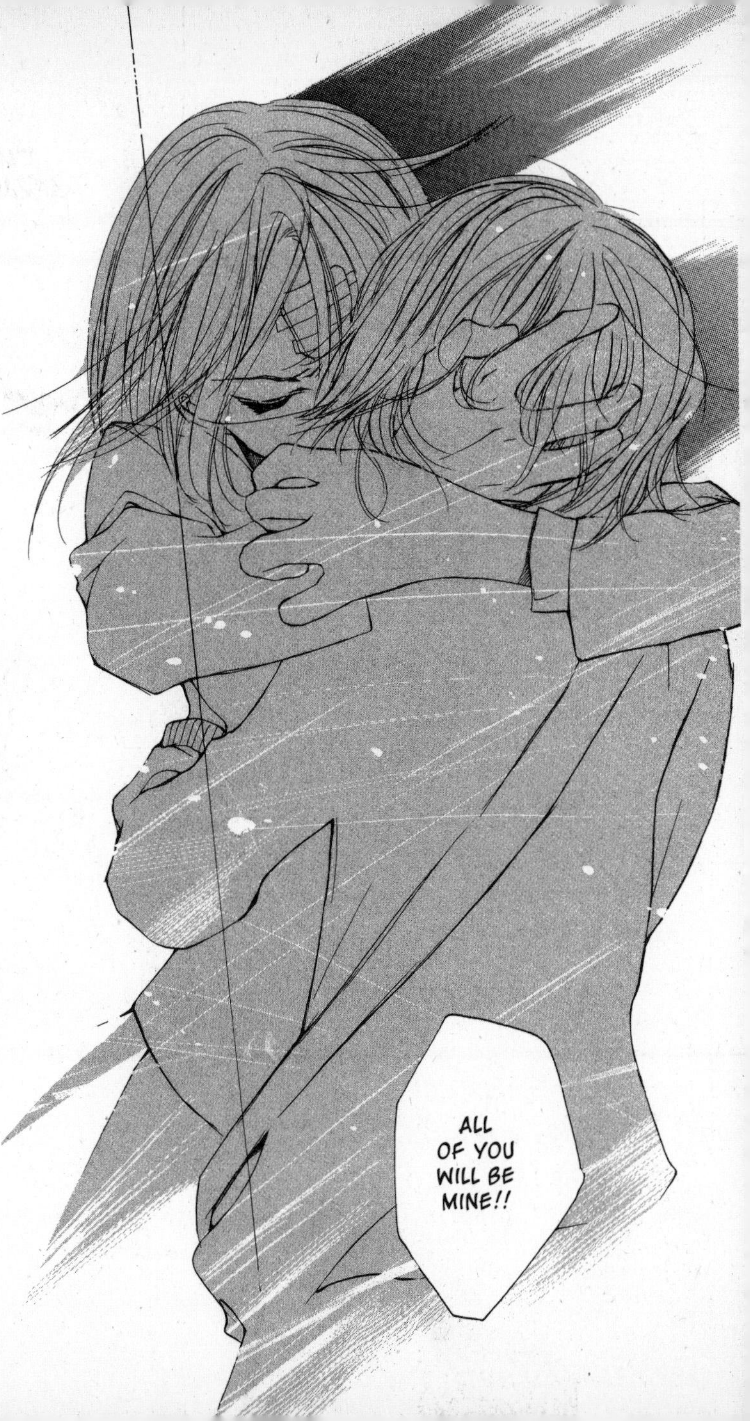
ALL OF YOU WILL BE MINE!!

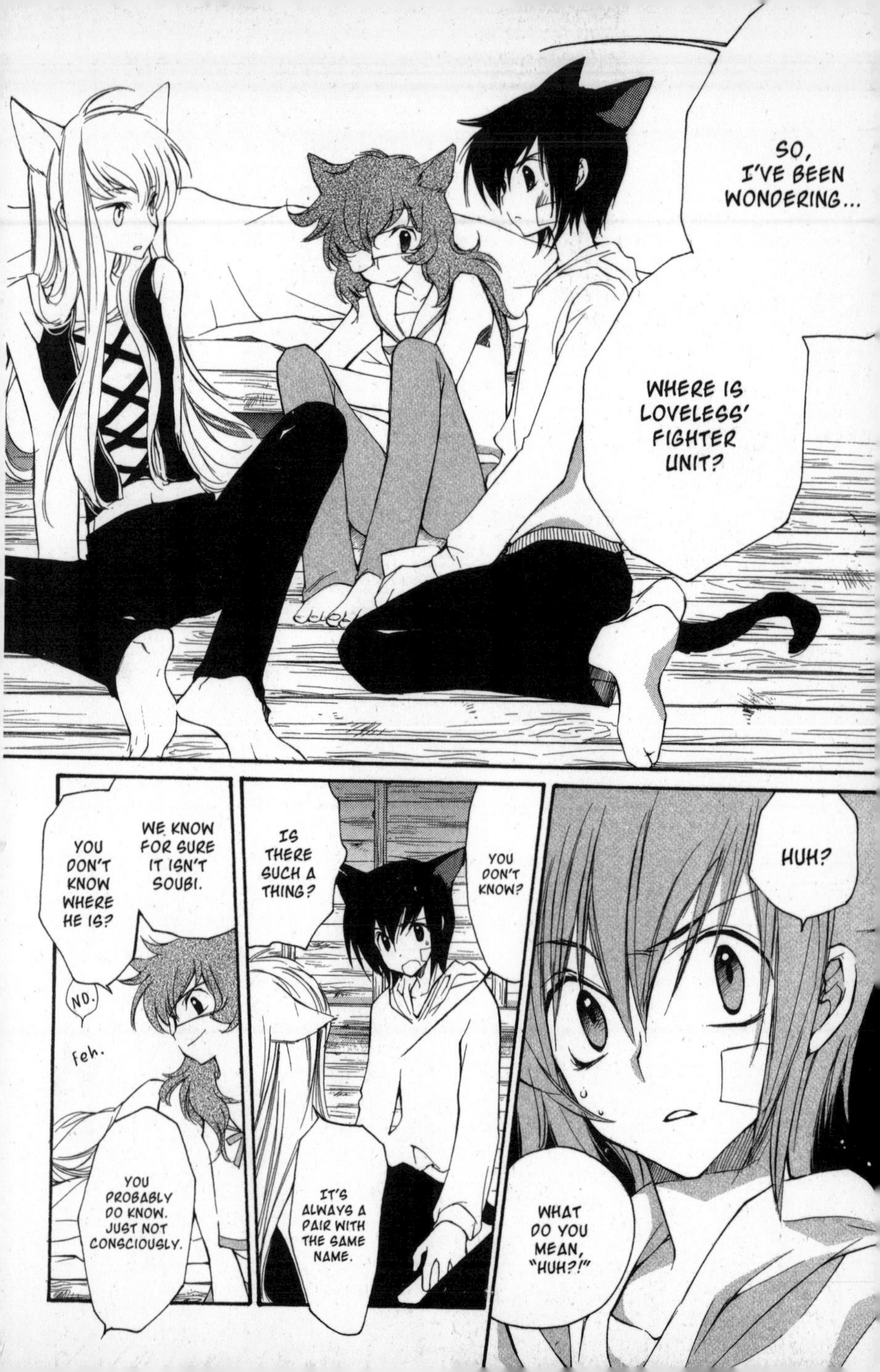
SO, I'VE BEEN WONDERING...
WHERE IS LOVELESS' FIGHTER UNIT?
HUH?
WHAT DO YOU MEAN, "HUH?!"
YOU DON'T KNOW?
IS THERE SUCH A THING?
IT'S ALWAYS A PAIR WITH THE SAME NAME.
WE KNOW FOR SURE IT ISN'T SOUBI.
YOU DON'T KNOW WHERE HE IS?
NO.
Feh.
YOU PROBABLY DO KNOW. JUST NOT CONSCIOUSLY.

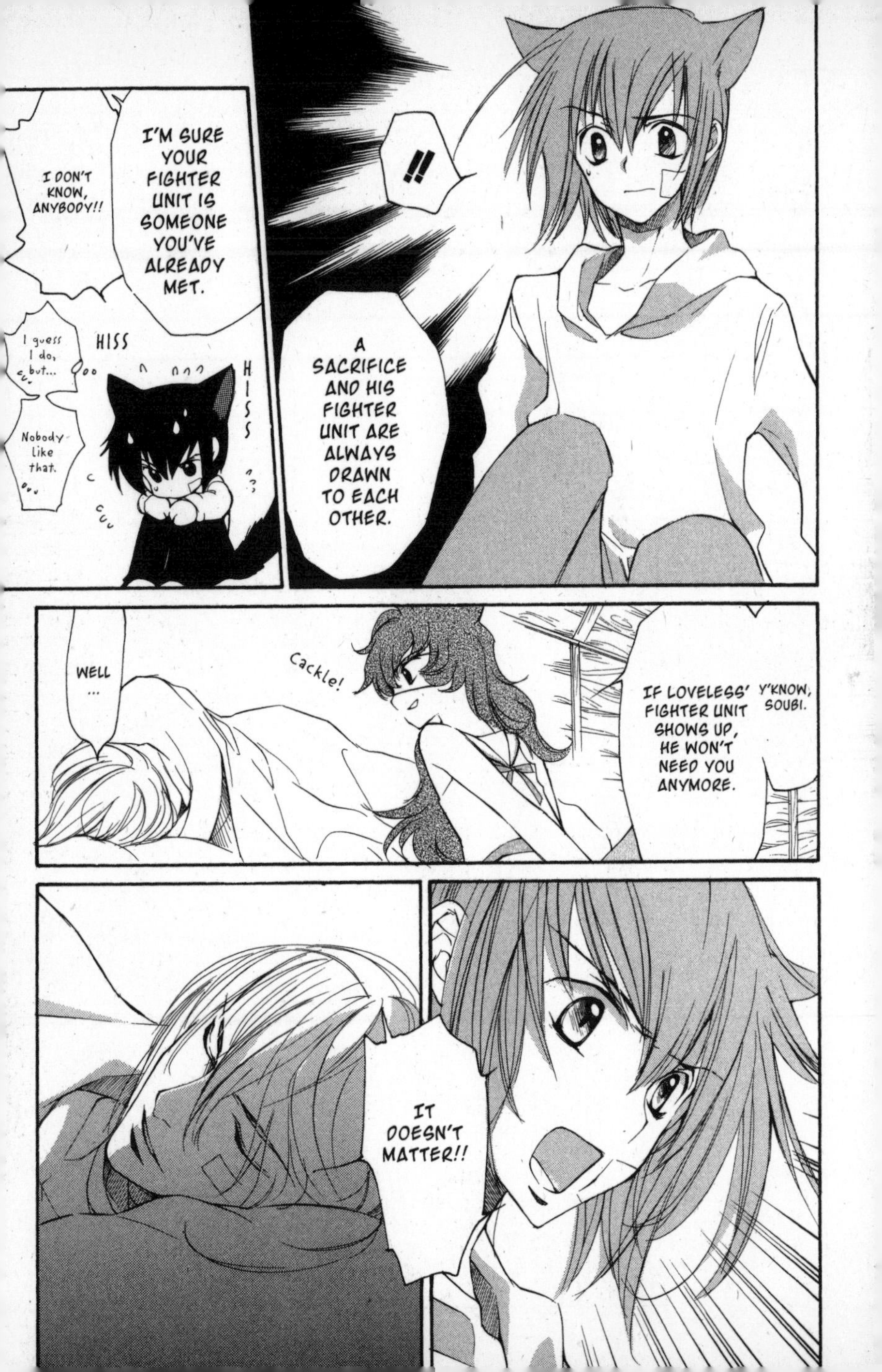
!!
A SACRIFICE AND HIS FIGHTER UNIT ARE ALWAYS DRAWN TO EACH OTHER.
I'M SURE YOUR FIGHTER UNIT IS SOMEONE YOU'VE ALREADY MET.
I DON'T KNOW, ANYBODY!!
HISS
HISS
I guess I do, but...
Nobody like that.
Y'KNOW, SOUBI.
IF LOVELESS' FIGHTER UNIT SHOWS UP, HE WON'T NEED YOU ANYMORE.
Cackle!
WELL ...
IT DOESN'T MATTER!!

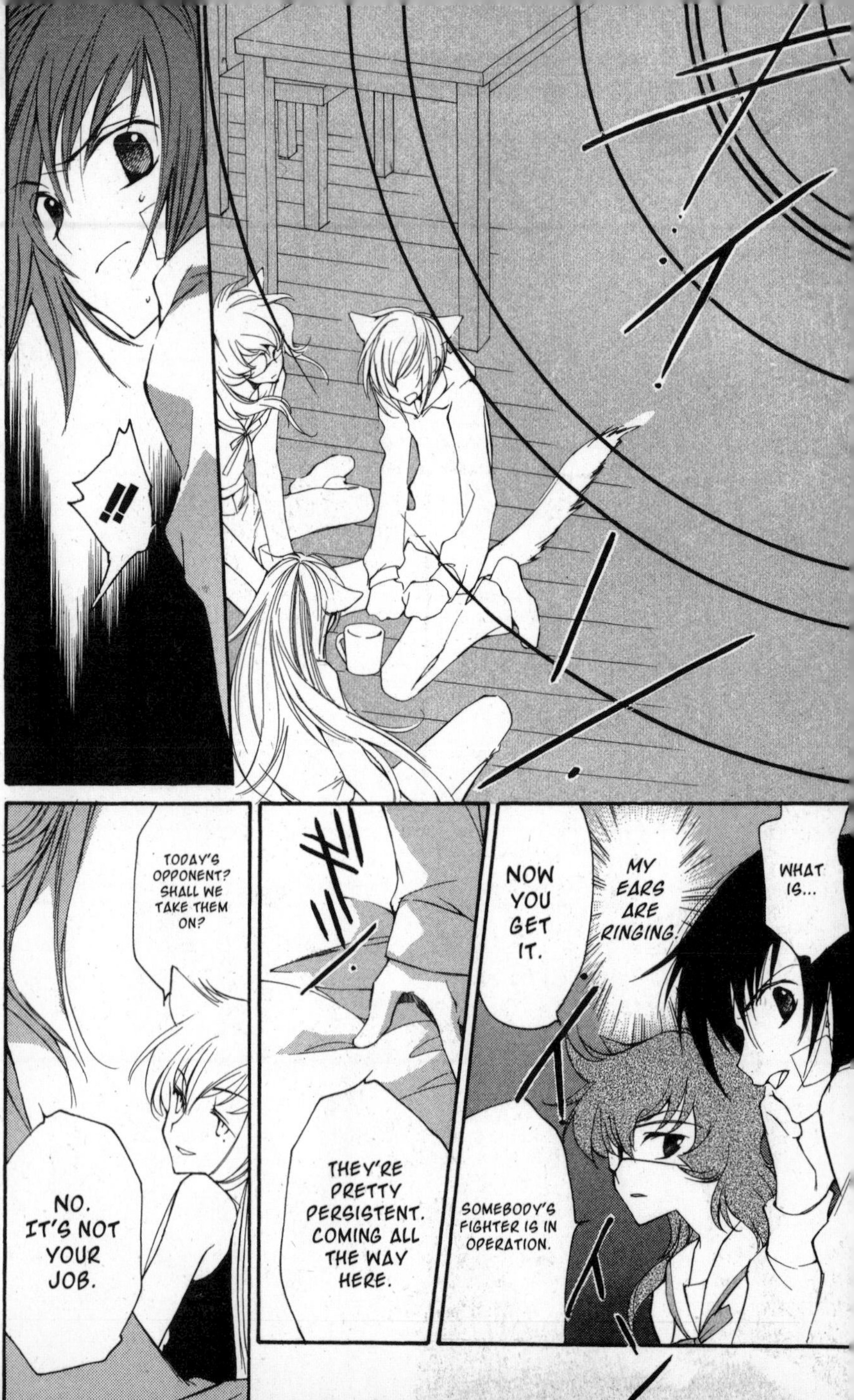
!!
WHAT IS...
MY EARS ARE RINGING!
NOW YOU GET IT.
SOMEBODY'S FIGHTER IS IN OPERATION.
THEY'RE PRETTY PERSISTENT. COMING ALL THE WAY HERE.
TODAY'S OPPONENT? SHALL WE TAKE THEM ON?
NO. IT'S NOT YOUR JOB.

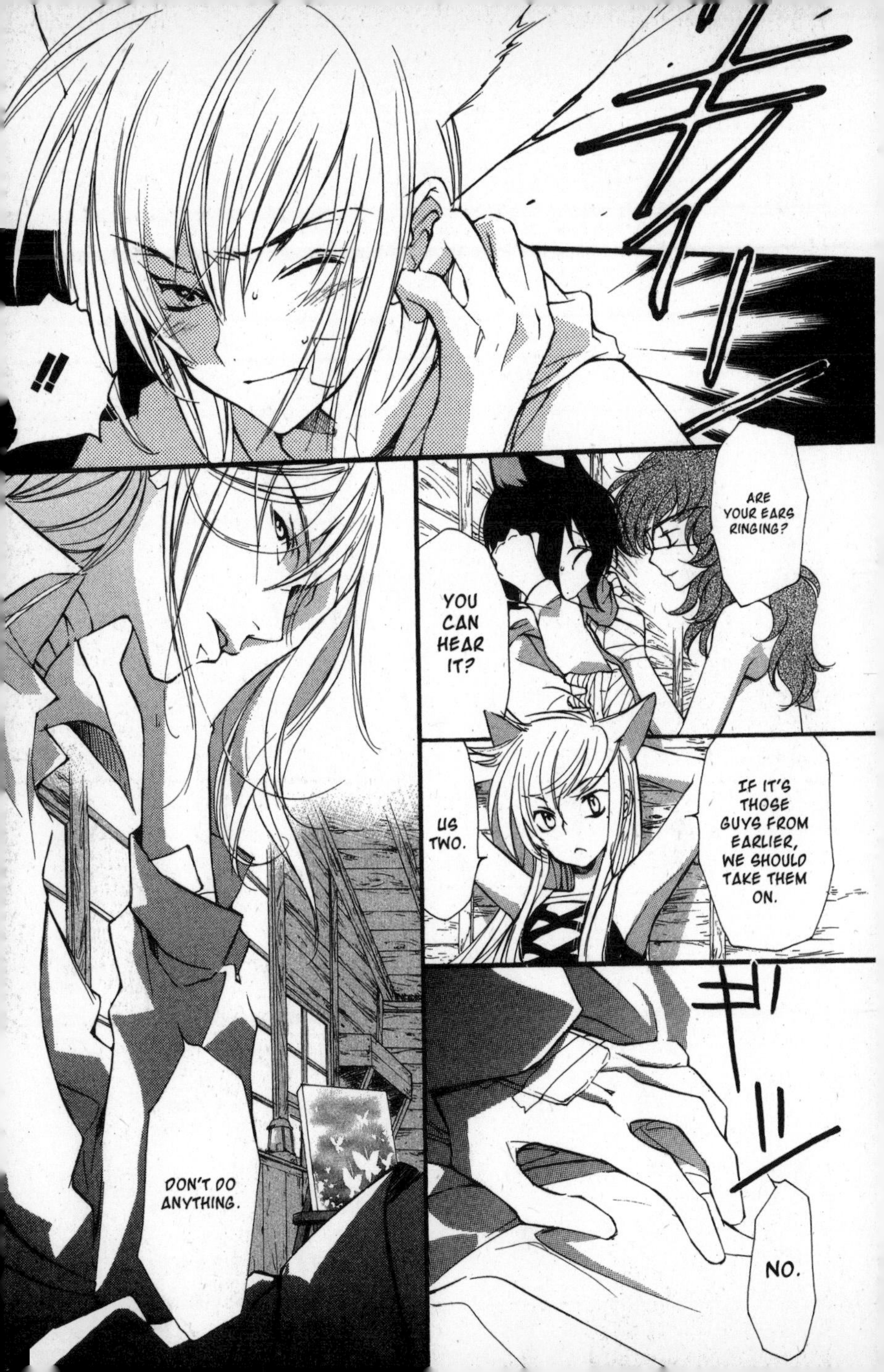
!!
ARE YOUR EARS RINGING?
YOU CAN HEAR IT?
IF IT'S THOSE GUYS FROM EARLIER, WE SHOULD TAKE THEM ON.
US TWO.
NO.
DON'T DO ANYTHING.

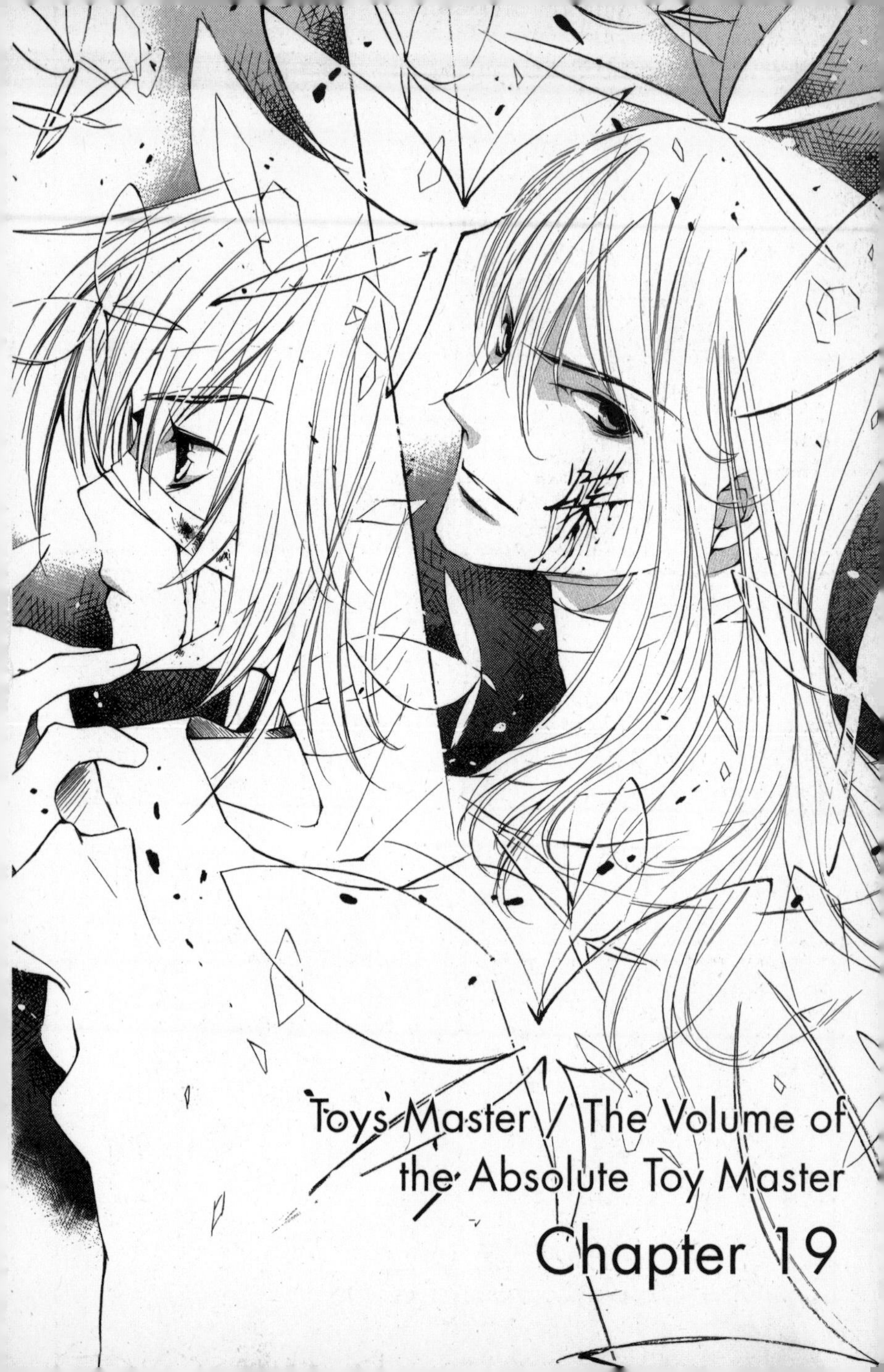
Toys Master / The Volume of
the Absolute Toy Master
Chapter 19

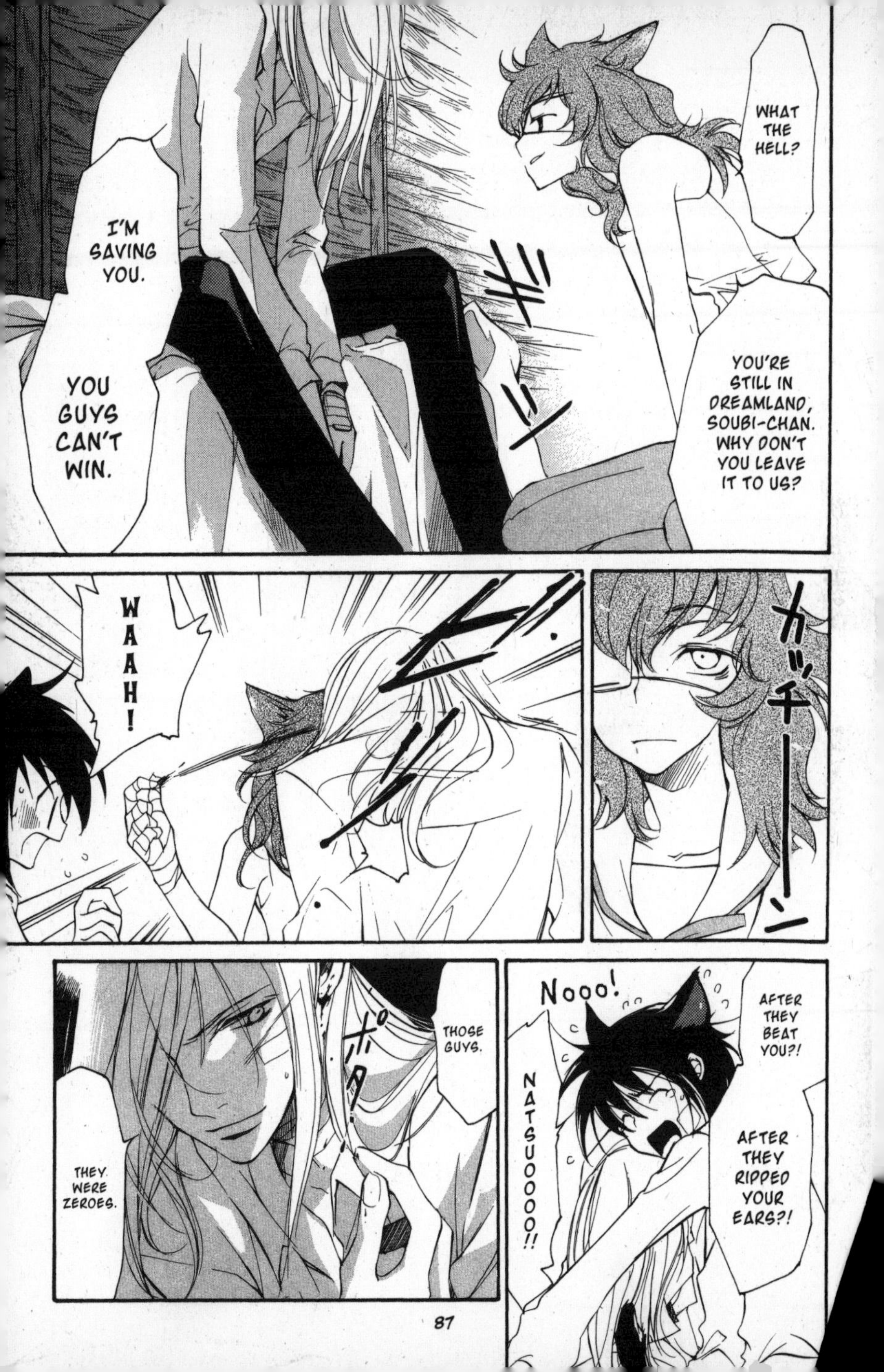
WHAT THE HELL?
YOU'RE STILL IN DREAMLAND, SOUBI-CHAN. WHY DON'T YOU LEAVE IT TO US?
I'M SAVING YOU.
YOU GUYS CAN'T WIN.
カッチーン
WAAAH!
AFTER THEY BEAT YOU?!
AFTER THEY RIPPED YOUR EARS?!
Nooo!
NATSUOOOOO!!
THOSE GUYS.
ポタ
THEY WERE ZEROES.

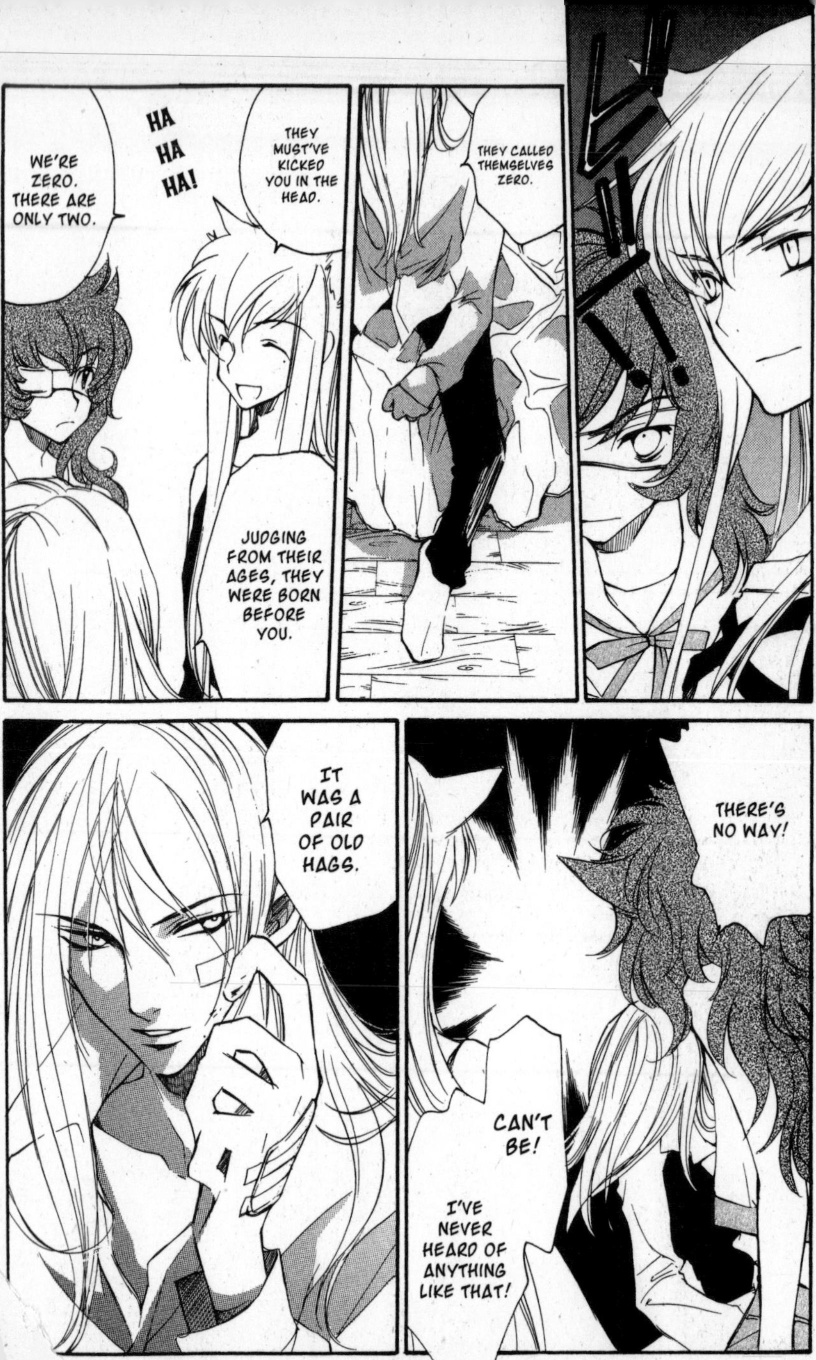

THEY CALLED THEMSELVES ZERO.
THEY MUST'VE KICKED YOU IN THE HEAD.
HA HA HA!
WE'RE ZERO. THERE ARE ONLY TWO.
JUDGING FROM THEIR AGES, THEY WERE BORN BEFORE YOU.
THERE'S NO WAY!
CAN'T BE!
I'VE NEVER HEARD OF ANYTHING LIKE THAT!
IT WAS A PAIR OF OLD HAGS.

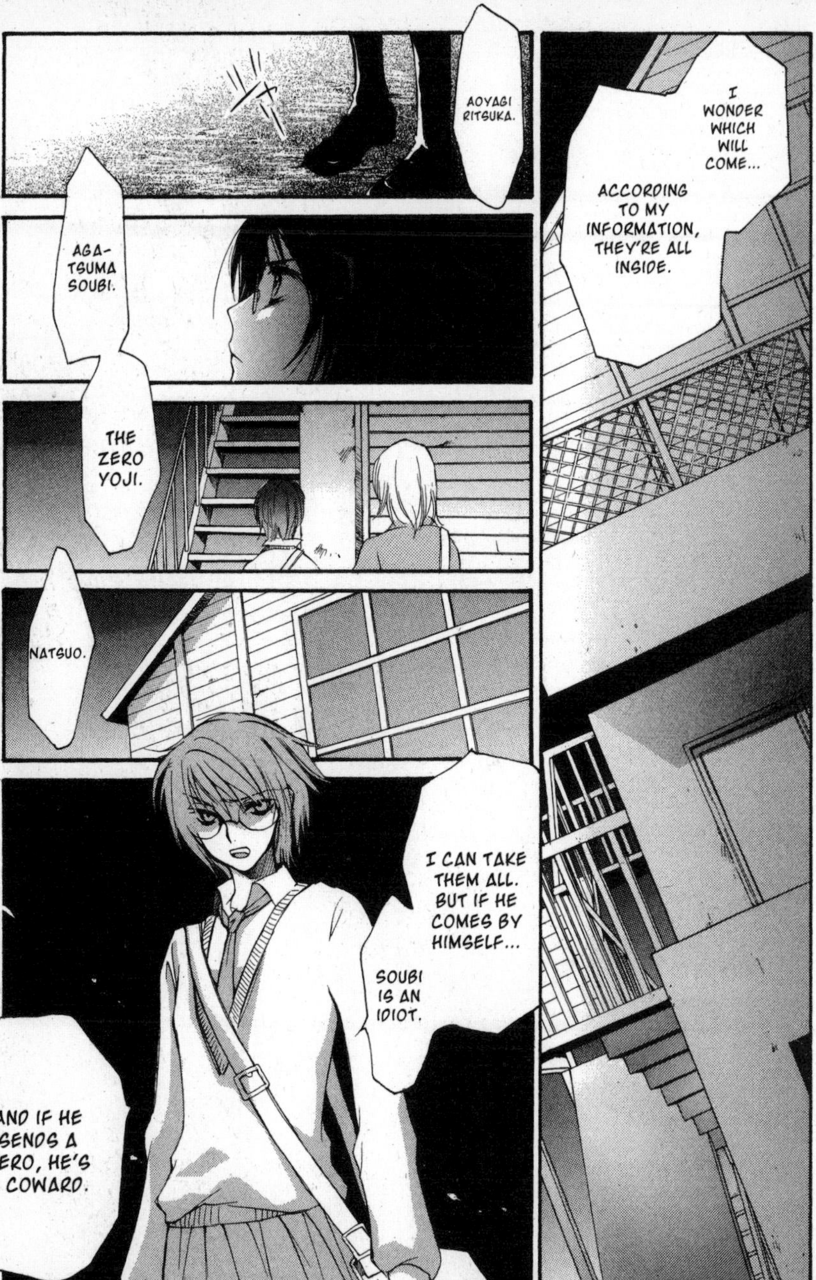
I WONDER WHICH WILL COME...
ACCORDING TO MY INFORMATION, THEY'RE ALL INSIDE.
AOYAGI RITSUKA.
AGA-TSUMA SOUBI.
THE ZERO YOJI.
NATSUO.
I CAN TAKE THEM ALL. BUT IF HE COMES BY HIMSELF...
SOUBI IS AN IDIOT.
AND IF HE SENDS A ZERO, HE'S A COWARD.

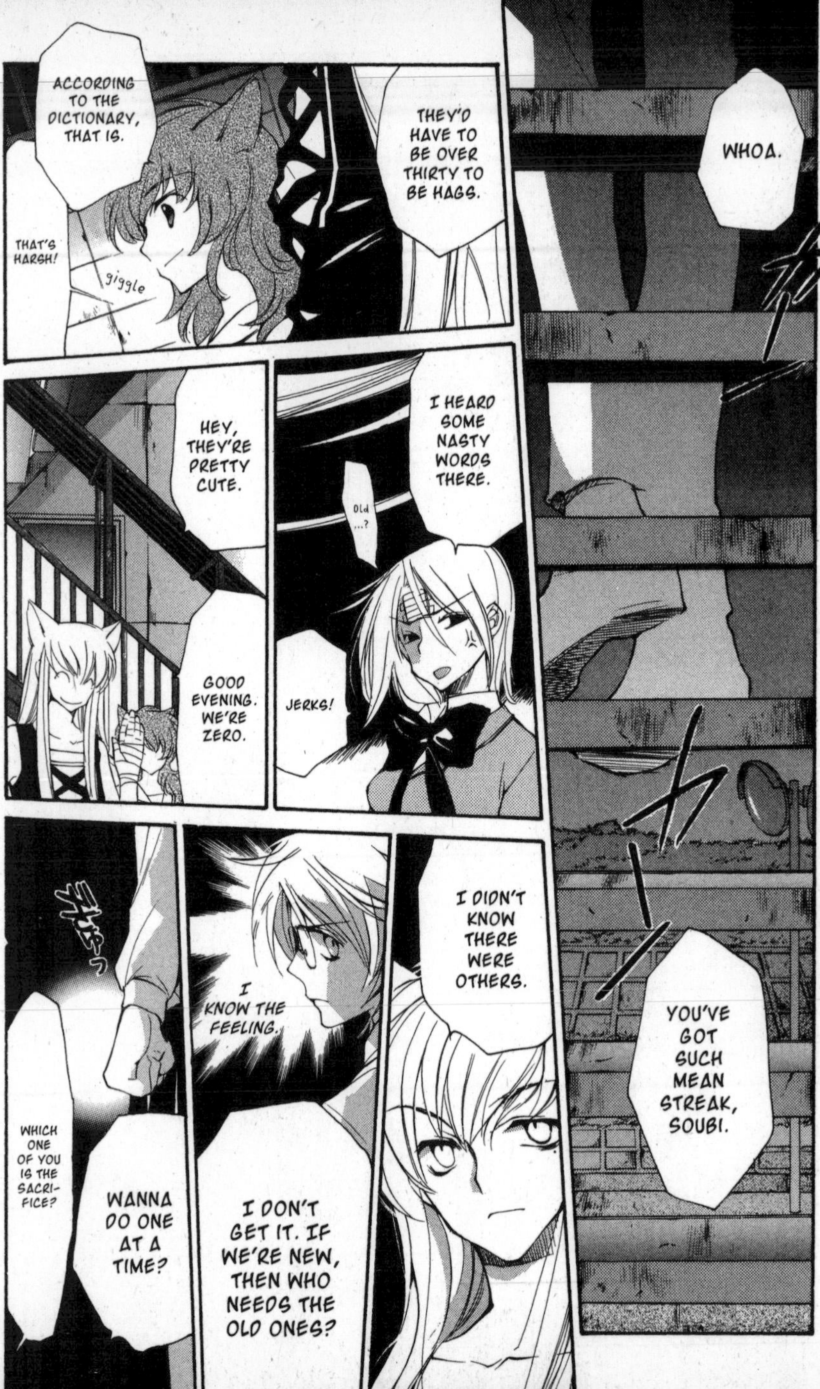
WHOA.
YOU'VE GOT SUCH MEAN STREAK, SOUBI.
THEY'D HAVE TO BE OVER THIRTY TO BE HAGS.
ACCORDING TO THE DICTIONARY, THAT IS.
THAT'S HARSH!
giggle
I HEARD SOME NASTY WORDS THERE.
Old ...?
JERKS!
HEY, THEY'RE PRETTY CUTE.
GOOD EVENING. WE'RE ZERO.
I DIDN'T KNOW THERE WERE OTHERS.
I DON'T GET IT. IF WE'RE NEW, THEN WHO NEEDS THE OLD ONES?
I KNOW THE FEELING.
WHICH ONE OF YOU IS THE SACRIFICE?
WANNA DO ONE AT A TIME?

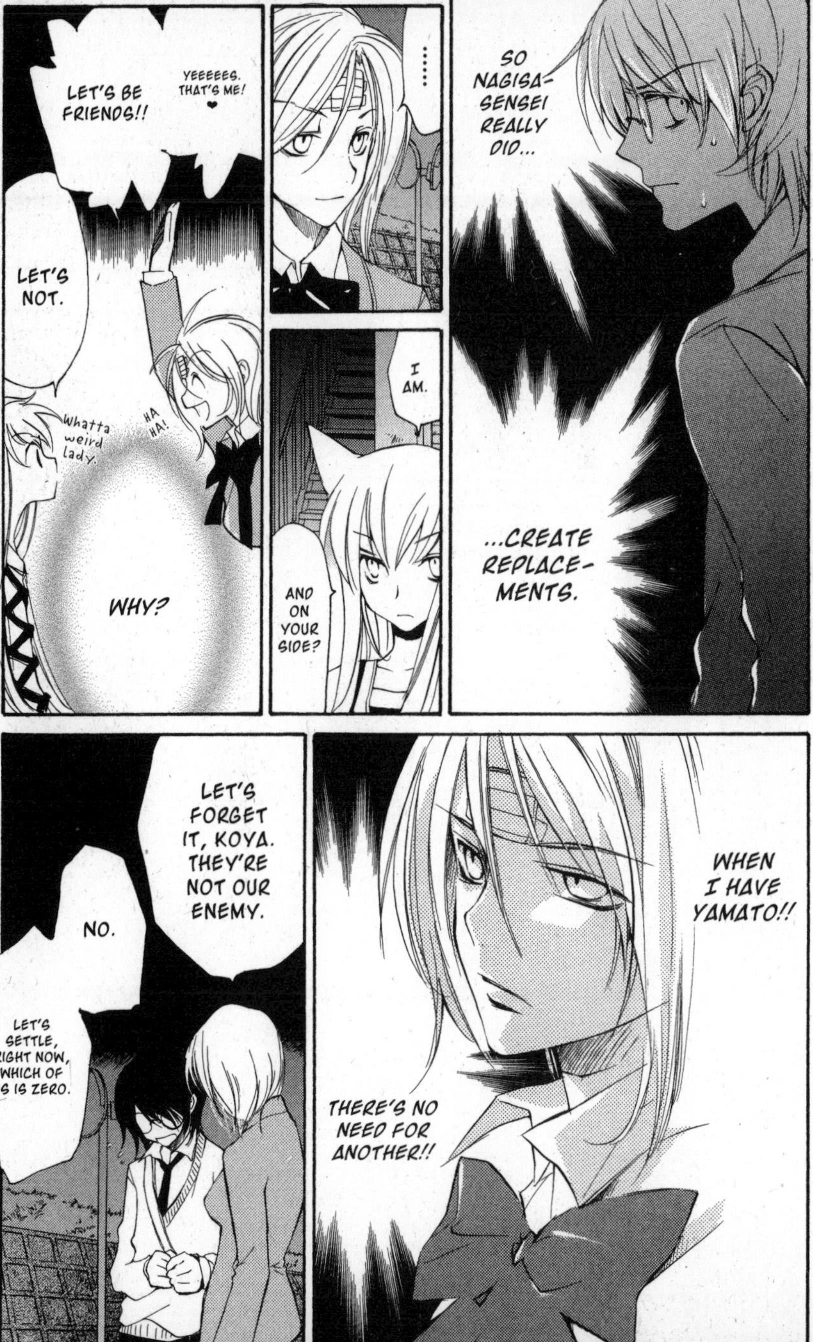

SO NAGISA-SENSEI REALLY DID...
...CREATE REPLACEMENTS.
......
I AM.
AND ON YOUR SIDE?
YEEEEEES. THAT'S ME! ❤
LET'S BE FRIENDS!!
LET'S NOT.
HA HA!
Whatta weird lady.
WHY?
WHEN I HAVE YAMATO!!
THERE'S NO NEED FOR ANOTHER!!
LET'S FORGET IT, KOYA. THEY'RE NOT OUR ENEMY.
NO.
LET'S SETTLE, RIGHT NOW, WHICH OF US IS ZERO.

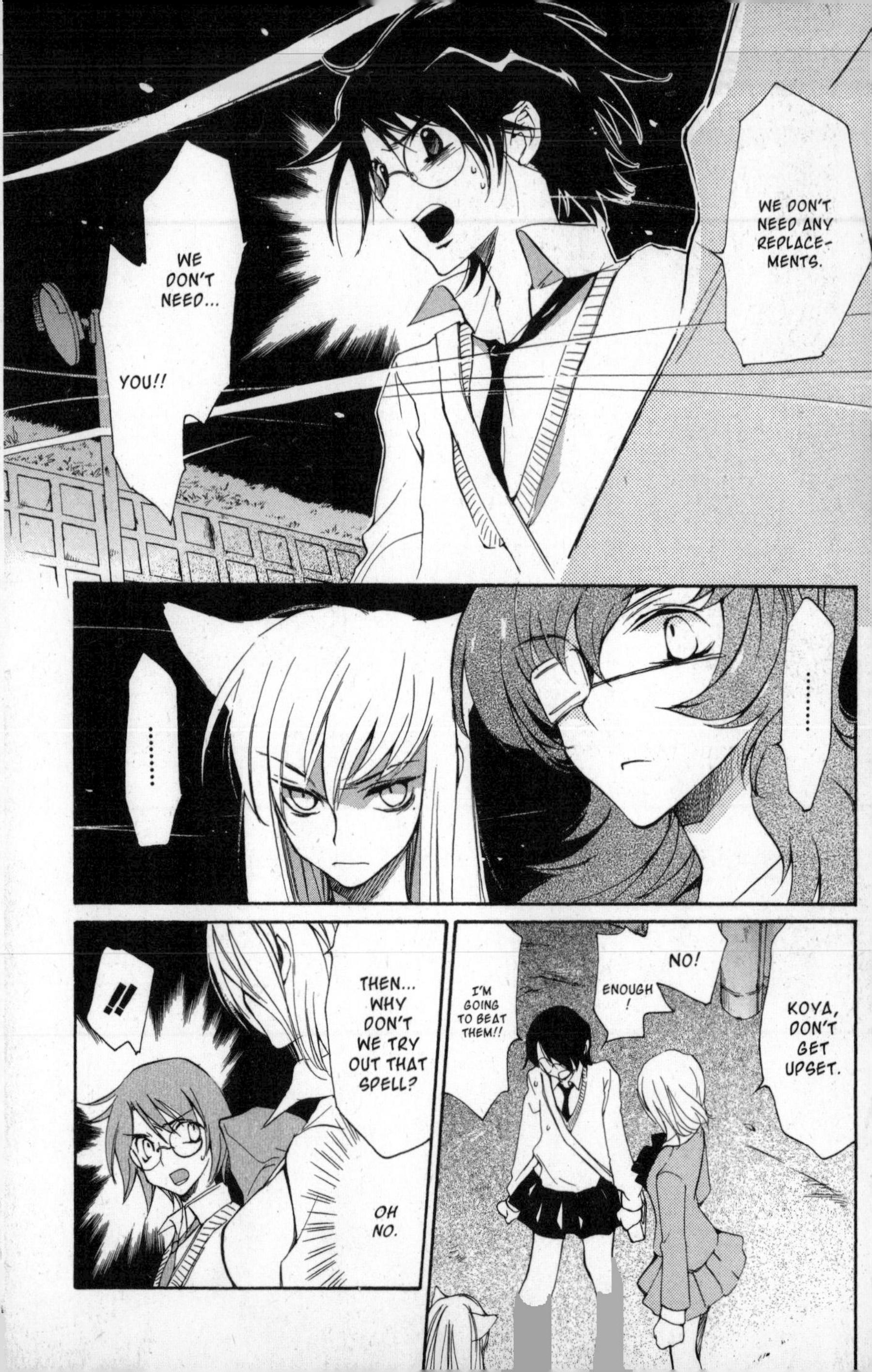
WE DON'T NEED ANY REPLACE-MENTS.
WE DON'T NEED...
YOU!!
......
......
KOYA, DON'T GET UPSET.
NO!
ENOUGH!
I'M GOING TO BEAT THEM!!
THEN... WHY DON'T WE TRY OUT THAT SPELL?
!!
OH NO.

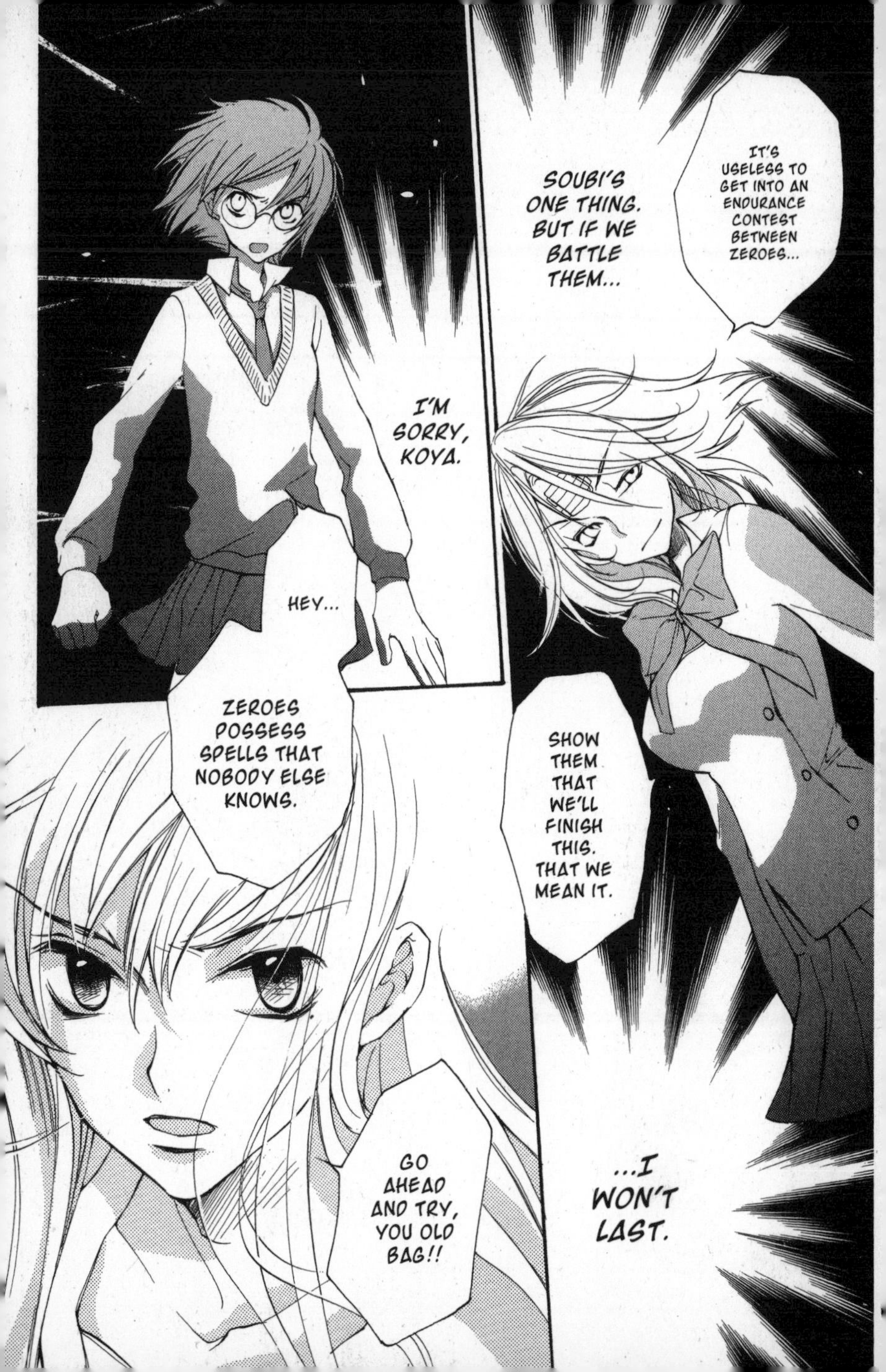
IT'S USELESS TO GET INTO AN ENDURANCE CONTEST BETWEEN ZEROES...
SOUBI'S ONE THING. BUT IF WE BATTLE THEM...
SHOW THEM THAT WE'LL FINISH THIS. THAT WE MEAN IT.
...I WON'T LAST.
I'M SORRY, KOYA.
HEY...
ZEROES POSSESS SPELLS THAT NOBODY ELSE KNOWS.
GO AHEAD AND TRY, YOU OLD BAG!!

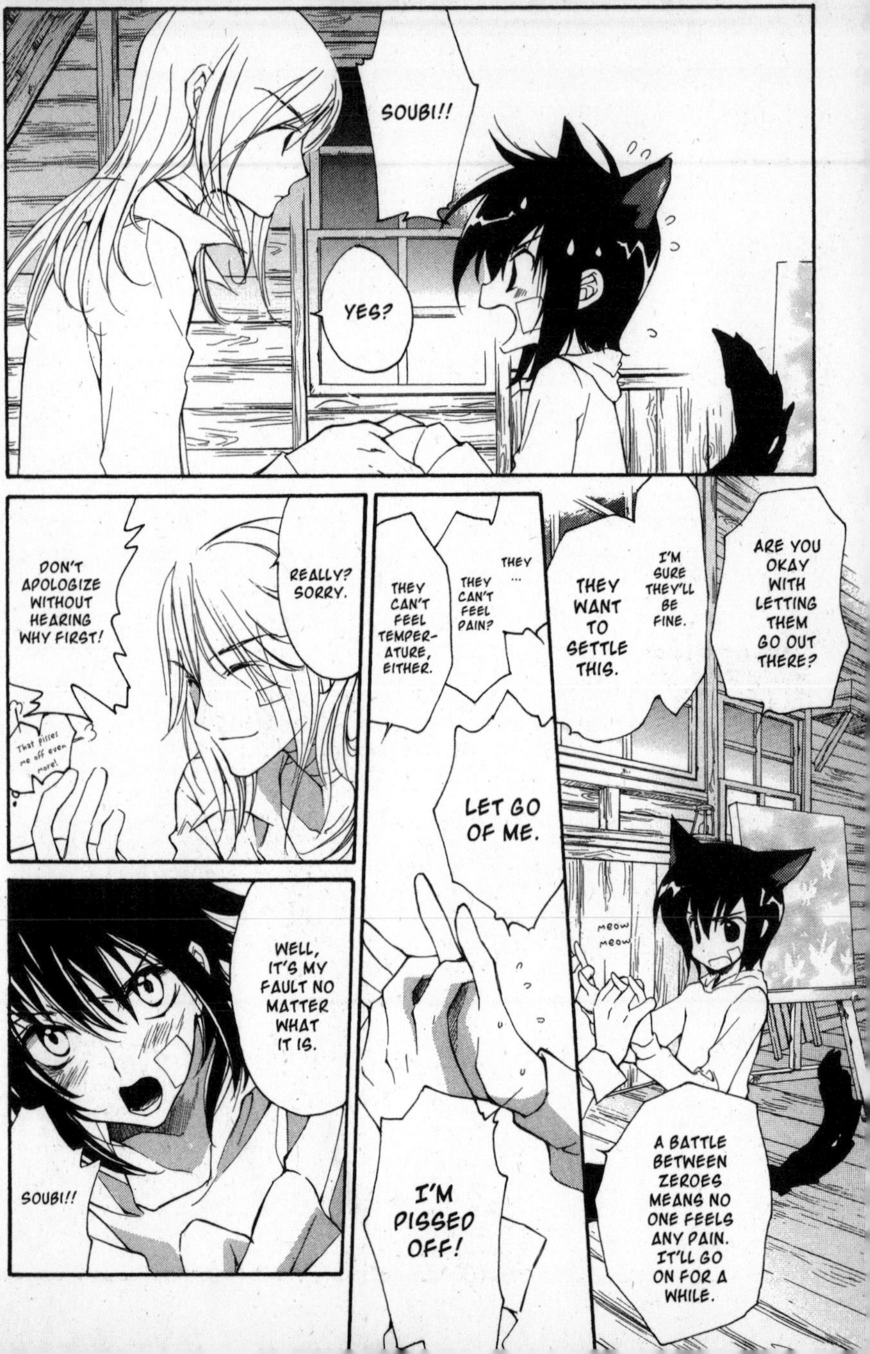
SOUBI!!
YES?
ARE YOU OKAY WITH LETTING THEM GO OUT THERE?
I'M SURE THEY'LL BE FINE.
THEY WANT TO SETTLE THIS.
THEY ...
THEY CAN'T FEEL PAIN?
THEY CAN'T FEEL TEMPER-ATURE, EITHER.
LET GO OF ME.
meow meow
A BATTLE BETWEEN ZEROES MEANS NO ONE FEELS ANY PAIN. IT'LL GO ON FOR A WHILE.
I'M PISSED OFF!
REALLY? SORRY.
DON'T APOLOGIZE WITHOUT HEARING WHY FIRST!
That pisses me off even more!
WELL, IT'S MY FAULT NO MATTER WHAT IT IS.
SOUBI!!

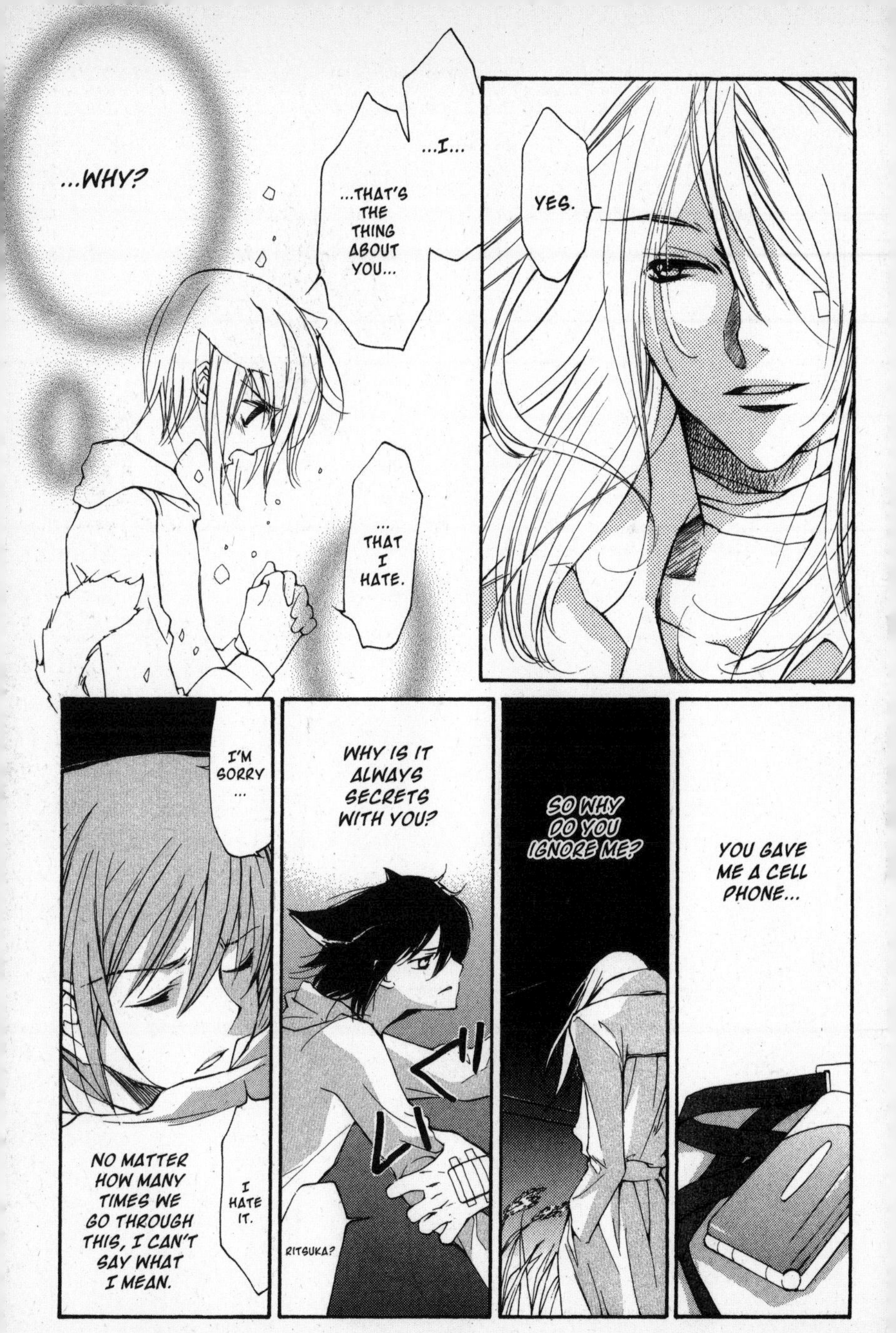
YES.
...I...
...THAT'S THE THING ABOUT YOU...
...WHY?
...THAT I HATE.
YOU GAVE ME A CELL PHONE...
SO WHY DO YOU IGNORE ME?
WHY IS IT ALWAYS SECRETS WITH YOU?
RITSUKA?
I'M SORRY...
I HATE IT.
NO MATTER HOW MANY TIMES WE GO THROUGH THIS, I CAN'T SAY WHAT I MEAN.

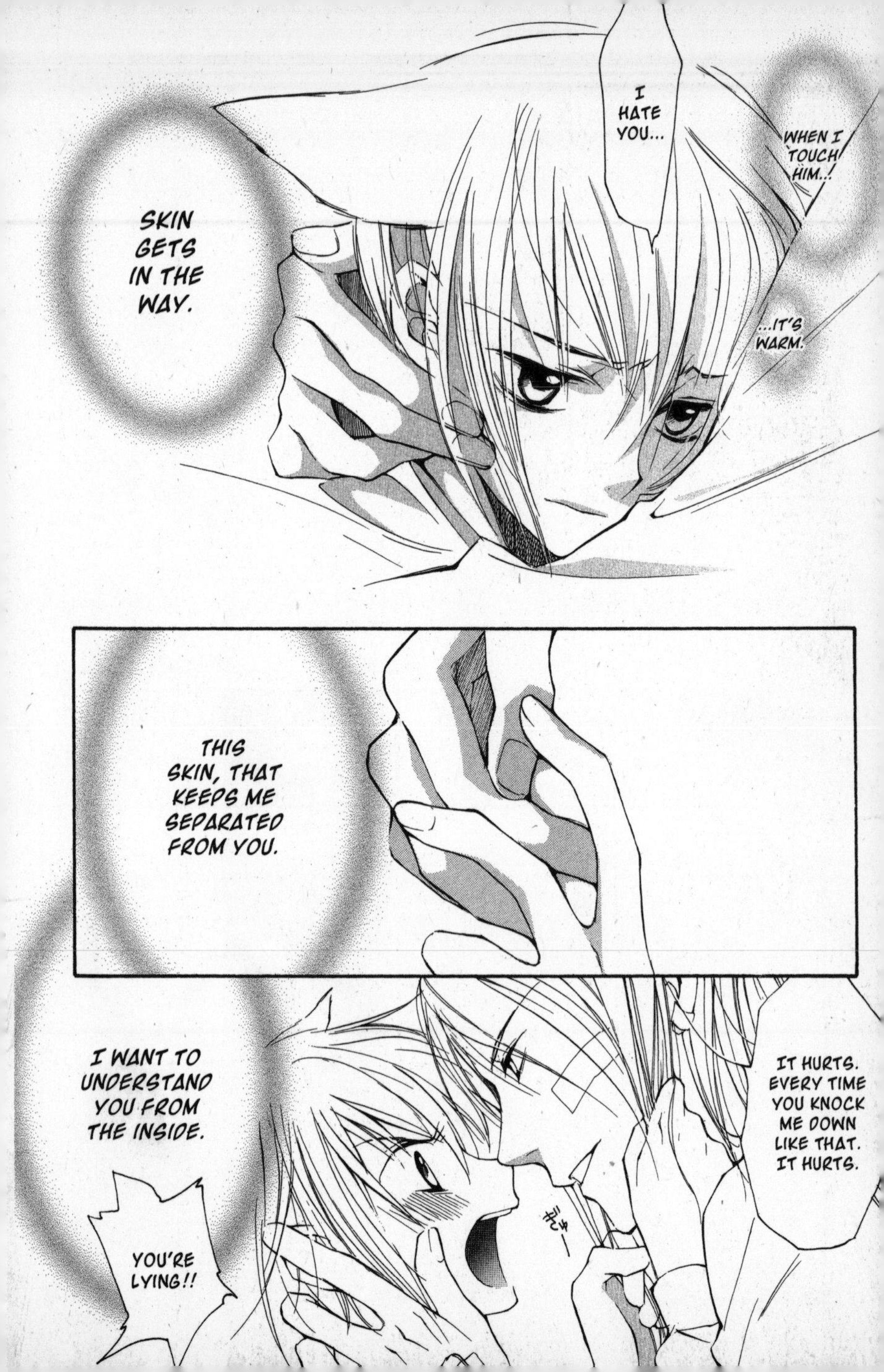
WHEN I TOUCH HIM..!
I HATE YOU...
...IT'S WARM.
SKIN GETS IN THE WAY.
THIS SKIN, THAT KEEPS ME SEPARATED FROM YOU.
IT HURTS. EVERY TIME YOU KNOCK ME DOWN LIKE THAT. IT HURTS.
I WANT TO UNDERSTAND YOU FROM THE INSIDE.
YOU'RE LYING!!

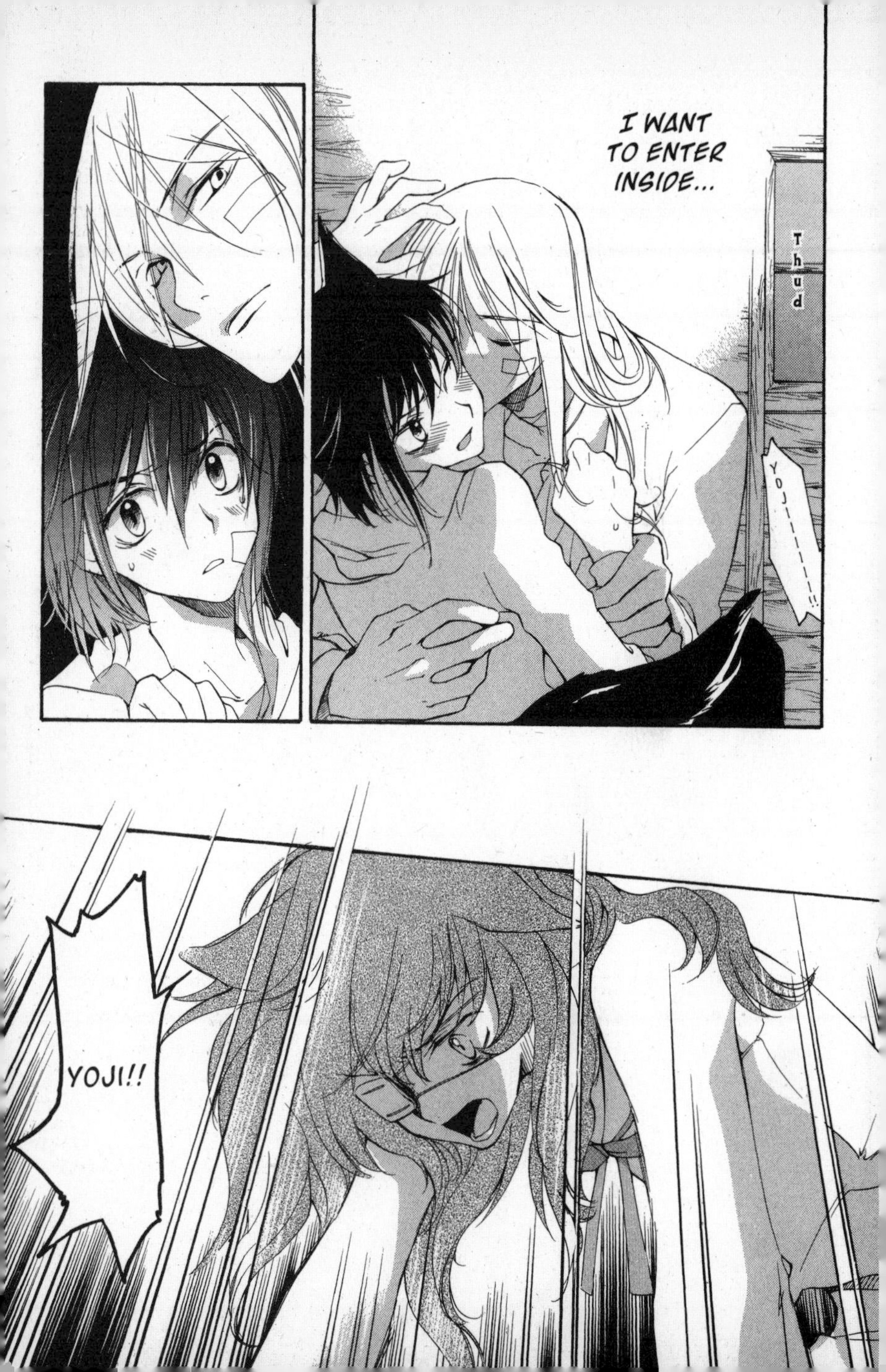
I WANT TO ENTER INSIDE...
Thud
YOJI-----!!
YOJI!!

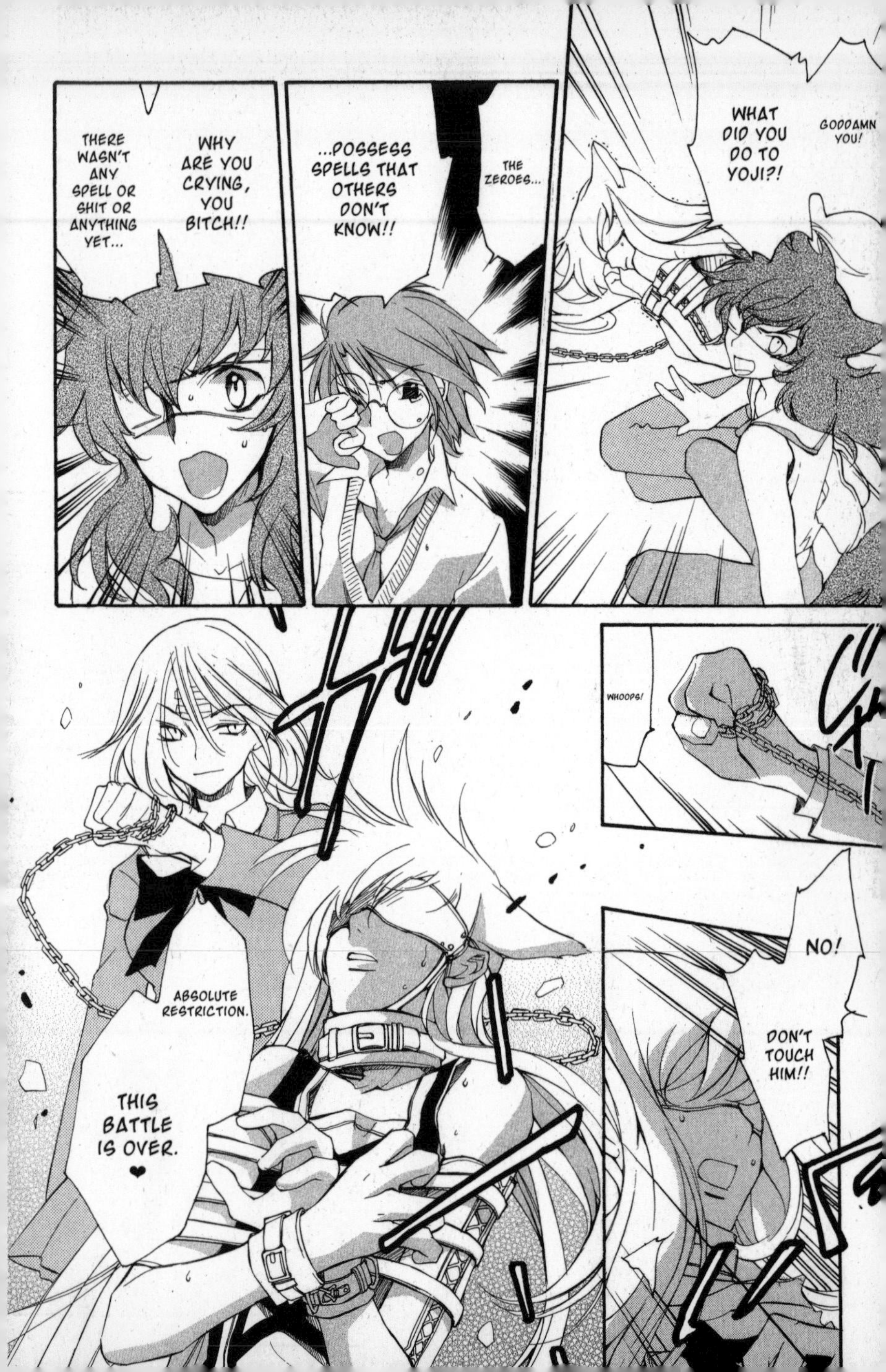
GODDAMN YOU!
WHAT DID YOU DO TO YOJI?!
THE ZEROES...
...POSSESS SPELLS THAT OTHERS DON'T KNOW!!
WHY ARE YOU CRYING, YOU BITCH!!
THERE WASN'T ANY SPELL OR SHIT OR ANYTHING YET...
WHOOPS!
NO!
DON'T TOUCH HIM!!
ABSOLUTE RESTRICTION.
THIS BATTLE IS OVER. ❤

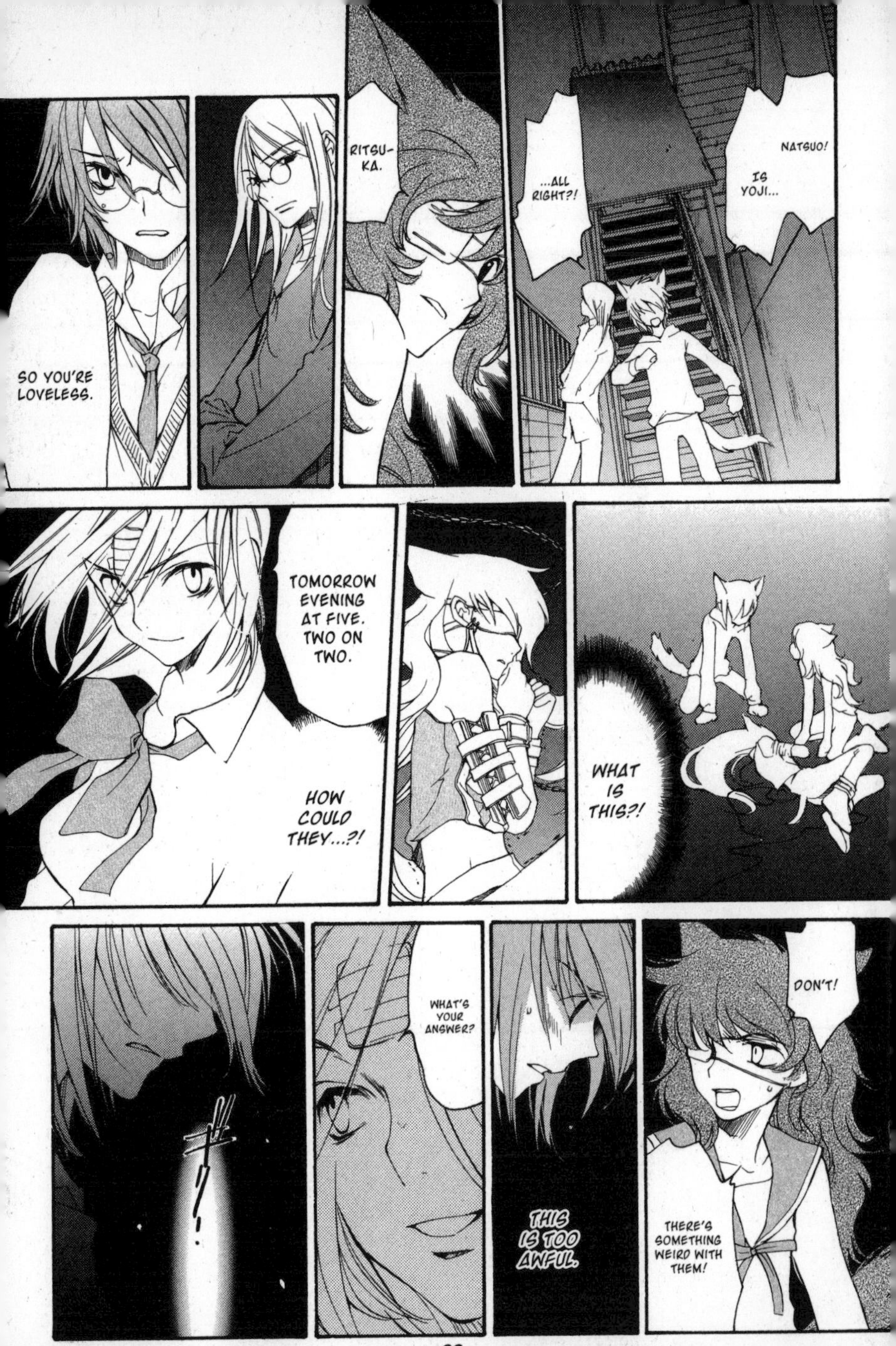
NATSUO!
IS YOJI...
...ALL RIGHT?!
RITSU-KA.
SO YOU'RE LOVELESS.
WHAT IS THIS?!
TOMORROW EVENING AT FIVE. TWO ON TWO.
HOW COULD THEY...?!
DON'T!
THERE'S SOMETHING WEIRD WITH THEM!
THIS IS TOO AWFUL.
WHAT'S YOUR ANSWER?

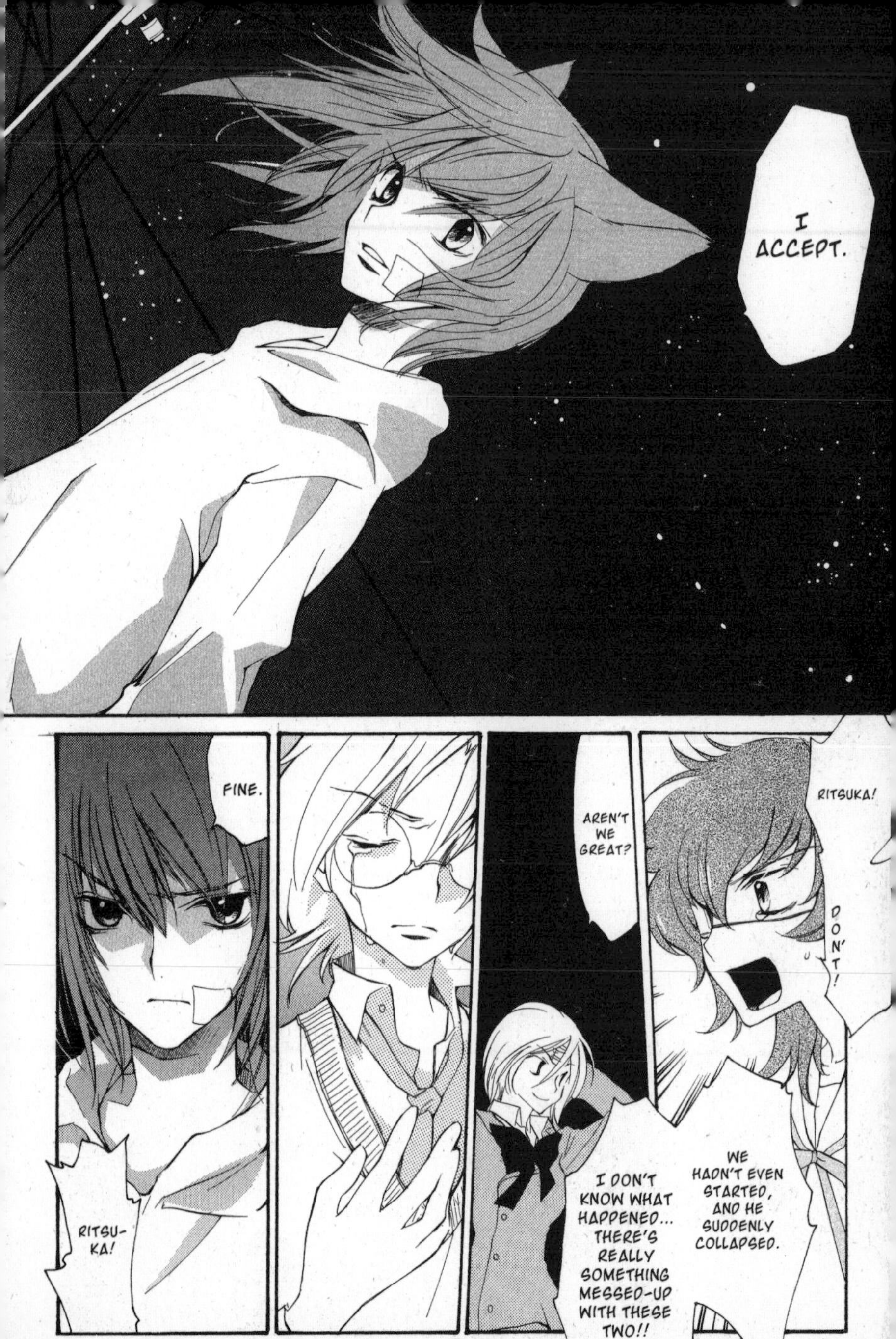
I ACCEPT.
RITSUKA!
DON'T!
AREN'T WE GREAT?
WE HADN'T EVEN STARTED, AND HE SUDDENLY COLLAPSED.
I DON'T KNOW WHAT HAPPENED... THERE'S REALLY SOMETHING MESSED-UP WITH THESE TWO!!
FINE.
RITSU-KA!

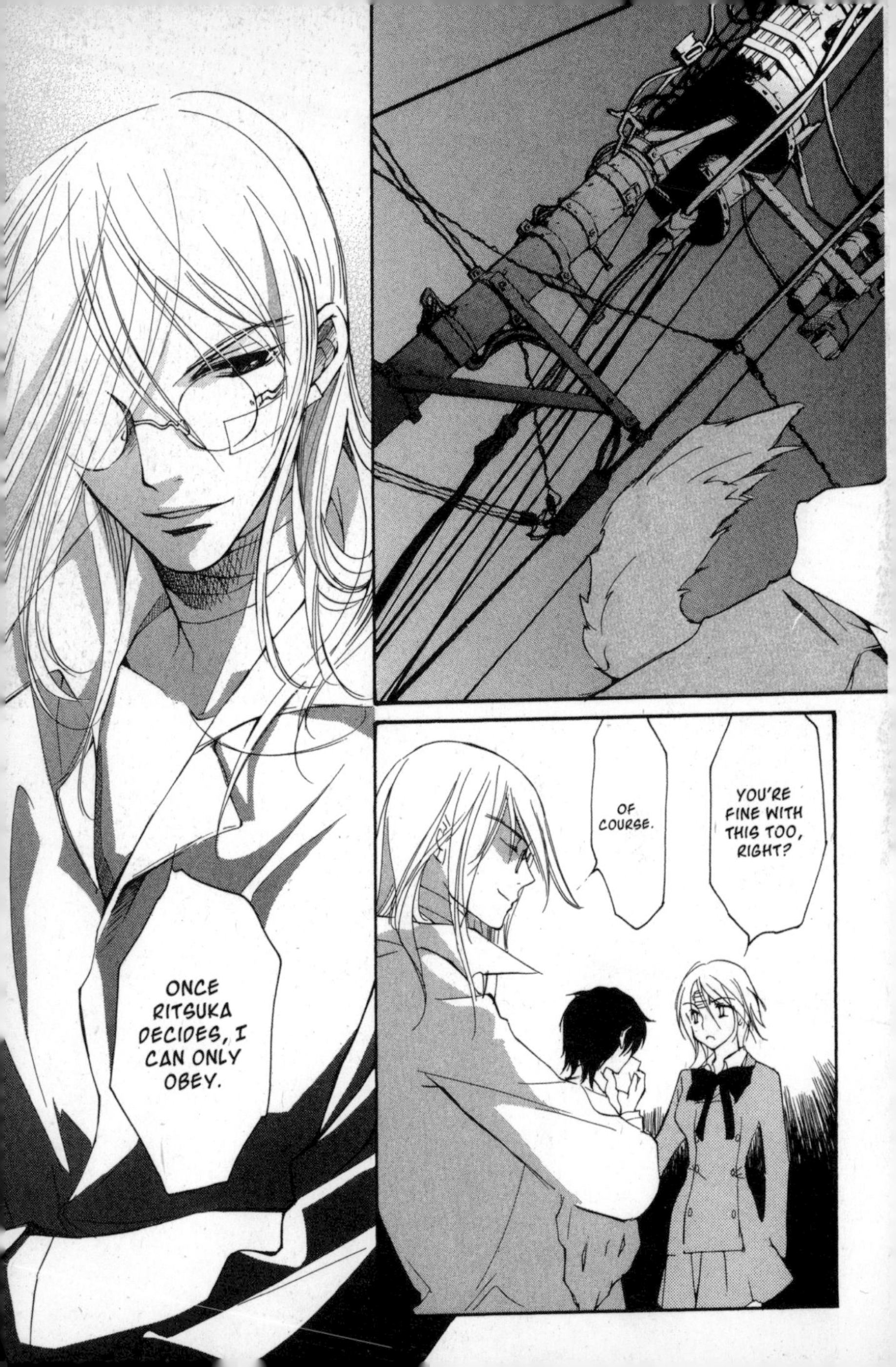
YOU'RE FINE WITH THIS TOO, RIGHT?
OF COURSE.
ONCE RITSUKA DECIDES, I CAN ONLY OBEY.

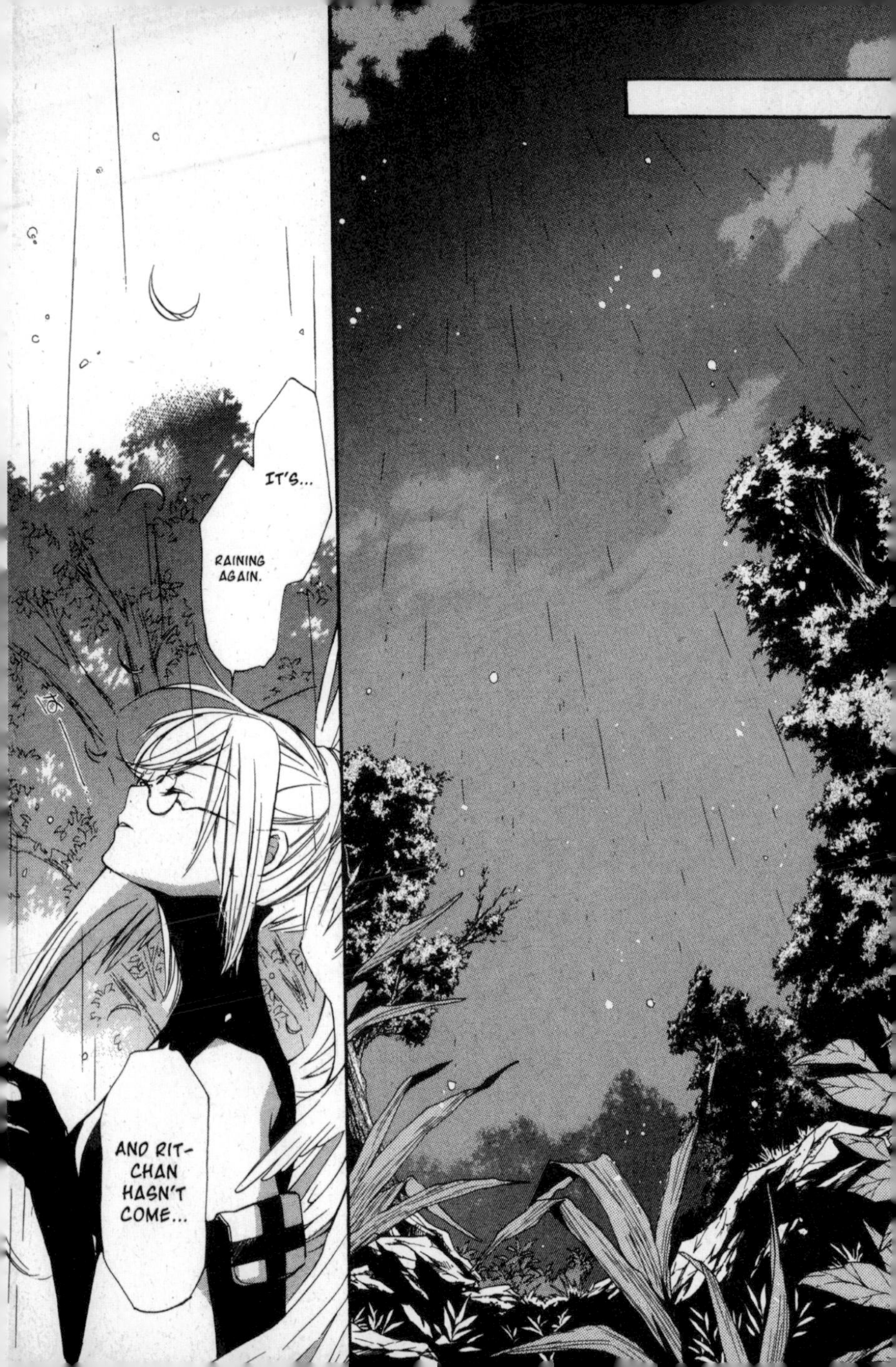
IT'S...
RAINING AGAIN.
AND RIT-CHAN HASN'T COME...

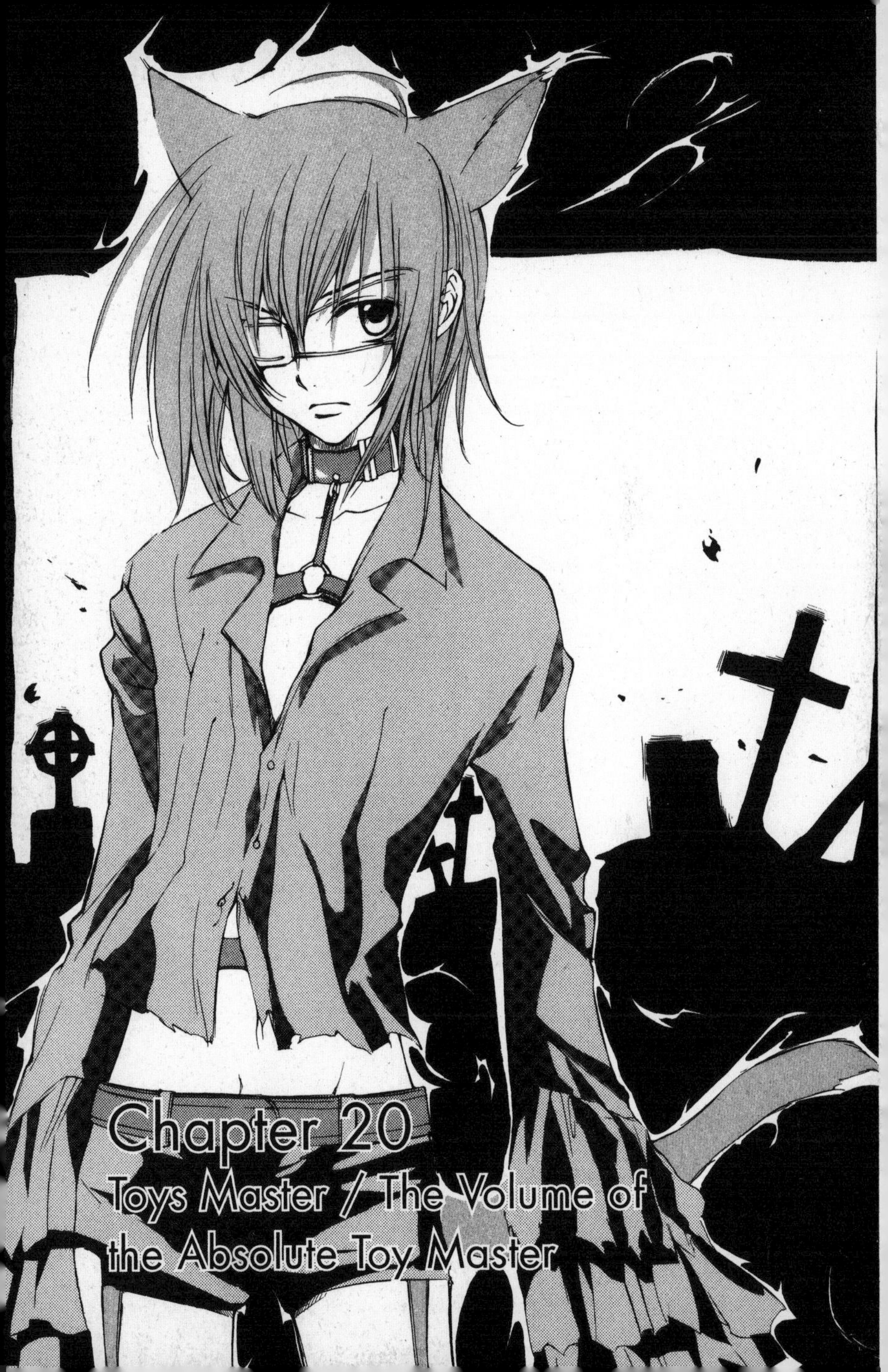
Chapter 20
Toys Master / The Volume of the Absolute Toy Master

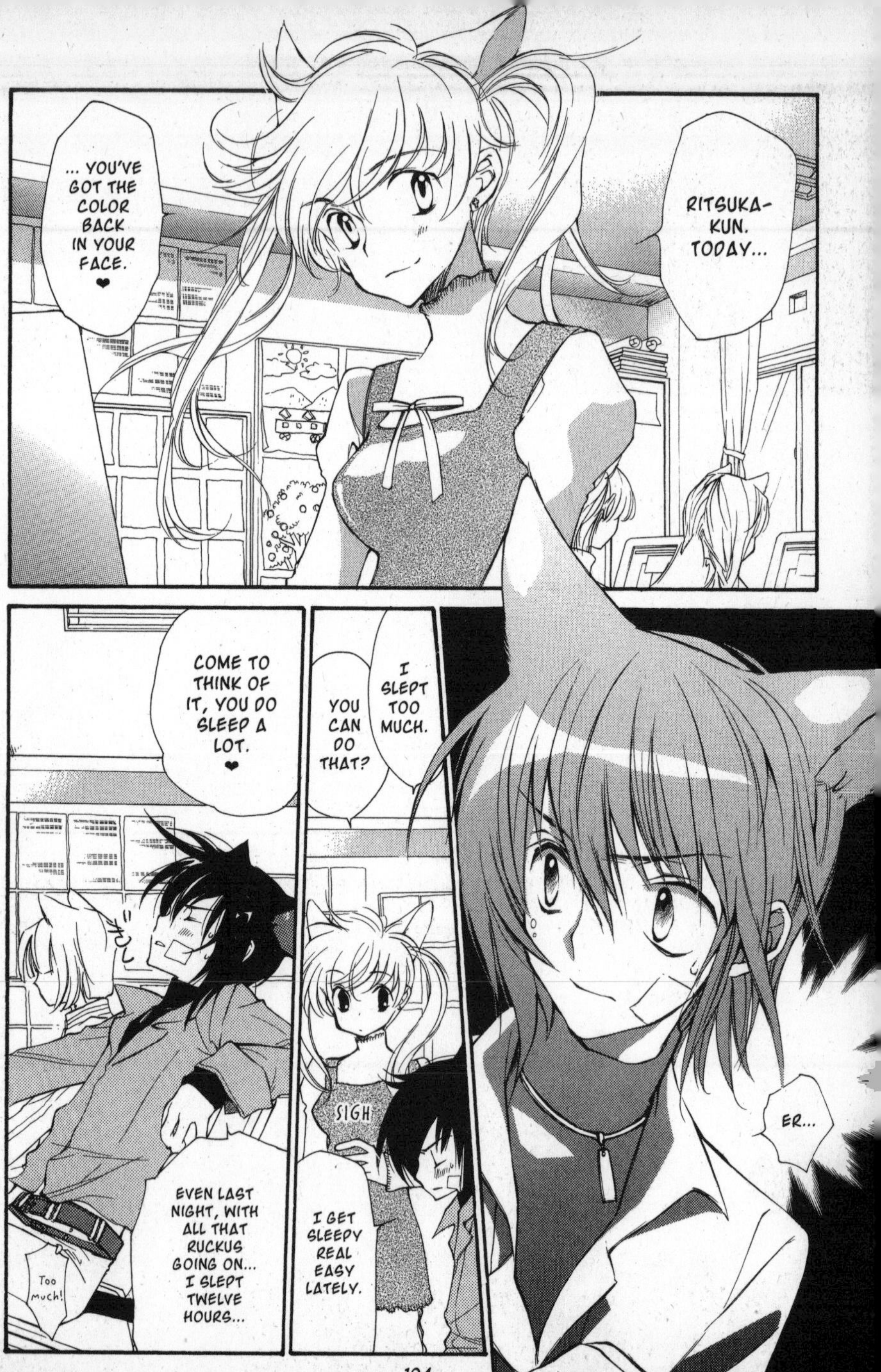
RITSUKA-KUN. TODAY...
... YOU'VE GOT THE COLOR BACK IN YOUR FACE. ❤
ER...
I SLEPT TOO MUCH.
YOU CAN DO THAT?
SIGH
I GET SLEEPY REAL EASY LATELY.
COME TO THINK OF IT, YOU DO SLEEP A LOT. ❤
EVEN LAST NIGHT, WITH ALL THAT RUCKUS GOING ON... I SLEPT TWELVE HOURS...
Too much!

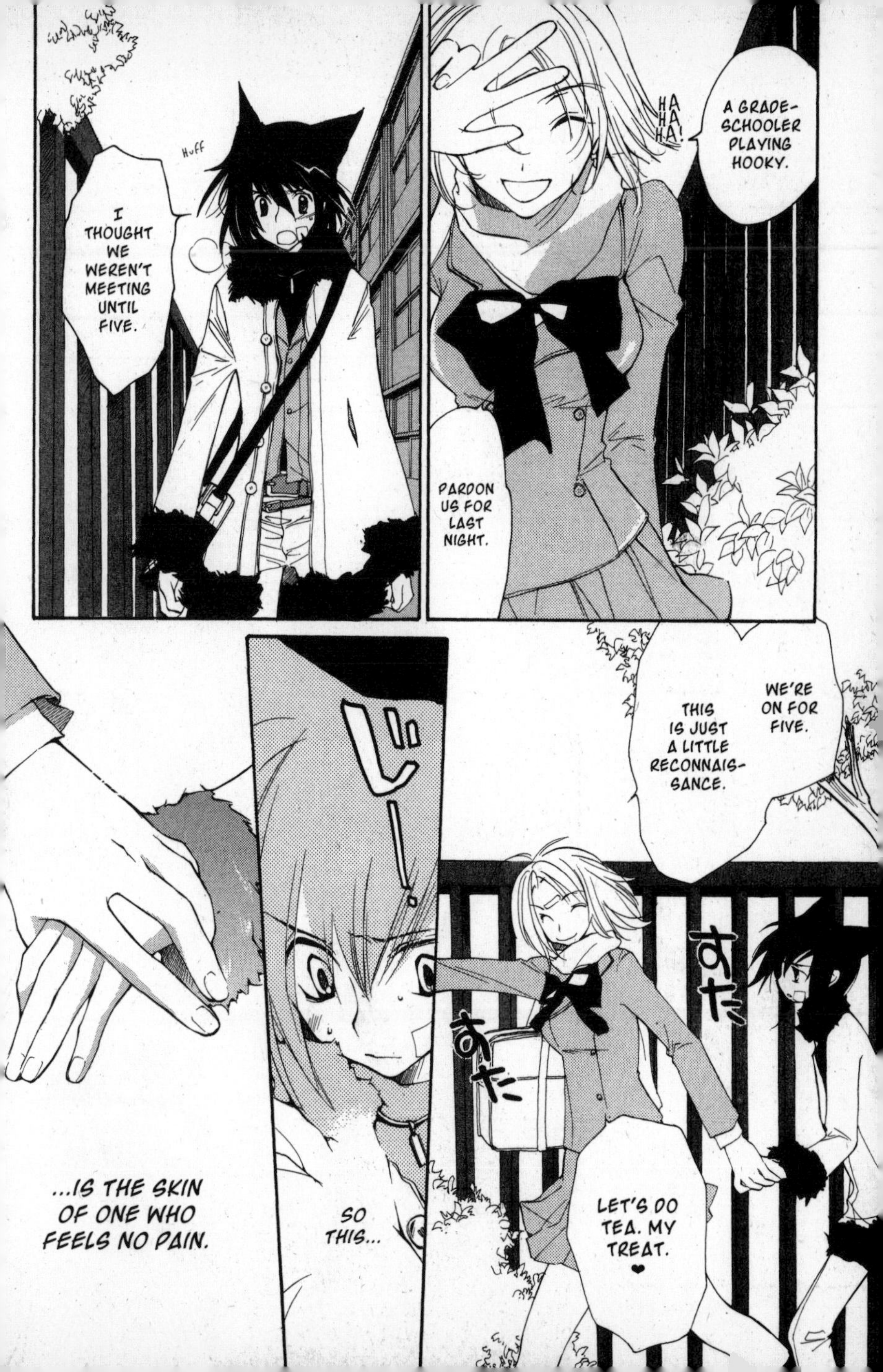
HA HA HA!
A GRADE-SCHOOLER PLAYING HOOKY.
PARDON US FOR LAST NIGHT.
Huff
I THOUGHT WE WEREN'T MEETING UNTIL FIVE.
WE'RE ON FOR FIVE.
THIS IS JUST A LITTLE RECONNAIS-SANCE.
すた
すた
LET'S DO TEA. MY TREAT. ❤
じー!
SO THIS...
...IS THE SKIN OF ONE WHO FEELS NO PAIN.

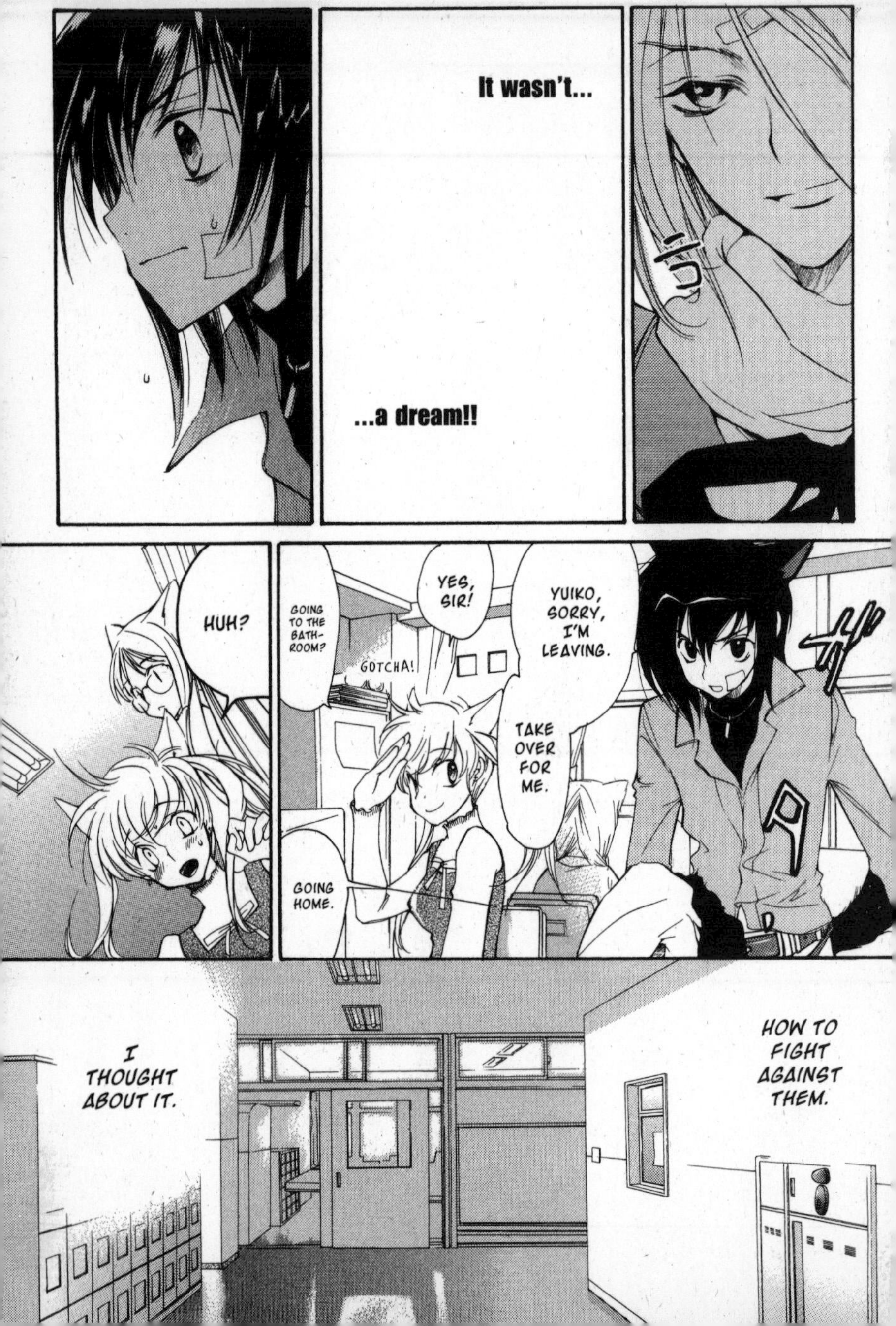
It wasn't...
...a dream!!
YUIKO, SORRY, I'M LEAVING.
TAKE OVER FOR ME.
YES, SIR!
GOING TO THE BATH-ROOM?
GOTCHA!
GOING HOME.
HUH?
HOW TO FIGHT AGAINST THEM.
I THOUGHT ABOUT IT.

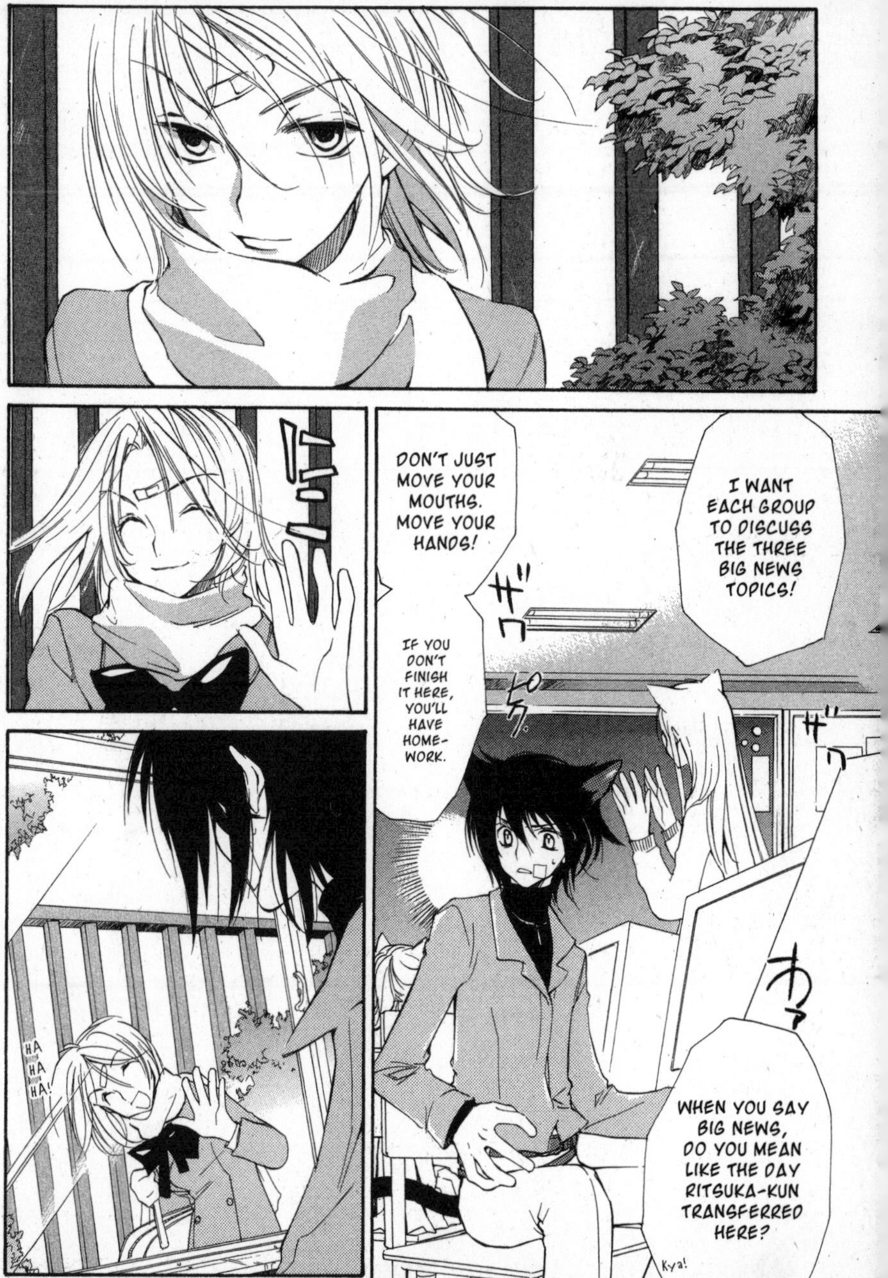
I WANT EACH GROUP TO DISCUSS THE THREE BIG NEWS TOPICS!
DON'T JUST MOVE YOUR MOUTHS. MOVE YOUR HANDS!
IF YOU DON'T FINISH IT HERE, YOU'LL HAVE HOME-WORK.
WHEN YOU SAY BIG NEWS, DO YOU MEAN LIKE THE DAY RITSUKA-KUN TRANSFERRED HERE?
Kya!
HA HA HA!

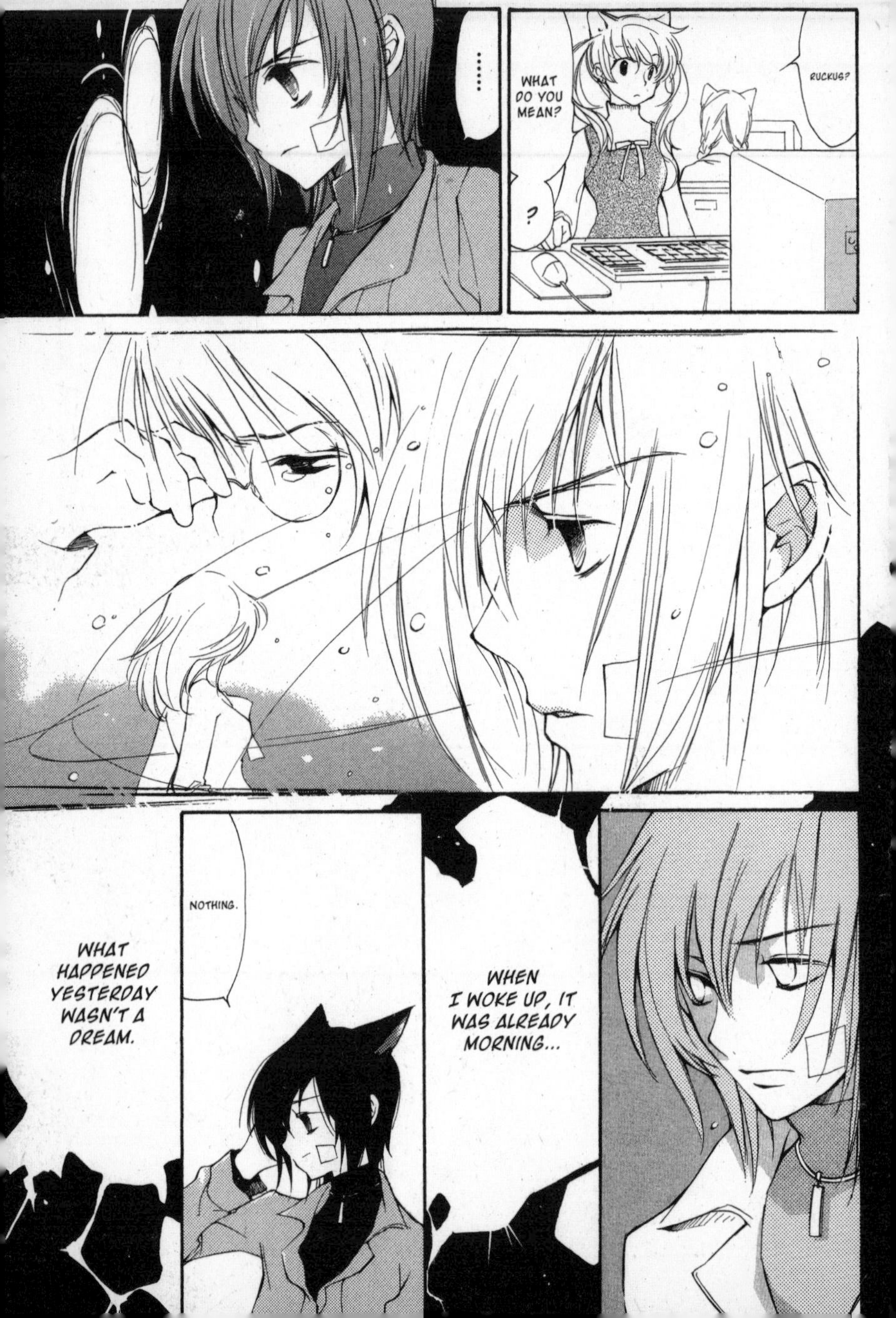

RUCKUS?
WHAT DO YOU MEAN?
?
......
WHEN I WOKE UP, IT WAS ALREADY MORNING...
NOTHING.
WHAT HAPPENED YESTERDAY WASN'T A DREAM.

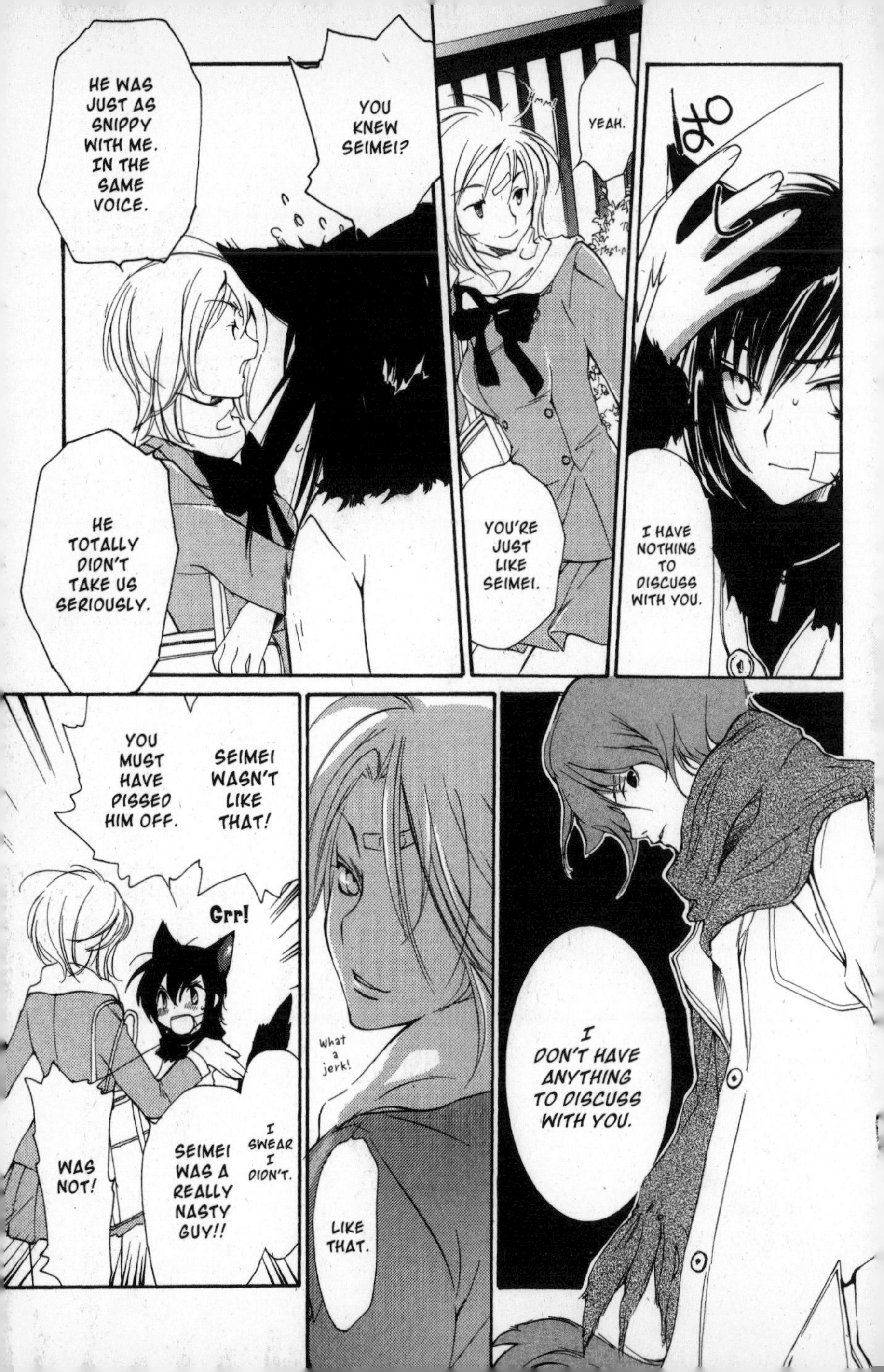

I HAVE NOTHING TO DISCUSS WITH YOU.
YEAH.
Hmm!
YOU'RE JUST LIKE SEIMEI.
YOU KNEW SEIMEI?
HE WAS JUST AS SNIPPY WITH ME. IN THE SAME VOICE.
HE TOTALLY DIDN'T TAKE US SERIOUSLY.
I DON'T HAVE ANYTHING TO DISCUSS WITH YOU.
What a jerk!
LIKE THAT.
SEIMEI WASN'T LIKE THAT!
YOU MUST HAVE PISSED HIM OFF.
Grr!
I SWEAR I DIDN'T.
SEIMEI WAS A REALLY NASTY GUY!!
WAS NOT!

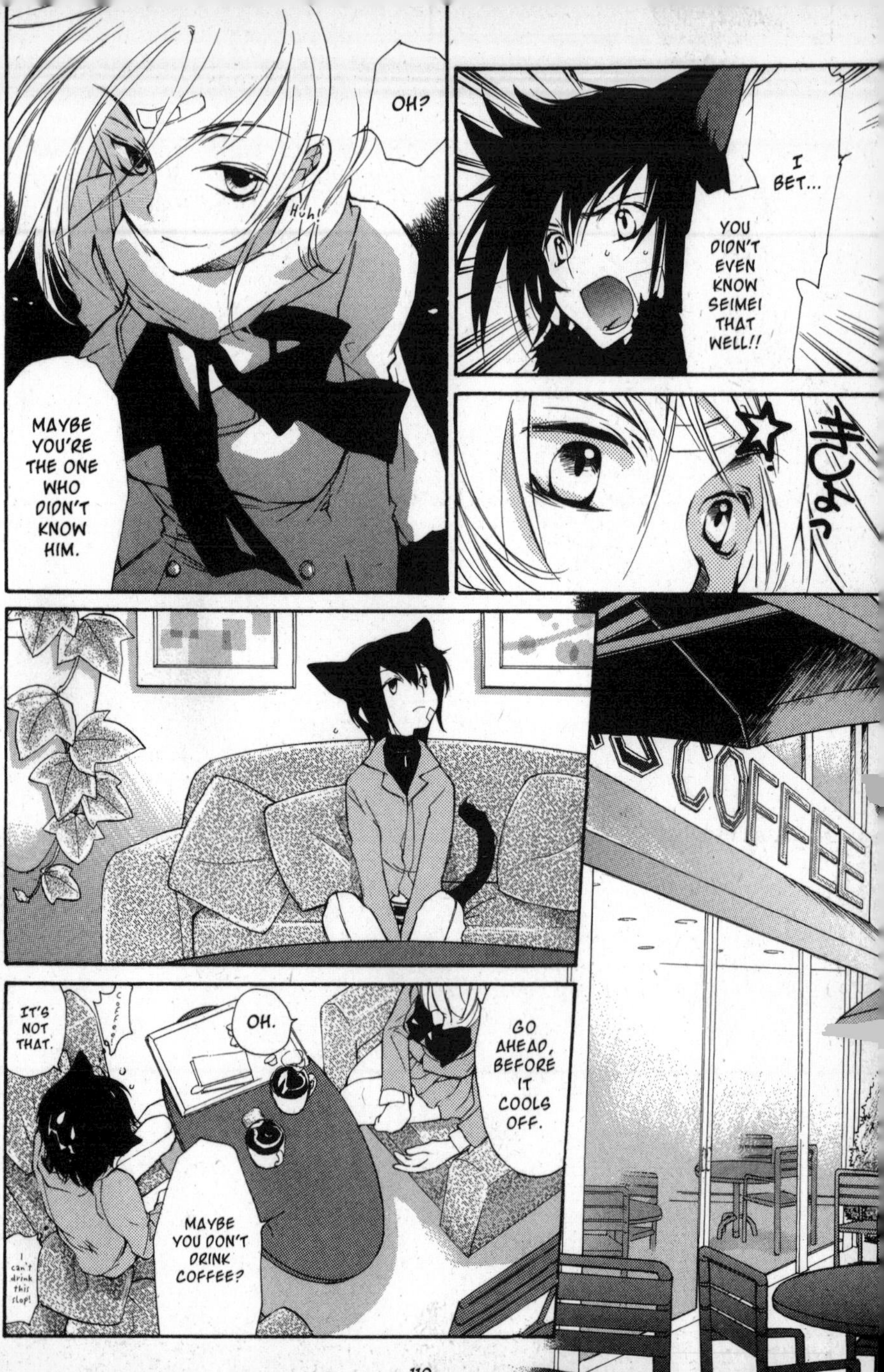

I BET...
YOU DIDN'T EVEN KNOW SEIMEI THAT WELL!!
OH?
Huh!
MAYBE YOU'RE THE ONE WHO DIDN'T KNOW HIM.
COFFEE
GO AHEAD, BEFORE IT COOLS OFF.
OH.
MAYBE YOU DON'T DRINK COFFEE?
IT'S NOT THAT.
Coffee!
I can't drink this slop!

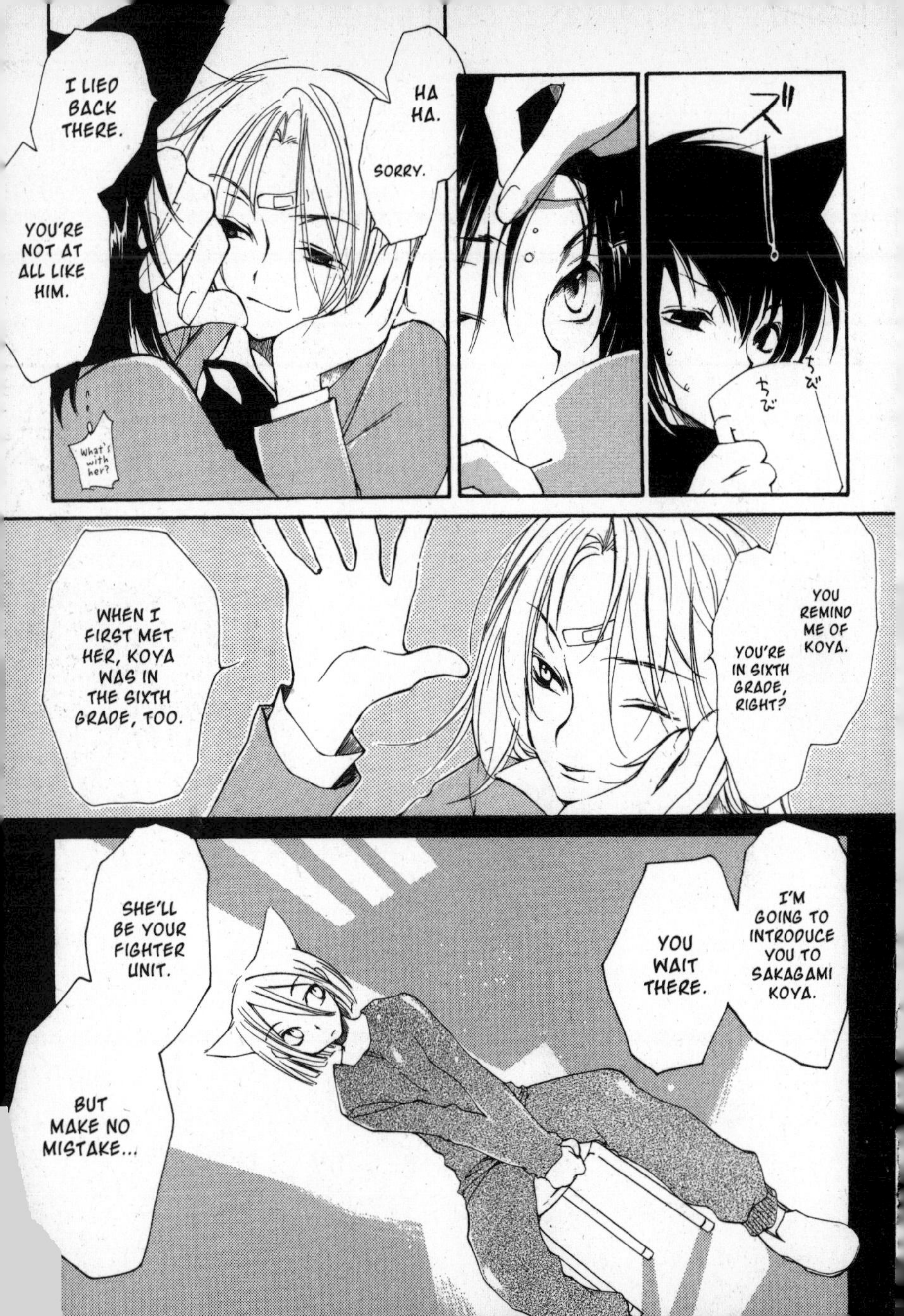
ズー
ちび
ちび
HA HA.
SORRY.
I LIED BACK THERE.
YOU'RE NOT AT ALL LIKE HIM.
What's with her?
YOU REMIND ME OF KOYA.
YOU'RE IN SIXTH GRADE, RIGHT?
WHEN I FIRST MET HER, KOYA WAS IN THE SIXTH GRADE, TOO.
I'M GOING TO INTRODUCE YOU TO SAKAGAMI KOYA.
YOU WAIT THERE.
SHE'LL BE YOUR FIGHTER UNIT.
BUT MAKE NO MISTAKE...

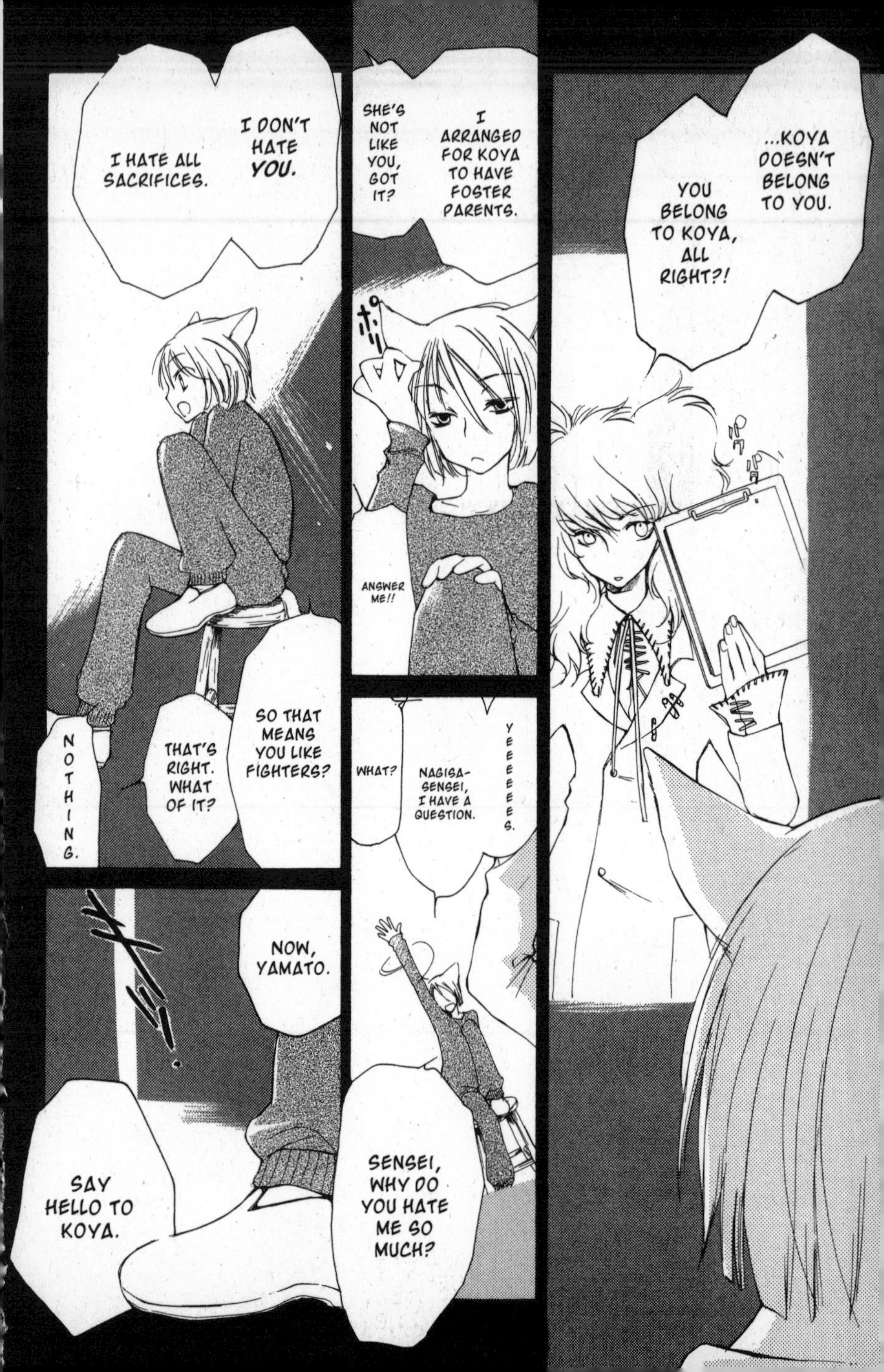
...KOYA DOESN'T BELONG TO YOU.
YOU BELONG TO KOYA, ALL RIGHT?!
I ARRANGED FOR KOYA TO HAVE FOSTER PARENTS.
SHE'S NOT LIKE YOU, GOT IT?
ANSWER ME!!
I DON'T HATE *YOU*.
I HATE ALL SACRIFICES.
SO THAT MEANS YOU LIKE FIGHTERS?
THAT'S RIGHT. WHAT OF IT?
NOTHING.
YEEEEEES.
NAGISA-SENSEI, I HAVE A QUESTION.
WHAT?
SENSEI, WHY DO YOU HATE ME SO MUCH?
NOW, YAMATO.
SAY HELLO TO KOYA.

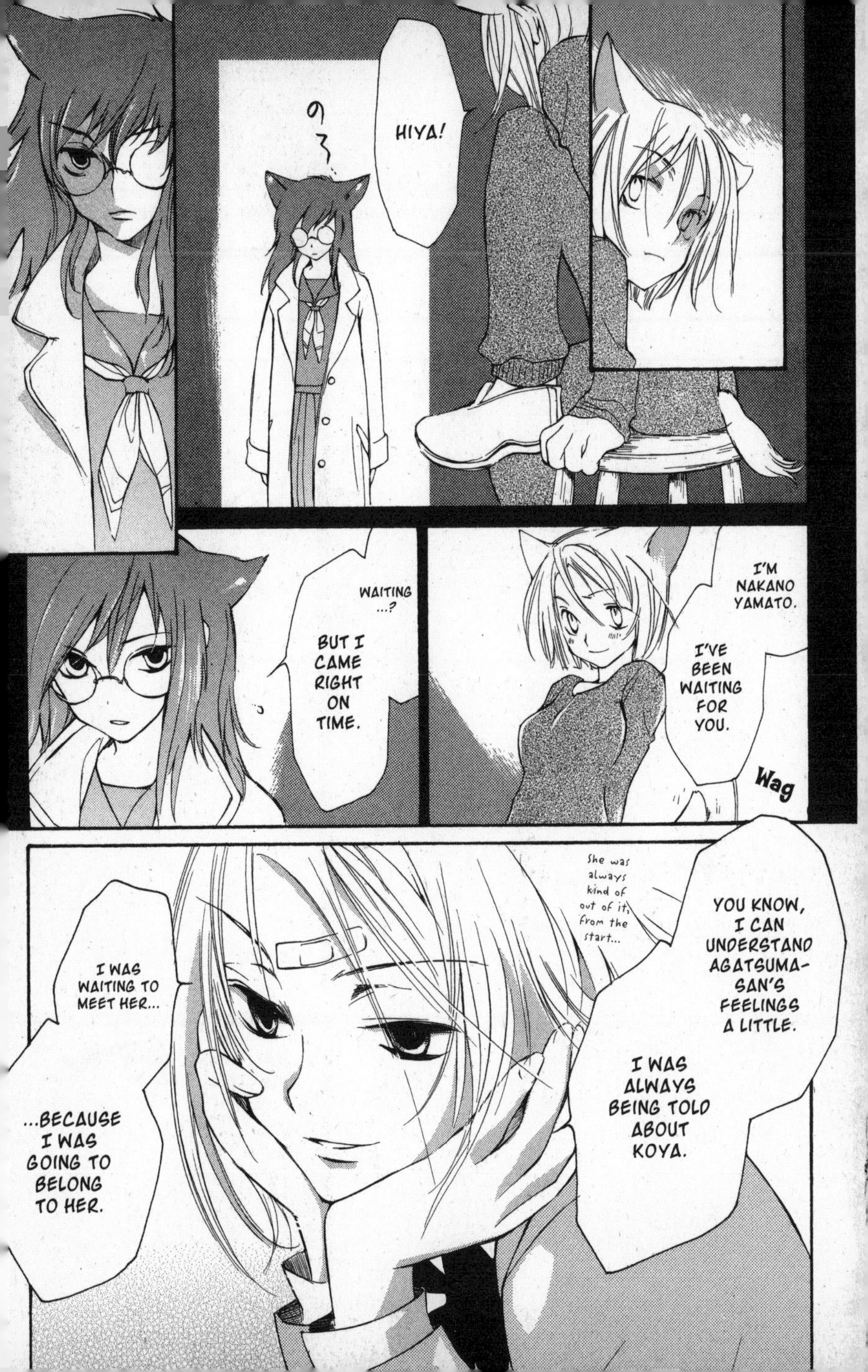
HIYA!
のろ…
I'M NAKANO YAMATO.
I'VE BEEN WAITING FOR YOU.
Wag
WAITING ...?
BUT I CAME RIGHT ON TIME.
YOU KNOW, I CAN UNDERSTAND AGATSUMA-SAN'S FEELINGS A LITTLE.
She was always kind of out of it, from the start...
I WAS ALWAYS BEING TOLD ABOUT KOYA.
I WAS WAITING TO MEET HER...
...BECAUSE I WAS GOING TO BELONG TO HER.

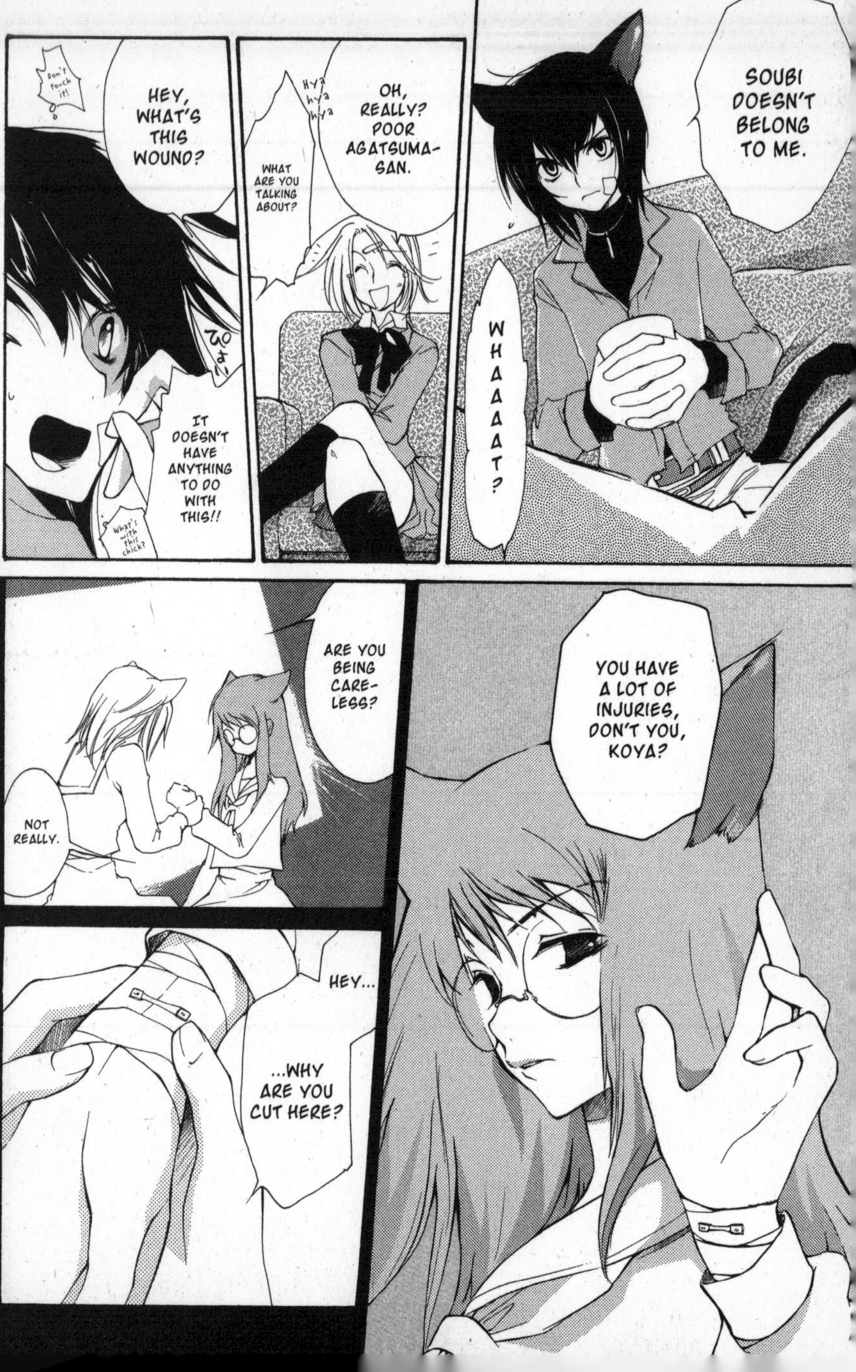
SOUBI DOESN'T BELONG TO ME.
WHAAAAAT?
OH, REALLY? POOR AGATSUMA-SAN.
Hya hya hya
WHAT ARE YOU TALKING ABOUT?
HEY, WHAT'S THIS WOUND?
Don't touch it!
IT DOESN'T HAVE ANYTHING TO DO WITH THIS!!
What's with this chick?
YOU HAVE A LOT OF INJURIES, DON'T YOU, KOYA?
ARE YOU BEING CARE-LESS?
NOT REALLY.
HEY...
...WHY ARE YOU CUT HERE?

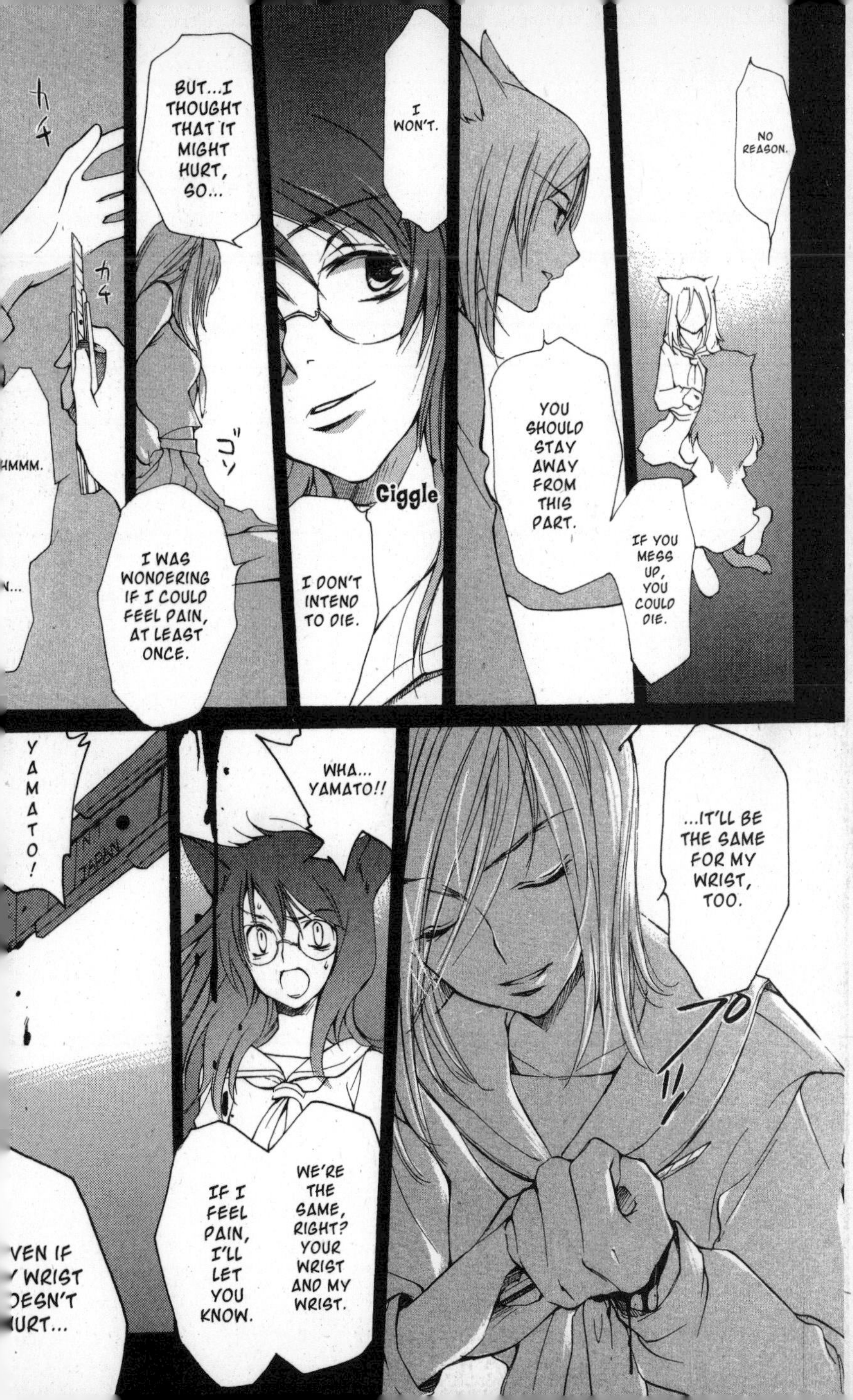
NO REASON.
YOU SHOULD STAY AWAY FROM THIS PART.
IF YOU MESS UP, YOU COULD DIE.
I WON'T.
Giggle
I DON'T INTEND TO DIE.
BUT...I THOUGHT THAT IT MIGHT HURT, SO...
I WAS WONDERING IF I COULD FEEL PAIN, AT LEAST ONCE.
カチ
カチ
HMMM.
N...
...IT'LL BE THE SAME FOR MY WRIST, TOO.
WHA... YAMATO!!
WE'RE THE SAME, RIGHT? YOUR WRIST AND MY WRIST.
IF I FEEL PAIN, I'LL LET YOU KNOW.
YAMATO!
VEN IF
Y WRIST
OESN'T
URT...

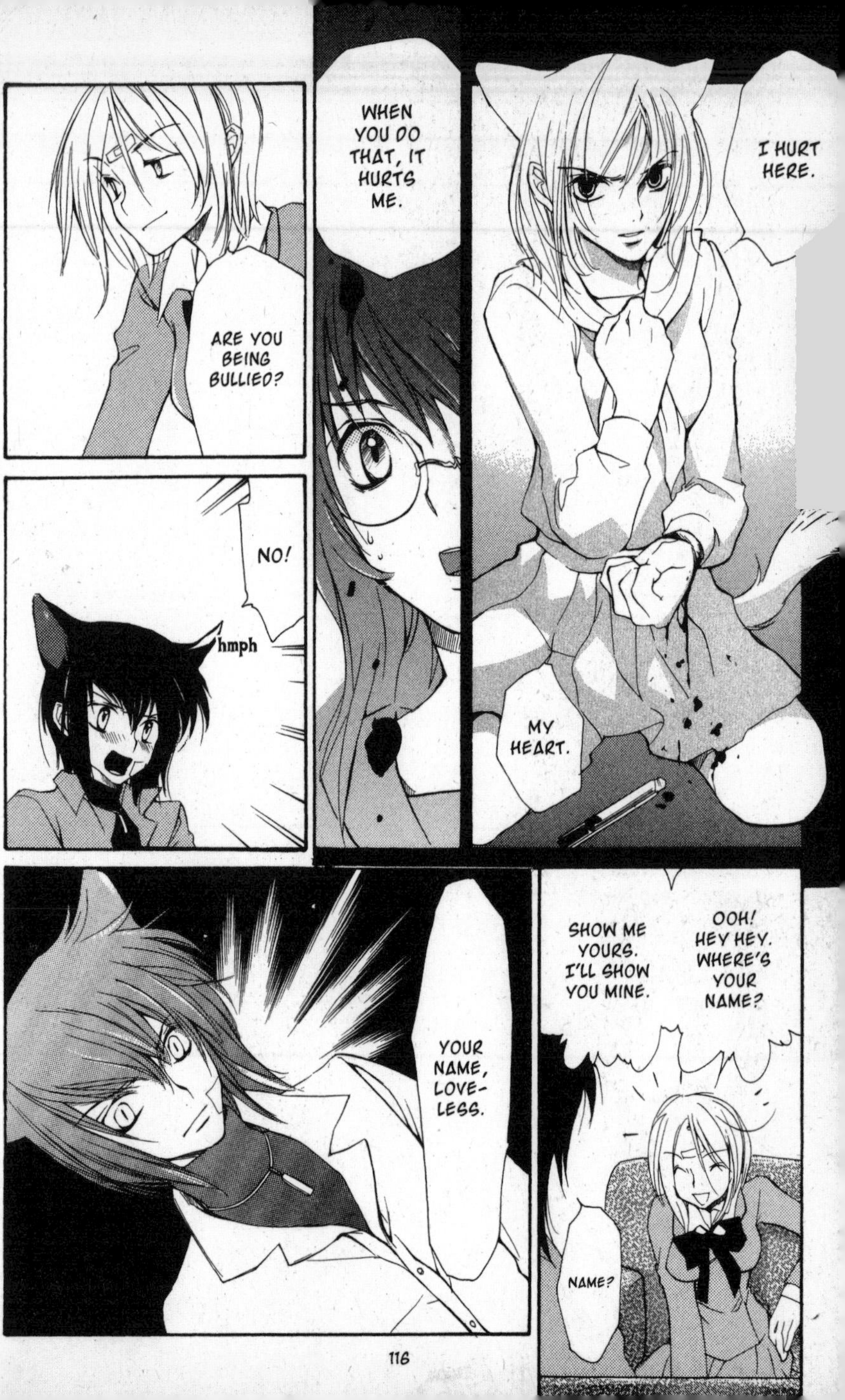
I HURT HERE.
MY HEART.
WHEN YOU DO THAT, IT HURTS ME.
ARE YOU BEING BULLIED?
NO!
hmph
OOH! HEY HEY. WHERE'S YOUR NAME?
SHOW ME YOURS. I'LL SHOW YOU MINE.
NAME?
YOUR NAME, LOVE-LESS.

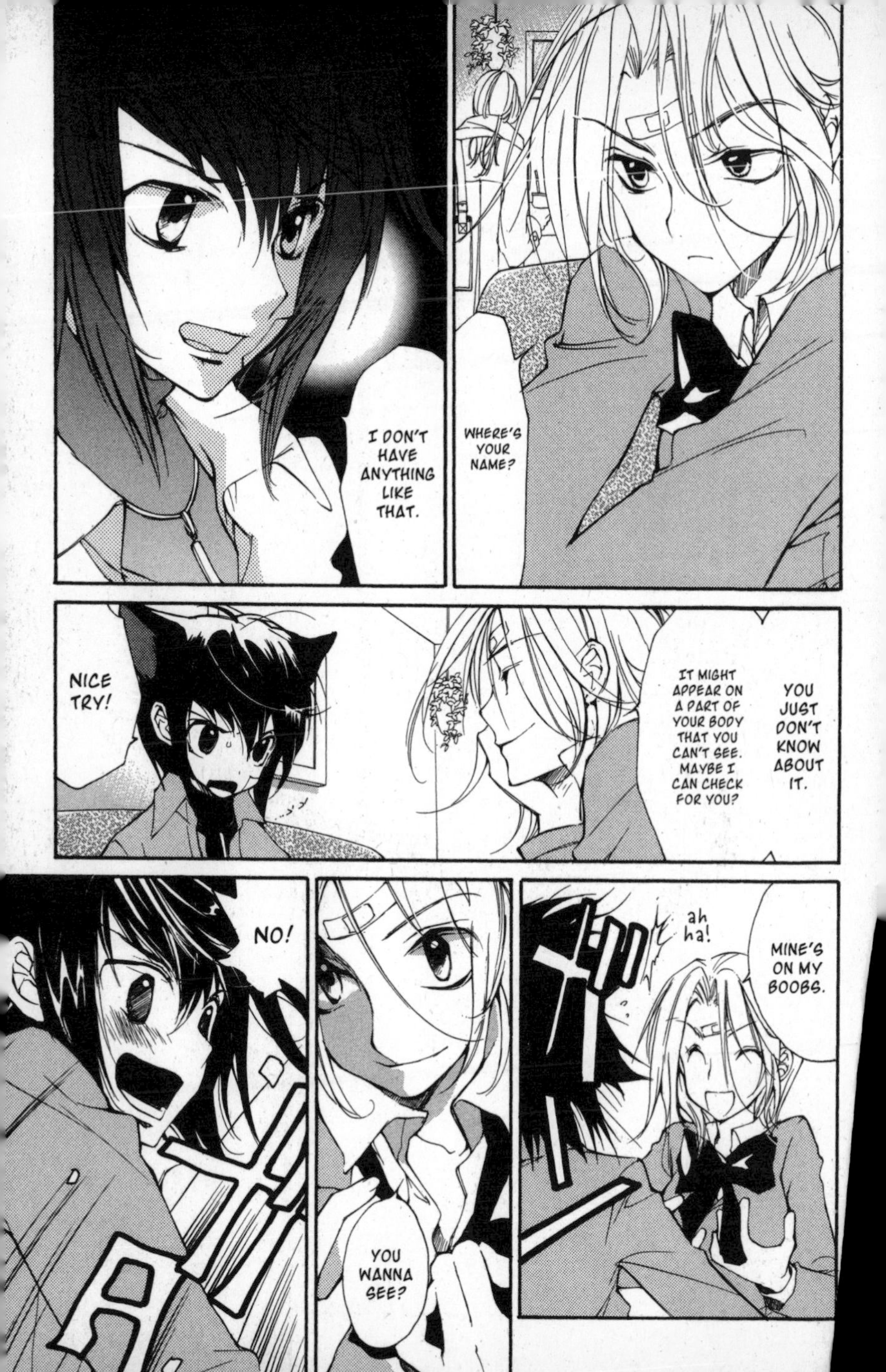
WHERE'S YOUR NAME?
I DON'T HAVE ANYTHING LIKE THAT.
YOU JUST DON'T KNOW ABOUT IT.
IT MIGHT APPEAR ON A PART OF YOUR BODY THAT YOU CAN'T SEE. MAYBE I CAN CHECK FOR YOU?
NICE TRY!
MINE'S ON MY BOOBS.
ah ha!
YOU WANNA SEE?
NO!

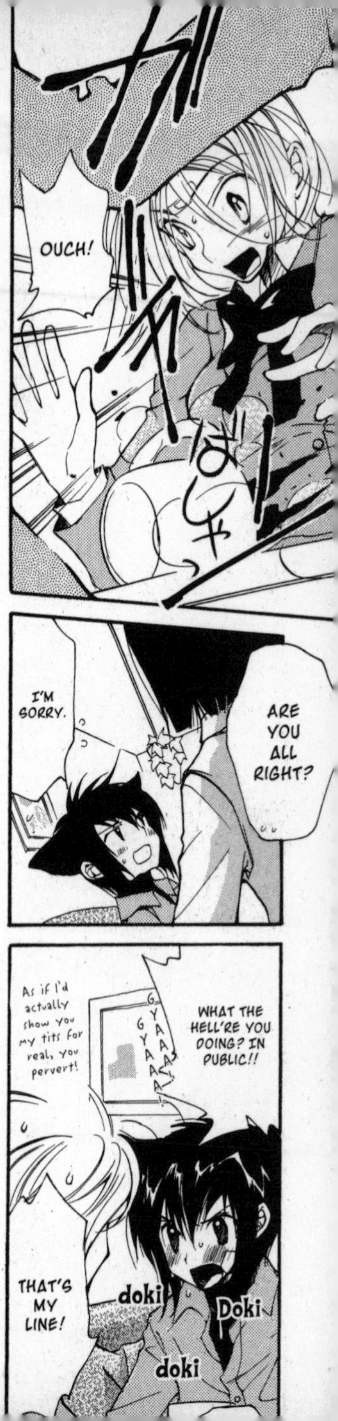
OUCH!
ARE YOU ALL RIGHT?
I'M SORRY.
WHAT THE HELL'RE YOU DOING? IN PUBLIC!!
GYAAAA!
As if I'd actually show you my tits for real, you pervert!
Doki
doki
THAT'S MY LINE!
doki

Toys Master / The Volume of the Absolute Toy Master

Chapter 21

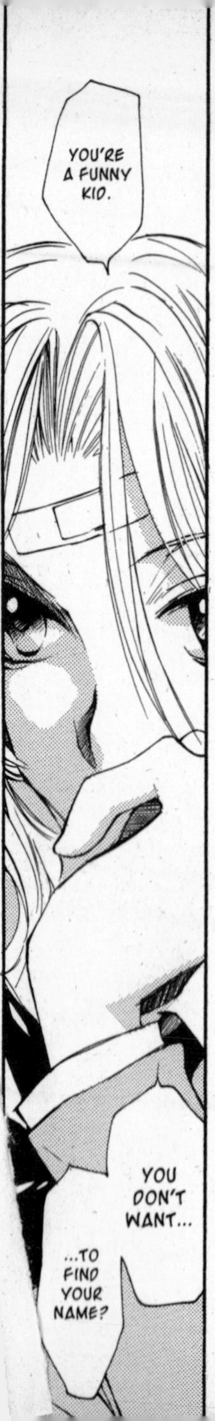
YOU'RE A FUNNY KID.
YOU DON'T WANT...
...TO FIND YOUR NAME?

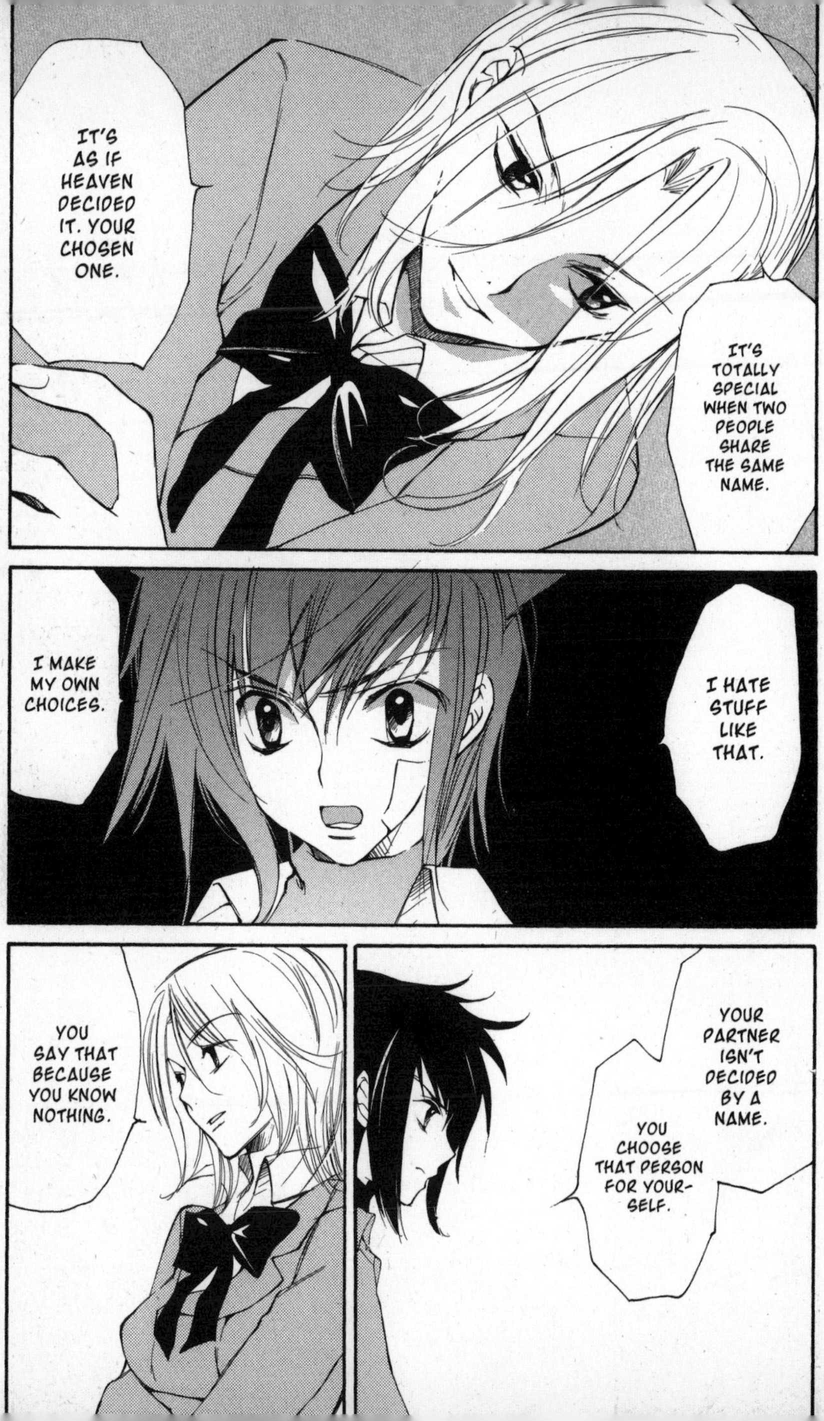
IT'S TOTALLY SPECIAL WHEN TWO PEOPLE SHARE THE SAME NAME.
IT'S AS IF HEAVEN DECIDED IT. YOUR CHOSEN ONE.
I HATE STUFF LIKE THAT.
I MAKE MY OWN CHOICES.
YOUR PARTNER ISN'T DECIDED BY A NAME.
YOU CHOOSE THAT PERSON FOR YOUR-SELF.
YOU SAY THAT BECAUSE YOU KNOW NOTHING.

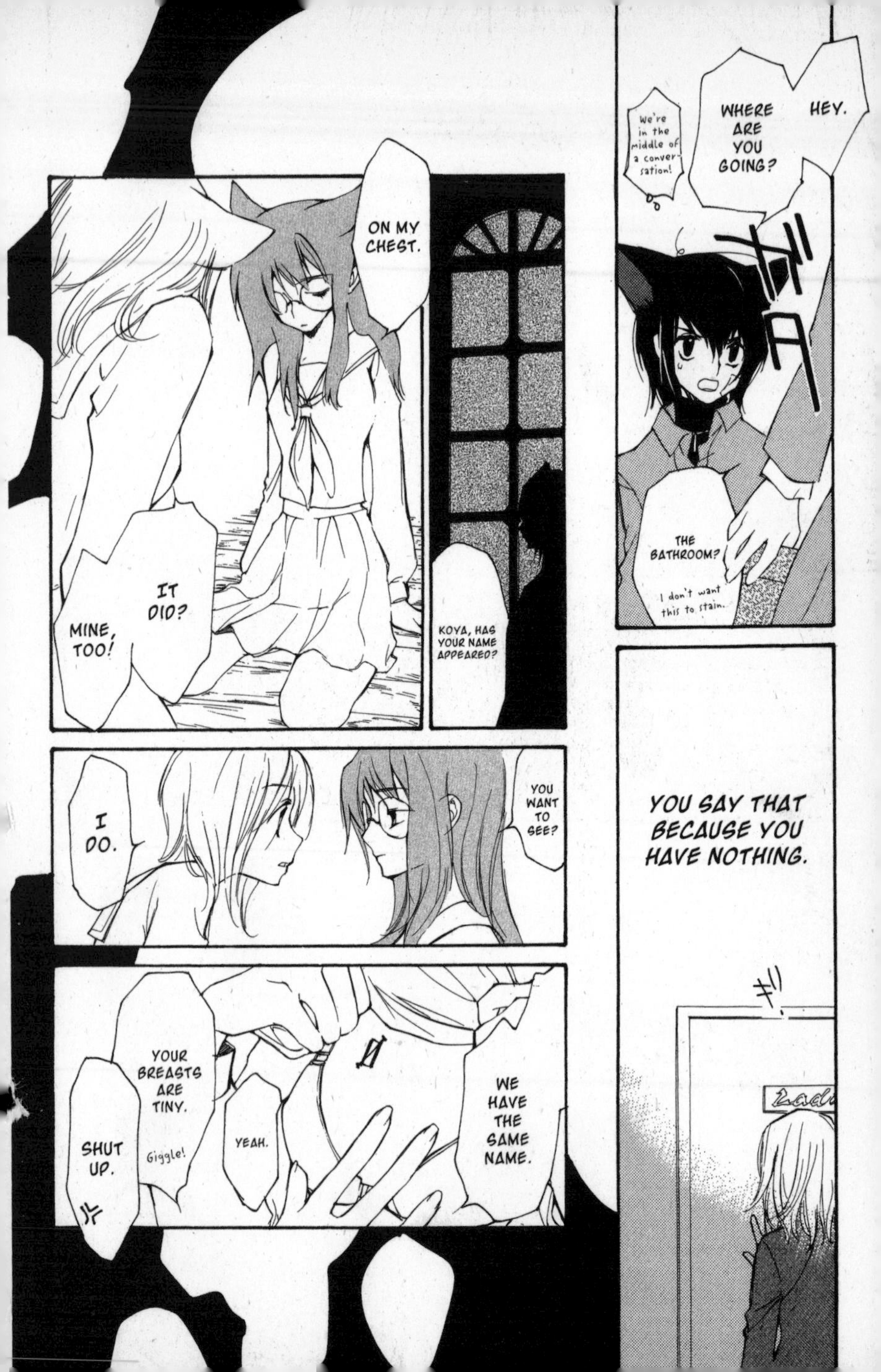
HEY.
WHERE ARE YOU GOING?
We're in the middle of a conversation!
THE BATHROOM?
I don't want this to stain.
YOU SAY THAT BECAUSE YOU HAVE NOTHING.
KOYA, HAS YOUR NAME APPEARED?
ON MY CHEST.
IT DID?
MINE, TOO!
YOU WANT TO SEE?
I DO.
WE HAVE THE SAME NAME.
YOUR BREASTS ARE TINY.
YEAH.
Giggle!
SHUT UP.

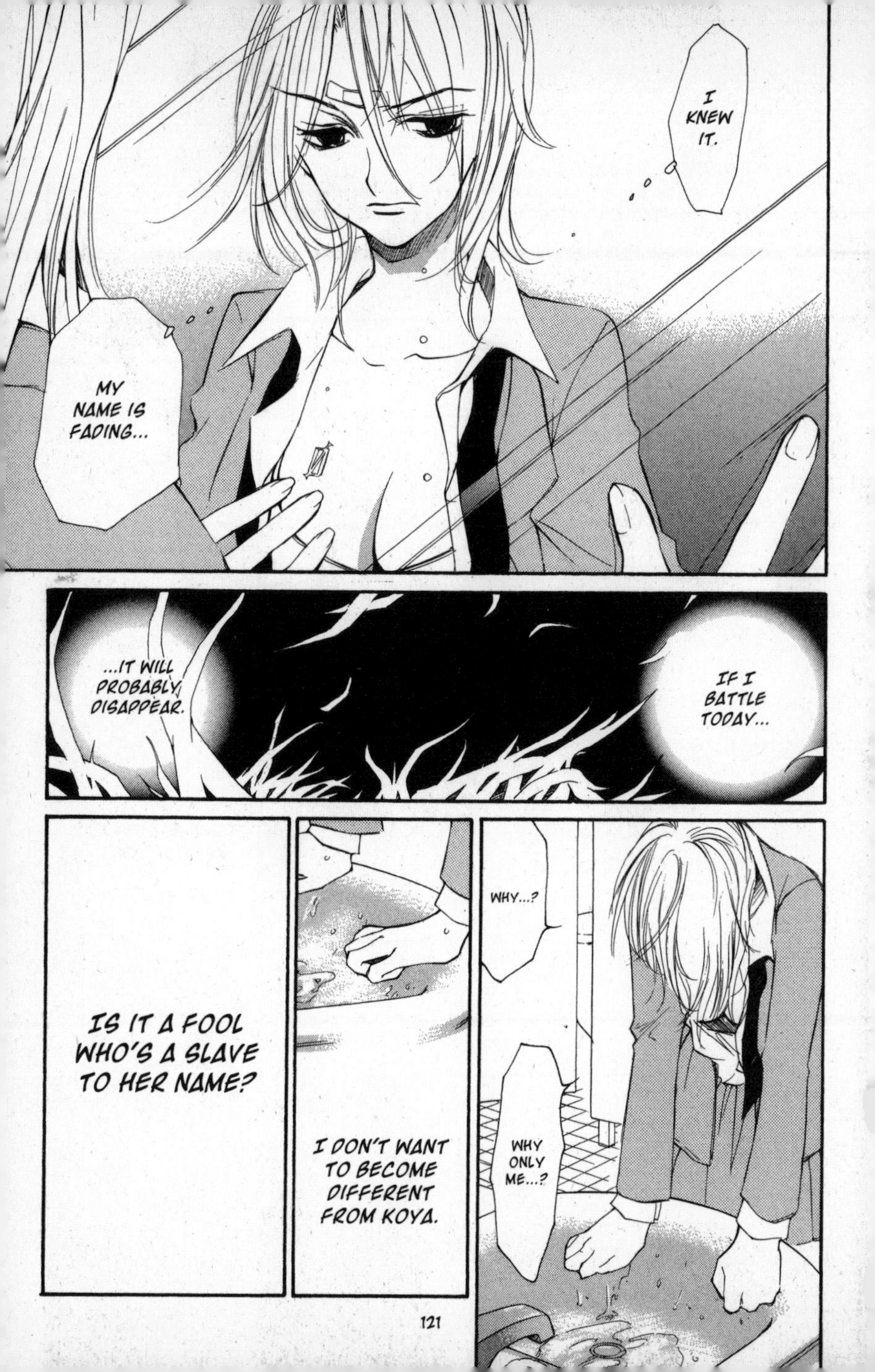
I KNEW IT.
MY NAME IS FADING...
IF I BATTLE TODAY...
...IT WILL PROBABLY DISAPPEAR.
WHY...?
WHY ONLY ME...?
I DON'T WANT TO BECOME DIFFERENT FROM KOYA.
IS IT A FOOL WHO'S A SLAVE TO HER NAME?

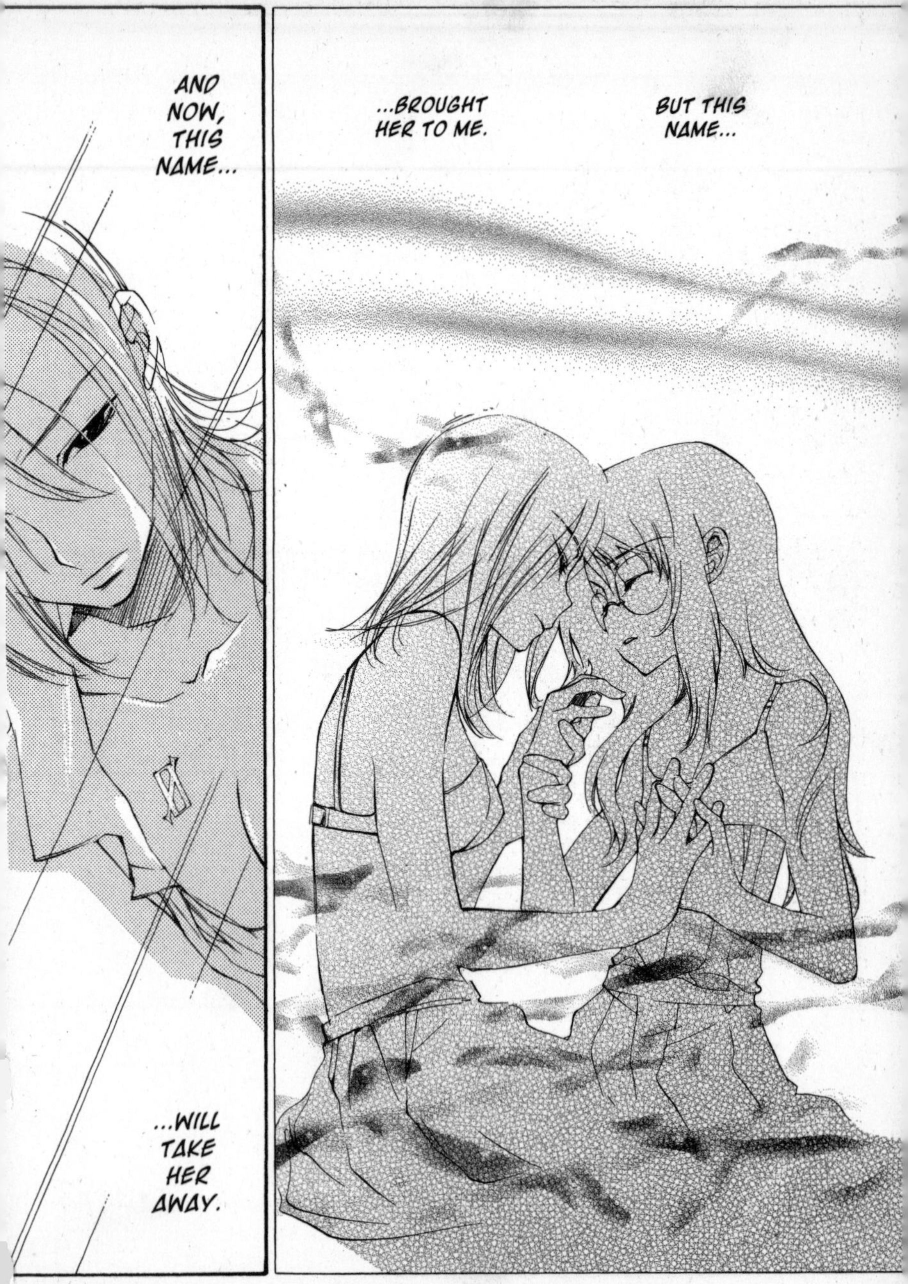
BUT THIS NAME...
...BROUGHT HER TO ME.
AND NOW, THIS NAME...
...WILL TAKE HER AWAY.

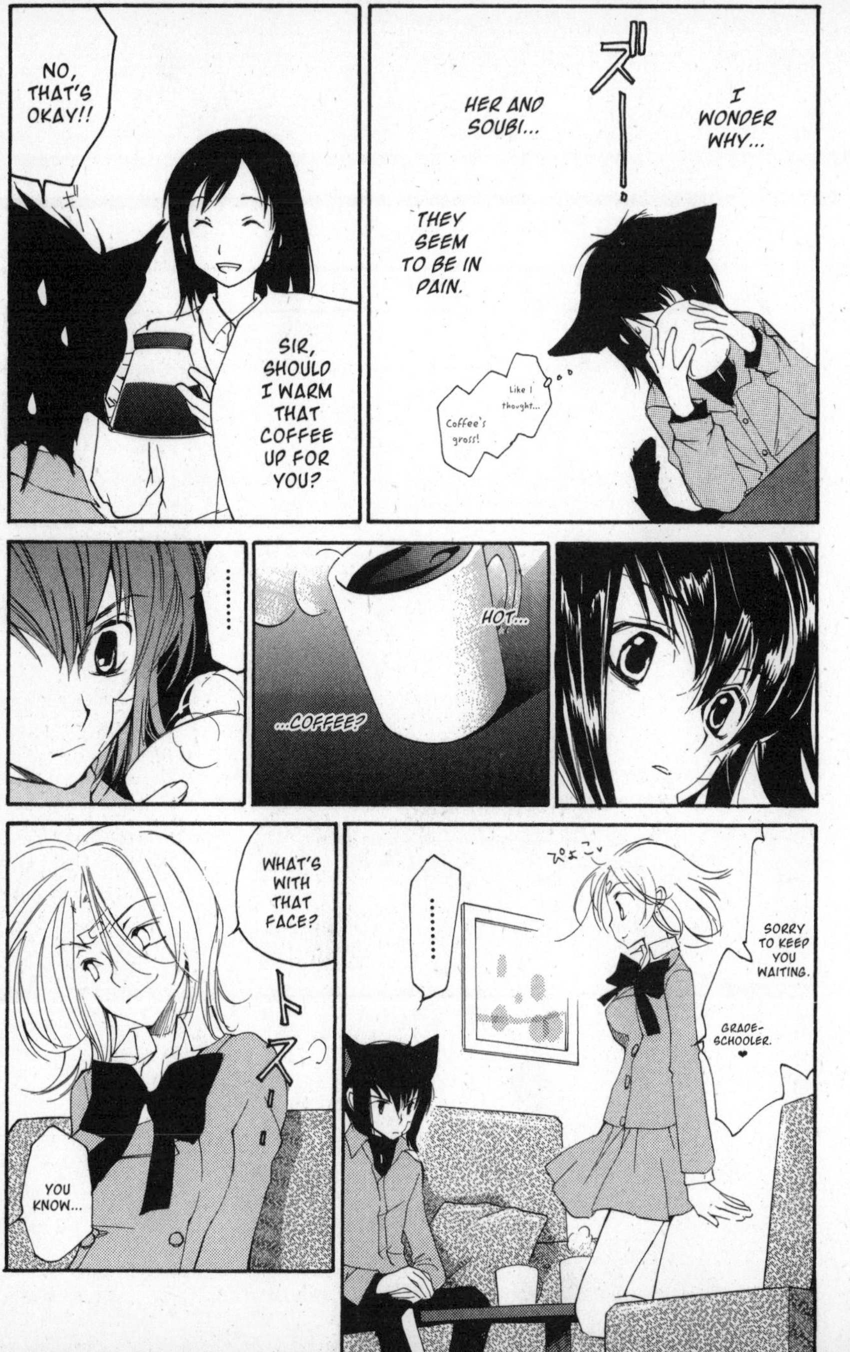

ズー！
I WONDER WHY...
HER AND SOUBI...
THEY SEEM TO BE IN PAIN.
Like I thought... Coffee's gross!
SIR, SHOULD I WARM THAT COFFEE UP FOR YOU?
NO, THAT'S OKAY!!
HOT...
...COFFEE?
......
SORRY TO KEEP YOU WAITING. GRADE-SCHOOLER. ❤
ぴょこ
......
WHAT'S WITH THAT FACE?
YOU KNOW...

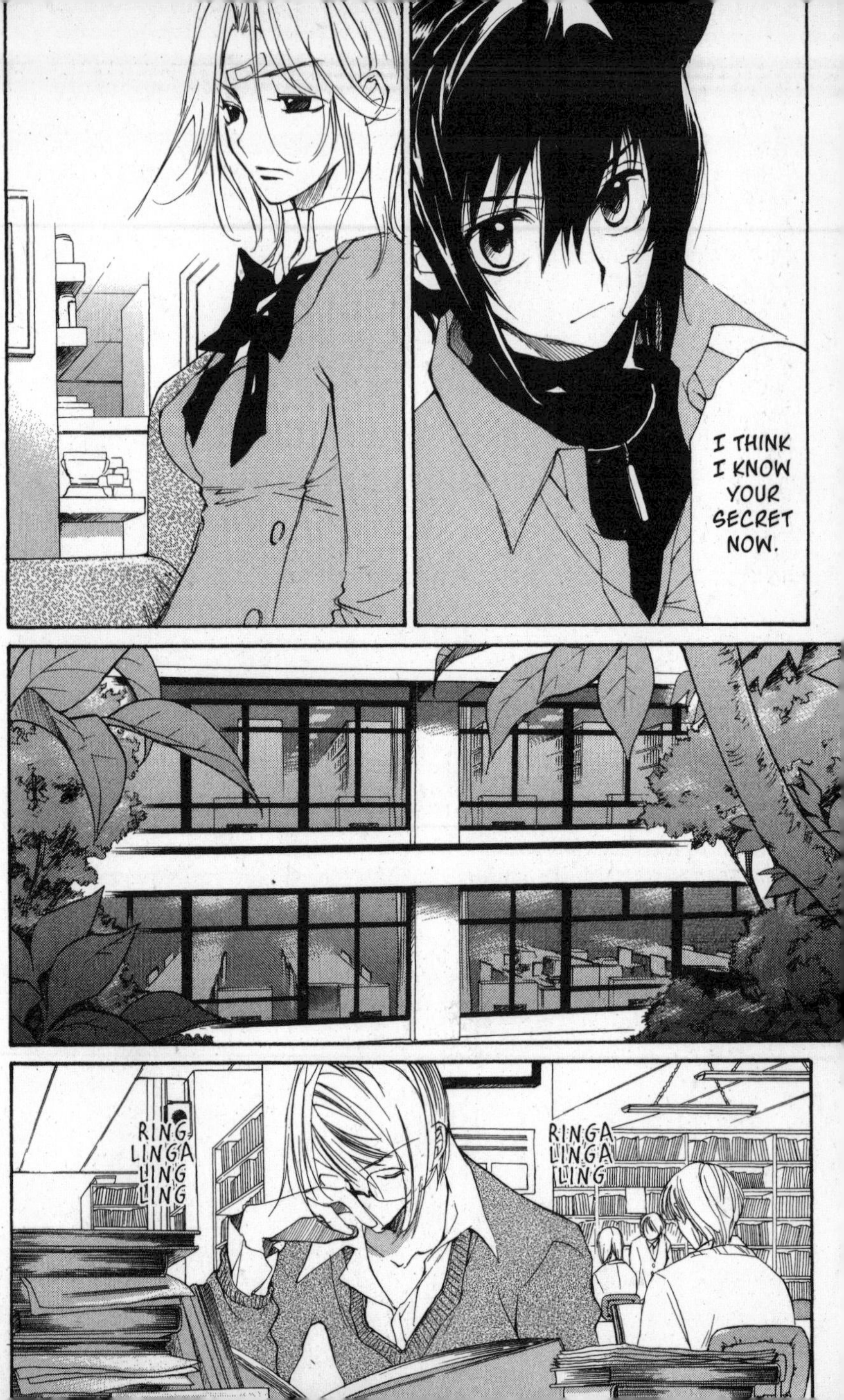
I THINK I KNOW YOUR SECRET NOW.
RINGA LINGA LING
RING LINGA LING LING

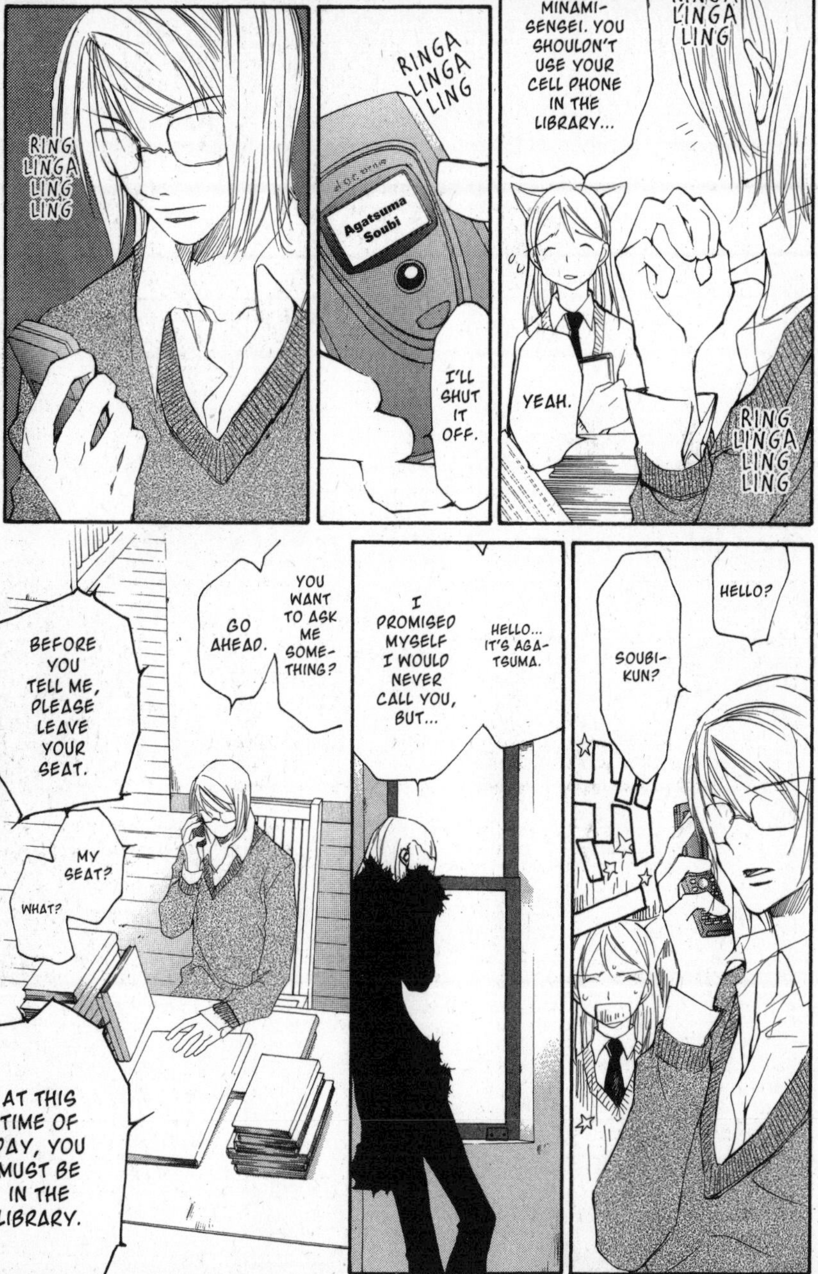
UH... MINAMI-SENSEI. YOU SHOULDN'T USE YOUR CELL PHONE IN THE LIBRARY...
RINGA LINGA LING
YEAH.
RING LINGA LING LING
RINGA LINGA LING
Agatsuma Soubi
I'LL SHUT IT OFF.
RING LINGA LING LING
HELLO?
SOUBI-KUN?
HELLO... IT'S AGA-TSUMA.
I PROMISED MYSELF I WOULD NEVER CALL YOU, BUT...
YOU WANT TO ASK ME SOME-THING?
GO AHEAD.
BEFORE YOU TELL ME, PLEASE LEAVE YOUR SEAT.
MY SEAT?
WHAT?
AT THIS TIME OF DAY, YOU MUST BE IN THE LIBRARY.

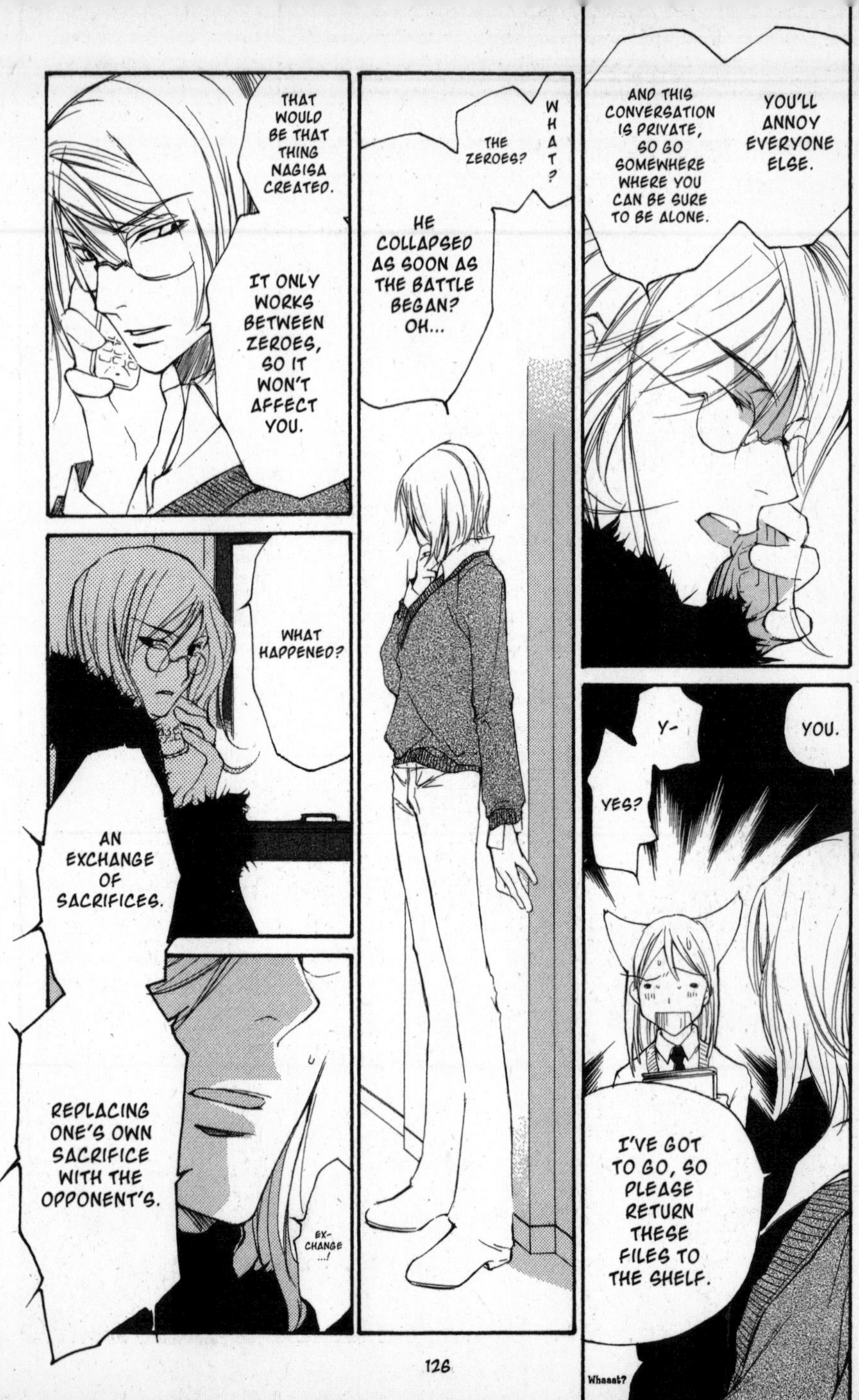
YOU'LL ANNOY EVERYONE ELSE.
AND THIS CONVERSATION IS PRIVATE, SO GO SOMEWHERE WHERE YOU CAN BE SURE TO BE ALONE.
YOU.
Y-
YES?
I'VE GOT TO GO, SO PLEASE RETURN THESE FILES TO THE SHELF.
Whaaat?
WHAT?
THE ZEROES?
HE COLLAPSED AS SOON AS THE BATTLE BEGAN? OH...
THAT WOULD BE THAT THING NAGISA CREATED.
IT ONLY WORKS BETWEEN ZEROES, SO IT WON'T AFFECT YOU.
WHAT HAPPENED?
AN EXCHANGE OF SACRIFICES.
REPLACING ONE'S OWN SACRIFICE WITH THE OPPONENT'S.
EX-CHANGE ...!

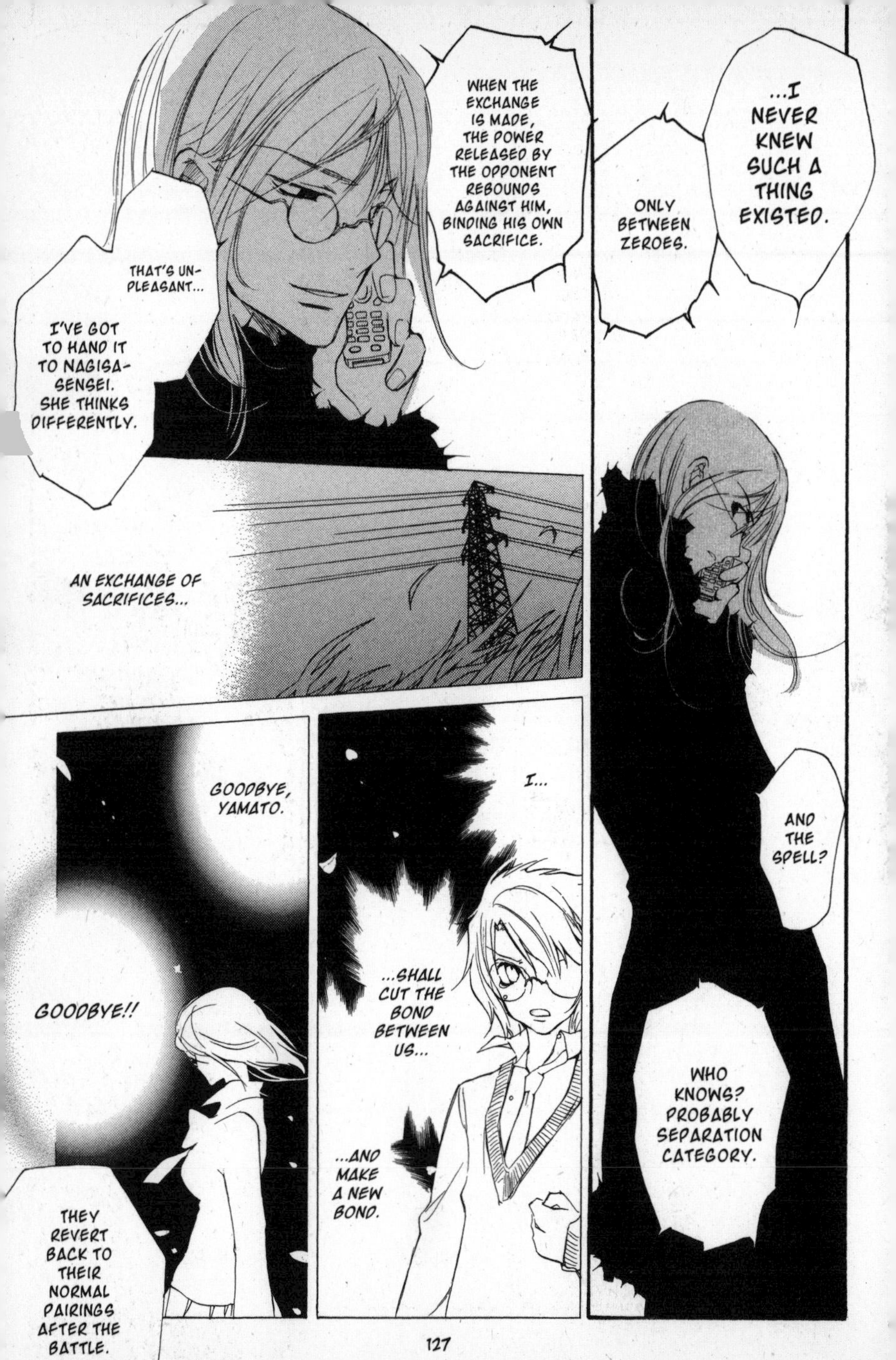

...I NEVER KNEW SUCH A THING EXISTED.
ONLY BETWEEN ZEROES.
AND THE SPELL?
WHO KNOWS? PROBABLY SEPARATION CATEGORY.
WHEN THE EXCHANGE IS MADE, THE POWER RELEASED BY THE OPPONENT REBOUNDS AGAINST HIM, BINDING HIS OWN SACRIFICE.
THAT'S UN-PLEASANT...
I'VE GOT TO HAND IT TO NAGISA-SENSEI. SHE THINKS DIFFERENTLY.
AN EXCHANGE OF SACRIFICES...
I...
...SHALL CUT THE BOND BETWEEN US...
...AND MAKE A NEW BOND.
GOODBYE, YAMATO.
GOODBYE!!
THEY REVERT BACK TO THEIR NORMAL PAIRINGS AFTER THE BATTLE.

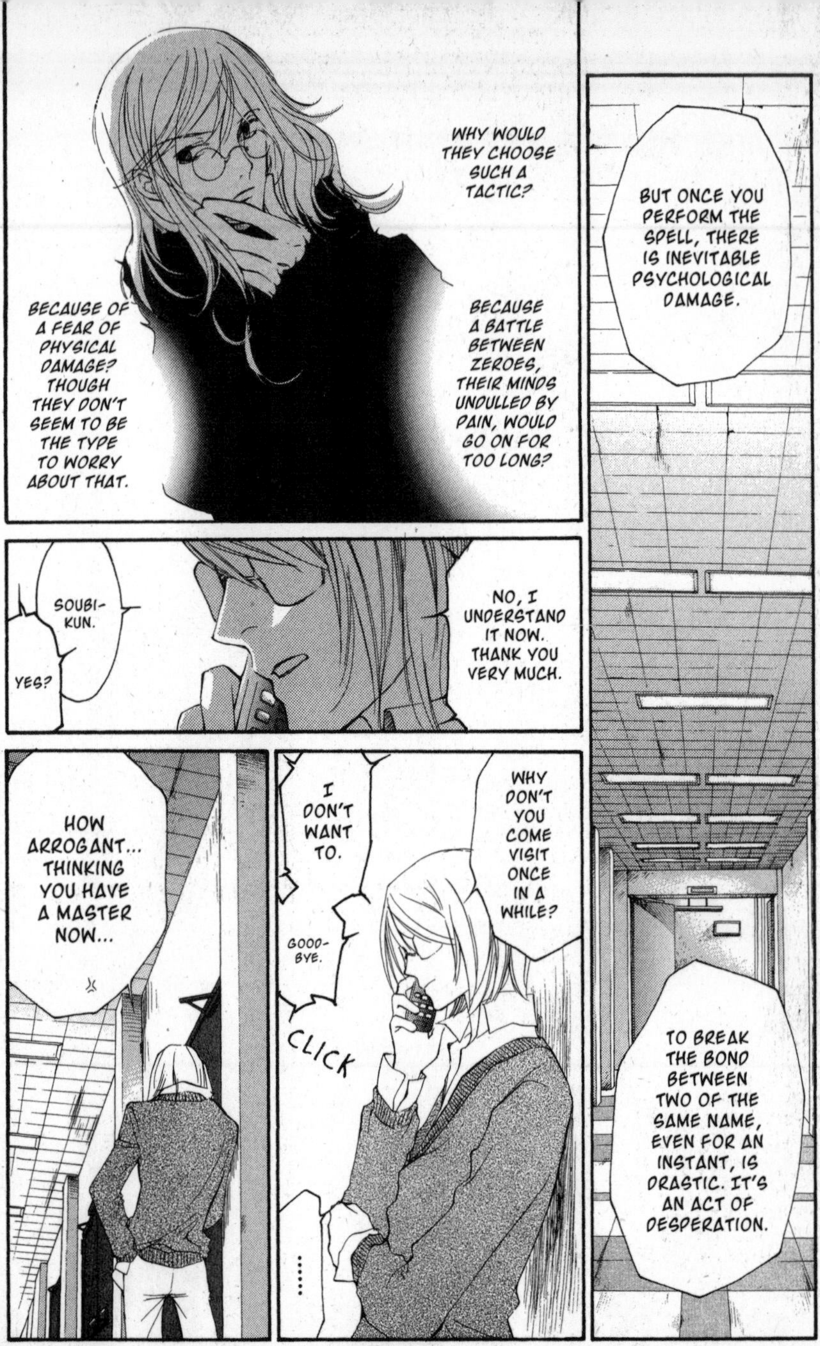
BUT ONCE YOU PERFORM THE SPELL, THERE IS INEVITABLE PSYCHOLOGICAL DAMAGE.
TO BREAK THE BOND BETWEEN TWO OF THE SAME NAME, EVEN FOR AN INSTANT, IS DRASTIC. IT'S AN ACT OF DESPERATION.
WHY WOULD THEY CHOOSE SUCH A TACTIC?
BECAUSE A BATTLE BETWEEN ZEROES, THEIR MINDS UNDULLED BY PAIN, WOULD GO ON FOR TOO LONG?
BECAUSE OF A FEAR OF PHYSICAL DAMAGE? THOUGH THEY DON'T SEEM TO BE THE TYPE TO WORRY ABOUT THAT.
NO, I UNDERSTAND IT NOW. THANK YOU VERY MUCH.
SOUBI-KUN.
YES?
WHY DON'T YOU COME VISIT ONCE IN A WHILE?
I DON'T WANT TO.
GOOD-BYE.
CLICK
......
HOW ARROGANT... THINKING YOU HAVE A MASTER NOW...

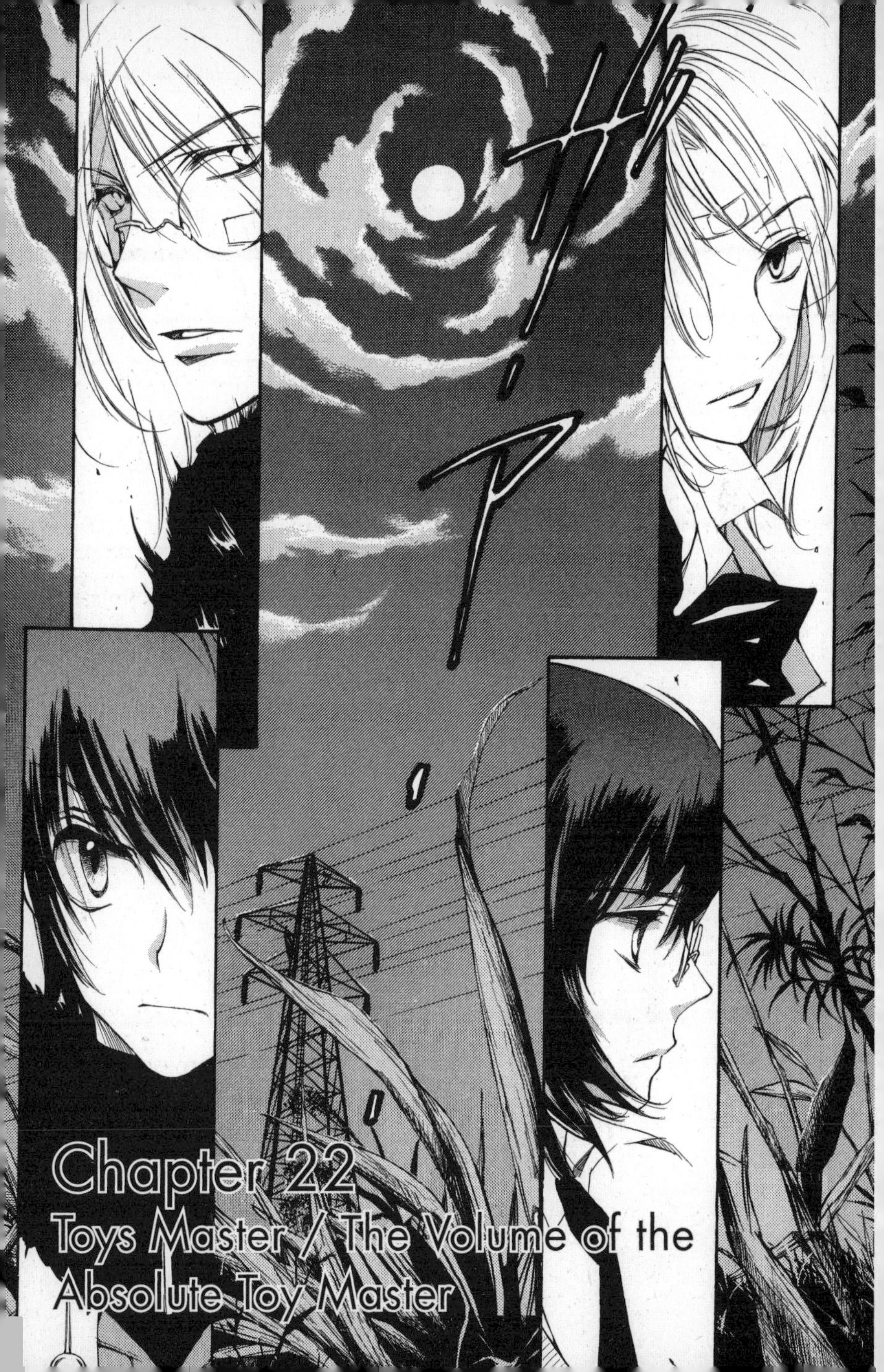

Chapter 22

Toys Master / The Volume of the Absolute Toy Master

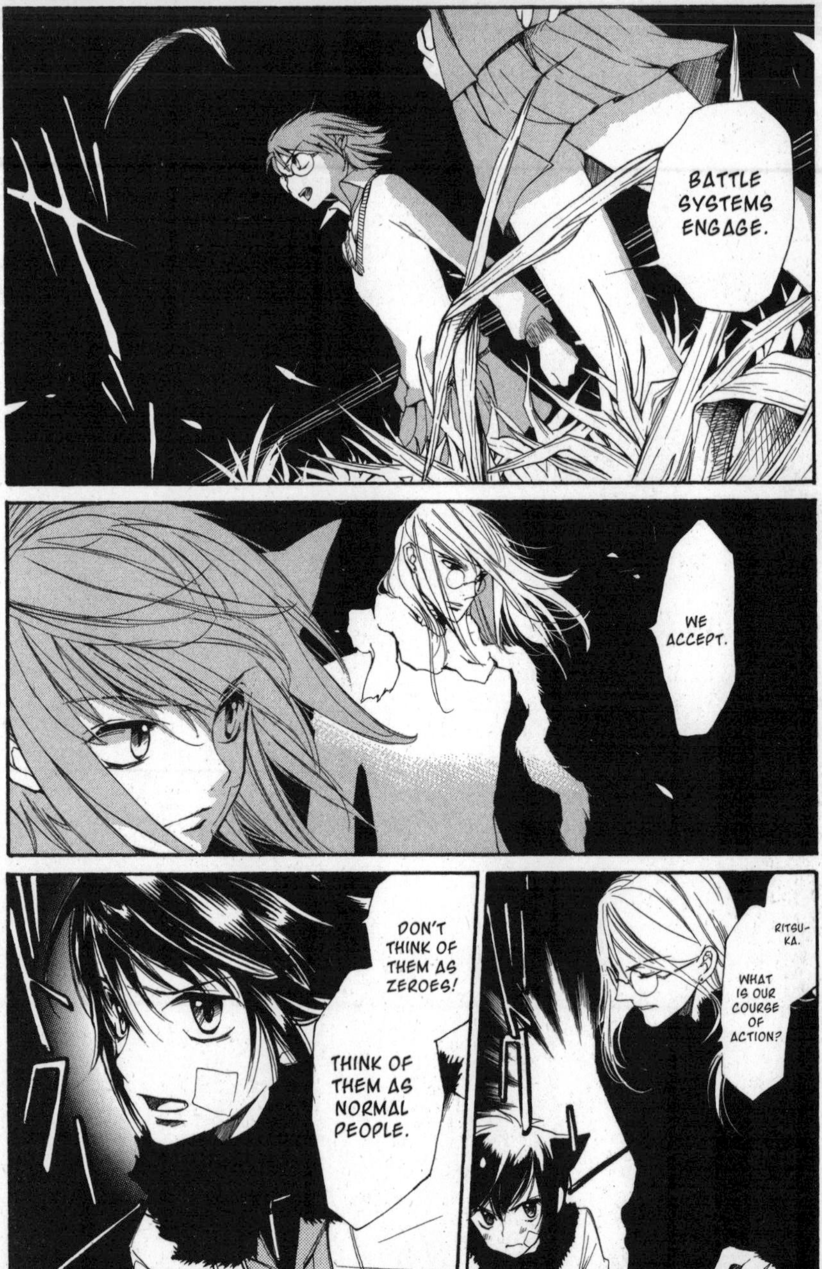
BATTLE SYSTEMS ENGAGE.
WE ACCEPT.
RITSU-KA.
WHAT IS OUR COURSE OF ACTION?
DON'T THINK OF THEM AS ZEROES!
THINK OF THEM AS NORMAL PEOPLE.

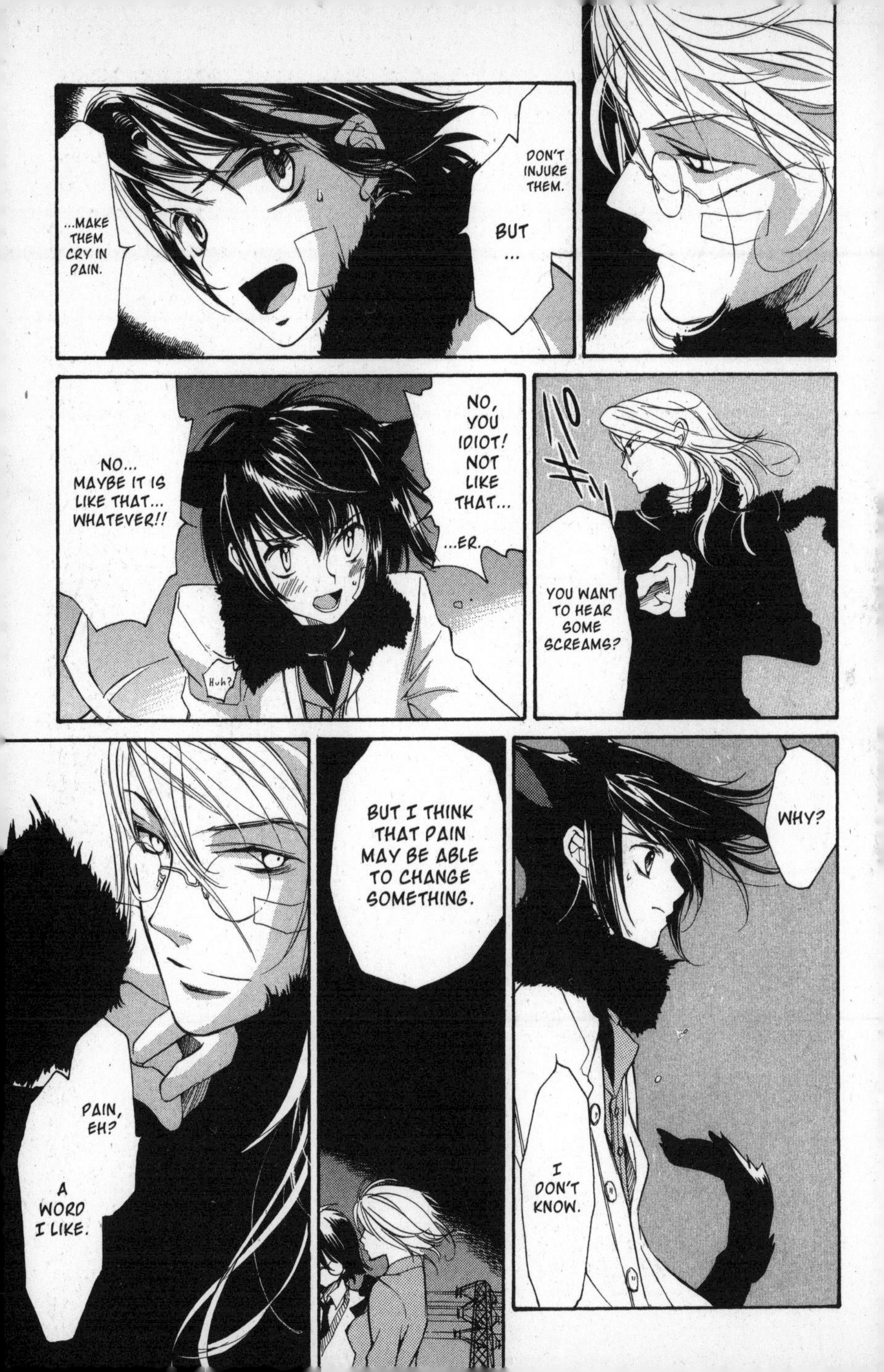
DON'T INJURE THEM.
BUT ...
...MAKE THEM CRY IN PAIN.
YOU WANT TO HEAR SOME SCREAMS?
NO, YOU IDIOT! NOT LIKE THAT...
...ER.
NO... MAYBE IT IS LIKE THAT... WHATEVER!!
Huh?
WHY?
I DON'T KNOW.
BUT I THINK THAT PAIN MAY BE ABLE TO CHANGE SOMETHING.
PAIN, EH?
A WORD I LIKE.

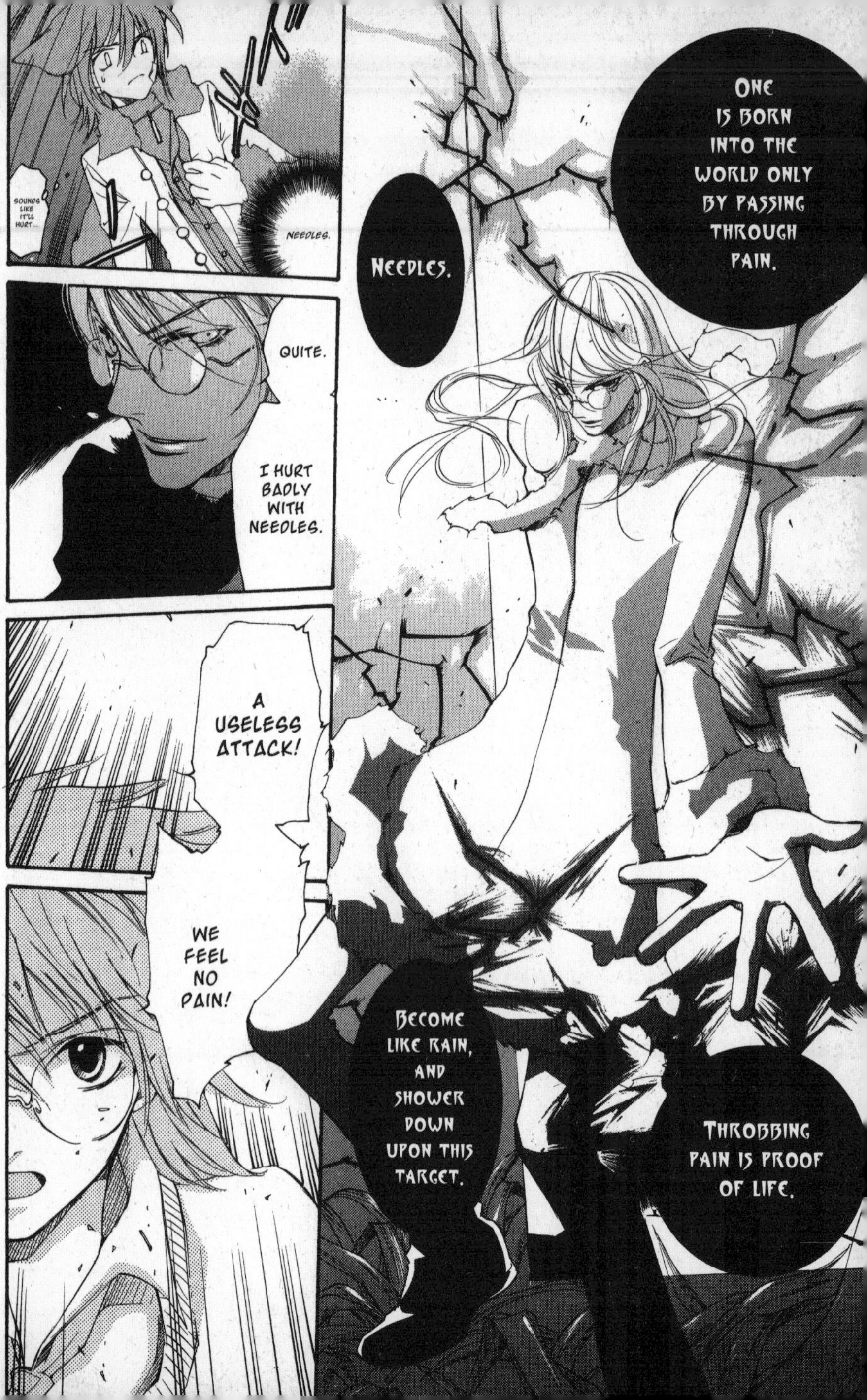
One is born into the world only by passing through pain.
Needles.
Throbbing pain is proof of life.
Become like rain, and shower down upon this target.
Needles.
Sounds like it'll hurt...
Quite.
I hurt badly with needles.
A useless attack!
We feel no pain!

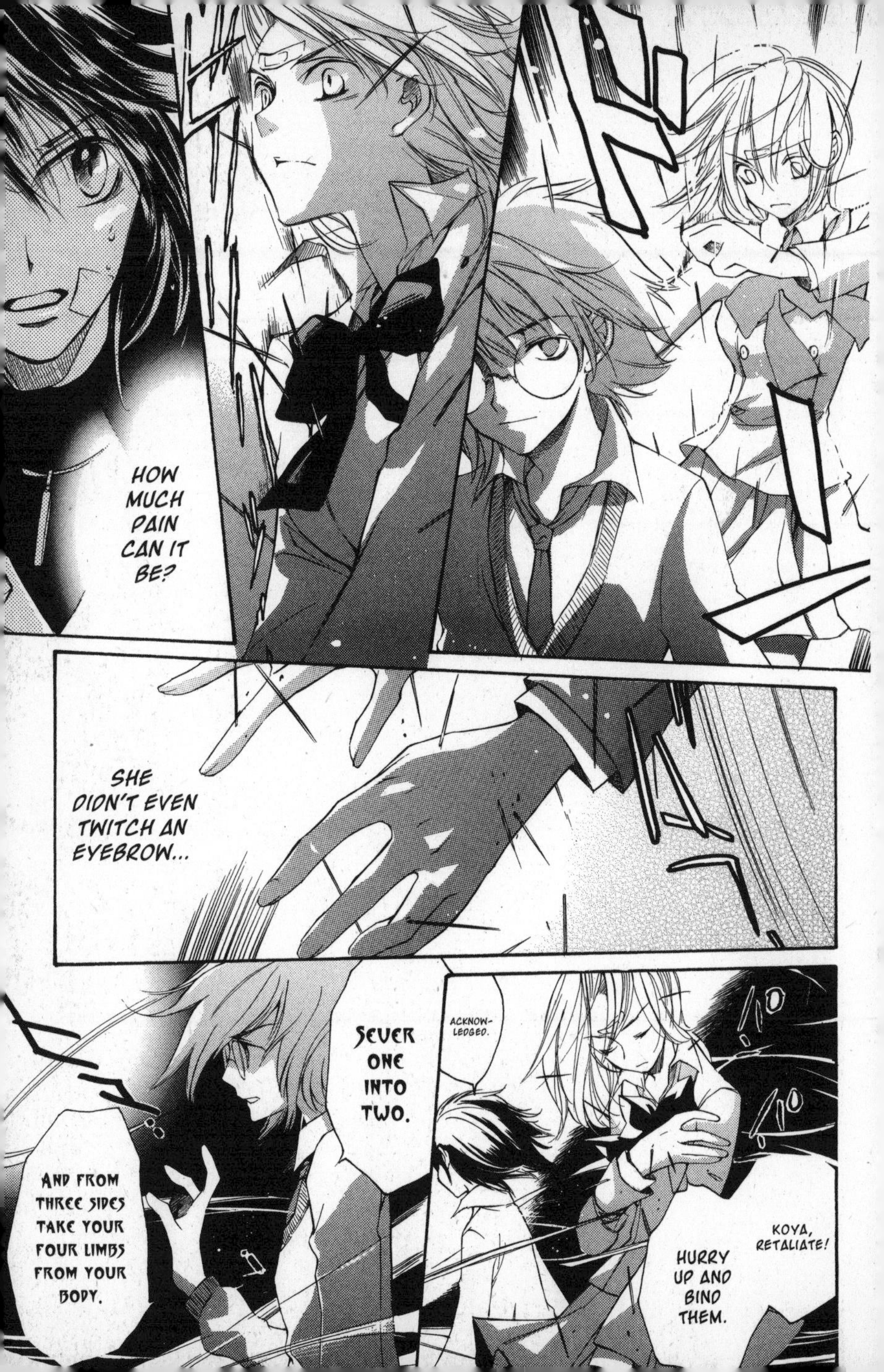
HOW MUCH PAIN CAN IT BE?
SHE DIDN'T EVEN TWITCH AN EYEBROW...
KOYA, RETALIATE!
HURRY UP AND BIND THEM.
ACKNOW-LEDGED.
SEVER ONE INTO TWO.
AND FROM THREE SIDES TAKE YOUR FOUR LIMBS FROM YOUR BODY.

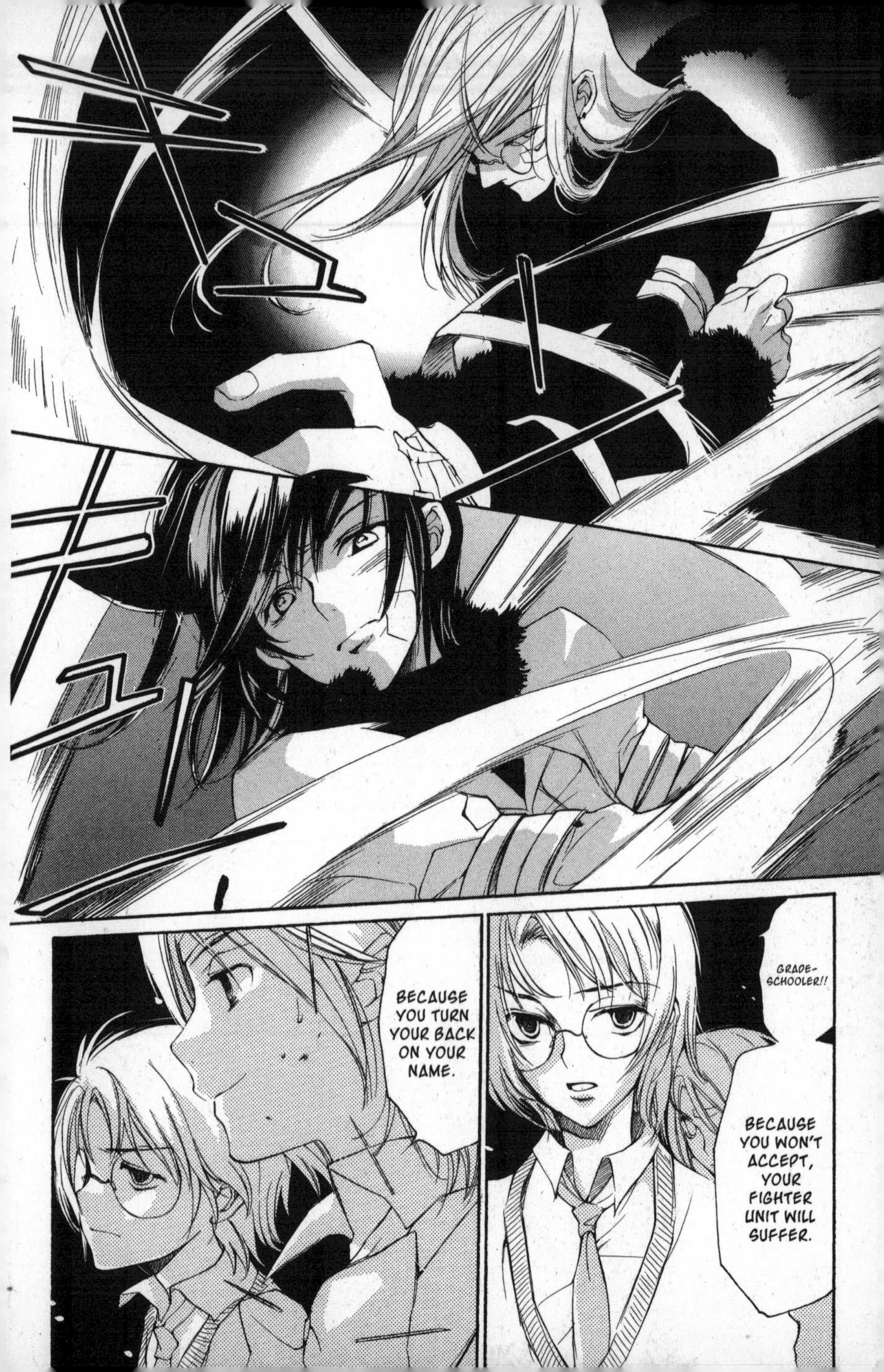
GRADE-SCHOOLER!!
BECAUSE YOU WON'T ACCEPT, YOUR FIGHTER UNIT WILL SUFFER.
BECAUSE YOU TURN YOUR BACK ON YOUR NAME.

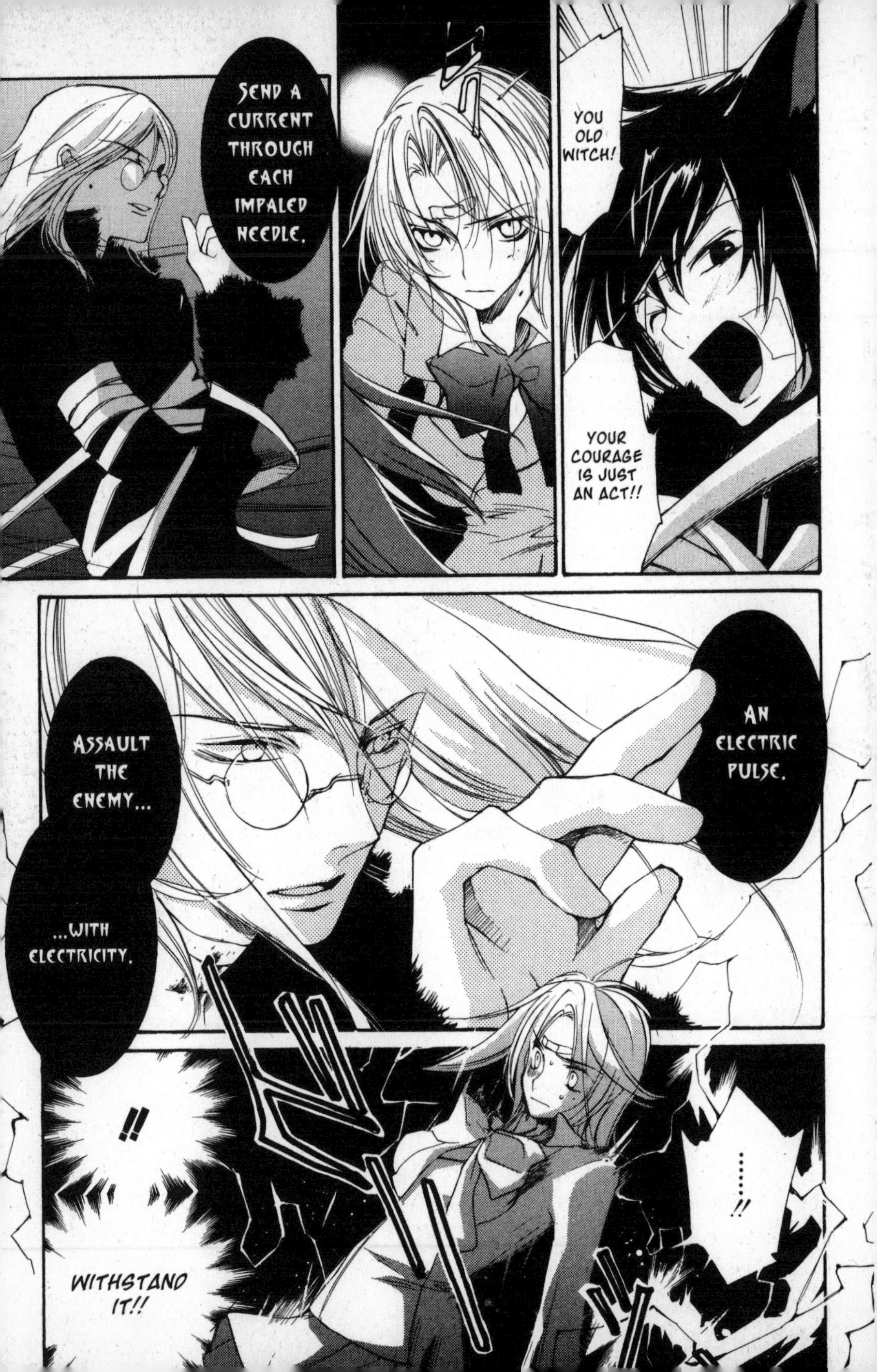
YOU OLD WITCH!
YOUR COURAGE IS JUST AN ACT!!
SEND A CURRENT THROUGH EACH IMPALED NEEDLE.
AN ELECTRIC PULSE.
ASSAULT THE ENEMY...
...WITH ELECTRICITY.
......!!
!!
WITHSTAND IT!!

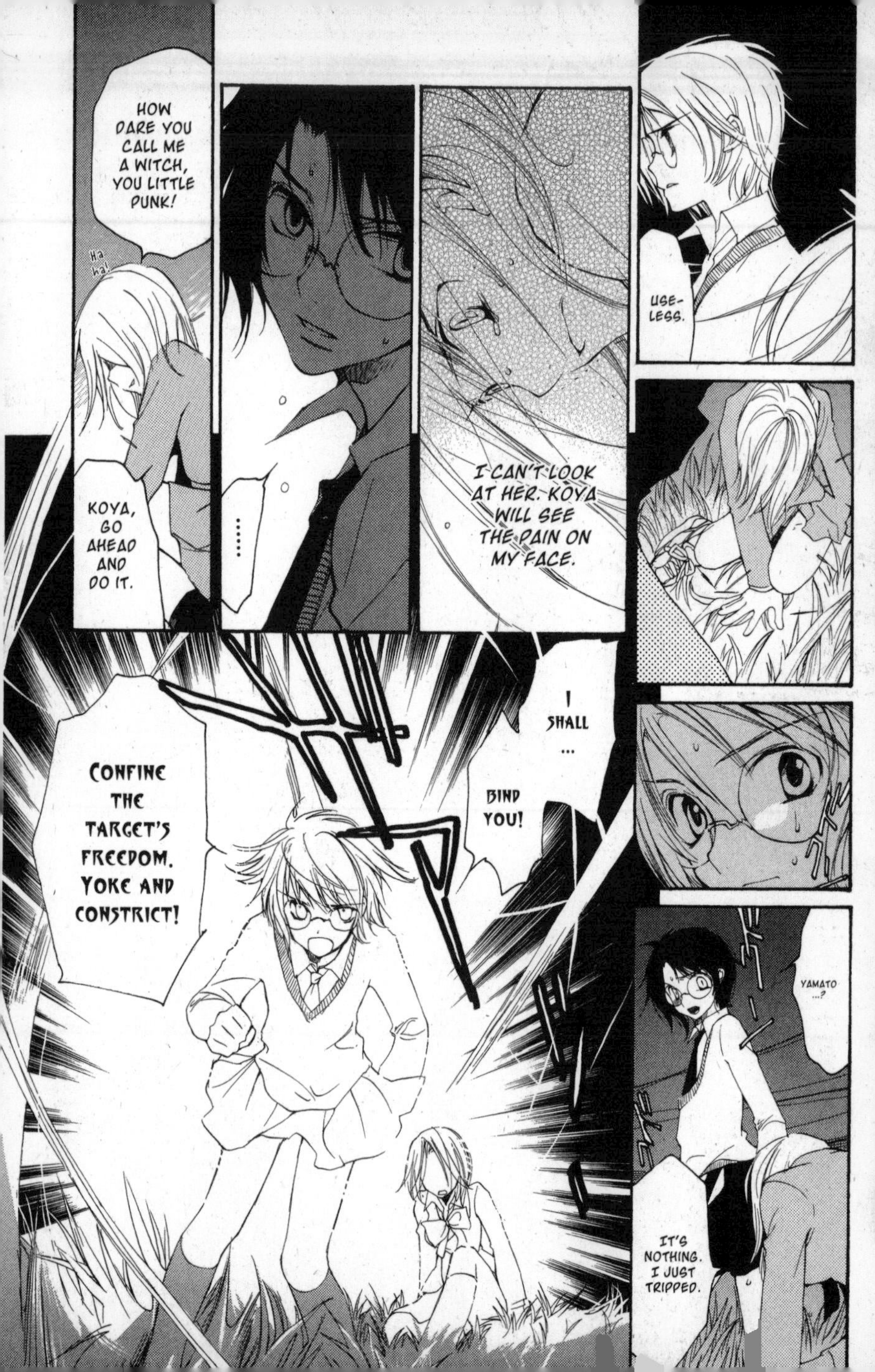
USE-LESS.
I CAN'T LOOK AT HER. KOYA WILL SEE THE PAIN ON MY FACE.
......
HOW DARE YOU CALL ME A WITCH, YOU LITTLE PUNK!
Ha ha!
KOYA, GO AHEAD AND DO IT.
I SHALL ...
BIND YOU!
CONFINE THE TARGET'S FREEDOM. YOKE AND CONSTRICT!
YAMATO ...?
IT'S NOTHING. I JUST TRIPPED.

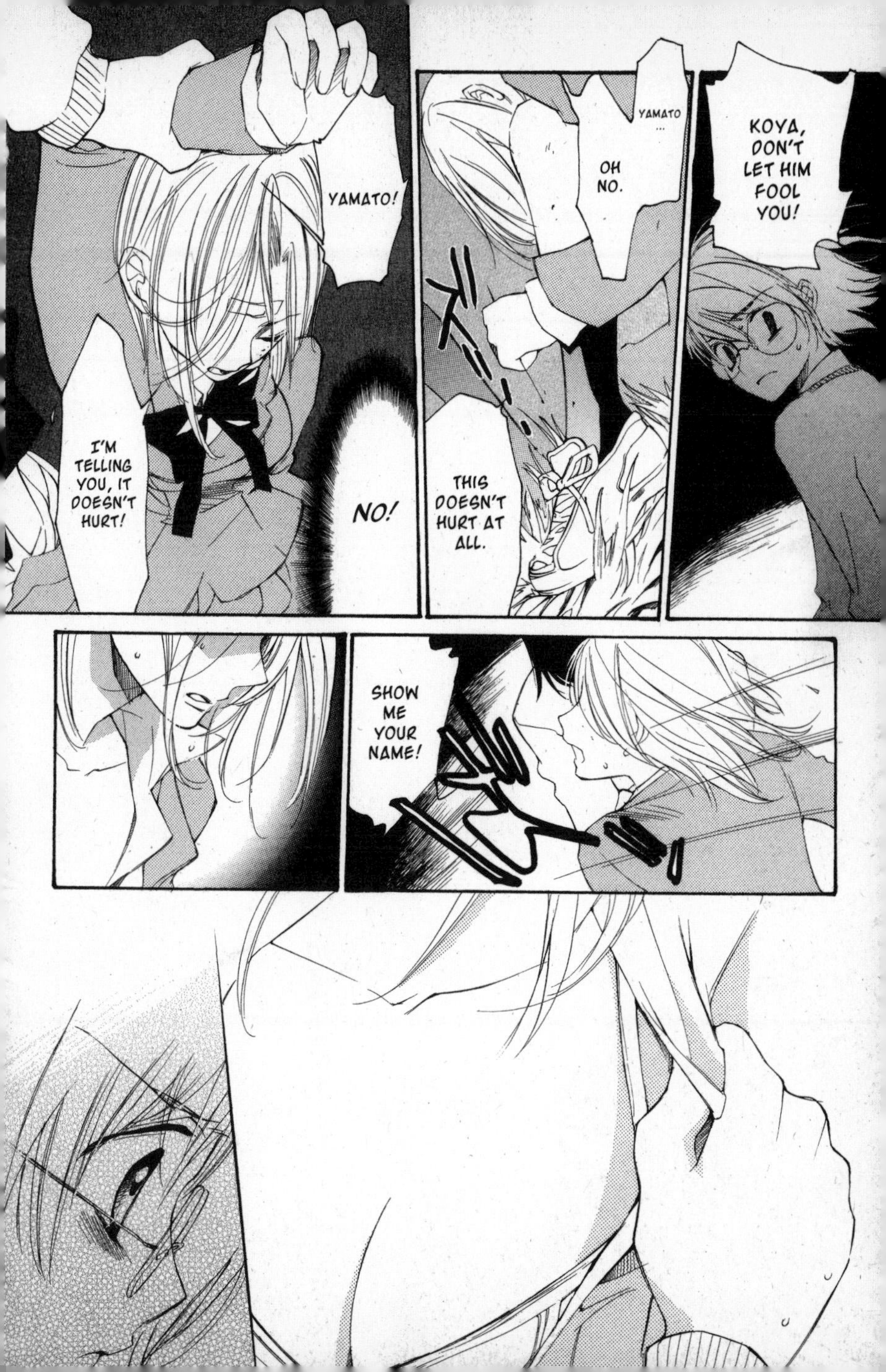
KOYA, DON'T LET HIM FOOL YOU!
YAMATO...
OH NO.
THIS DOESN'T HURT AT ALL.
YAMATO!
I'M TELLING YOU, IT DOESN'T HURT!
NO!
SHOW ME YOUR NAME!

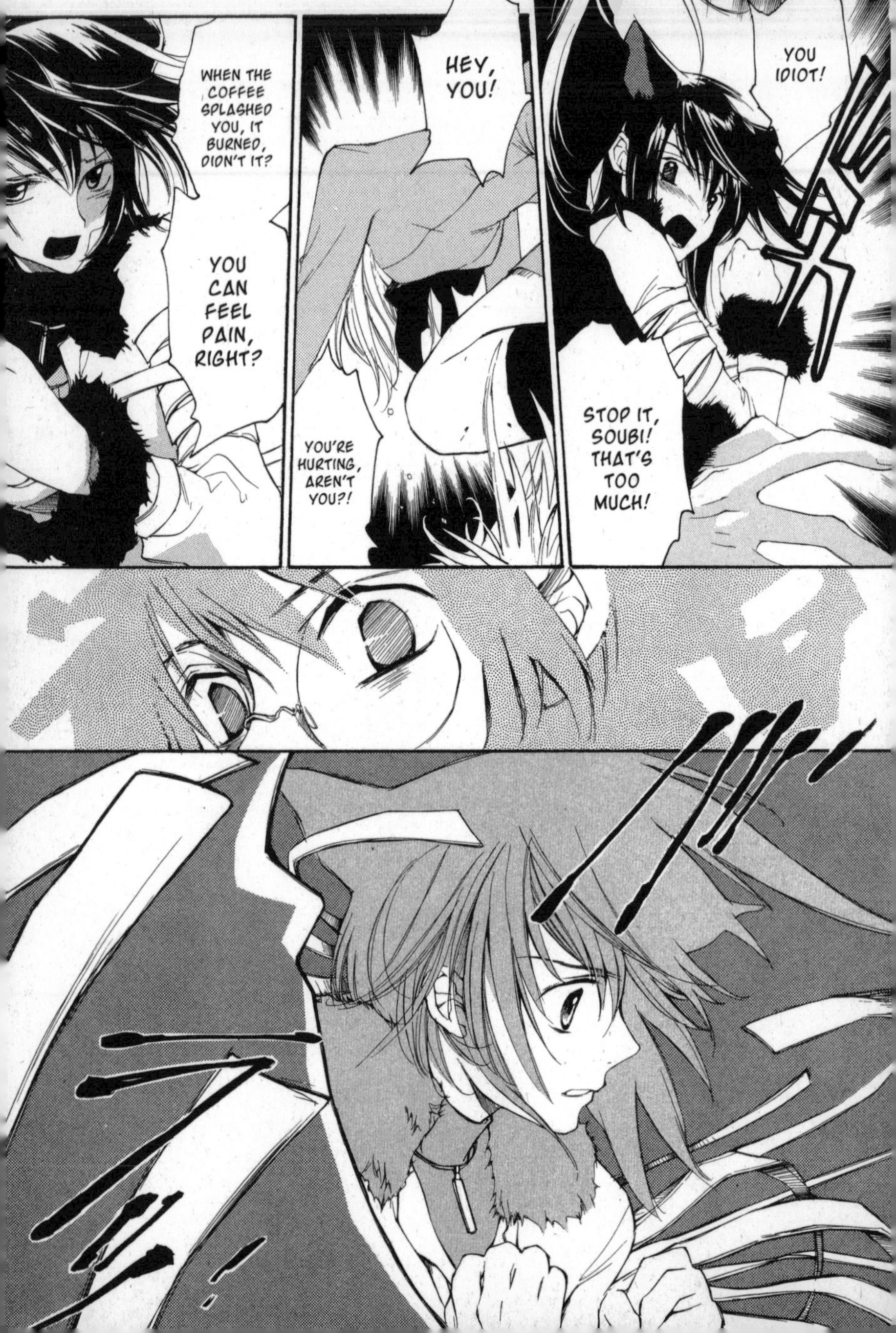
YOU IDIOT!
STOP IT, SOUBI! THAT'S TOO MUCH!
HEY, YOU!
YOU'RE HURTING, AREN'T YOU?!
WHEN THE COFFEE SPLASHED YOU, IT BURNED, DIDN'T IT?
YOU CAN FEEL PAIN, RIGHT?

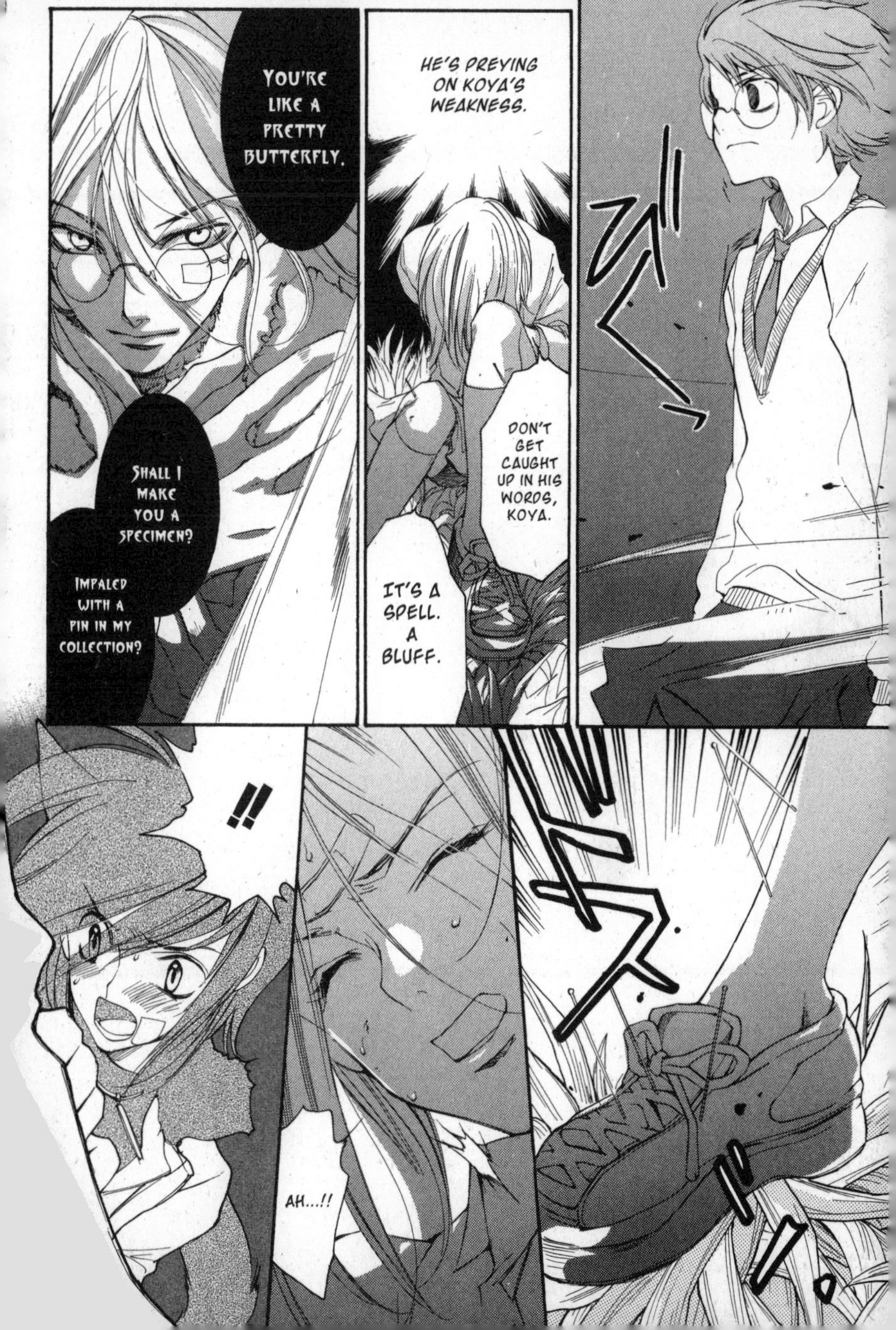
HE'S PREYING ON KOYA'S WEAKNESS.
DON'T GET CAUGHT UP IN HIS WORDS, KOYA.
IT'S A SPELL. A BLUFF.
YOU'RE LIKE A PRETTY BUTTERFLY.
SHALL I MAKE YOU A SPECIMEN?
IMPALED WITH A PIN IN MY COLLECTION?
AH...!!
!!

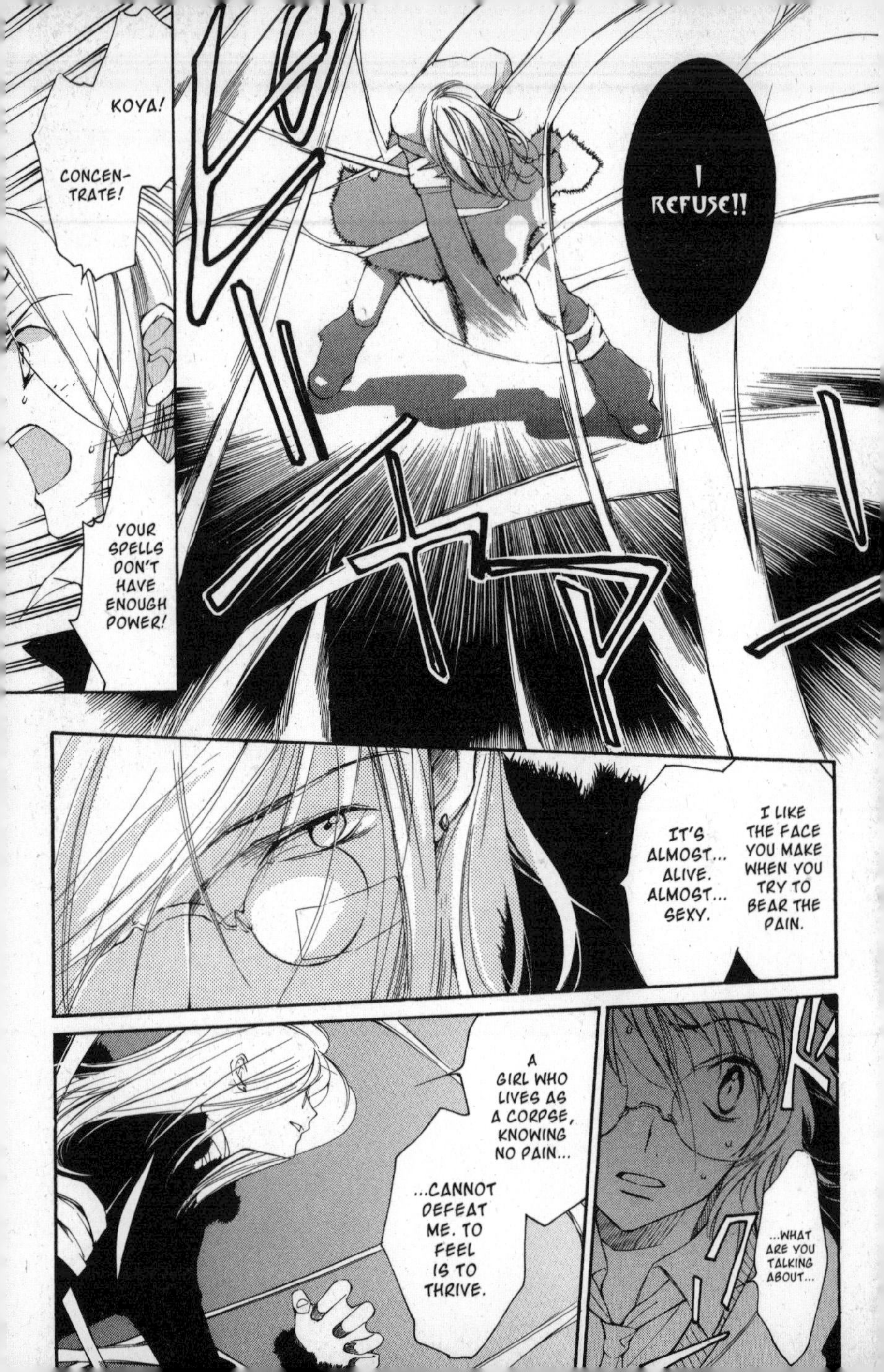
I REFUSE!!
KOYA!
CONCENTRATE!
YOUR SPELLS DON'T HAVE ENOUGH POWER!
I LIKE THE FACE YOU MAKE WHEN YOU TRY TO BEAR THE PAIN.
IT'S ALMOST... ALIVE. ALMOST... SEXY.
...WHAT ARE YOU TALKING ABOUT...
A GIRL WHO LIVES AS A CORPSE, KNOWING NO PAIN...
...CANNOT DEFEAT ME. TO FEEL IS TO THRIVE.

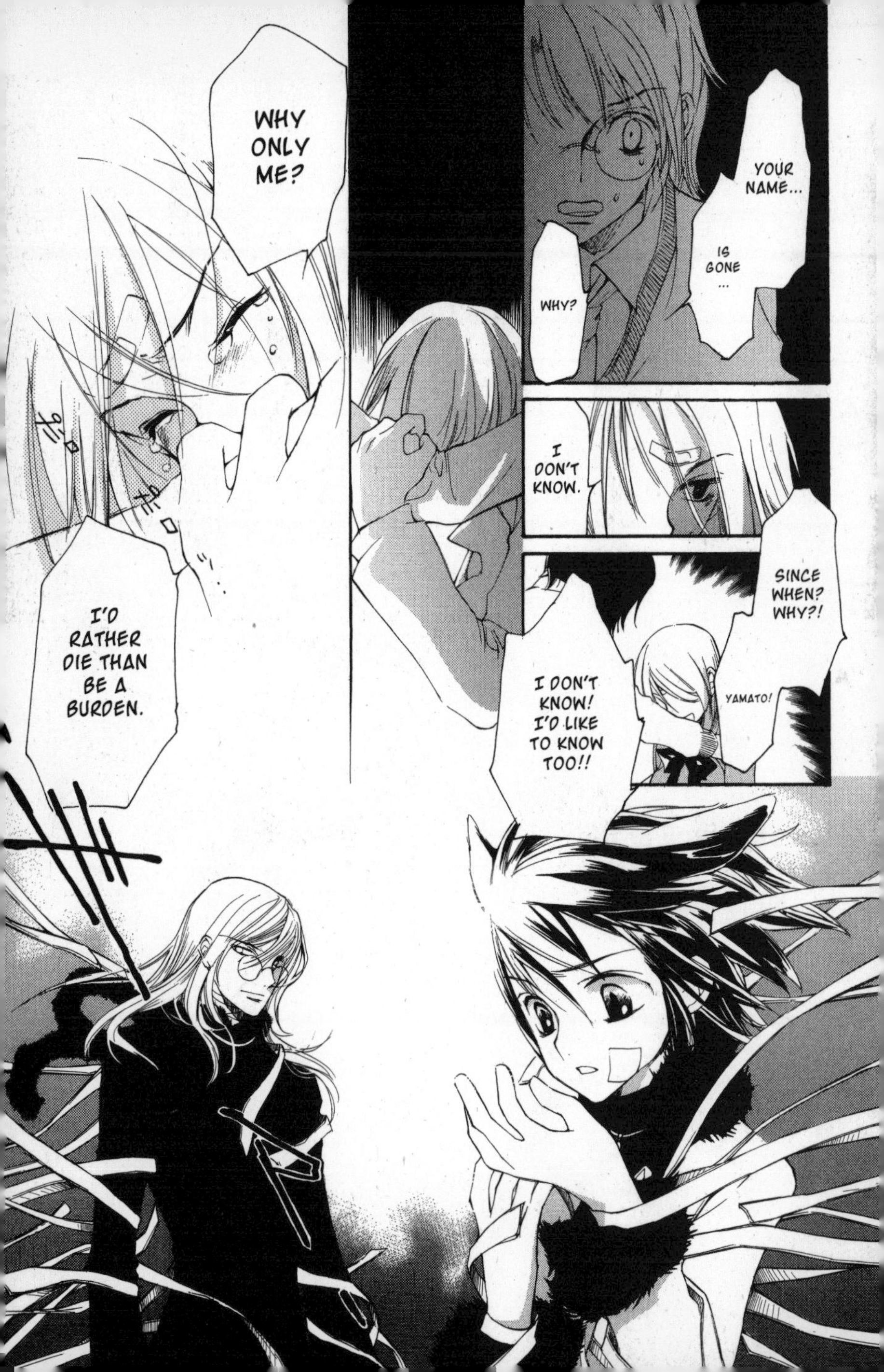
YOUR NAME...
IS GONE ...
WHY?
I DON'T KNOW.
SINCE WHEN? WHY?!
YAMATO!
I DON'T KNOW! I'D LIKE TO KNOW TOO!!
WHY ONLY ME?
I'D RATHER DIE THAN BE A BURDEN.

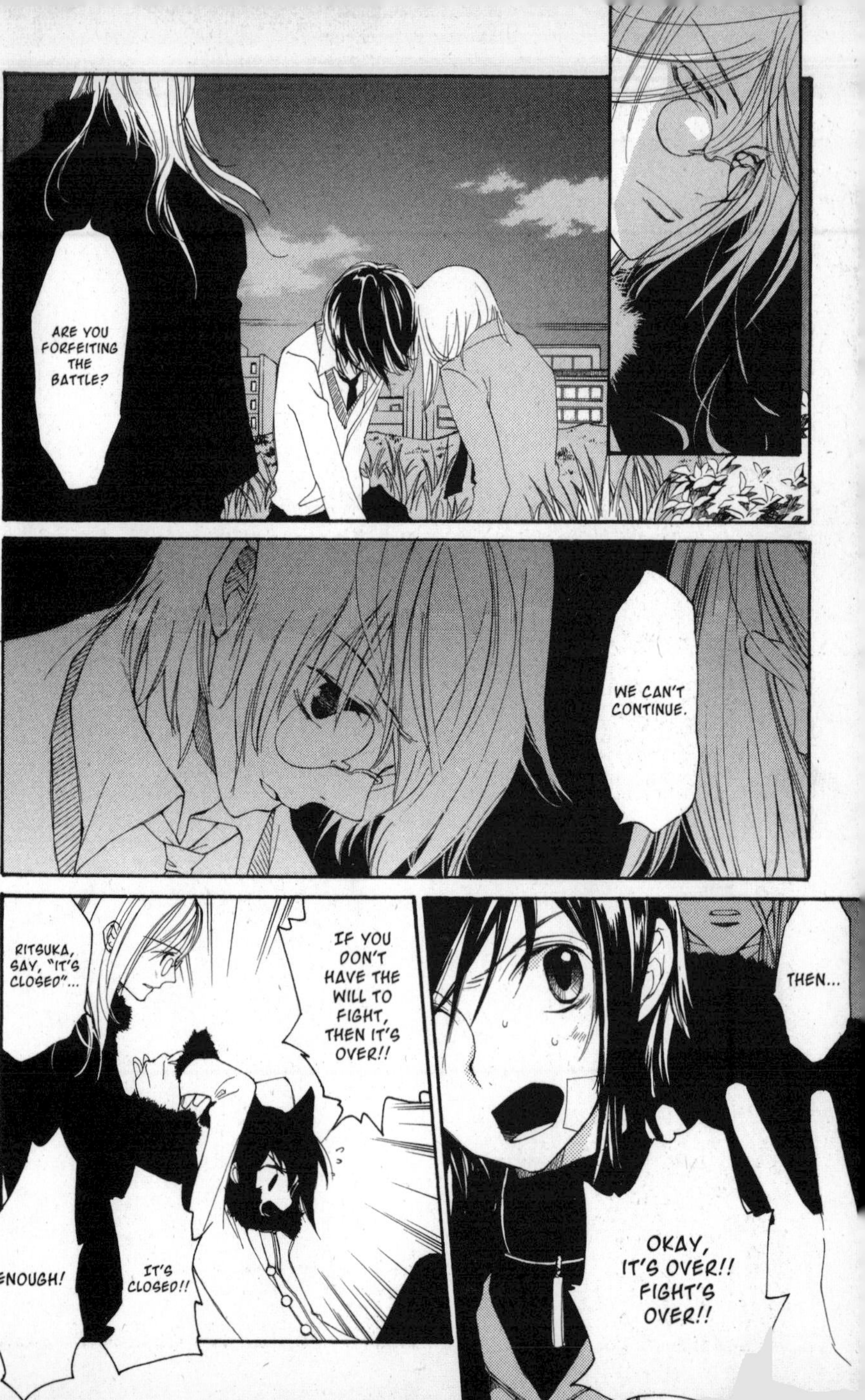
ARE YOU FORFEITING THE BATTLE?
WE CAN'T CONTINUE.
THEN...
OKAY, IT'S OVER!! FIGHT'S OVER!!
IF YOU DON'T HAVE THE WILL TO FIGHT, THEN IT'S OVER!!
RITSUKA, SAY, "IT'S CLOSED"...
IT'S CLOSED!!
ENOUGH!

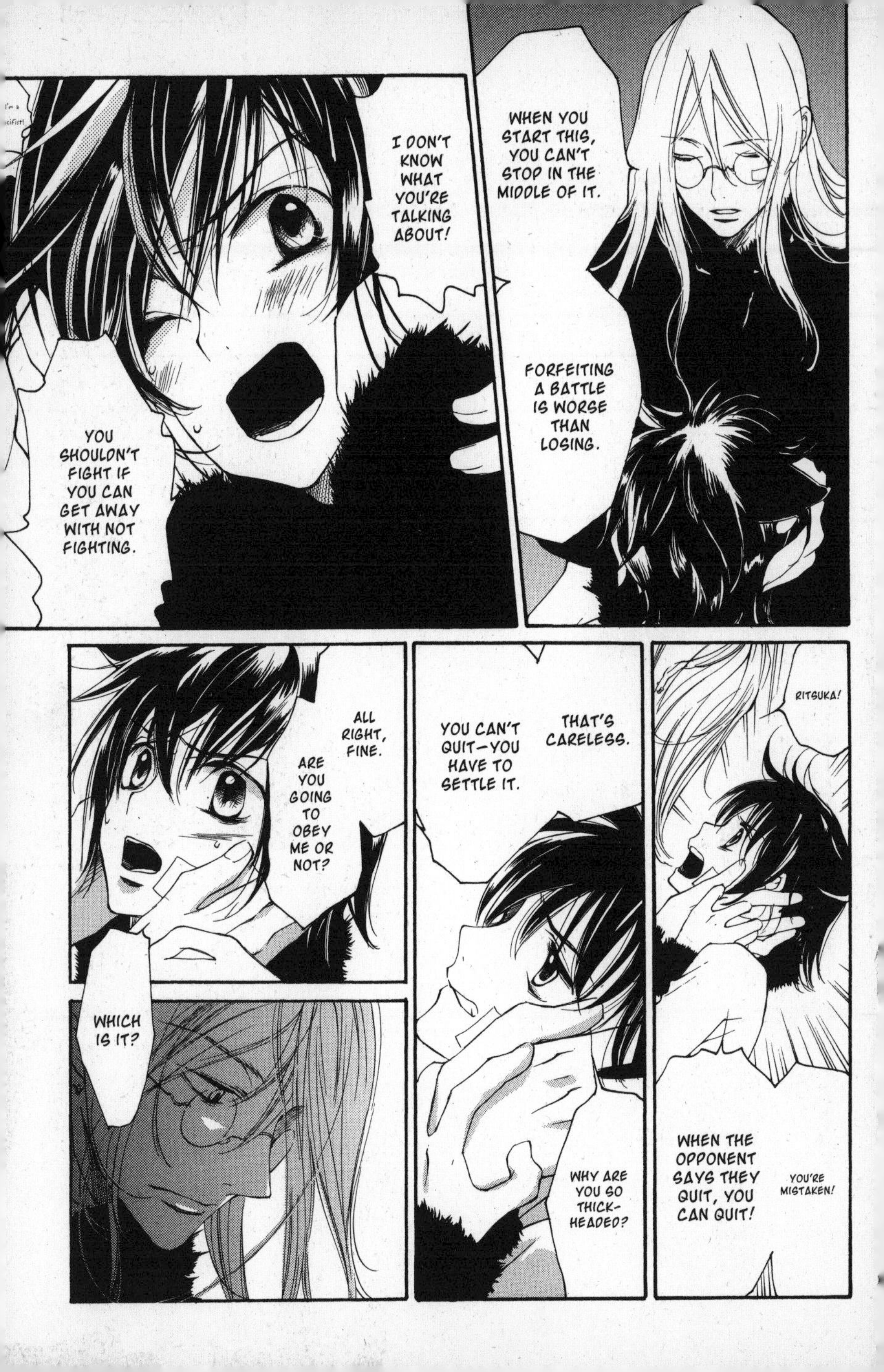

WHEN YOU START THIS, YOU CAN'T STOP IN THE MIDDLE OF IT.
FORFEITING A BATTLE IS WORSE THAN LOSING.
I DON'T KNOW WHAT YOU'RE TALKING ABOUT!
YOU SHOULDN'T FIGHT IF YOU CAN GET AWAY WITH NOT FIGHTING.
RITSUKA!
YOU'RE MISTAKEN!
WHEN THE OPPONENT SAYS THEY QUIT, YOU CAN QUIT!
THAT'S CARELESS.
YOU CAN'T QUIT—YOU HAVE TO SETTLE IT.
WHY ARE YOU SO THICK-HEADED?
ALL RIGHT, FINE.
ARE YOU GOING TO OBEY ME OR NOT?
WHICH IS IT?

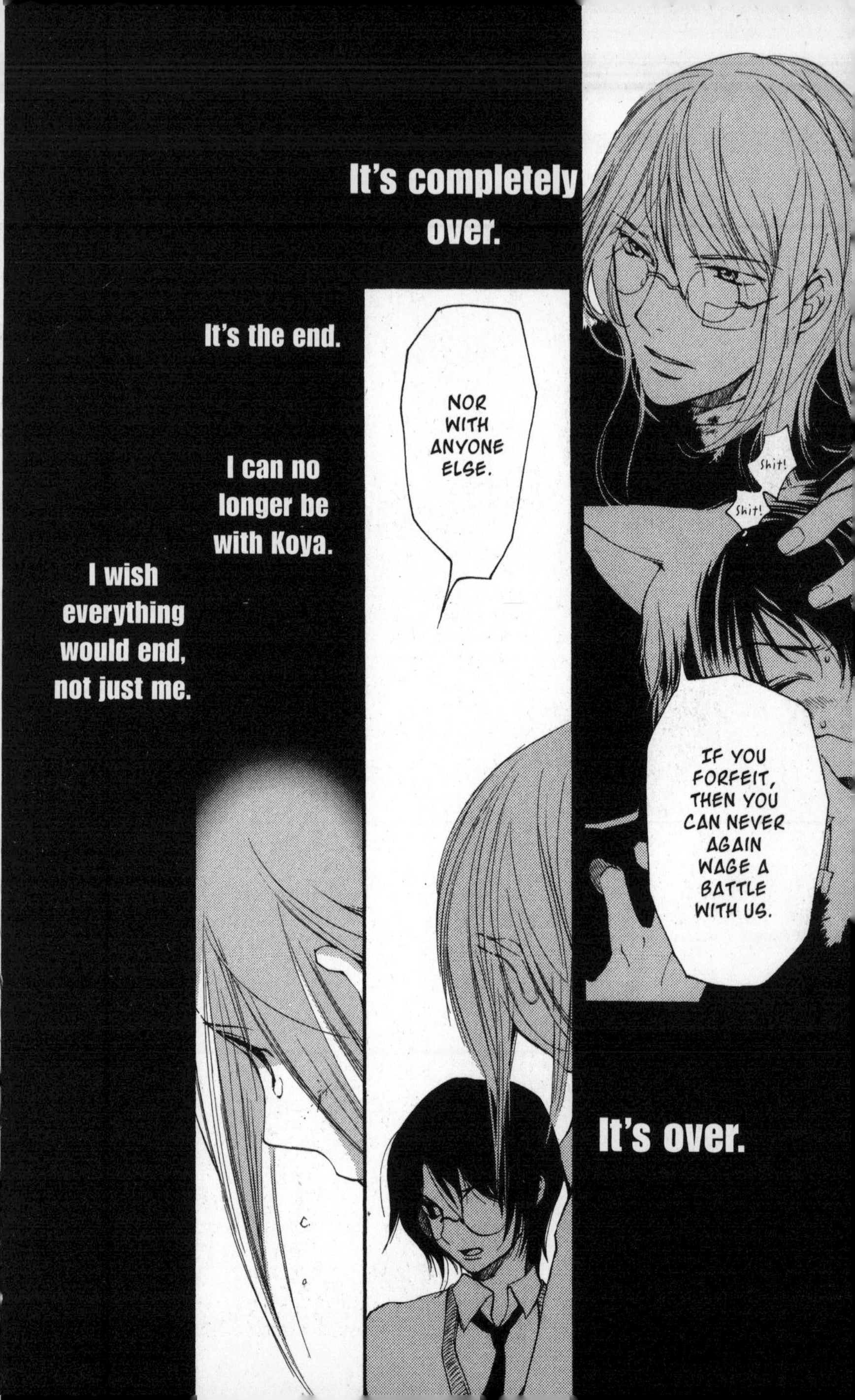
It's completely over.
Shit!
Shit!
IF YOU FORFEIT, THEN YOU CAN NEVER AGAIN WAGE A BATTLE WITH US.
It's over.
NOR WITH ANYONE ELSE.
It's the end.
I can no longer be with Koya.
I wish everything would end, not just me.

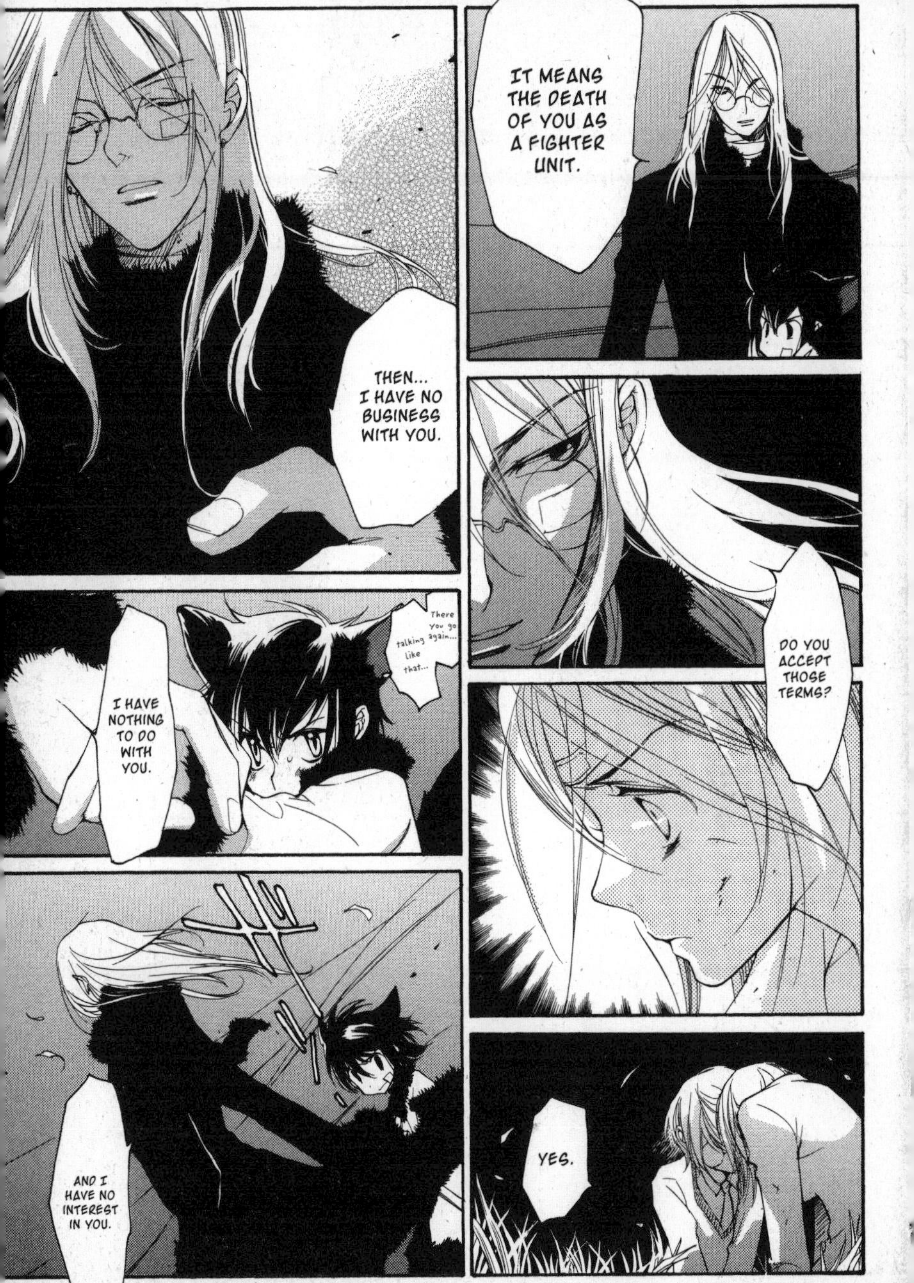
IT MEANS THE DEATH OF YOU AS A FIGHTER UNIT.
DO YOU ACCEPT THOSE TERMS?
YES.
THEN... I HAVE NO BUSINESS WITH YOU.
I HAVE NOTHING TO DO WITH YOU.
There you go talking again... like that...
AND I HAVE NO INTEREST IN YOU.

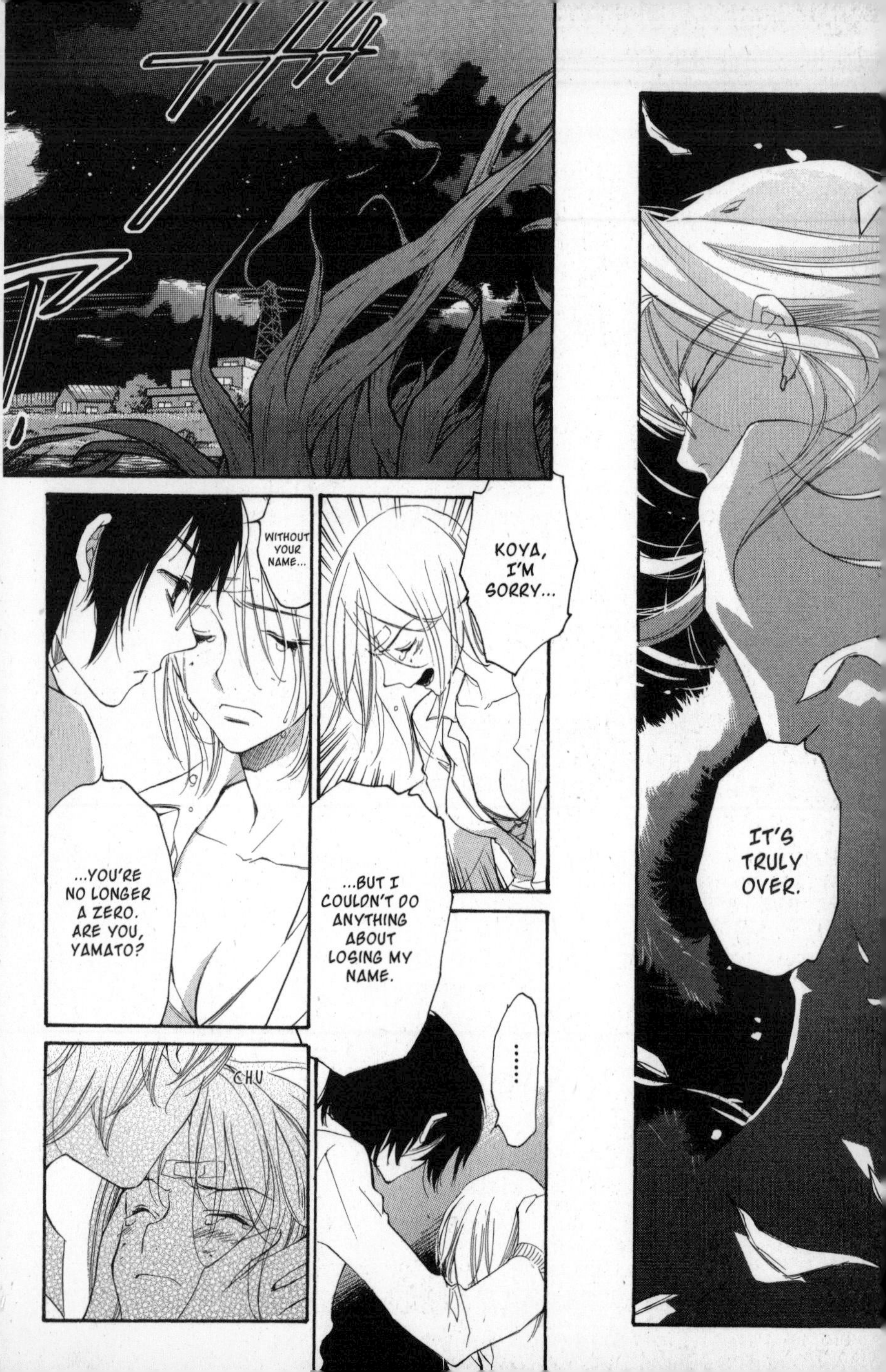
IT'S TRULY OVER.
KOYA, I'M SORRY...
...BUT I COULDN'T DO ANYTHING ABOUT LOSING MY NAME.
WITHOUT YOUR NAME...
...YOU'RE NO LONGER A ZERO. ARE YOU, YAMATO?
......
CHU

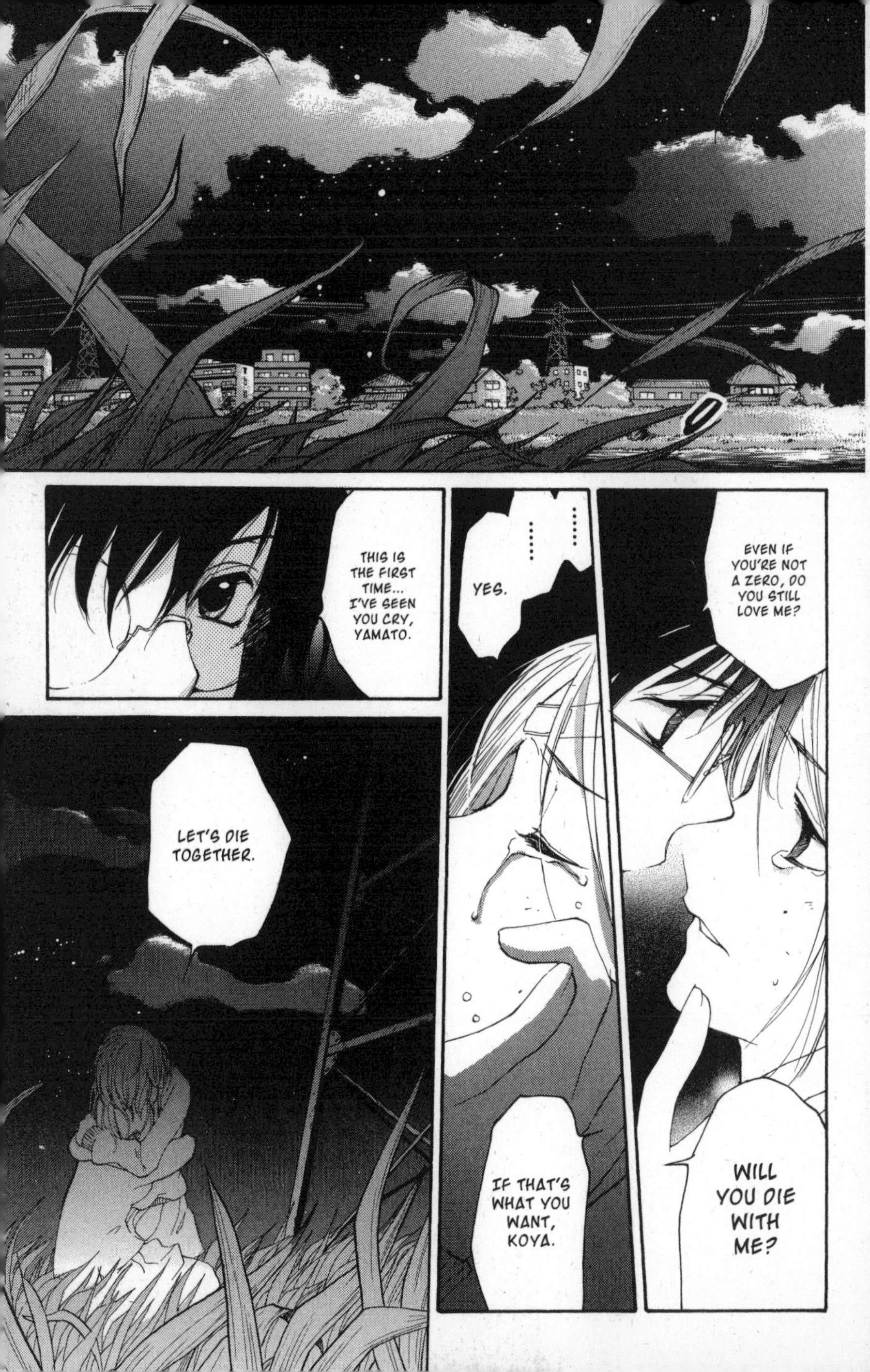
EVEN IF YOU'RE NOT A ZERO, DO YOU STILL LOVE ME?
WILL YOU DIE WITH ME?
......
YES.
IF THAT'S WHAT YOU WANT, KOYA.
THIS IS THE FIRST TIME... I'VE SEEN YOU CRY, YAMATO.
LET'S DIE TOGETHER.

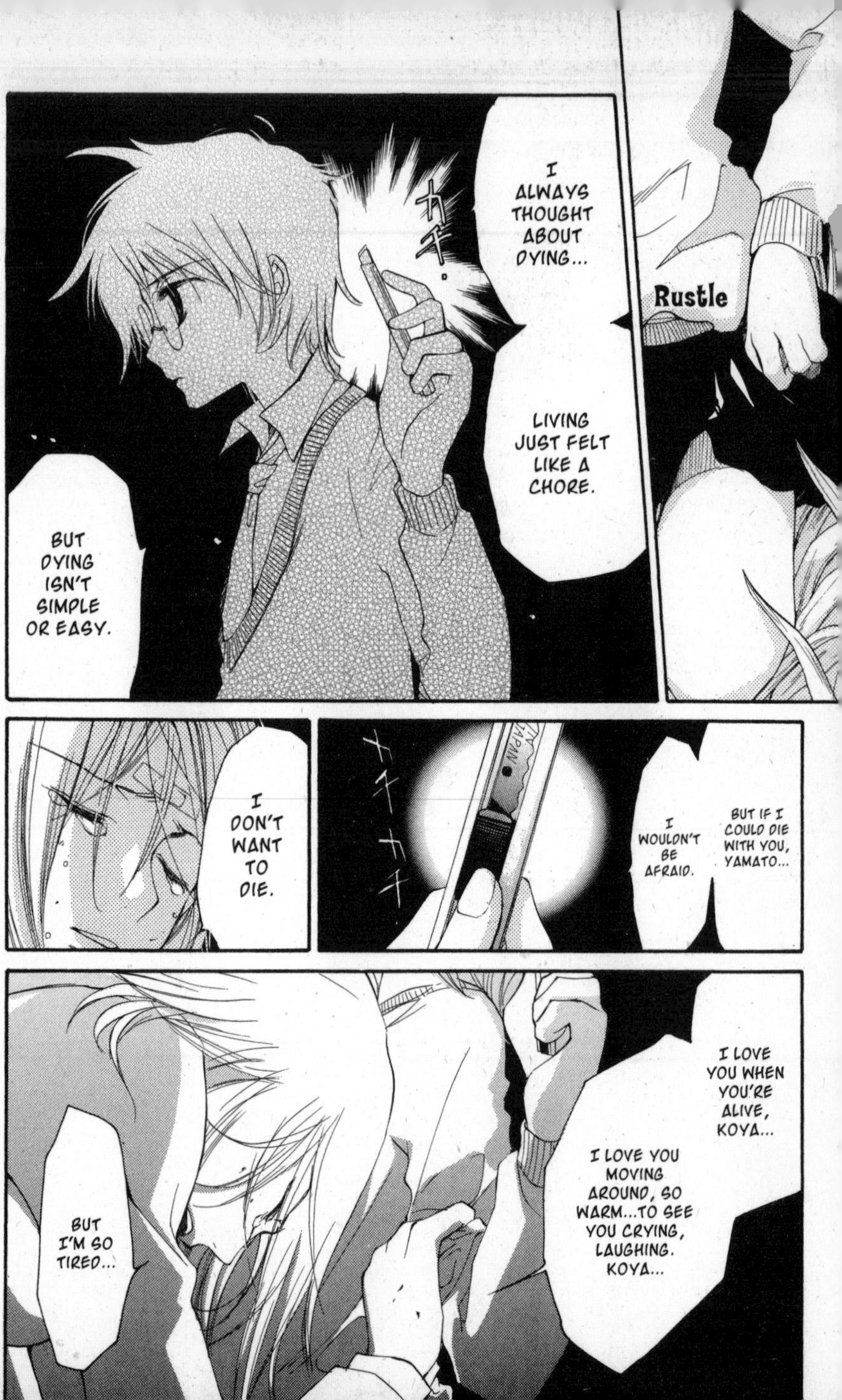
Rustle
I ALWAYS THOUGHT ABOUT DYING...
カチ。
LIVING JUST FELT LIKE A CHORE.
BUT DYING ISN'T SIMPLE OR EASY.
BUT IF I COULD DIE WITH YOU, YAMATO...
I WOULDN'T BE AFRAID.
I DON'T WANT TO DIE.
I LOVE YOU WHEN YOU'RE ALIVE, KOYA...
I LOVE YOU MOVING AROUND, SO WARM...TO SEE YOU CRYING, LAUGHING. KOYA...
BUT I'M SO TIRED...

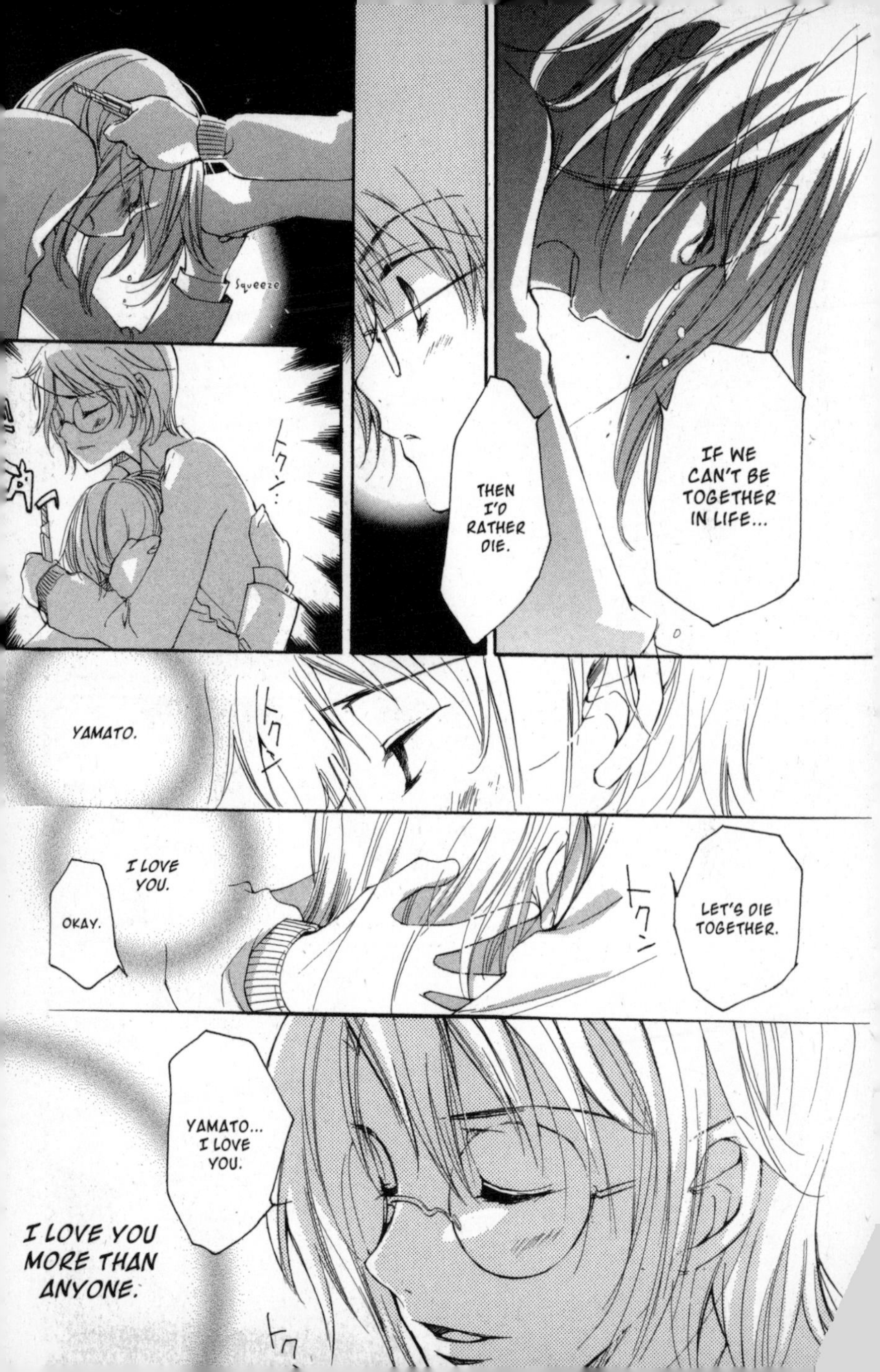
IF WE CAN'T BE TOGETHER IN LIFE...
THEN I'D RATHER DIE.
Squeeze
YAMATO.
LET'S DIE TOGETHER.
I LOVE YOU.
OKAY.
YAMATO... I LOVE YOU.
I LOVE YOU MORE THAN ANYONE.

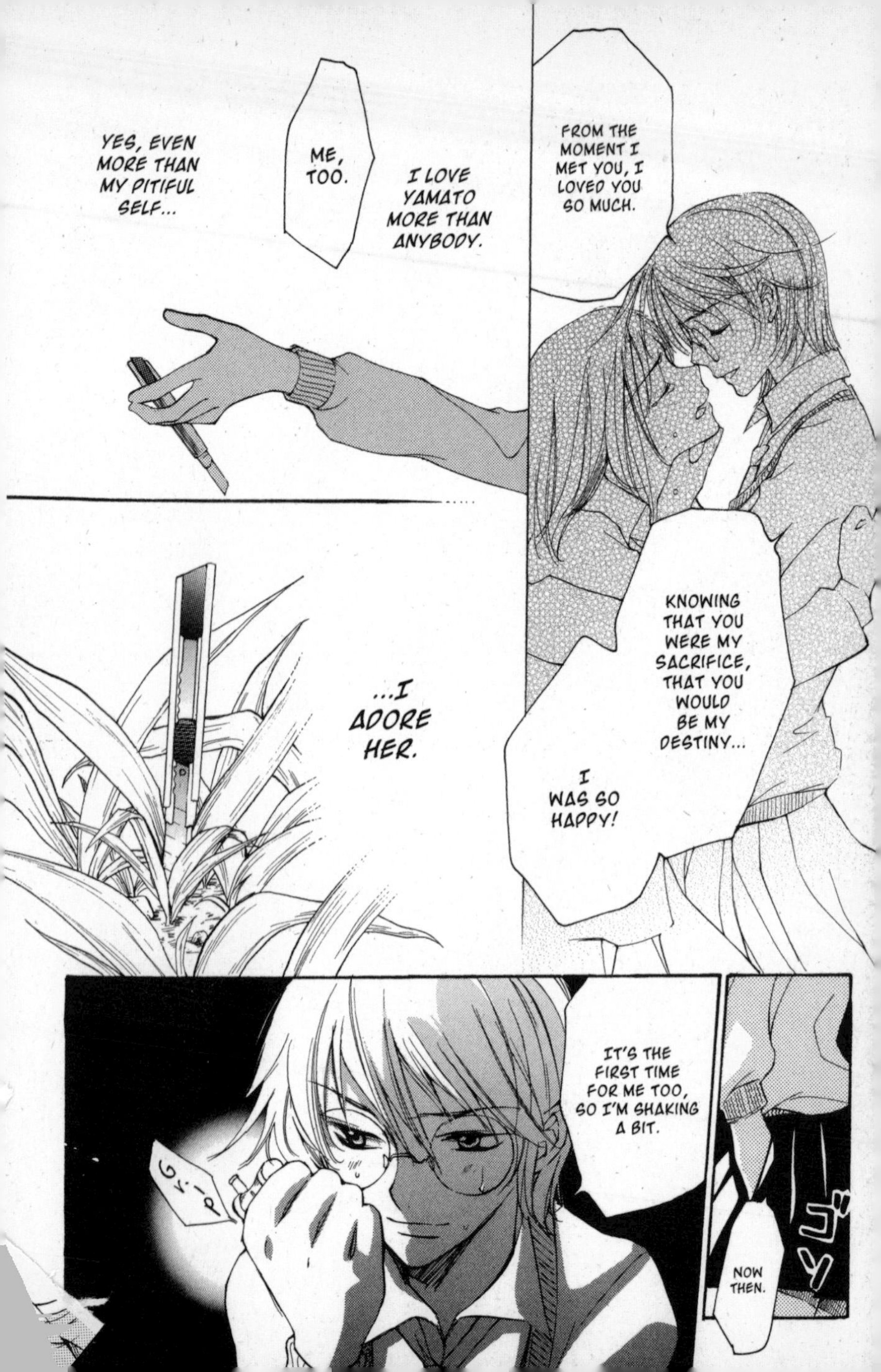
FROM THE MOMENT I MET YOU, I LOVED YOU SO MUCH.
KNOWING THAT YOU WERE MY SACRIFICE, THAT YOU WOULD BE MY DESTINY...
I WAS SO HAPPY!
ME, TOO.
I LOVE YAMATO MORE THAN ANYBODY.
YES, EVEN MORE THAN MY PITIFUL SELF...
...I ADORE HER.
NOW THEN.
IT'S THE FIRST TIME FOR ME TOO, SO I'M SHAKING A BIT.

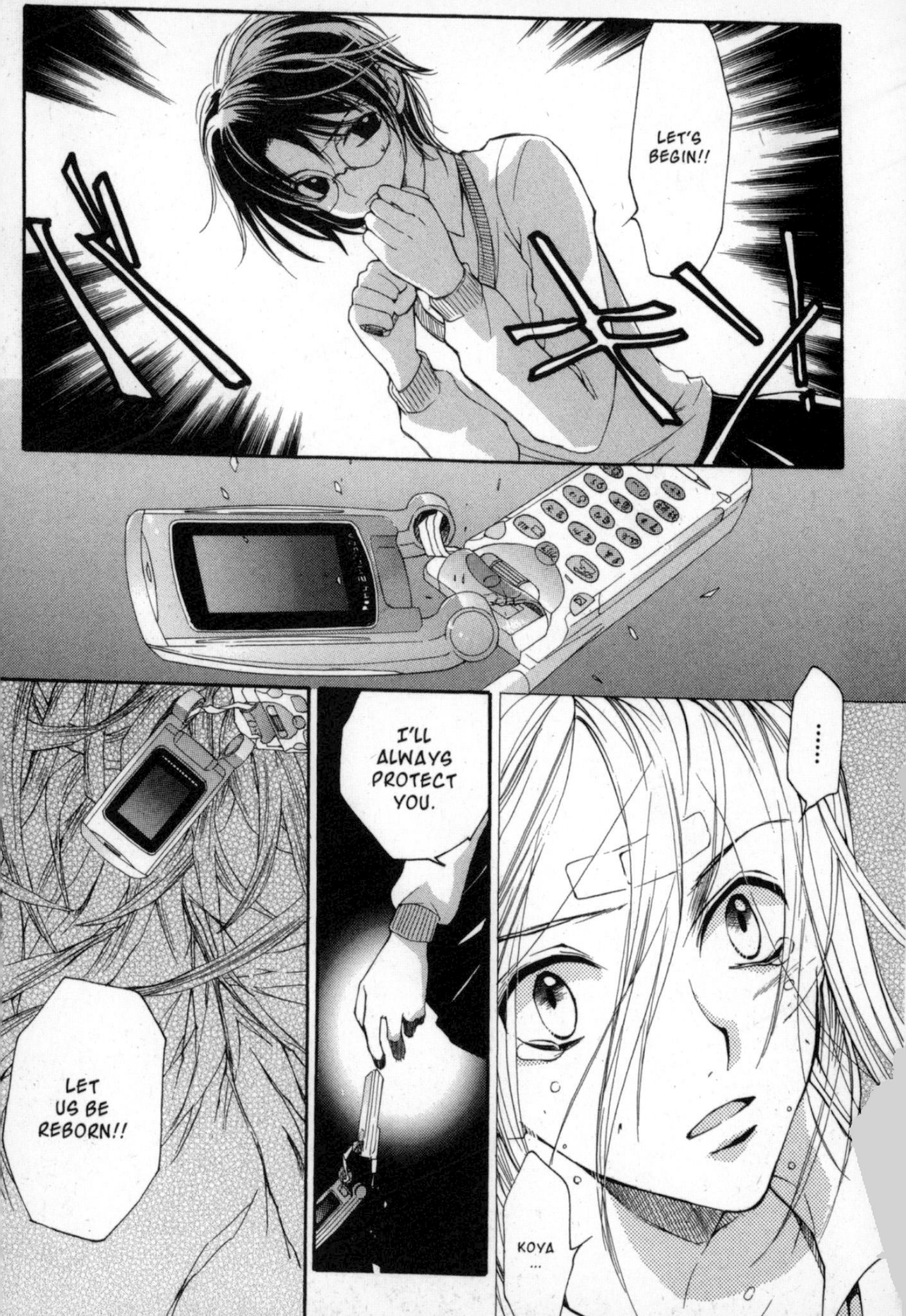
LET'S BEGIN!!
......
KOYA ...
I'LL ALWAYS PROTECT YOU.
LET US BE REBORN!!

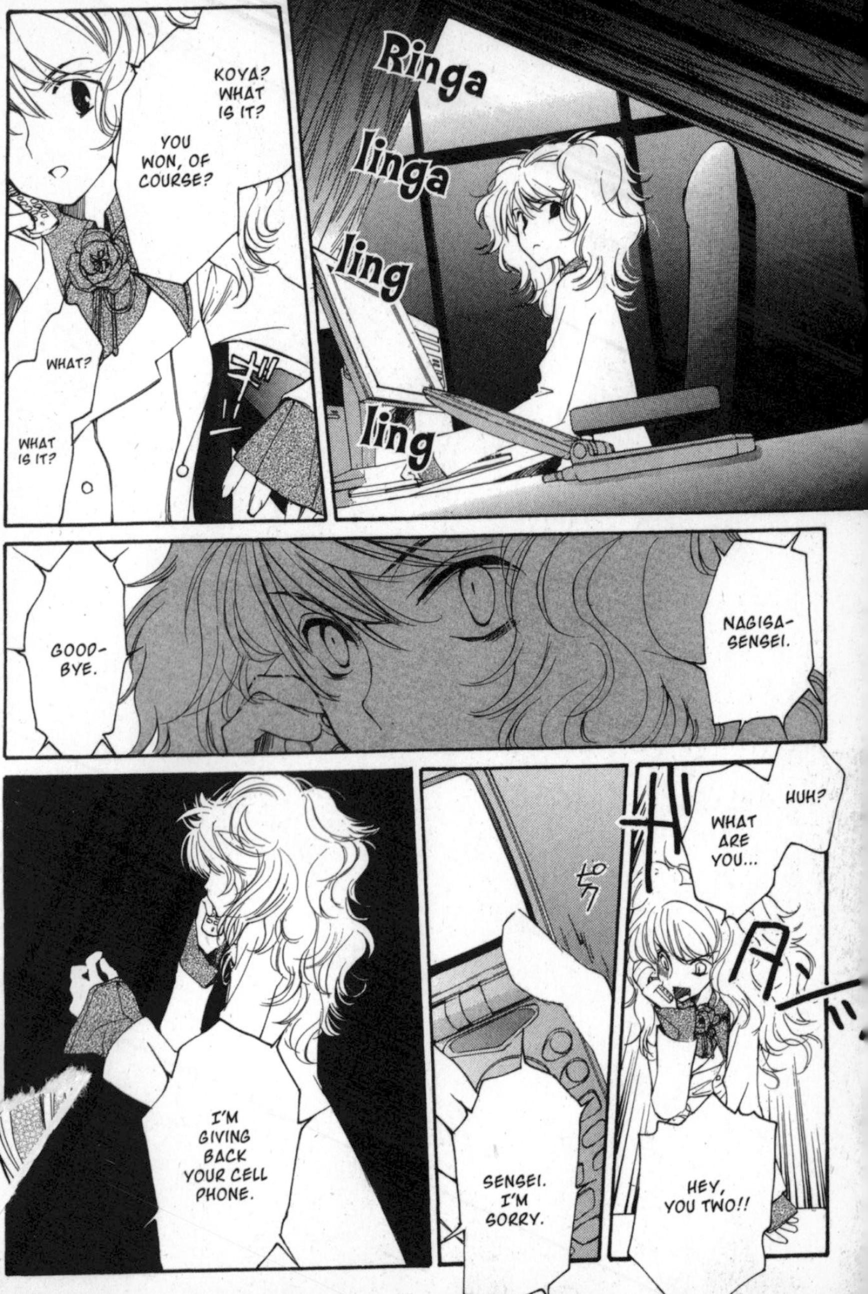
Ringa
linga
ling
ling
KOYA? WHAT IS IT?
YOU WON, OF COURSE?
WHAT?
WHAT IS IT?
NAGISA-SENSEI.
GOOD-BYE.
HUH?
WHAT ARE YOU...
HEY, YOU TWO!!
SENSEI. I'M SORRY.
I'M GIVING BACK YOUR CELL PHONE.

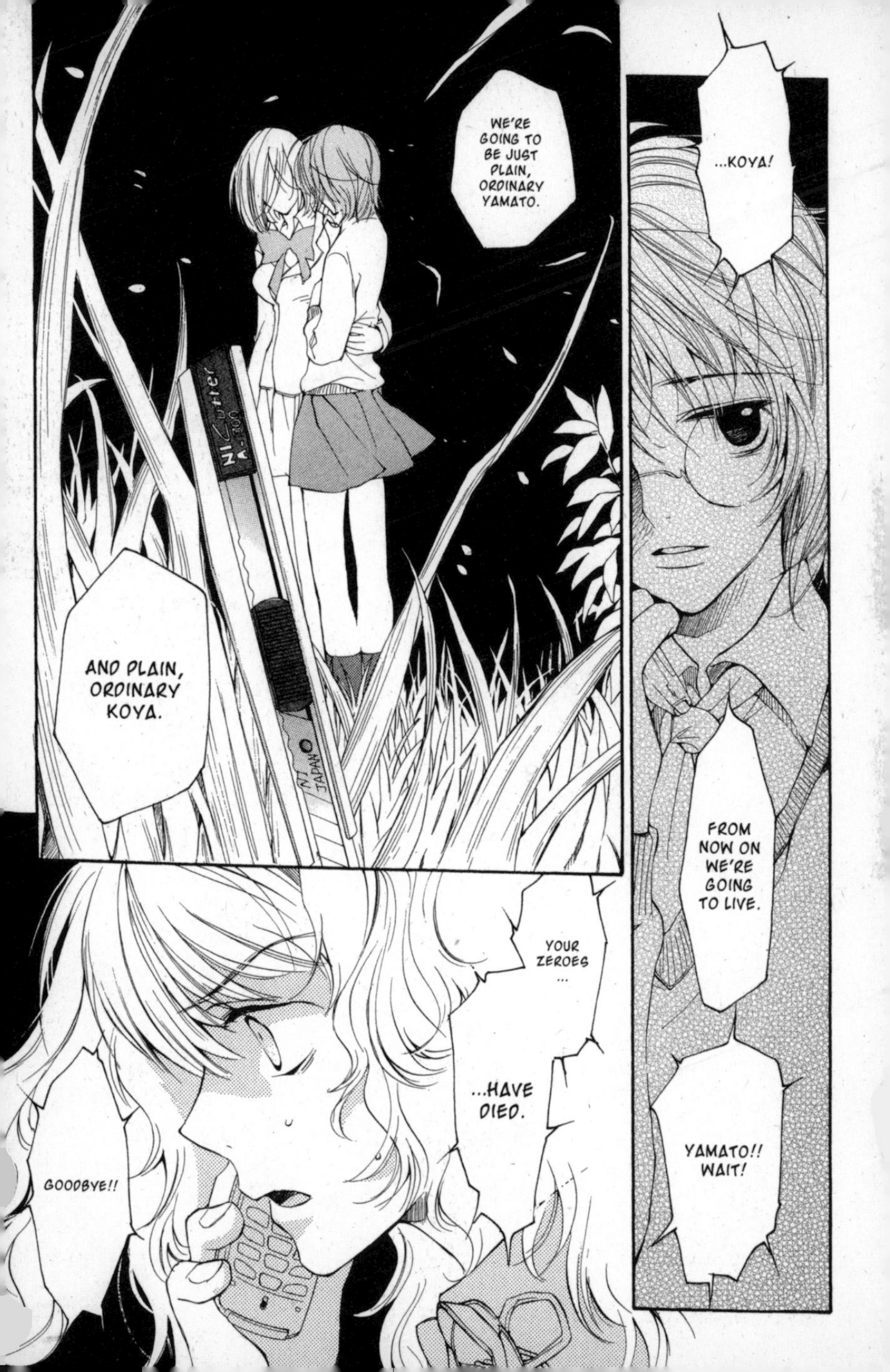
WE'RE GOING TO BE JUST PLAIN, ORDINARY YAMATO.
AND PLAIN, ORDINARY KOYA.
...KOYA!
FROM NOW ON WE'RE GOING TO LIVE.
YOUR ZEROES ...
...HAVE DIED.
GOODBYE!!
YAMATO!! WAIT!

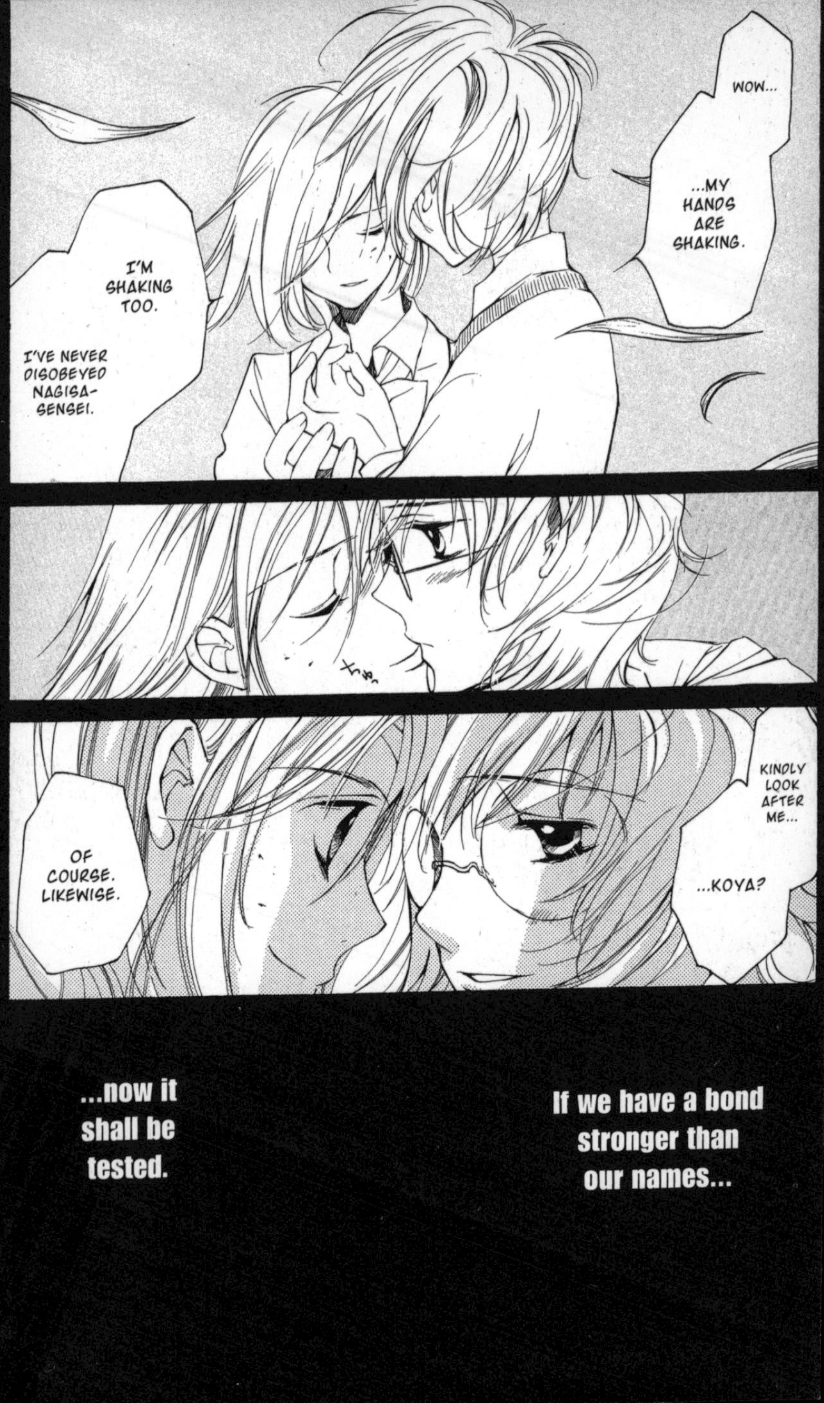
WOW...
...MY HANDS ARE SHAKING.
I'M SHAKING TOO.
I'VE NEVER DISOBEYED NAGISA-SENSEI.
KINDLY LOOK AFTER ME...
...KOYA?
OF COURSE. LIKEWISE.
If we have a bond stronger than our names...
...now it shall be tested.

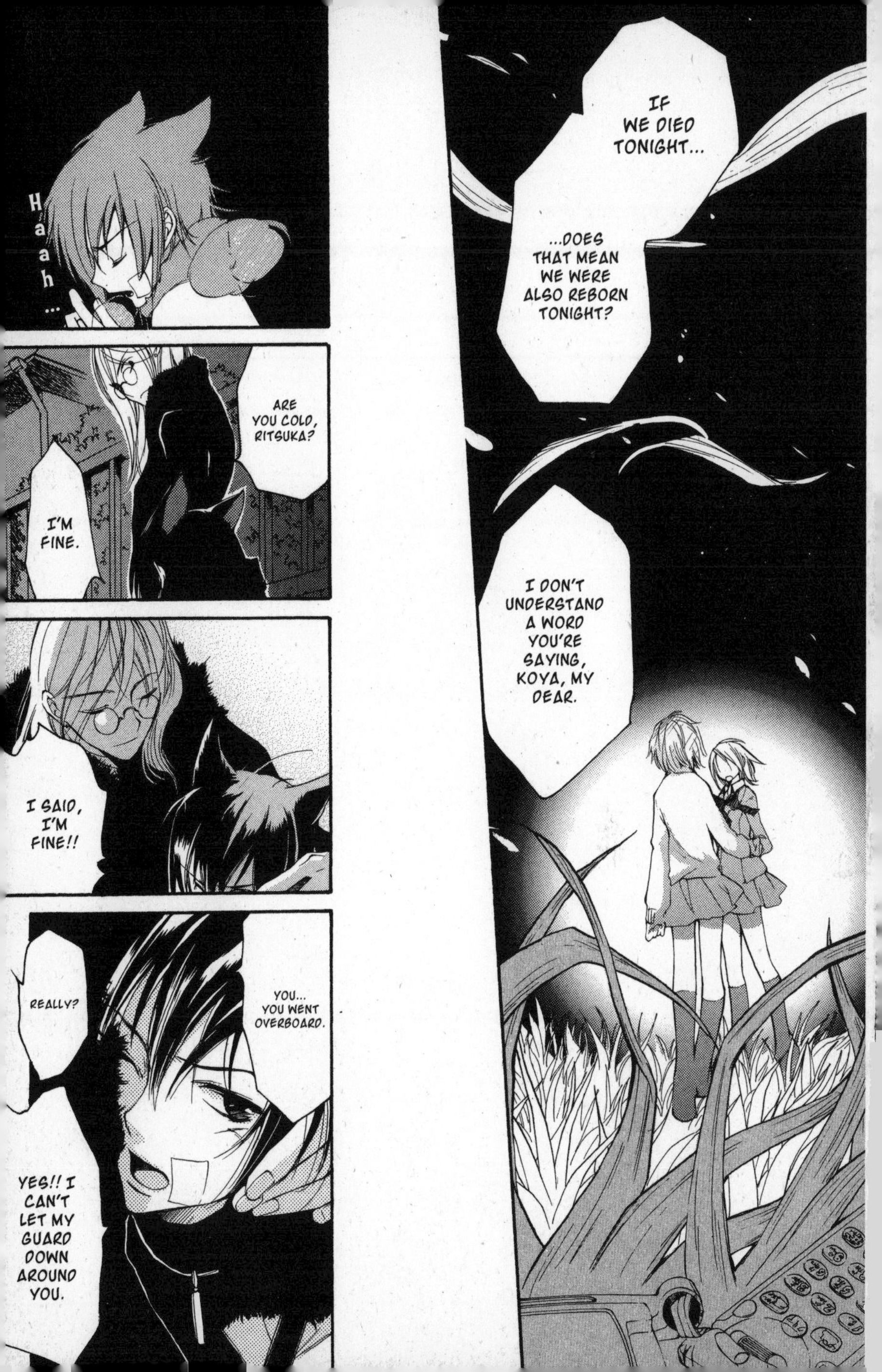
IF WE DIED TONIGHT...
...DOES THAT MEAN WE WERE ALSO REBORN TONIGHT?
I DON'T UNDERSTAND A WORD YOU'RE SAYING, KOYA, MY DEAR.
Haah...
ARE YOU COLD, RITSUKA?
I'M FINE.
I SAID, I'M FINE!!
YOU... YOU WENT OVERBOARD.
REALLY?
YES!! I CAN'T LET MY GUARD DOWN AROUND YOU.

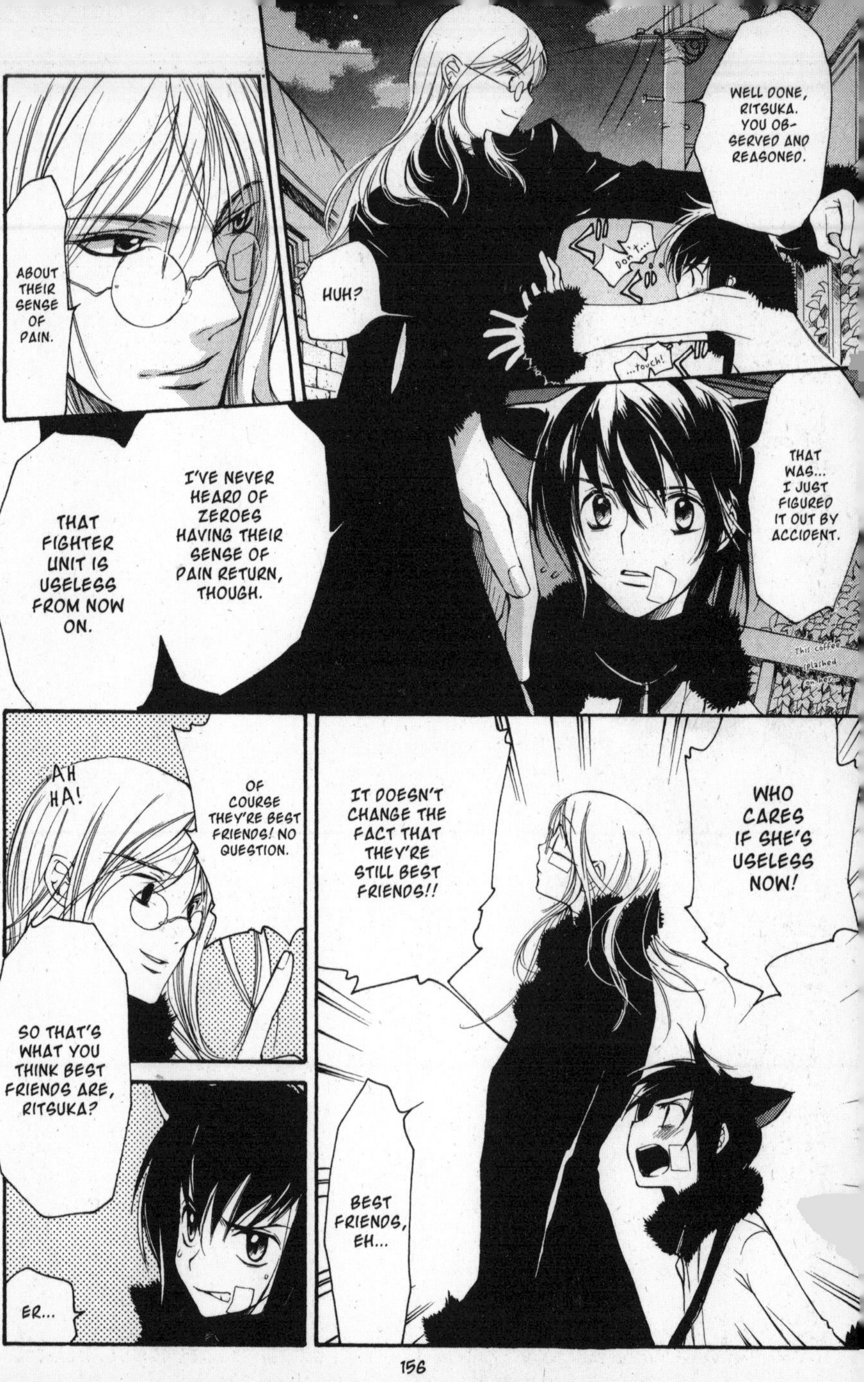
WELL DONE, RITSUKA. YOU OB-SERVED AND REASONED.
HUH?
Don't...
...touch!
ABOUT THEIR SENSE OF PAIN.
THAT WAS... I JUST FIGURED IT OUT BY ACCIDENT.
This coffee splashed on her...
I'VE NEVER HEARD OF ZEROES HAVING THEIR SENSE OF PAIN RETURN, THOUGH.
THAT FIGHTER UNIT IS USELESS FROM NOW ON.
WHO CARES IF SHE'S USELESS NOW!
IT DOESN'T CHANGE THE FACT THAT THEY'RE STILL BEST FRIENDS!!
BEST FRIENDS, EH...
OF COURSE THEY'RE BEST FRIENDS! NO QUESTION.
AH HA!
SO THAT'S WHAT YOU THINK BEST FRIENDS ARE, RITSUKA?
ER...

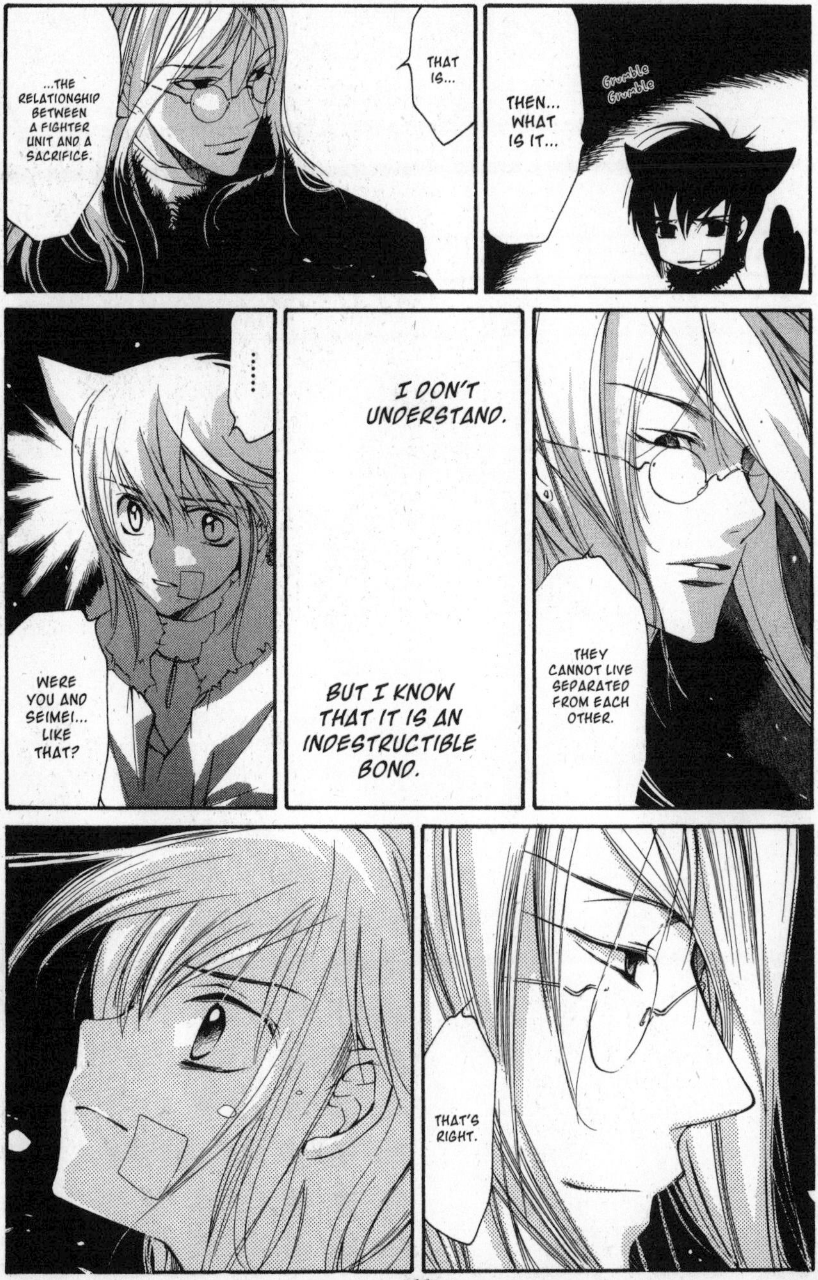
Grumble Grumble
THEN... WHAT IS IT...
THAT IS...
...THE RELATIONSHIP BETWEEN A FIGHTER UNIT AND A SACRIFICE.
THEY CANNOT LIVE SEPARATED FROM EACH OTHER.
I DON'T UNDERSTAND.
BUT I KNOW THAT IT IS AN INDESTRUCTIBLE BOND.
......
WERE YOU AND SEIMEI... LIKE THAT?
THAT'S RIGHT.

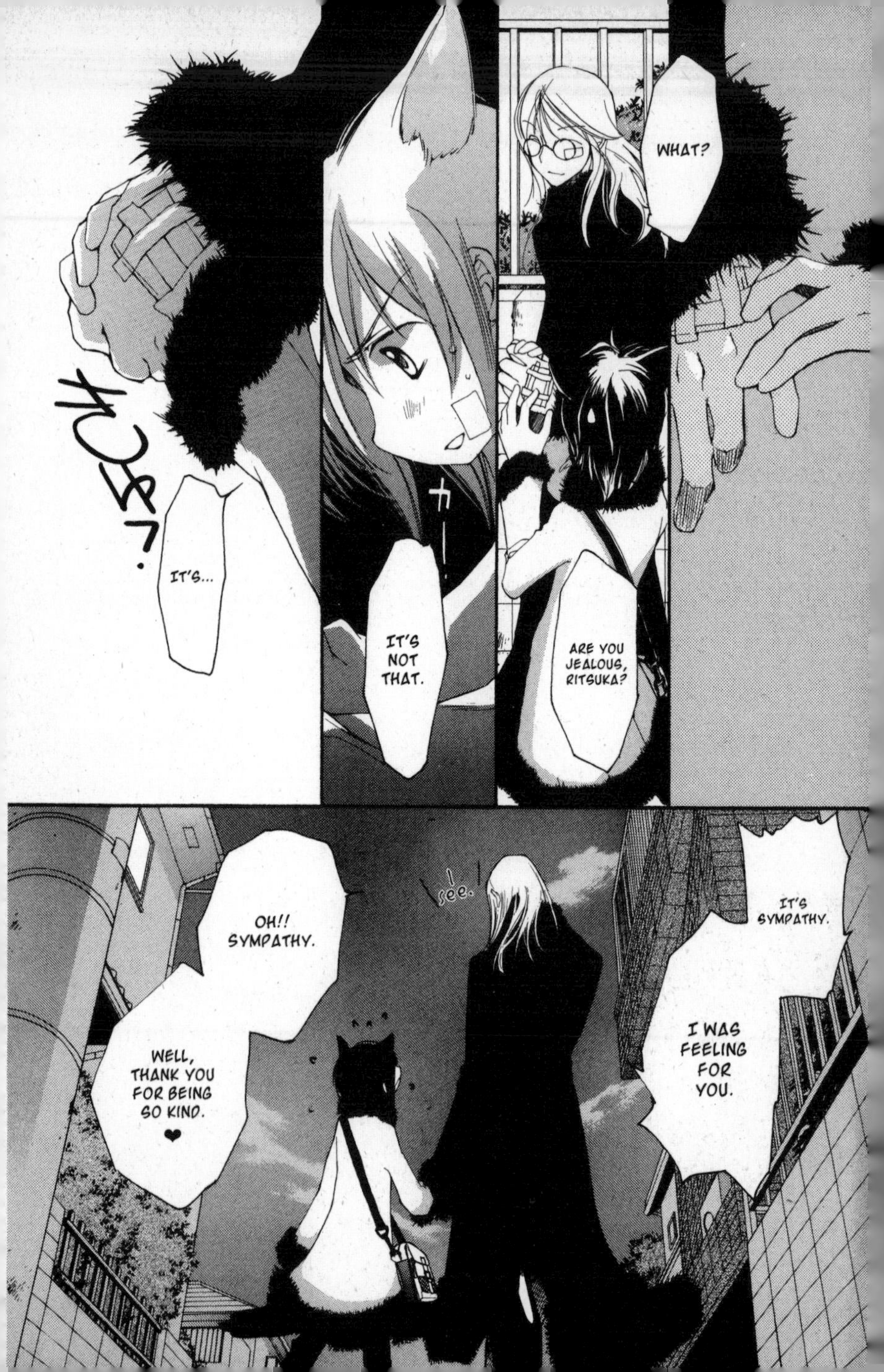
WHAT?
ARE YOU JEALOUS, RITSUKA?
IT'S NOT THAT.
IT'S...
IT'S SYMPATHY.
I WAS FEELING FOR YOU.
I see.
OH!! SYMPATHY.
WELL, THANK YOU FOR BEING SO KIND. ❤

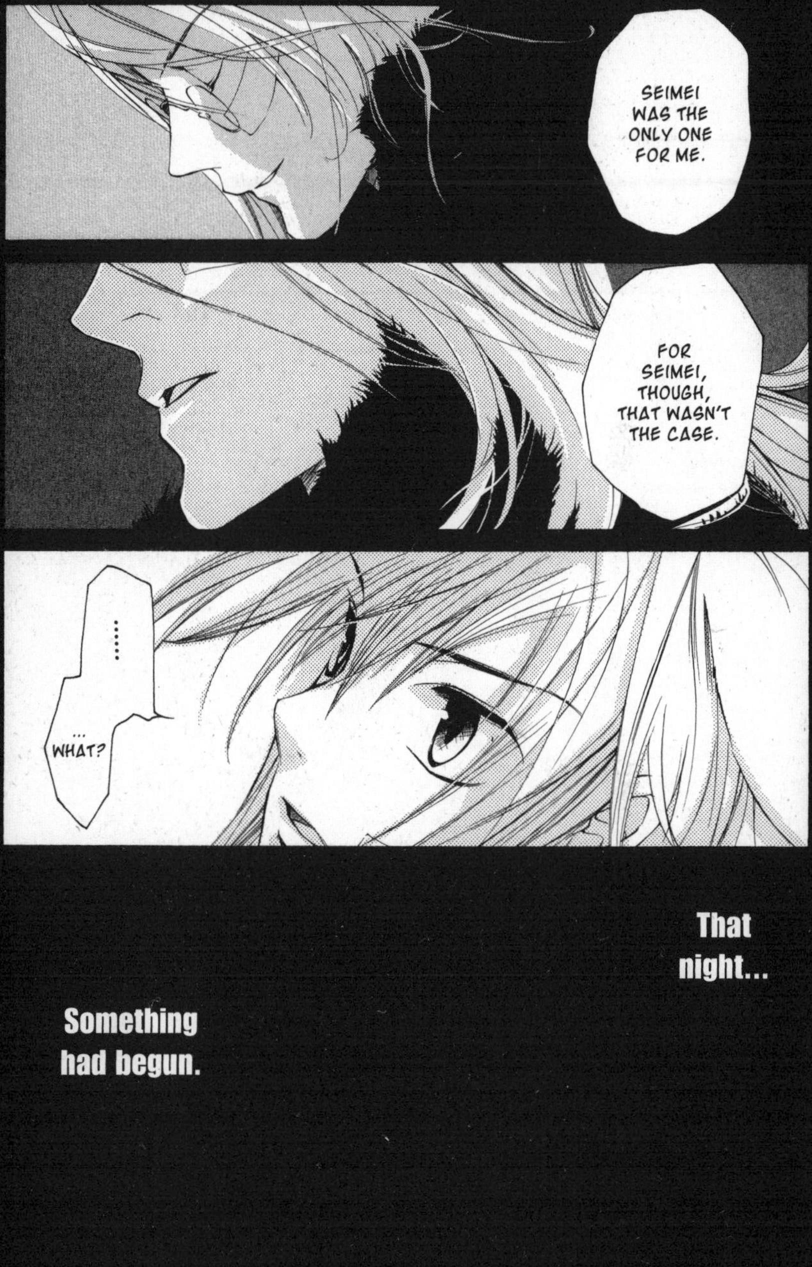
SEIMEI WAS THE ONLY ONE FOR ME.
FOR SEIMEI, THOUGH, THAT WASN'T THE CASE.
......
... WHAT?
That night...
Something had begun.

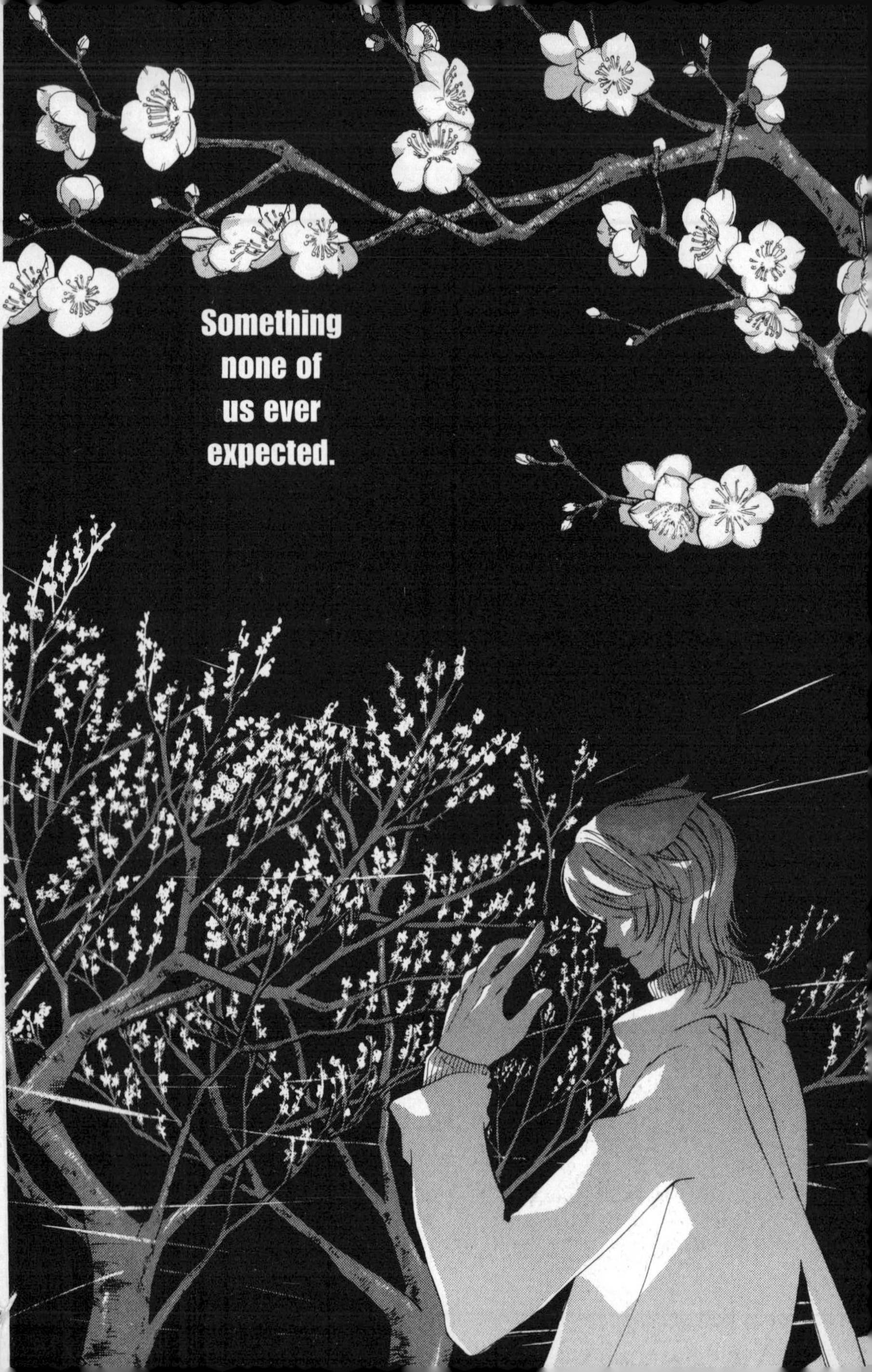
Something none of us ever expected.

A Girl Named Osamu

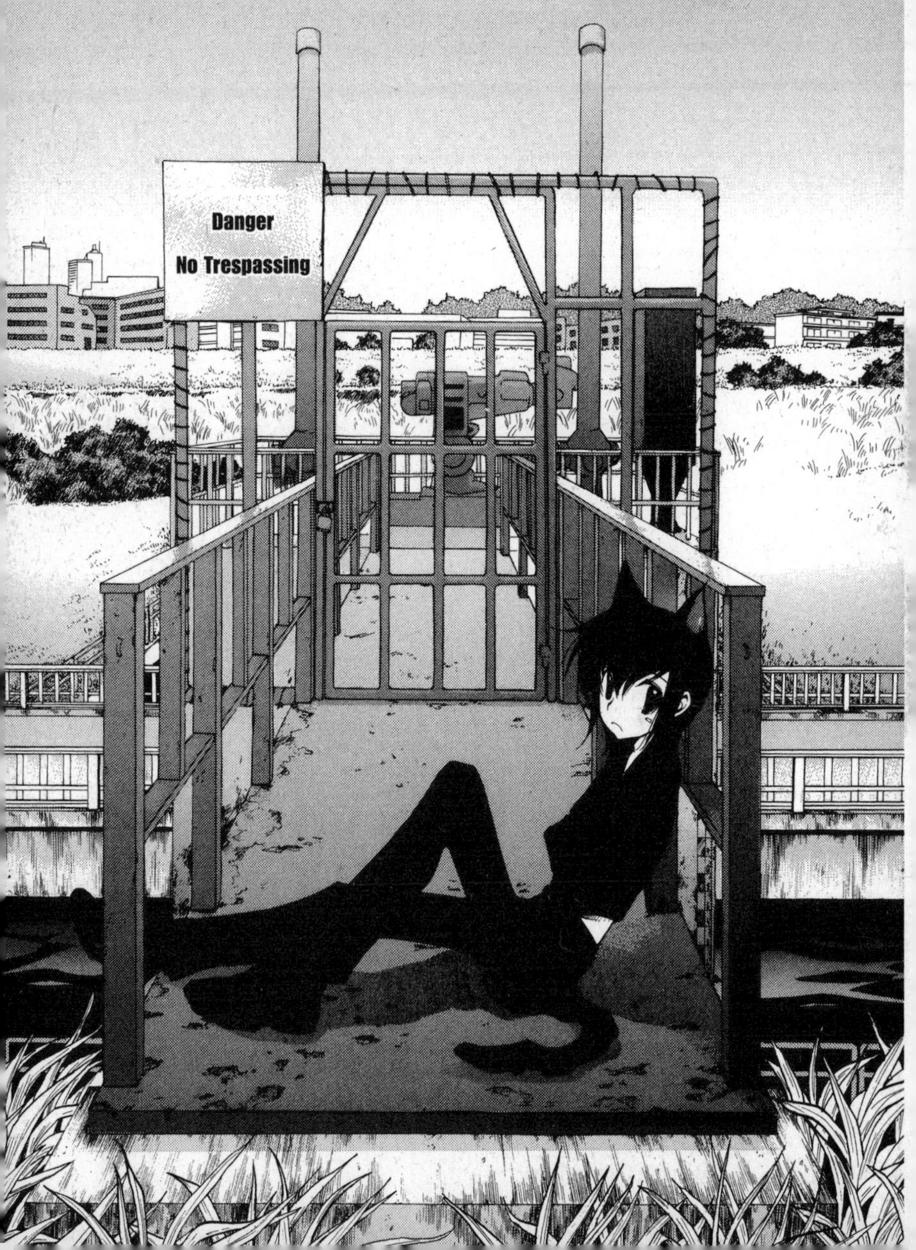
Danger
No Trespassing

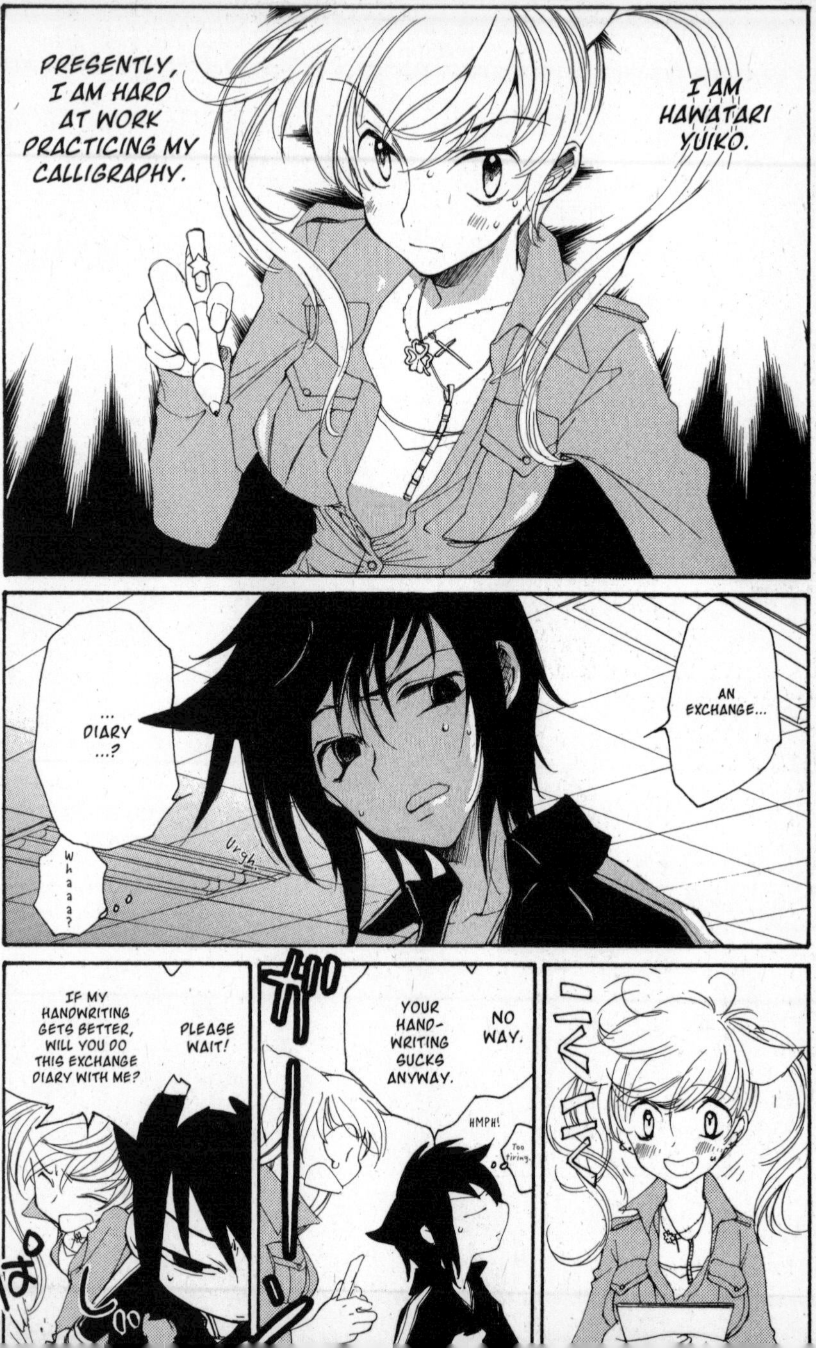
I AM HAWATARI YUIKO.
PRESENTLY, I AM HARD AT WORK PRACTICING MY CALLIGRAPHY.
AN EXCHANGE...
... DIARY ...?
Urgh.
Whaaaa?
NO WAY.
YOUR HAND-WRITING SUCKS ANYWAY.
HMPH!
Too tiring.
PLEASE WAIT!
IF MY HANDWRITING GETS BETTER, WILL YOU DO THIS EXCHANGE DIARY WITH ME?

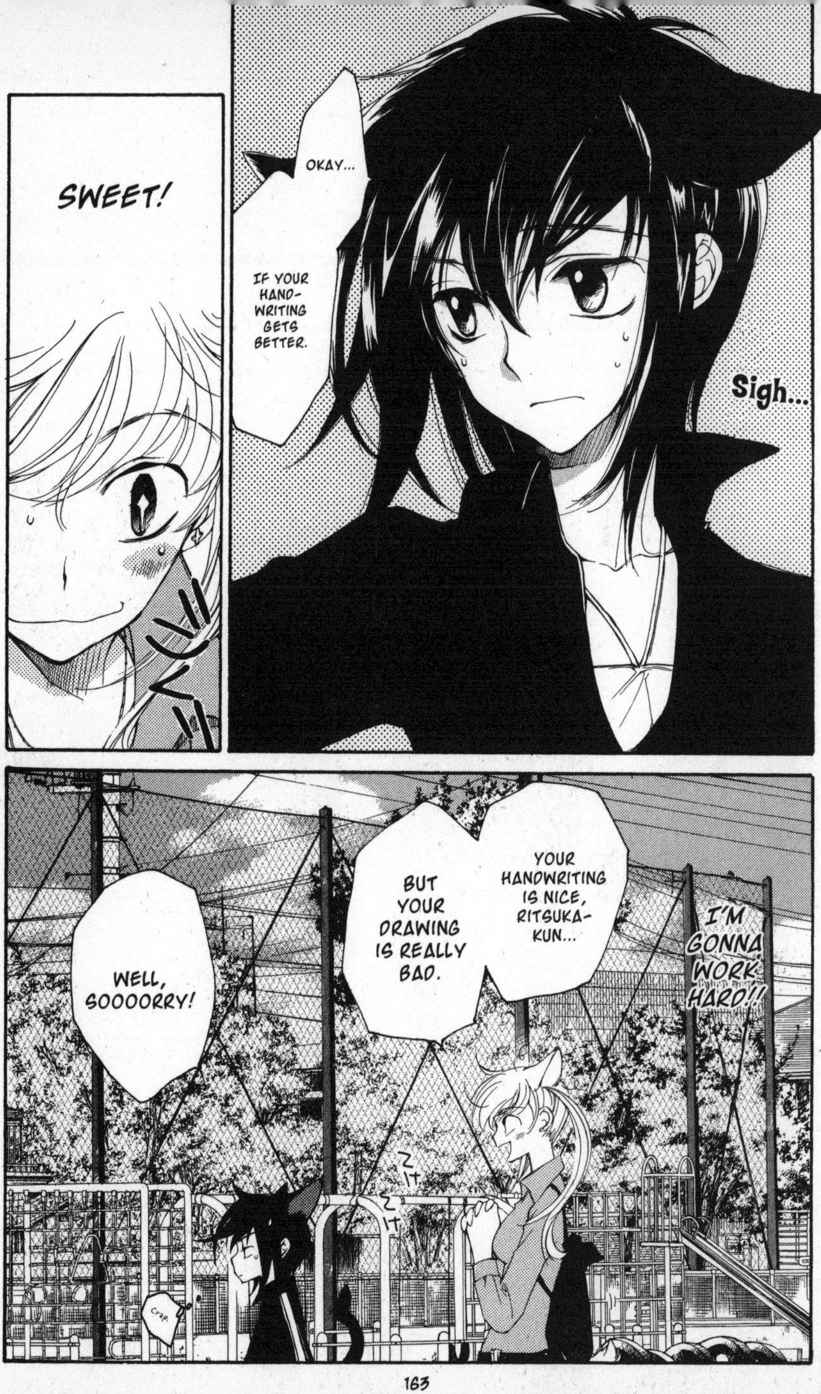
OKAY...
IF YOUR HAND-WRITING GETS BETTER.
Sigh...
SWEET!
I'M GONNA WORK HARD!!
YOUR HANDWRITING IS NICE, RITSUKA-KUN...
BUT YOUR DRAWING IS REALLY BAD.
WELL, SOOOORRY!
Crap.

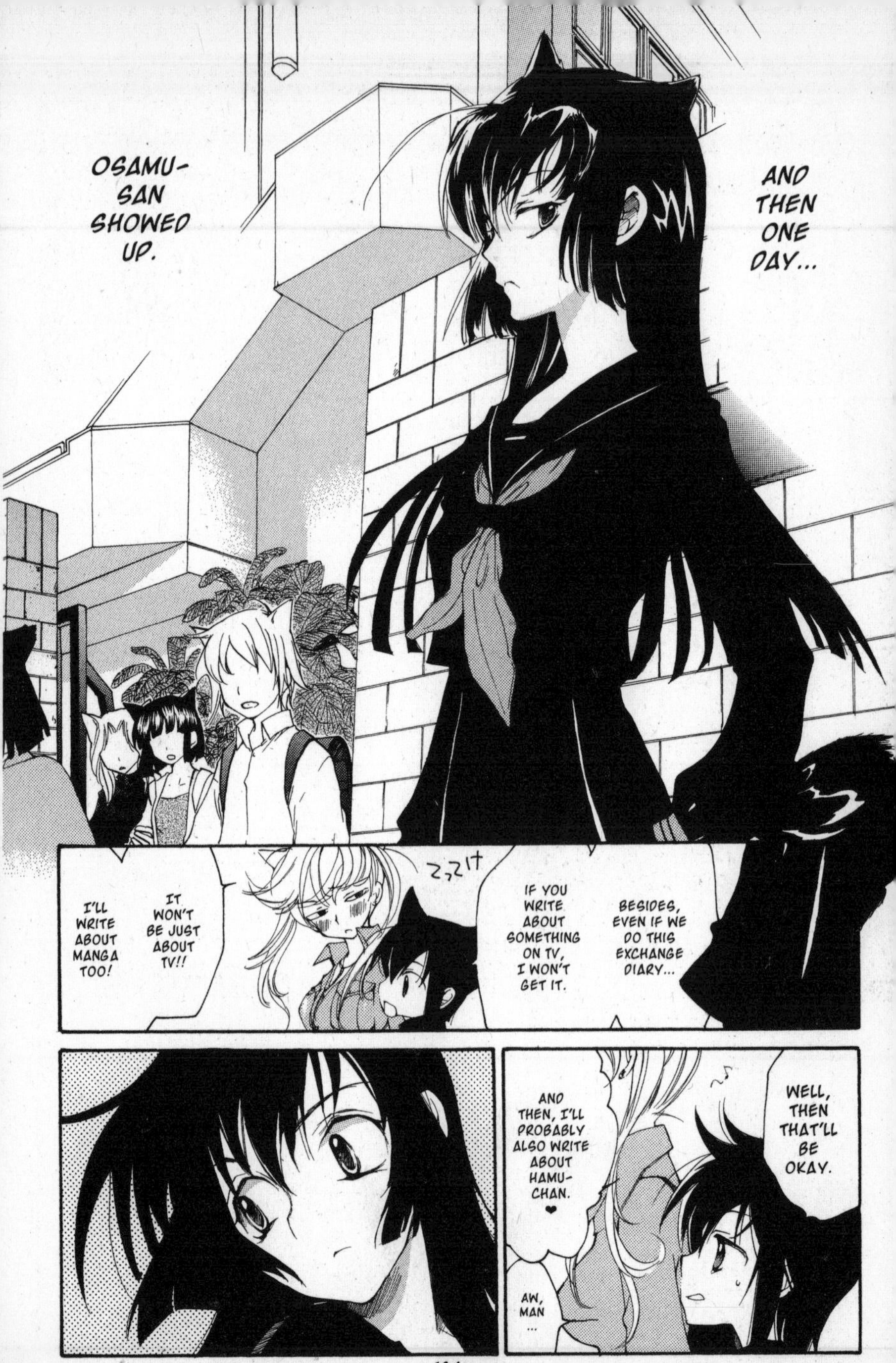
AND THEN ONE DAY...
OSAMU-SAN SHOWED UP.
BESIDES, EVEN IF WE DO THIS EXCHANGE DIARY...
IF YOU WRITE ABOUT SOMETHING ON TV, I WON'T GET IT.
IT WON'T BE JUST ABOUT TV!!
I'LL WRITE ABOUT MANGA TOO!
WELL, THEN THAT'LL BE OKAY.
AND THEN, I'LL PROBABLY ALSO WRITE ABOUT HAMU-CHAN. ❤
AW, MAN ...

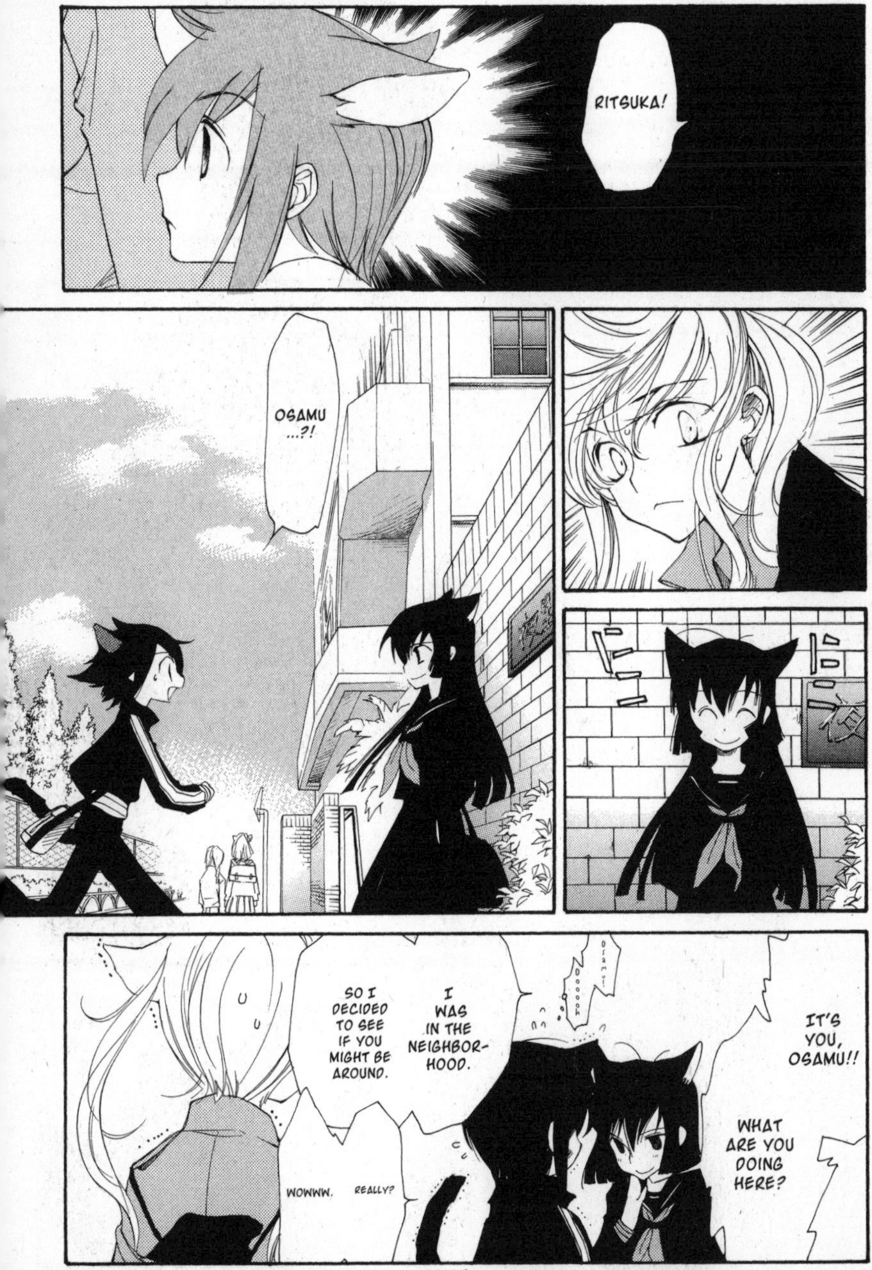
RITSUKA!
OSAMU ...?!
IT'S YOU, OSAMU!!
WHAT ARE YOU DOING HERE?
I WAS IN THE NEIGHBOR-HOOD.
SO I DECIDED TO SEE IF YOU MIGHT BE AROUND.
REALLY?
WOWWW.

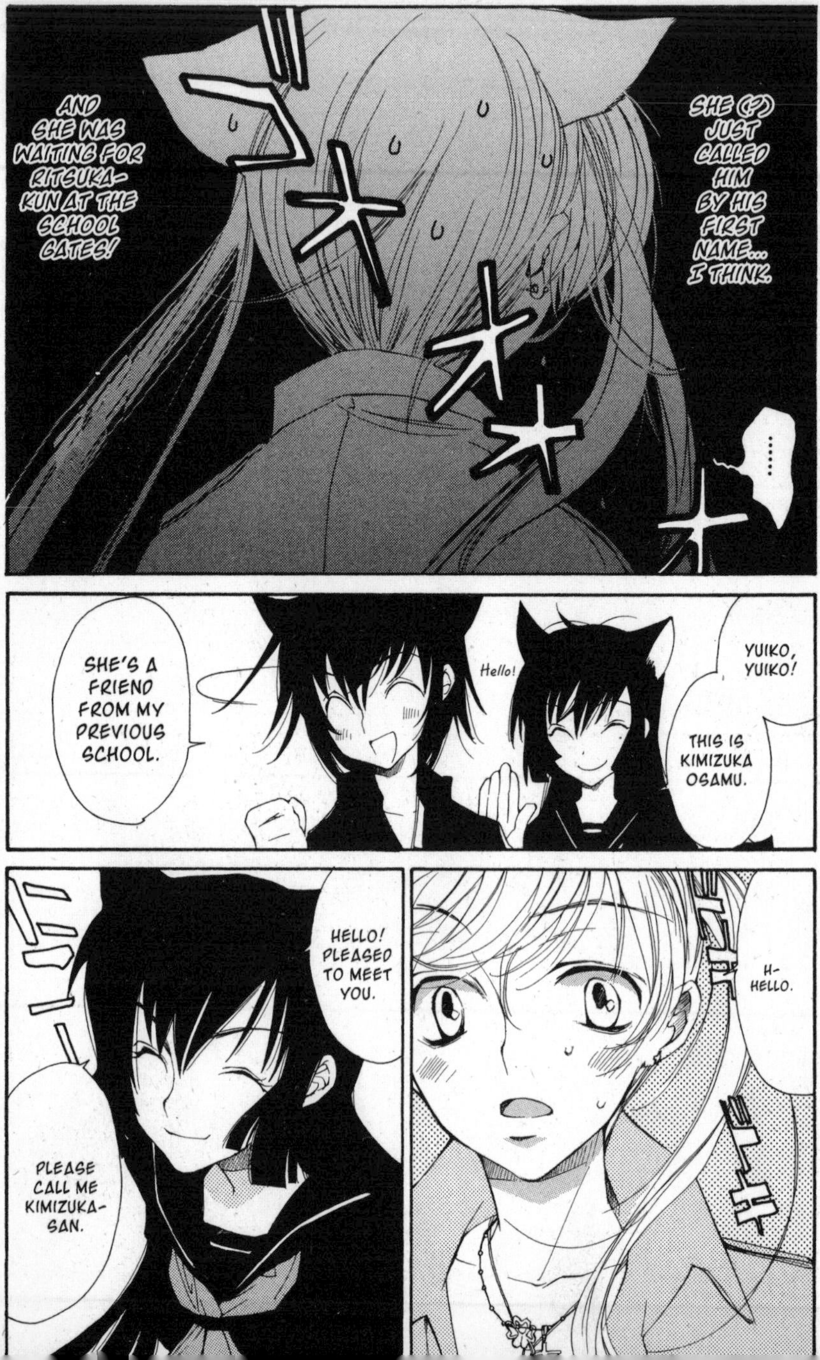
SHE (?) JUST CALLED HIM BY HIS FIRST NAME... I THINK.
AND SHE WAS WAITING FOR RITSUKA-KUN AT THE SCHOOL GATES!
......
YUIKO, YUIKO!
THIS IS KIMIZUKA OSAMU.
Hello!
SHE'S A FRIEND FROM MY PREVIOUS SCHOOL.
H-HELLO.
HELLO! PLEASED TO MEET YOU.
PLEASE CALL ME KIMIZUKA-SAN.

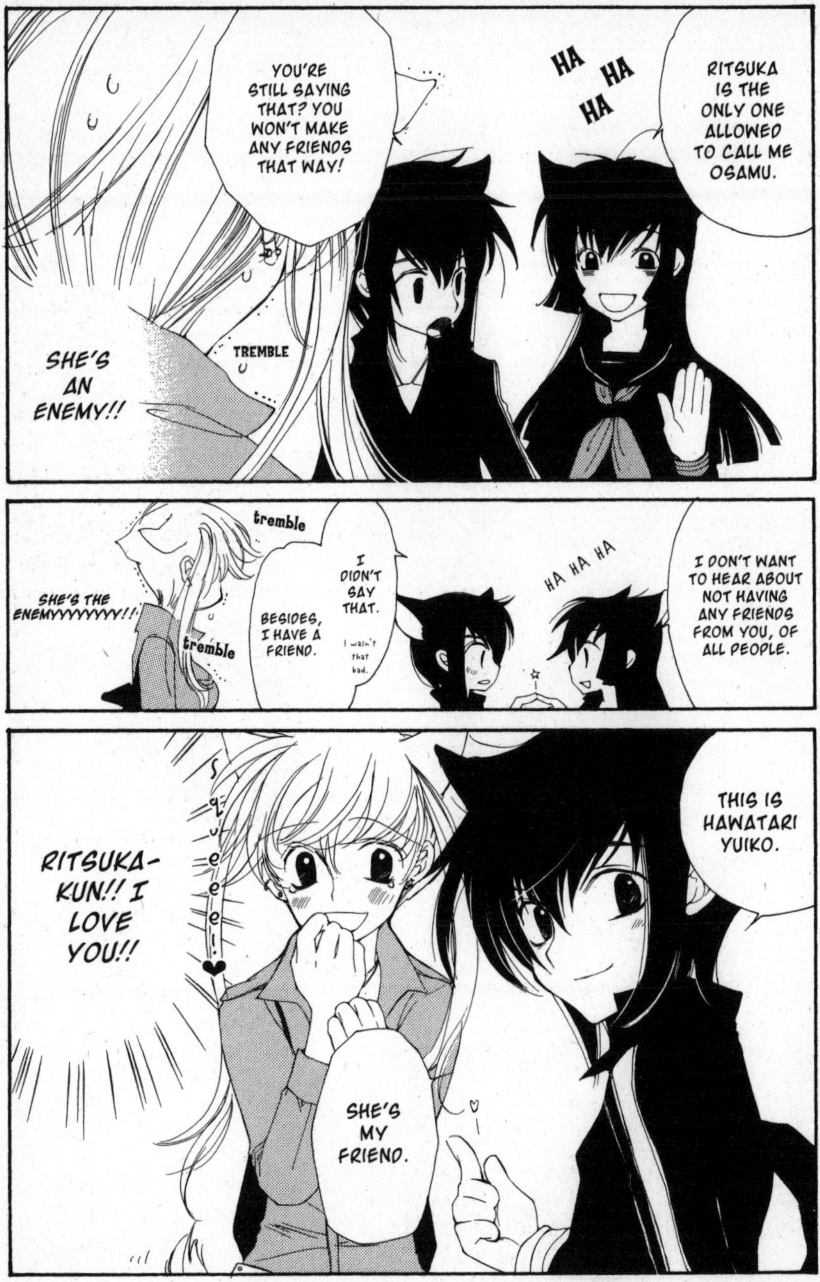
RITSUKA IS THE ONLY ONE ALLOWED TO CALL ME OSAMU.
HA HA HA
YOU'RE STILL SAYING THAT? YOU WON'T MAKE ANY FRIENDS THAT WAY!
TREMBLE
SHE'S AN ENEMY!!
I DON'T WANT TO HEAR ABOUT NOT HAVING ANY FRIENDS FROM YOU, OF ALL PEOPLE.
HA HA HA
I DIDN'T SAY THAT.
I wasn't that bad.
BESIDES, I HAVE A FRIEND.
tremble
tremble
SHE'S THE ENEMYYYYYYYY!!
THIS IS HAWATARI YUIKO.
SHE'S MY FRIEND.
squeeeee!
RITSUKA-KUN!! I LOVE YOU!!

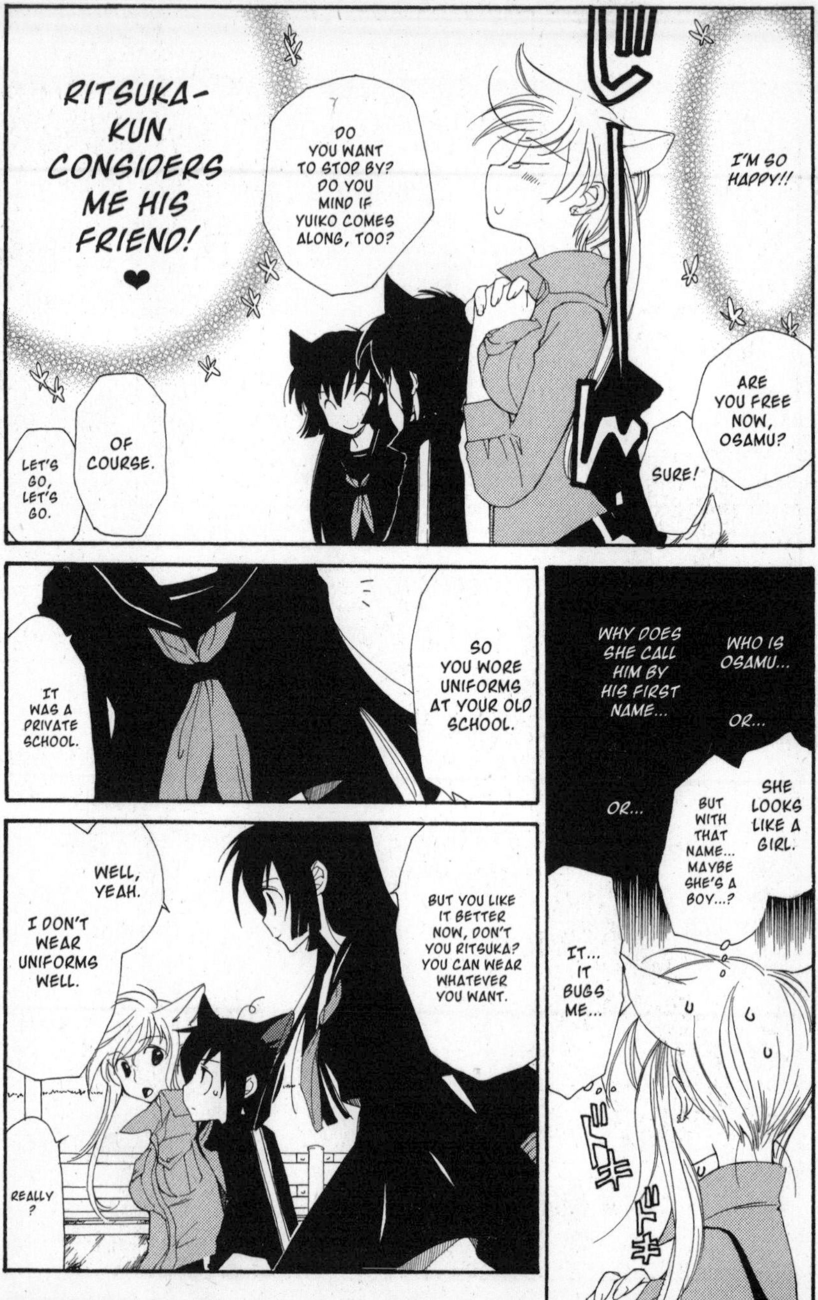
I'M SO HAPPY!!
DO YOU WANT TO STOP BY? DO YOU MIND IF YUIKO COMES ALONG, TOO?
RITSUKA-KUN CONSIDERS ME HIS FRIEND! ❤
ARE YOU FREE NOW, OSAMU?
SURE!
OF COURSE.
LET'S GO, LET'S GO.
WHO IS OSAMU...
OR...
WHY DOES SHE CALL HIM BY HIS FIRST NAME...
OR...
SHE LOOKS LIKE A GIRL.
BUT WITH THAT NAME... MAYBE SHE'S A BOY...?
IT... IT BUGS ME...
SO YOU WORE UNIFORMS AT YOUR OLD SCHOOL.
IT WAS A PRIVATE SCHOOL.
BUT YOU LIKE IT BETTER NOW, DON'T YOU RITSUKA? YOU CAN WEAR WHATEVER YOU WANT.
WELL, YEAH.
I DON'T WEAR UNIFORMS WELL.
REALLY?

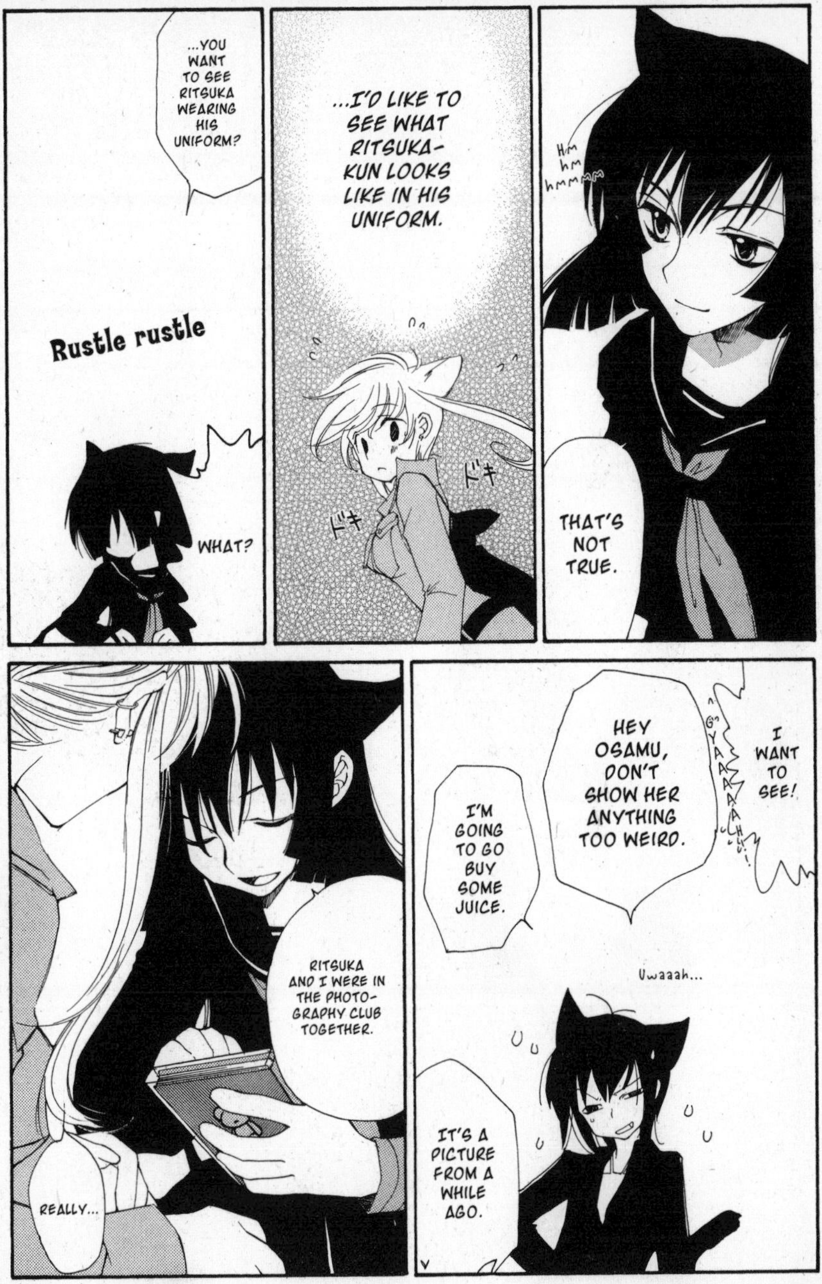
Hm hm hmmmm
THAT'S NOT TRUE.
...I'D LIKE TO SEE WHAT RITSUKA-KUN LOOKS LIKE IN HIS UNIFORM.
ドキ
ドキ
...YOU WANT TO SEE RITSUKA WEARING HIS UNIFORM?
Rustle rustle
WHAT?
I WANT TO SEE!
HEY OSAMU, DON'T SHOW HER ANYTHING TOO WEIRD.
I'M GOING TO GO BUY SOME JUICE.
Uwaaah...
IT'S A PICTURE FROM A WHILE AGO.
RITSUKA AND I WERE IN THE PHOTOGRAPHY CLUB TOGETHER.
REALLY...

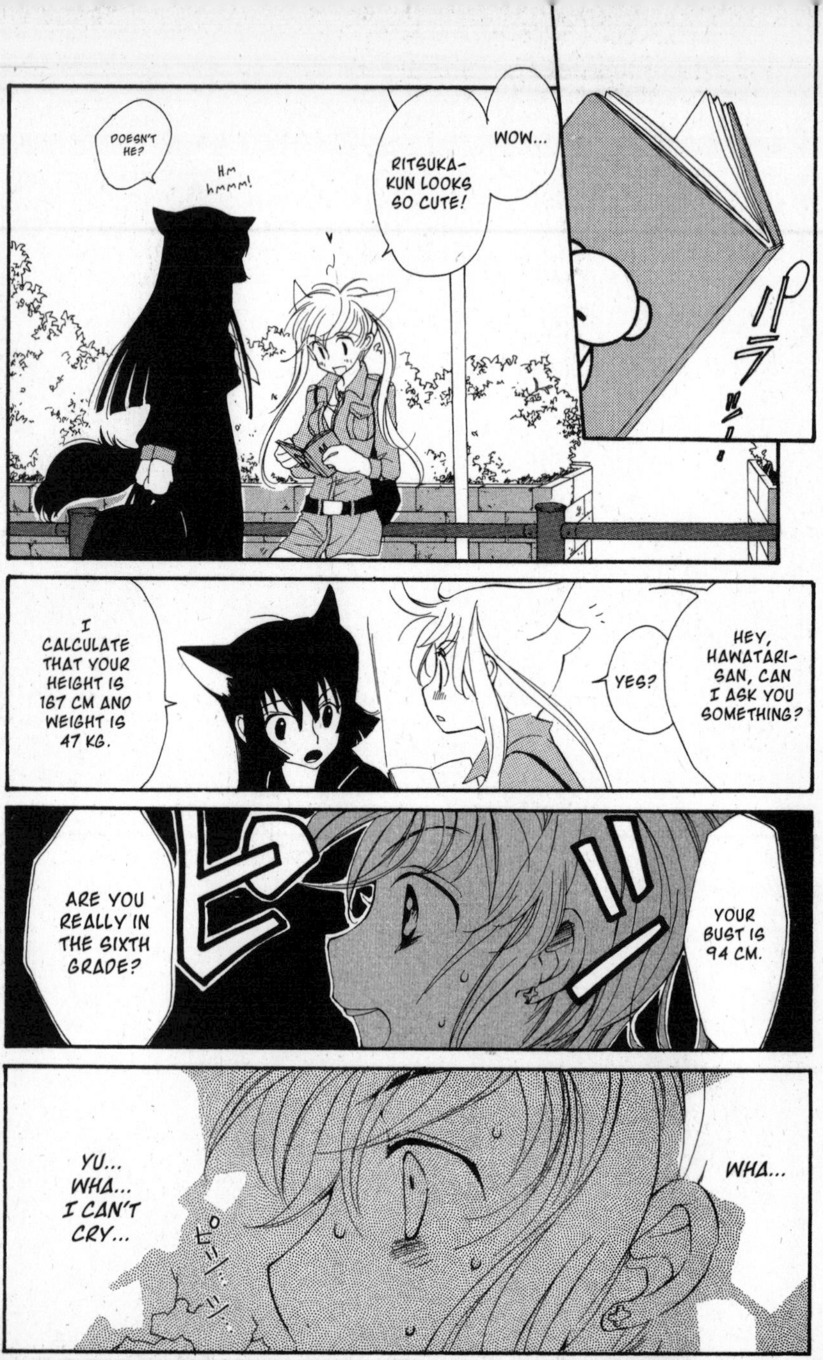
パラ
WOW... RITSUKA-KUN LOOKS SO CUTE!
Hm hmmm!
DOESN'T HE?
HEY, HAWATARI-SAN, CAN I ASK YOU SOMETHING?
YES?
I CALCULATE THAT YOUR HEIGHT IS 167 CM AND WEIGHT IS 47 KG.
YOUR BUST IS 94 CM.
ARE YOU REALLY IN THE SIXTH GRADE?
WHA...
YU... WHA... I CAN'T CRY...

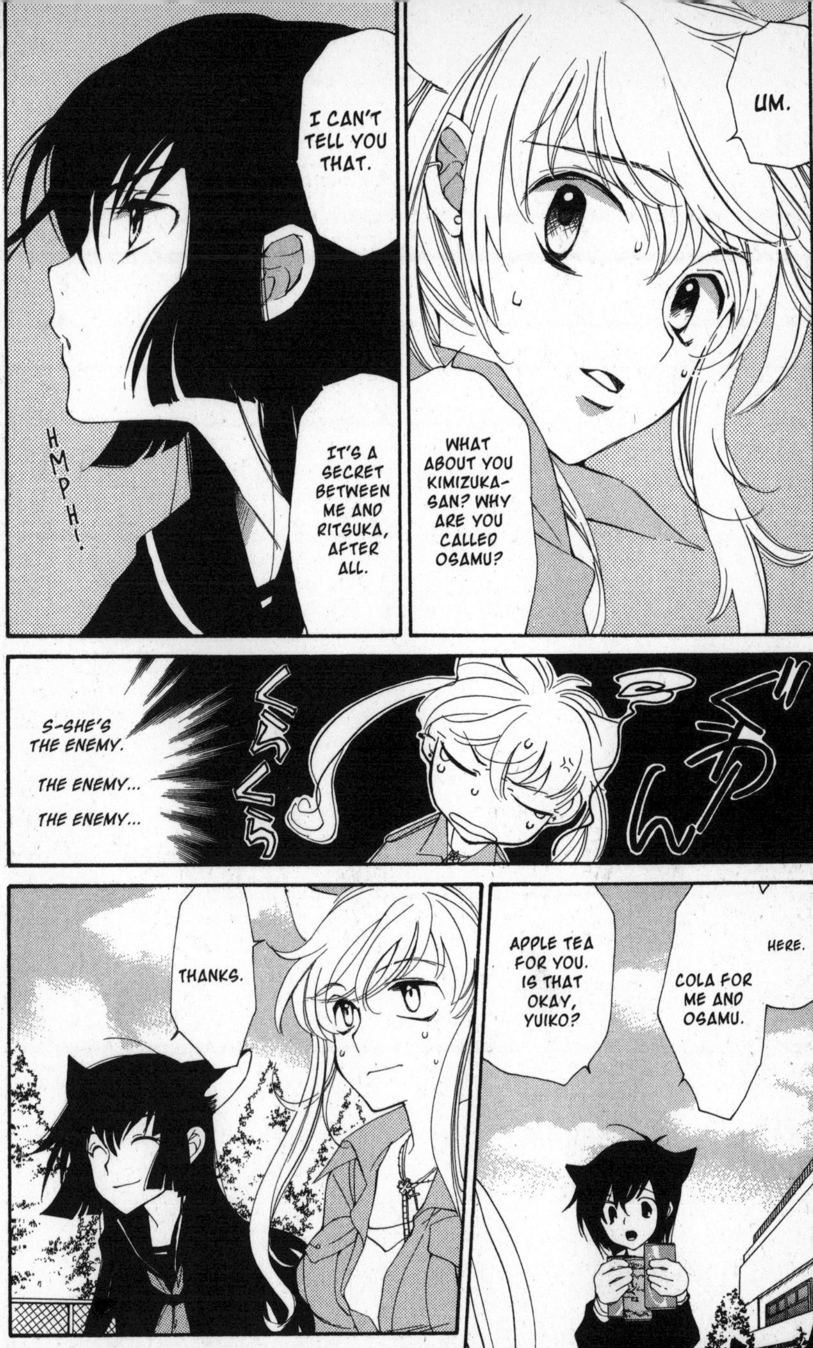
UM.
WHAT ABOUT YOU KIMIZUKA-SAN? WHY ARE YOU CALLED OSAMU?
I CAN'T TELL YOU THAT.
IT'S A SECRET BETWEEN ME AND RITSUKA, AFTER ALL.
HMPH!
S-SHE'S THE ENEMY.
THE ENEMY...
THE ENEMY...
HERE.
COLA FOR ME AND OSAMU.
APPLE TEA FOR YOU. IS THAT OKAY, YUIKO?
THANKS.

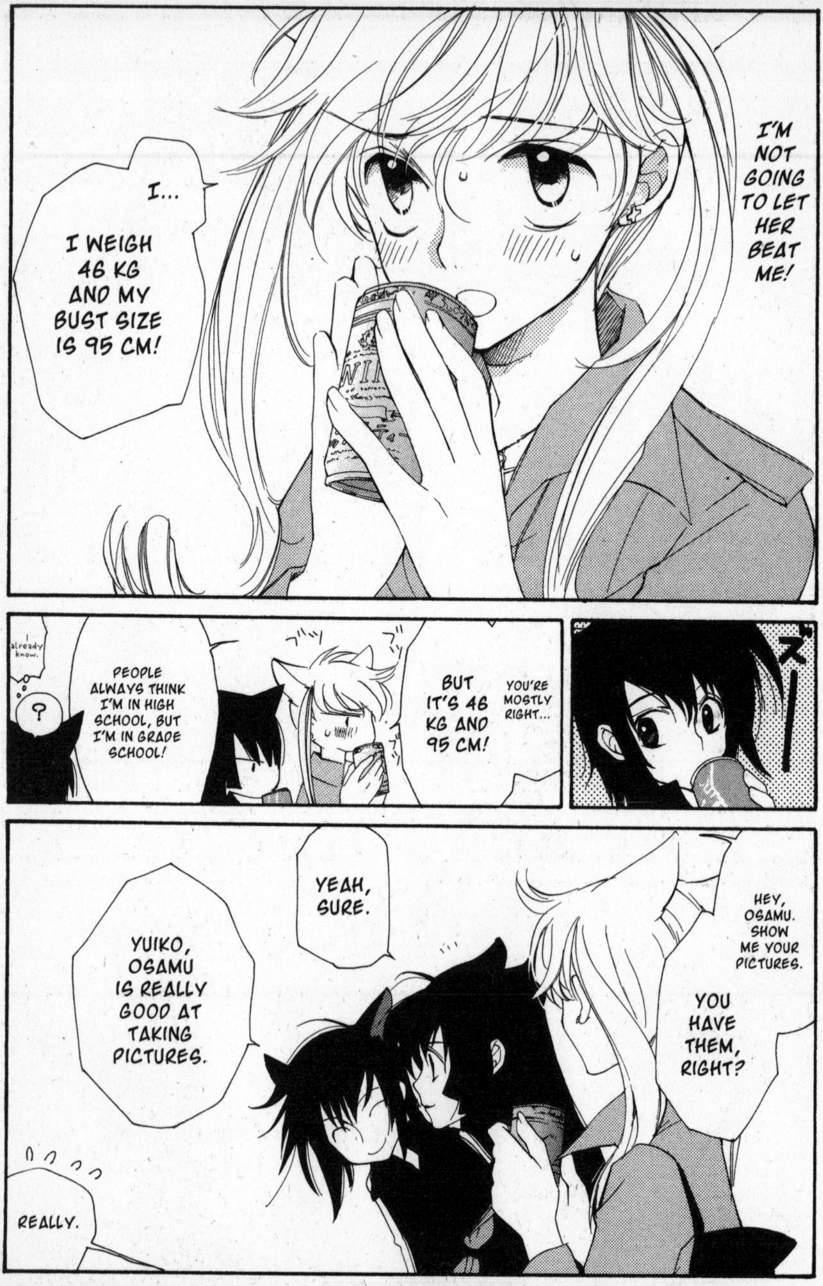
I'M NOT GOING TO LET HER BEAT ME!
I...
I WEIGH 46 KG AND MY BUST SIZE IS 95 CM!
ズー
YOU'RE MOSTLY RIGHT...
BUT IT'S 46 KG AND 95 CM!
PEOPLE ALWAYS THINK I'M IN HIGH SCHOOL, BUT I'M IN GRADE SCHOOL!
I already know.
?
HEY, OSAMU. SHOW ME YOUR PICTURES.
YOU HAVE THEM, RIGHT?
YEAH, SURE.
YUIKO, OSAMU IS REALLY GOOD AT TAKING PICTURES.
REALLY.

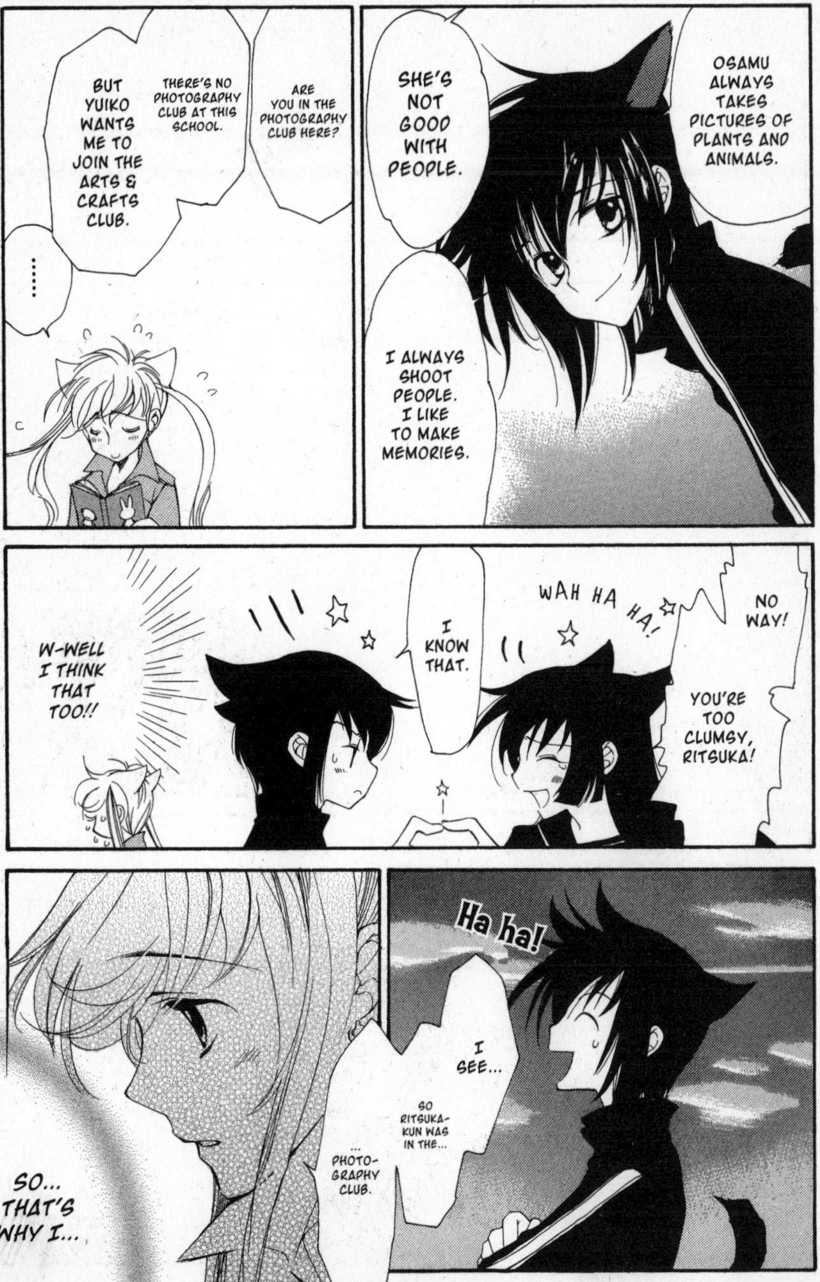
OSAMU ALWAYS TAKES PICTURES OF PLANTS AND ANIMALS.
SHE'S NOT GOOD WITH PEOPLE.
I ALWAYS SHOOT PEOPLE. I LIKE TO MAKE MEMORIES.
ARE YOU IN THE PHOTOGRAPHY CLUB HERE?
THERE'S NO PHOTOGRAPHY CLUB AT THIS SCHOOL.
BUT YUIKO WANTS ME TO JOIN THE ARTS & CRAFTS CLUB.
......
NO WAY!
YOU'RE TOO CLUMSY, RITSUKA!
WAH HA HA!
I KNOW THAT.
W-WELL I THINK THAT TOO!!
Ha ha!
I SEE...
SO RITSUKA-KUN WAS IN THE...
...PHOTOGRAPHY CLUB.
SO... THAT'S WHY I...

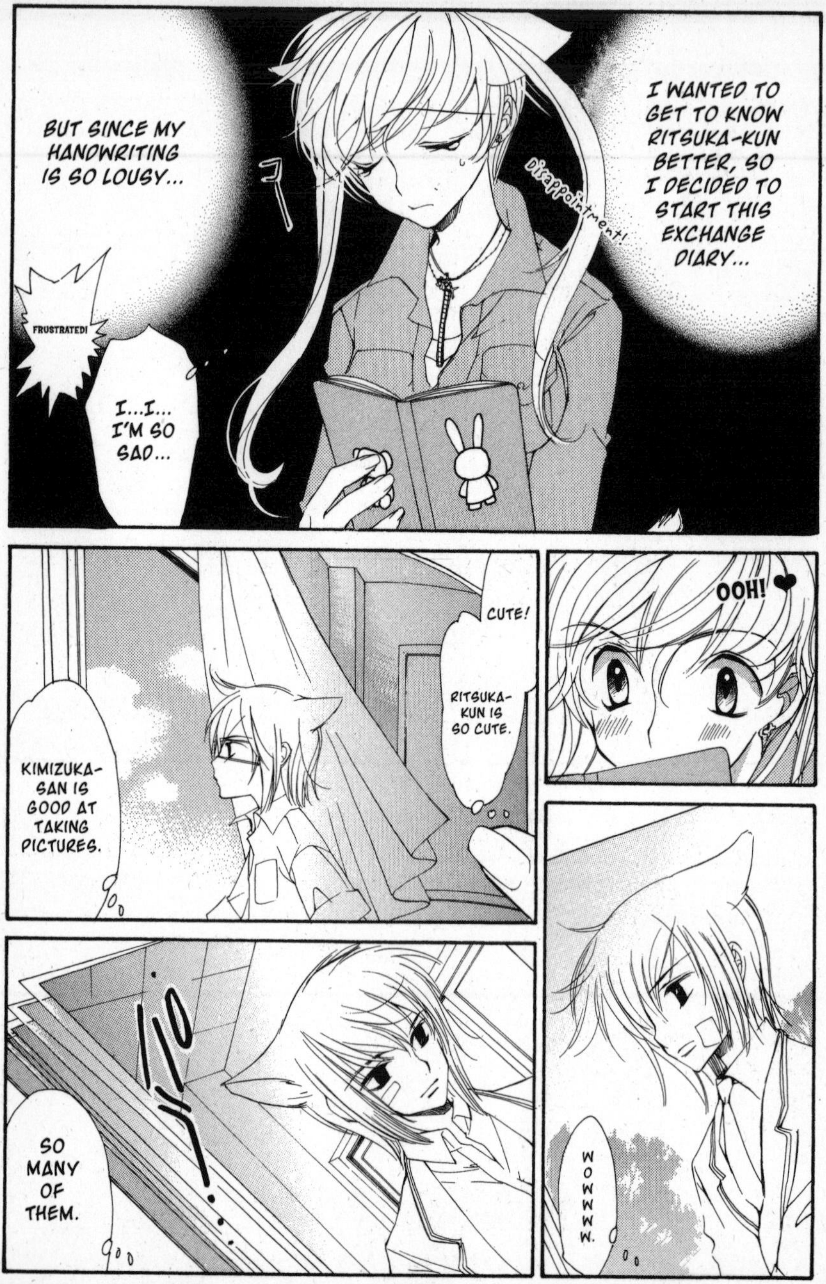

I WANTED TO GET TO KNOW RITSUKA-KUN BETTER, SO I DECIDED TO START THIS EXCHANGE DIARY...
Disappointment!
BUT SINCE MY HANDWRITING IS SO LOUSY...
FRUSTRATED!
I...I... I'M SO SAD...
OOH!
CUTE!
RITSUKA-KUN IS SO CUTE.
KIMIZUKA-SAN IS GOOD AT TAKING PICTURES.
WOWWWW.
SO MANY OF THEM.

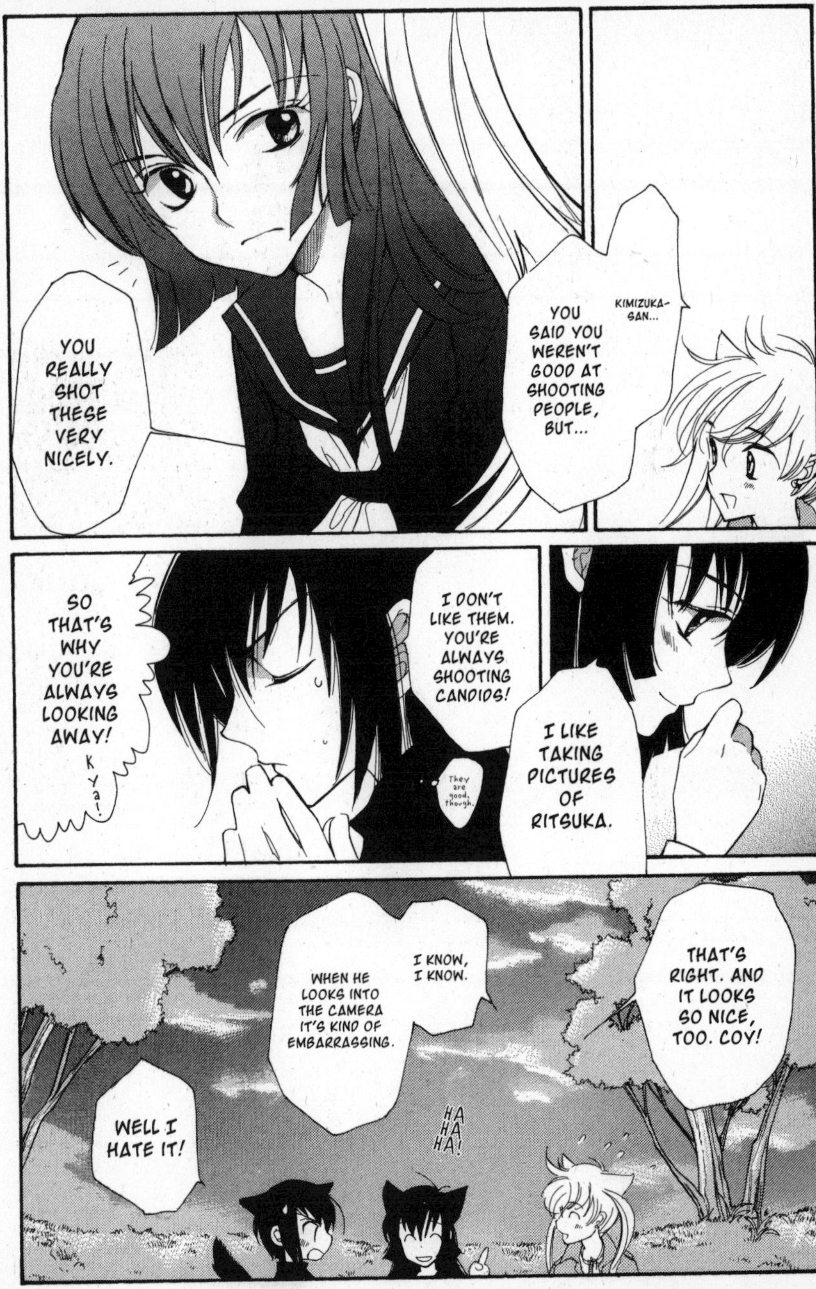
KIMIZUKA-SAN...
YOU SAID YOU WEREN'T GOOD AT SHOOTING PEOPLE, BUT...
YOU REALLY SHOT THESE VERY NICELY.
I LIKE TAKING PICTURES OF RITSUKA.
I DON'T LIKE THEM. YOU'RE ALWAYS SHOOTING CANDIDS!
They are good, though.
SO THAT'S WHY YOU'RE ALWAYS LOOKING AWAY!
Kya!
THAT'S RIGHT. AND IT LOOKS SO NICE, TOO. COY!
I KNOW, I KNOW.
WHEN HE LOOKS INTO THE CAMERA IT'S KIND OF EMBARRASSING.
HA HA HA!
WELL I HATE IT!

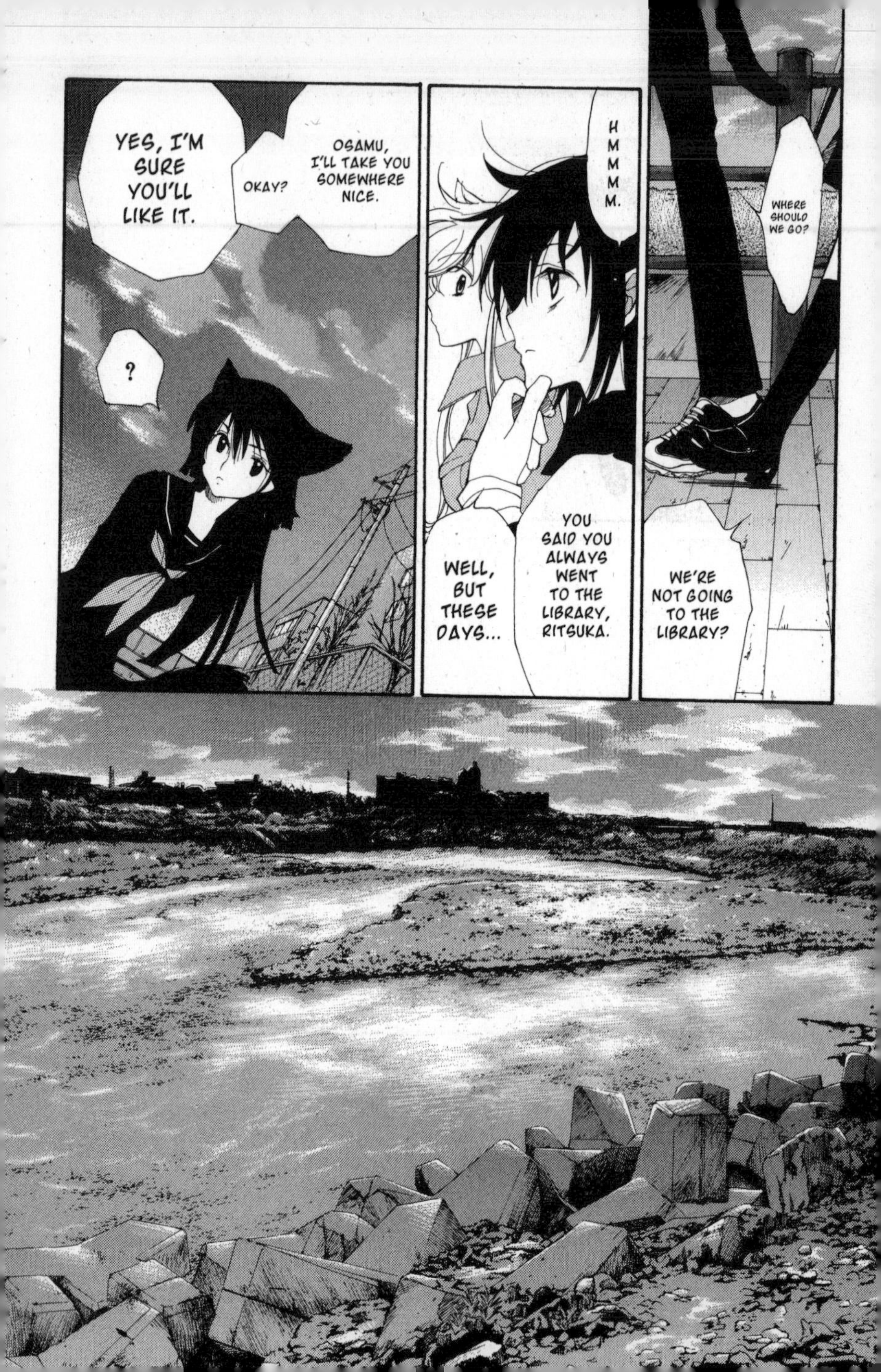
WHERE SHOULD WE GO?
WE'RE NOT GOING TO THE LIBRARY?
HMMMM.
YOU SAID YOU ALWAYS WENT TO THE LIBRARY, RITSUKA.
WELL, BUT THESE DAYS...
OSAMU, I'LL TAKE YOU SOMEWHERE NICE.
OKAY?
YES, I'M SURE YOU'LL LIKE IT.
?

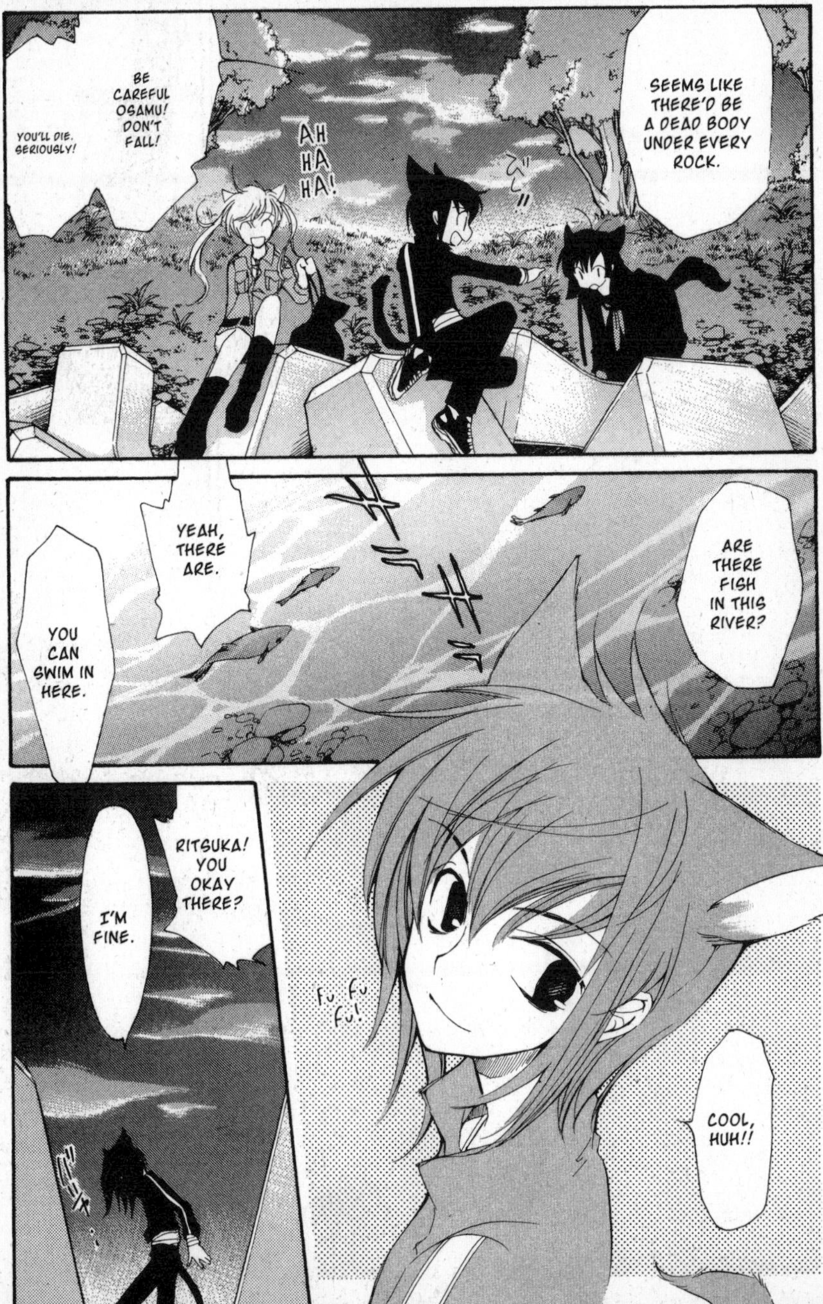
SEEMS LIKE THERE'D BE A DEAD BODY UNDER EVERY ROCK.
AH HA HA!
BE CAREFUL OSAMU! DON'T FALL!
YOU'LL DIE. SERIOUSLY!
ARE THERE FISH IN THIS RIVER?
YEAH, THERE ARE.
YOU CAN SWIM IN HERE.
COOL, HUH!!
FU FU FU!
RITSUKA! YOU OKAY THERE?
I'M FINE.

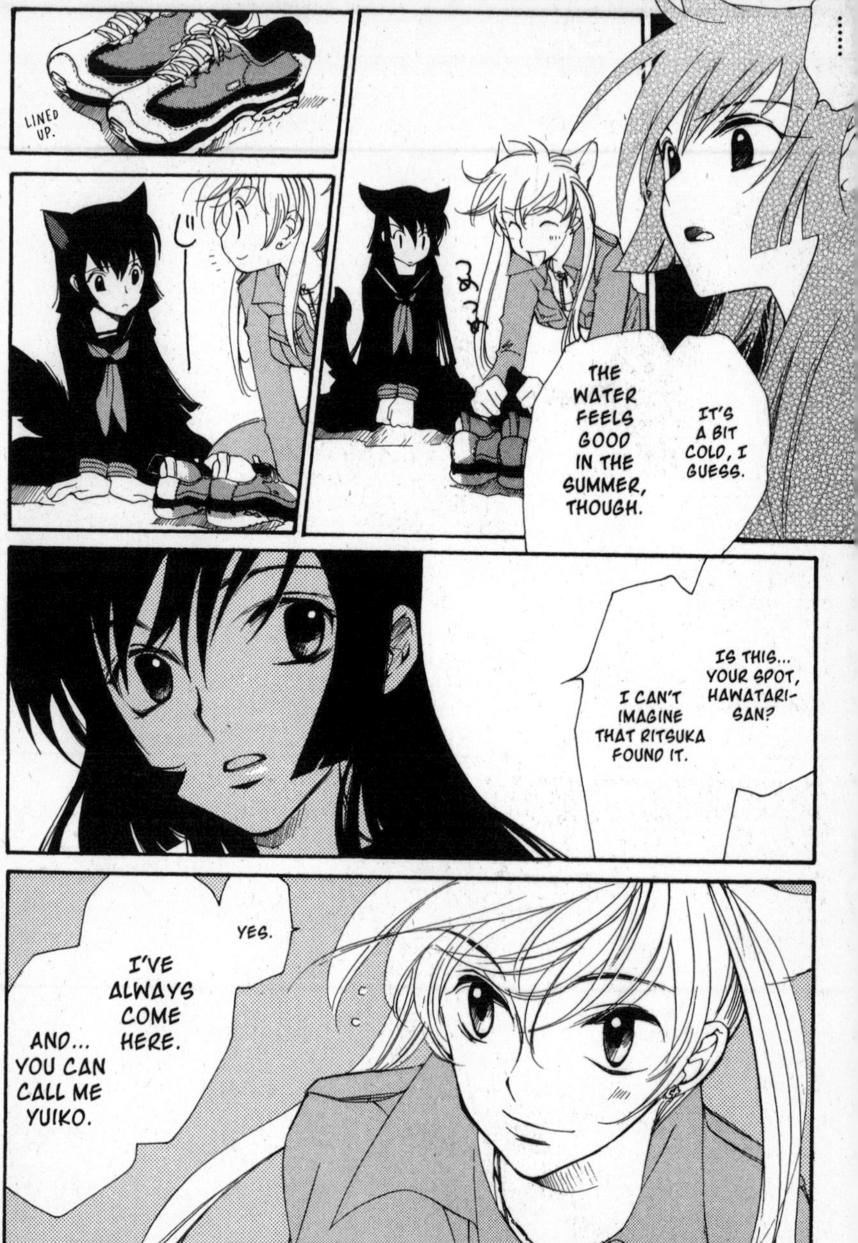
....
IT'S A BIT COLD, I GUESS.
THE WATER FEELS GOOD IN THE SUMMER, THOUGH.
LINED UP.
IS THIS... YOUR SPOT, HAWATARI-SAN?
I CAN'T IMAGINE THAT RITSUKA FOUND IT.
YES.
I'VE ALWAYS COME HERE.
AND... YOU CAN CALL ME YUIKO.

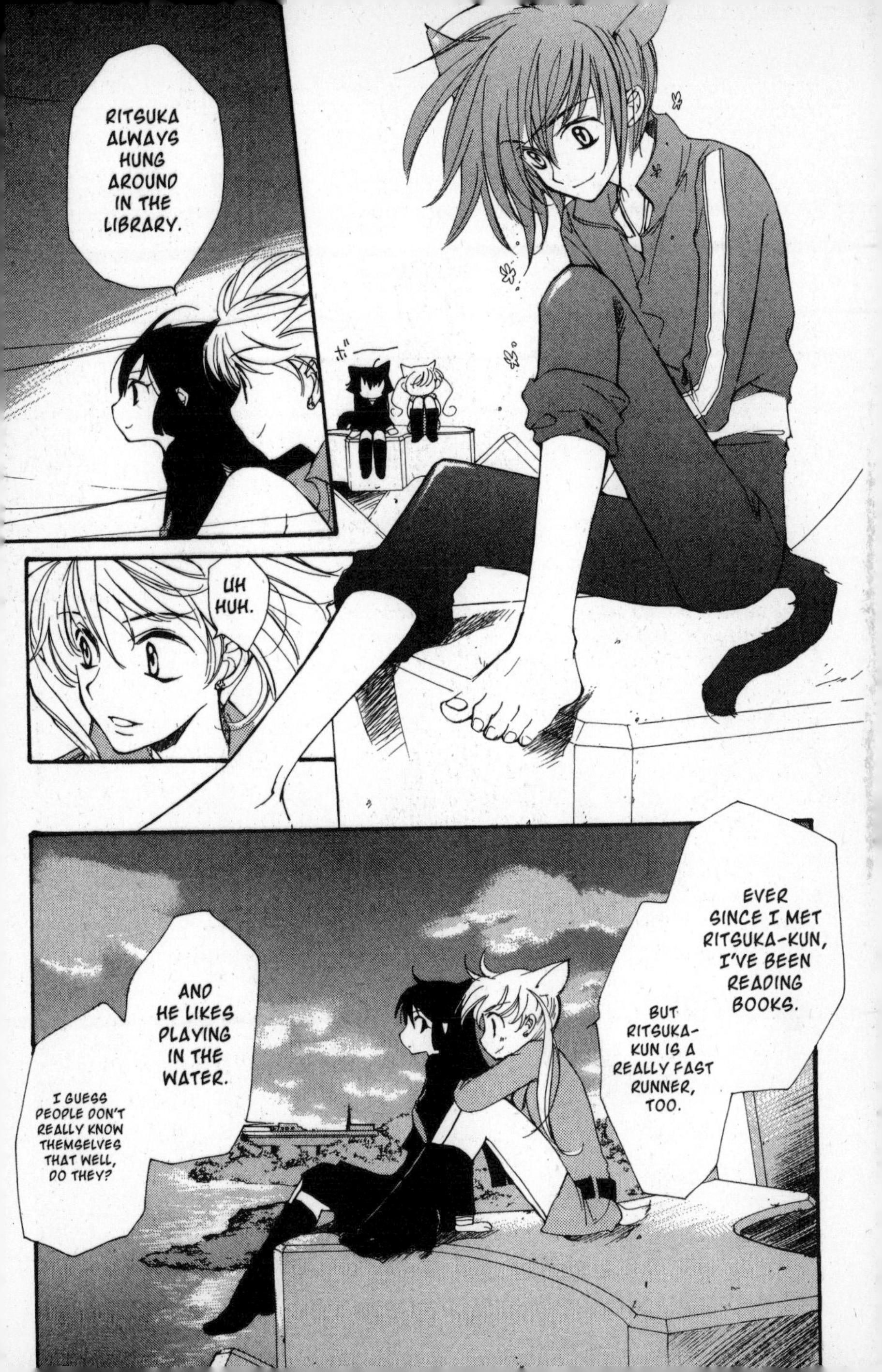
RITSUKA ALWAYS HUNG AROUND IN THE LIBRARY.
UH HUH.
EVER SINCE I MET RITSUKA-KUN, I'VE BEEN READING BOOKS.
BUT RITSUKA-KUN IS A REALLY FAST RUNNER, TOO.
AND HE LIKES PLAYING IN THE WATER.
I GUESS PEOPLE DON'T REALLY KNOW THEMSELVES THAT WELL, DO THEY?

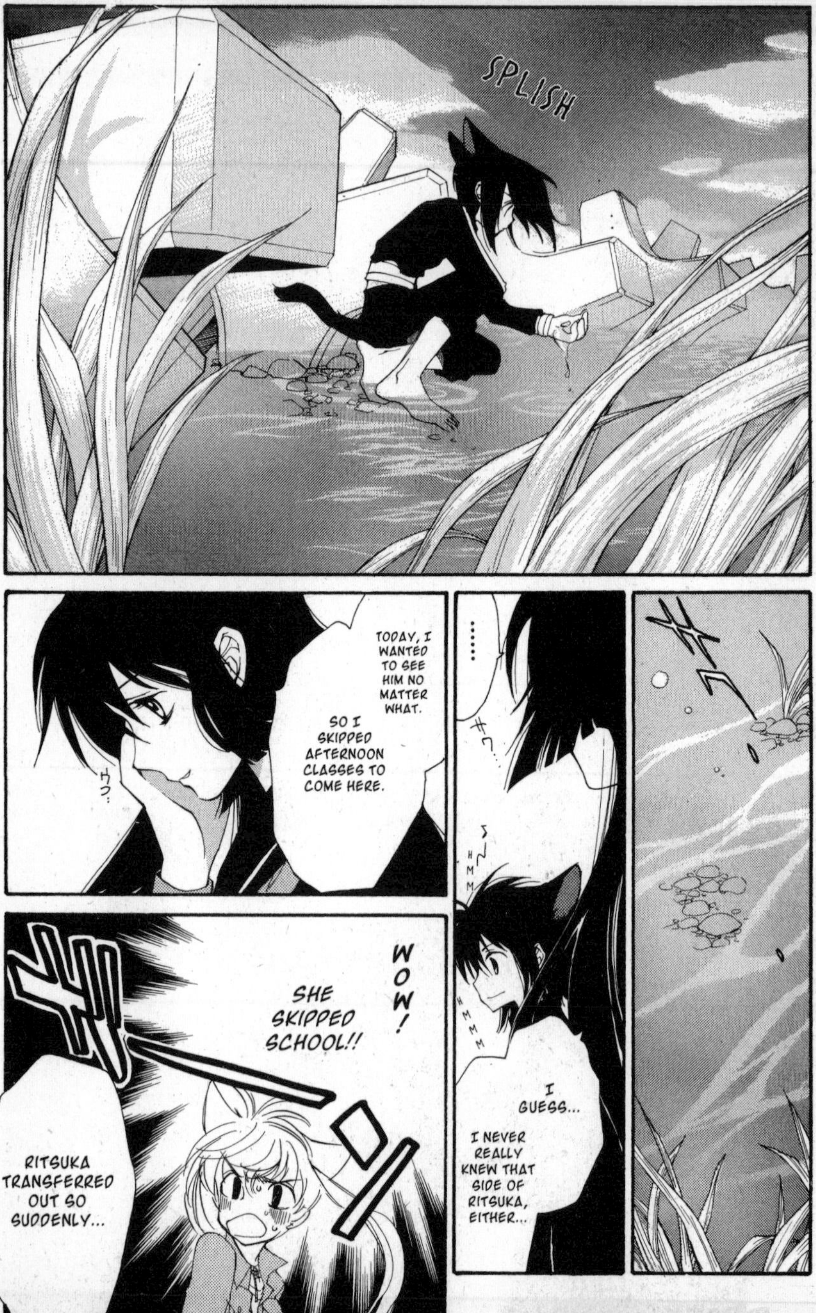
SPLISH
......
HMM
HMM
I GUESS...
I NEVER REALLY KNEW THAT SIDE OF RITSUKA, EITHER...
TODAY, I WANTED TO SEE HIM NO MATTER WHAT.
SO I SKIPPED AFTERNOON CLASSES TO COME HERE.
WOW!
SHE SKIPPED SCHOOL!!
RITSUKA TRANSFERRED OUT SO SUDDENLY...

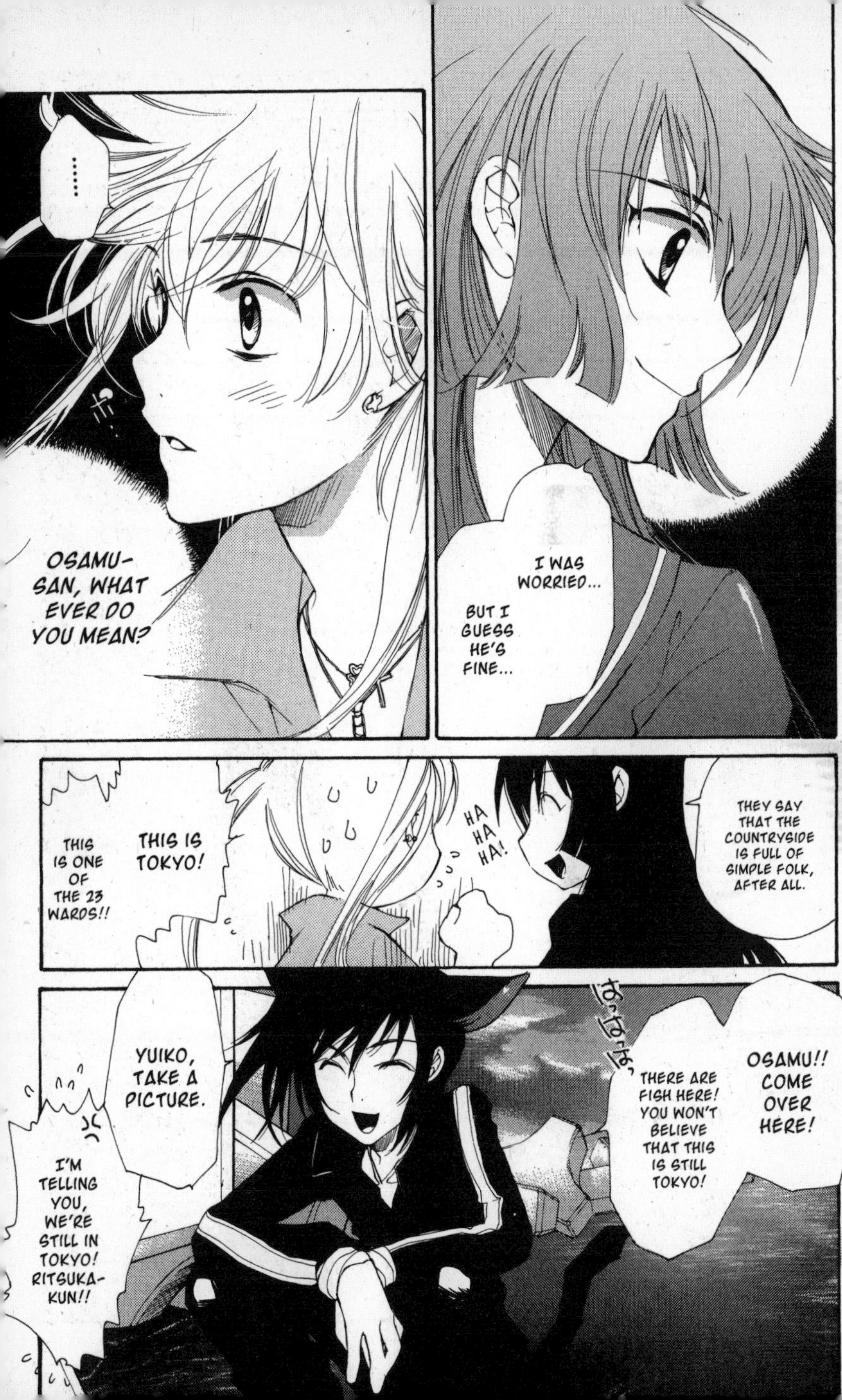
I WAS WORRIED...
BUT I GUESS HE'S FINE...
......
OSAMU-SAN, WHAT EVER DO YOU MEAN?
THEY SAY THAT THE COUNTRYSIDE IS FULL OF SIMPLE FOLK, AFTER ALL.
HA HA HA!
THIS IS TOKYO!
THIS IS ONE OF THE 23 WARDS!!
OSAMU!! COME OVER HERE!
THERE ARE FISH HERE! YOU WON'T BELIEVE THAT THIS IS STILL TOKYO!
YUIKO, TAKE A PICTURE.
I'M TELLING YOU, WE'RE STILL IN TOKYO! RITSUKA-KUN!!

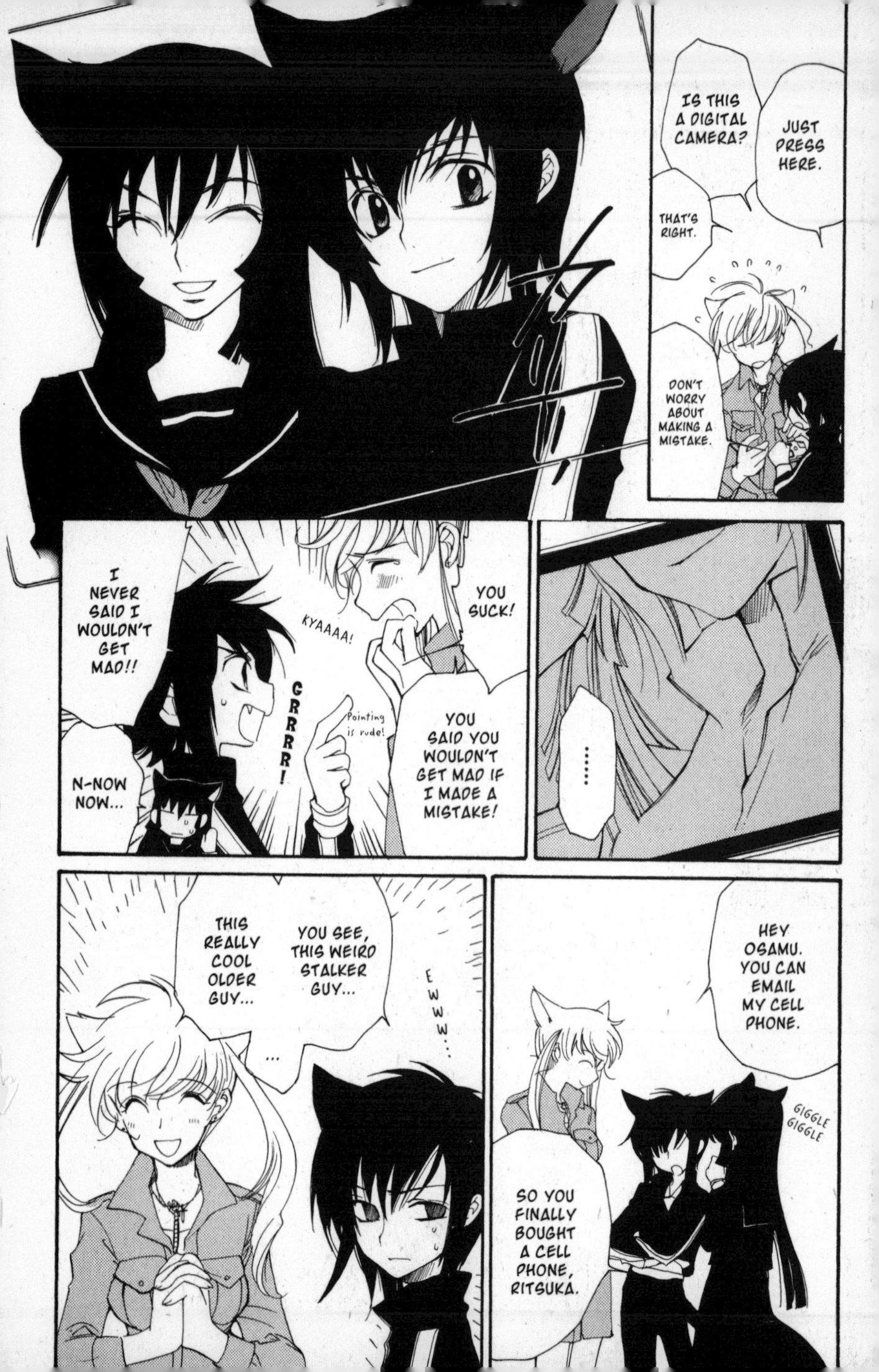
IS THIS A DIGITAL CAMERA?
JUST PRESS HERE.
THAT'S RIGHT.
DON'T WORRY ABOUT MAKING A MISTAKE.
......
YOU SUCK!
KYAAAA!
YOU SAID YOU WOULDN'T GET MAD IF I MADE A MISTAKE!
Pointing is rude!
GRRRR!
I NEVER SAID I WOULDN'T GET MAD!!
N-NOW NOW...
HEY OSAMU. YOU CAN EMAIL MY CELL PHONE.
GIGGLE GIGGLE
SO YOU FINALLY BOUGHT A CELL PHONE, RITSUKA.
EWWW...
YOU SEE, THIS WEIRD STALKER GUY...
THIS REALLY COOL OLDER GUY...
...

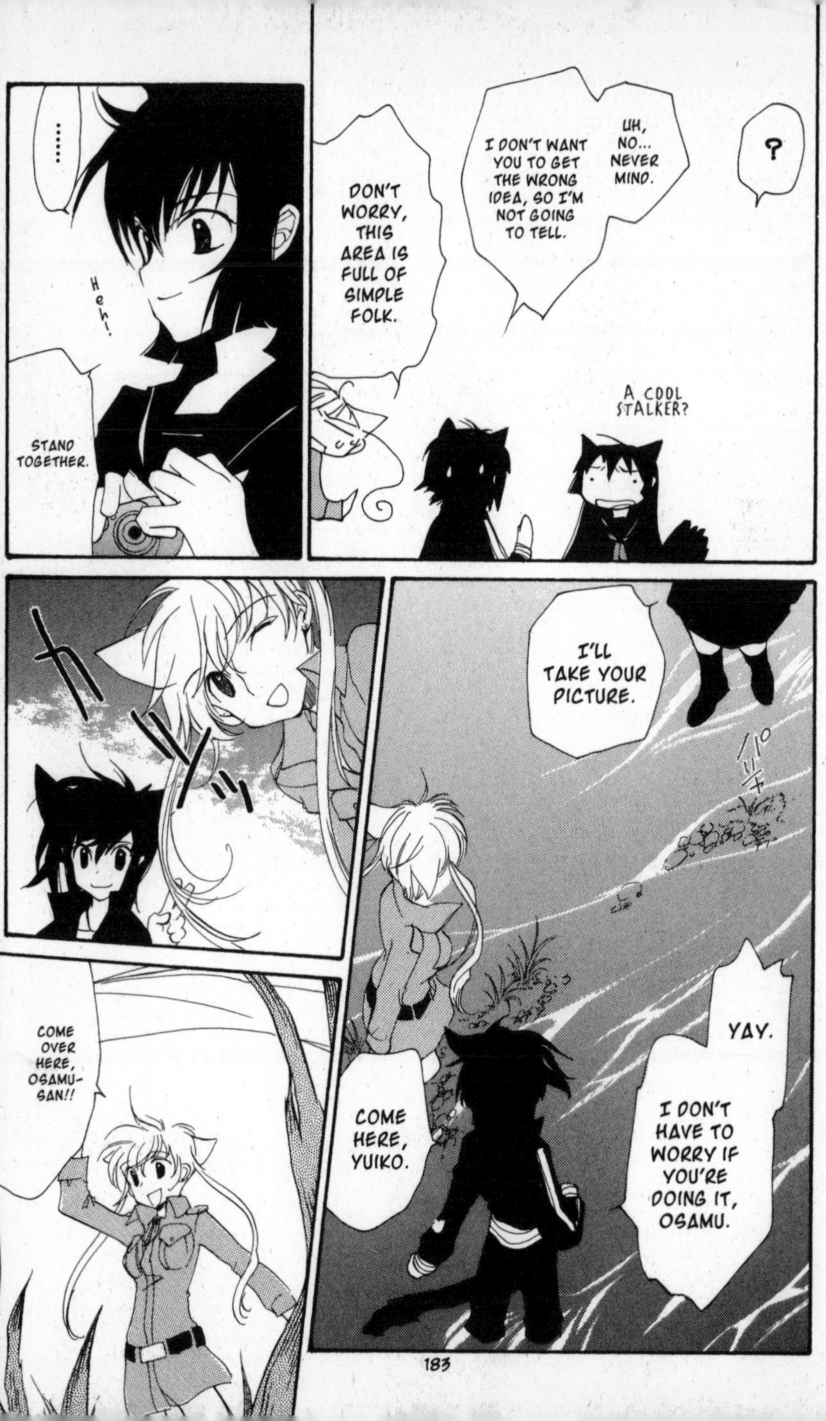
?
UH, NO... NEVER MIND.
I DON'T WANT YOU TO GET THE WRONG IDEA, SO I'M NOT GOING TO TELL.
DON'T WORRY, THIS AREA IS FULL OF SIMPLE FOLK.
A COOL STALKER?
......
Heh!
STAND TOGETHER.
I'LL TAKE YOUR PICTURE.
YAY.
I DON'T HAVE TO WORRY IF YOU'RE DOING IT, OSAMU.
COME HERE, YUIKO.
COME OVER HERE, OSAMU-SAN!!

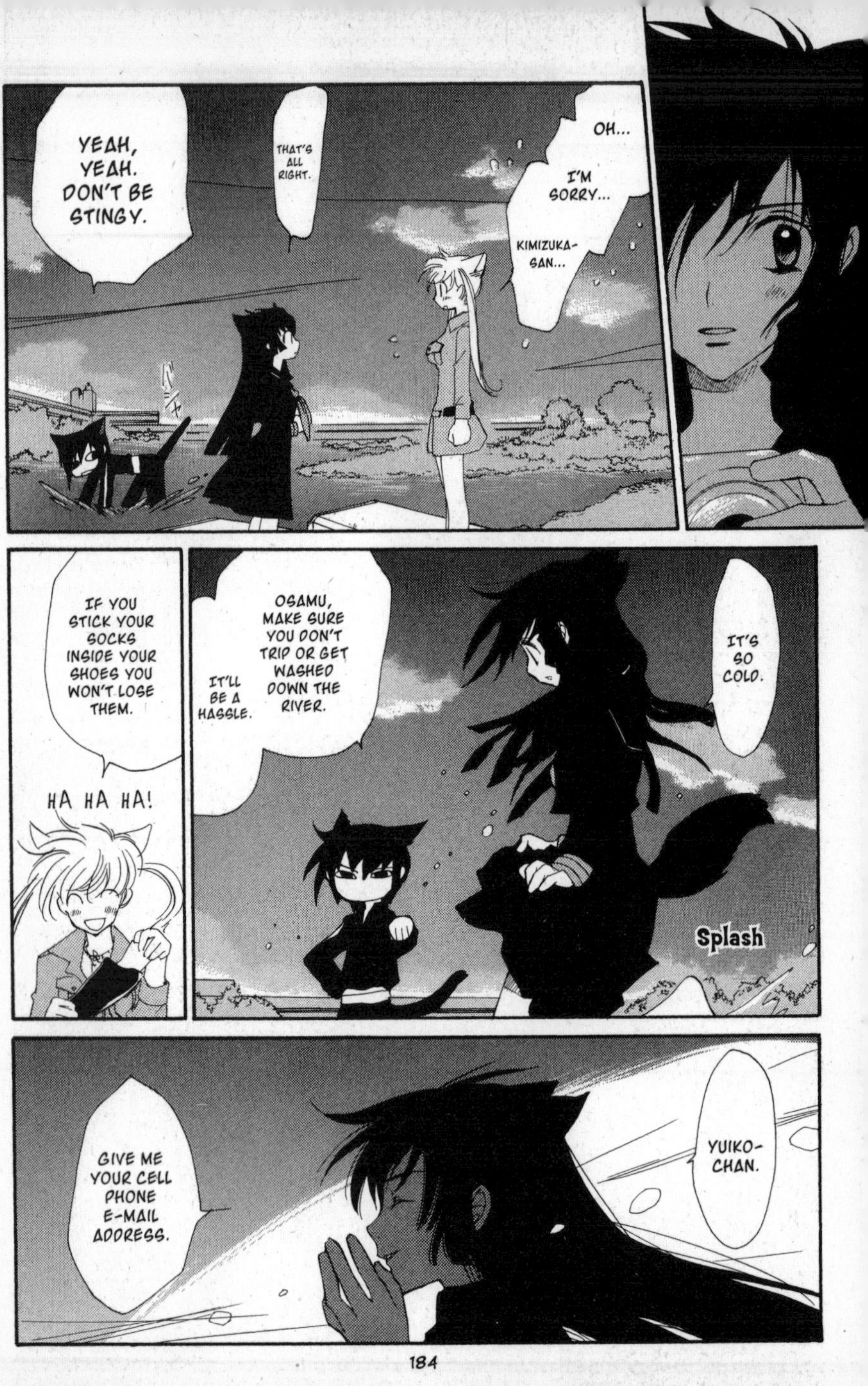
OH... I'M SORRY... KIMIZUKA-SAN...
THAT'S ALL RIGHT.
YEAH, YEAH. DON'T BE STINGY.
IT'S SO COLD.
OSAMU, MAKE SURE YOU DON'T TRIP OR GET WASHED DOWN THE RIVER.
IT'LL BE A HASSLE.
Splash
IF YOU STICK YOUR SOCKS INSIDE YOUR SHOES YOU WON'T LOSE THEM.
HA HA HA!
YUIKO-CHAN.
GIVE ME YOUR CELL PHONE E-MAIL ADDRESS.

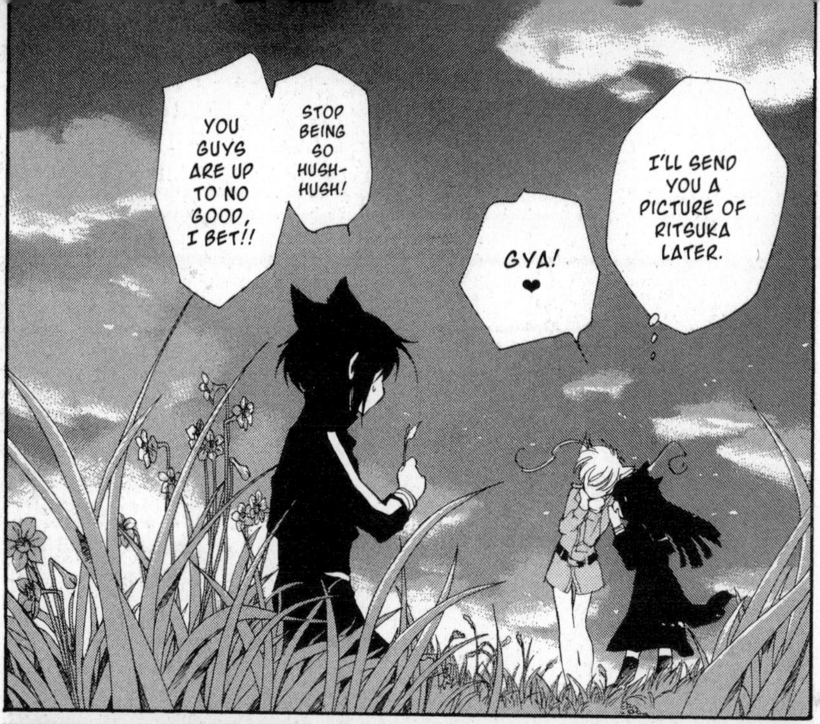
I'LL SEND YOU A PICTURE OF RITSUKA LATER.
GYA! ❤
STOP BEING SO HUSH-HUSH!
YOU GUYS ARE UP TO NO GOOD, I BET!!

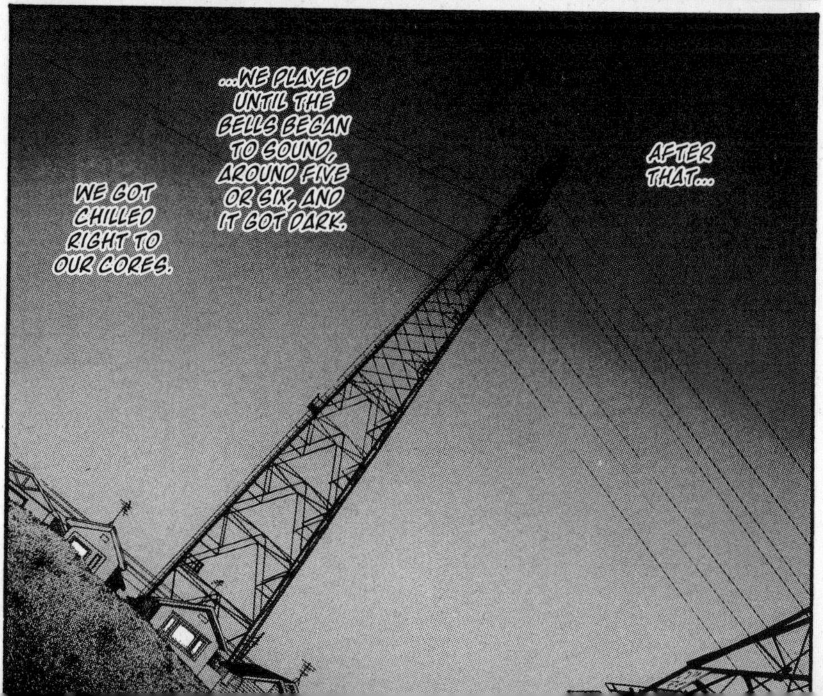
AFTER THAT...
...WE PLAYED UNTIL THE BELLS BEGAN TO SOUND, AROUND FIVE OR SIX, AND IT GOT DARK.
WE GOT CHILLED RIGHT TO OUR CORES.

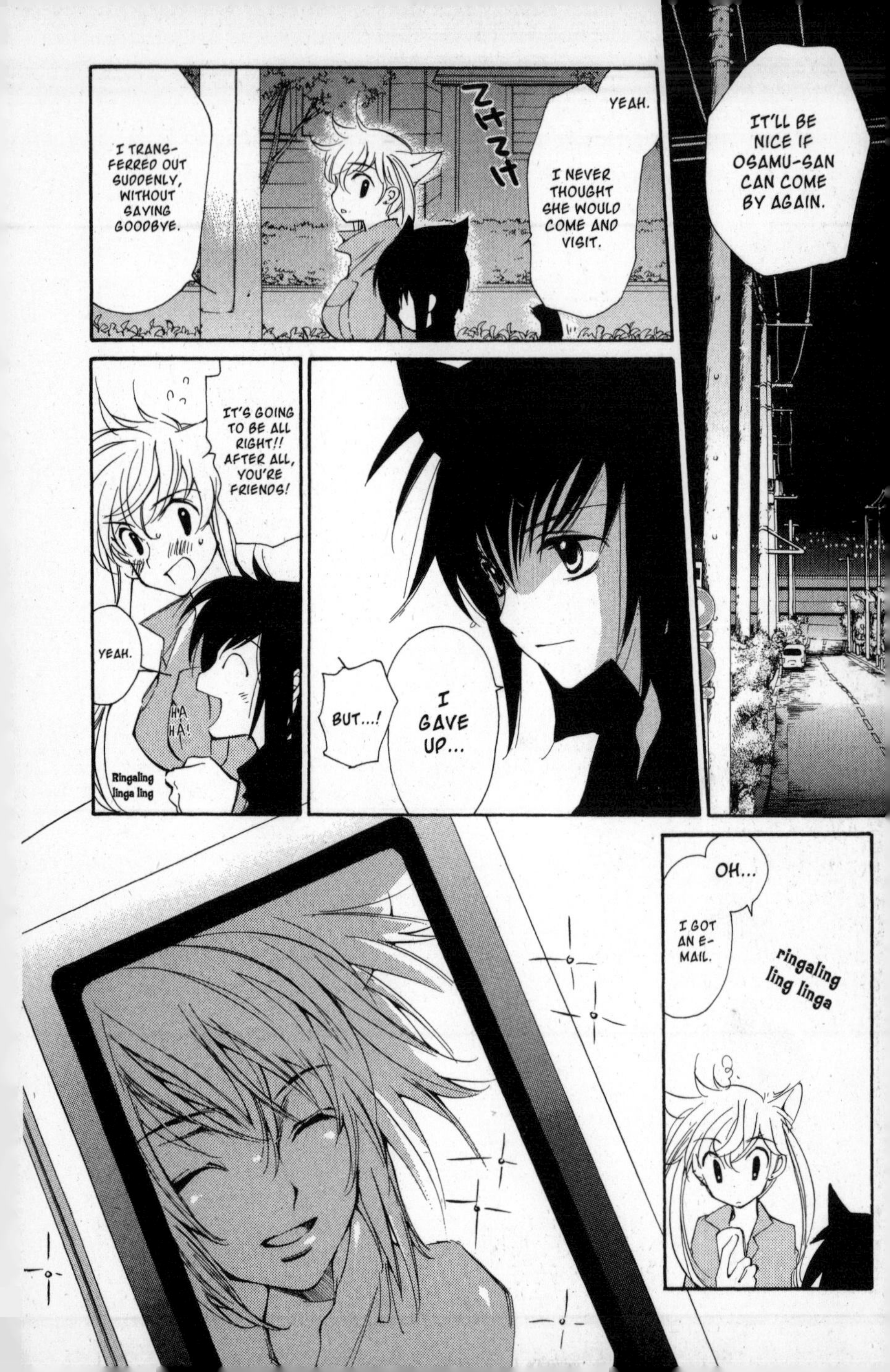
IT'LL BE NICE IF OSAMU-SAN CAN COME BY AGAIN.
YEAH.
I NEVER THOUGHT SHE WOULD COME AND VISIT.
てけてけ
I TRANS-FERRED OUT SUDDENLY, WITHOUT SAYING GOODBYE.
I GAVE UP...
BUT...!
IT'S GOING TO BE ALL RIGHT!! AFTER ALL, YOU'RE FRIENDS!
YEAH.
HA HA!
Ringaling linga ling
OH...
I GOT AN E-MAIL.
ringaling ling linga

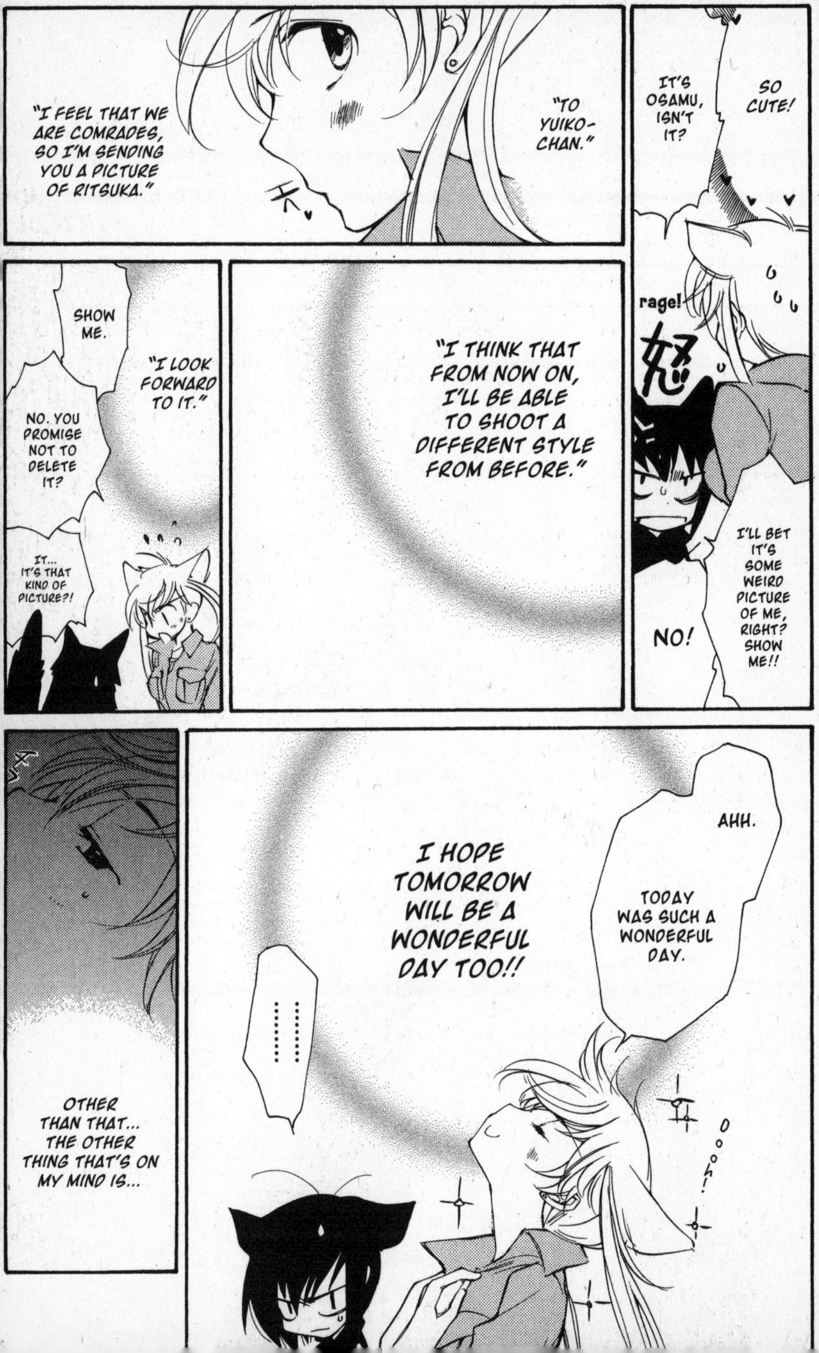
SO CUTE!
IT'S OSAMU, ISN'T IT?
rage!
I'LL BET IT'S SOME WEIRD PICTURE OF ME, RIGHT? SHOW ME!!
NO!
"TO YUIKO-CHAN."
"I FEEL THAT WE ARE COMRADES, SO I'M SENDING YOU A PICTURE OF RITSUKA."
"I THINK THAT FROM NOW ON, I'LL BE ABLE TO SHOOT A DIFFERENT STYLE FROM BEFORE."
"I LOOK FORWARD TO IT."
SHOW ME.
NO. YOU PROMISE NOT TO DELETE IT?
IT... IT'S THAT KIND OF PICTURE?!
AHH.
TODAY WAS SUCH A WONDERFUL DAY.
I HOPE TOMORROW WILL BE A WONDERFUL DAY TOO!!
......
Oooh!
OTHER THAN THAT... THE OTHER THING THAT'S ON MY MIND IS...

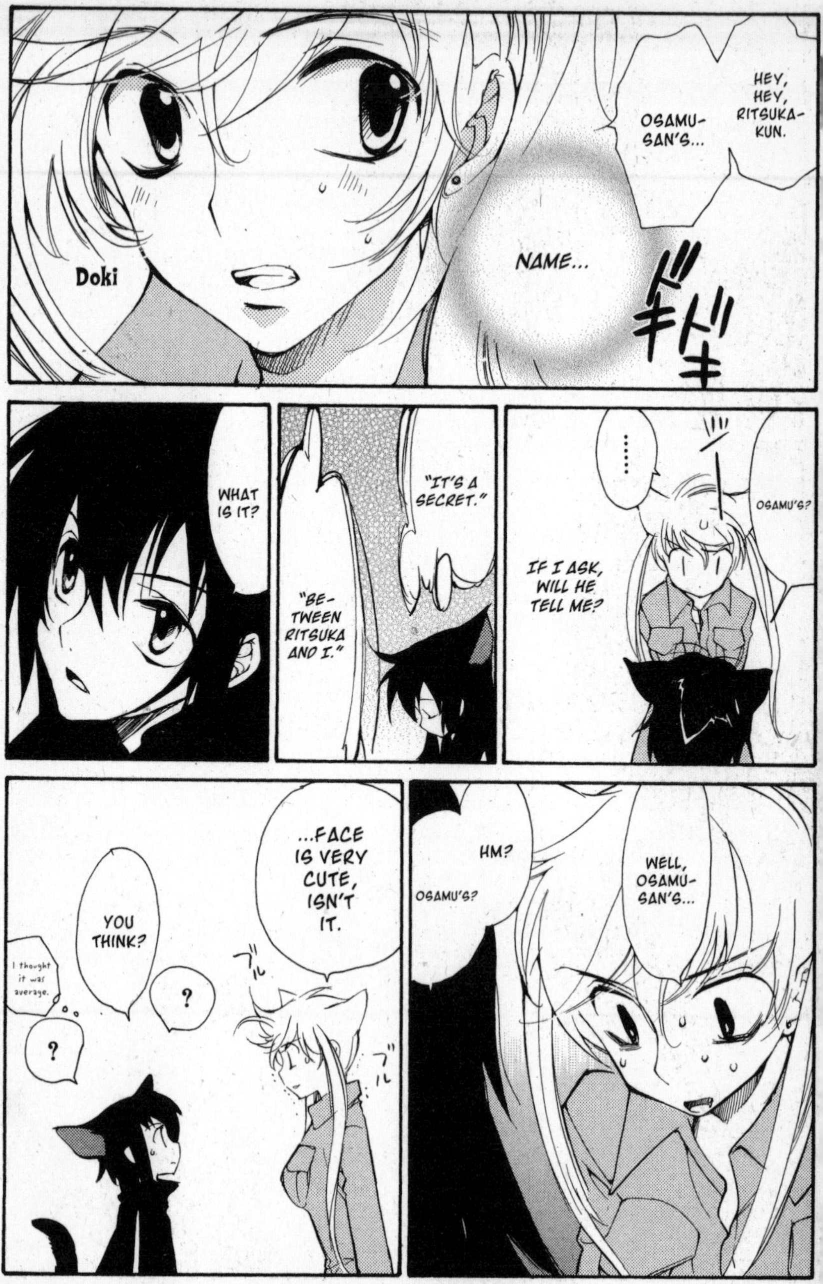
HEY, HEY, RITSUKA-KUN.
OSAMU-SAN'S...
NAME...
ドキドキ
Doki
......
OSAMU'S?
IF I ASK, WILL HE TELL ME?
"IT'S A SECRET."
"BE-TWEEN RITSUKA AND I."
WHAT IS IT?
WELL, OSAMU-SAN'S...
HM?
OSAMU'S?
...FACE IS VERY CUTE, ISN'T IT.
ブル
ブル
YOU THINK?
?
?
I thought it was average.

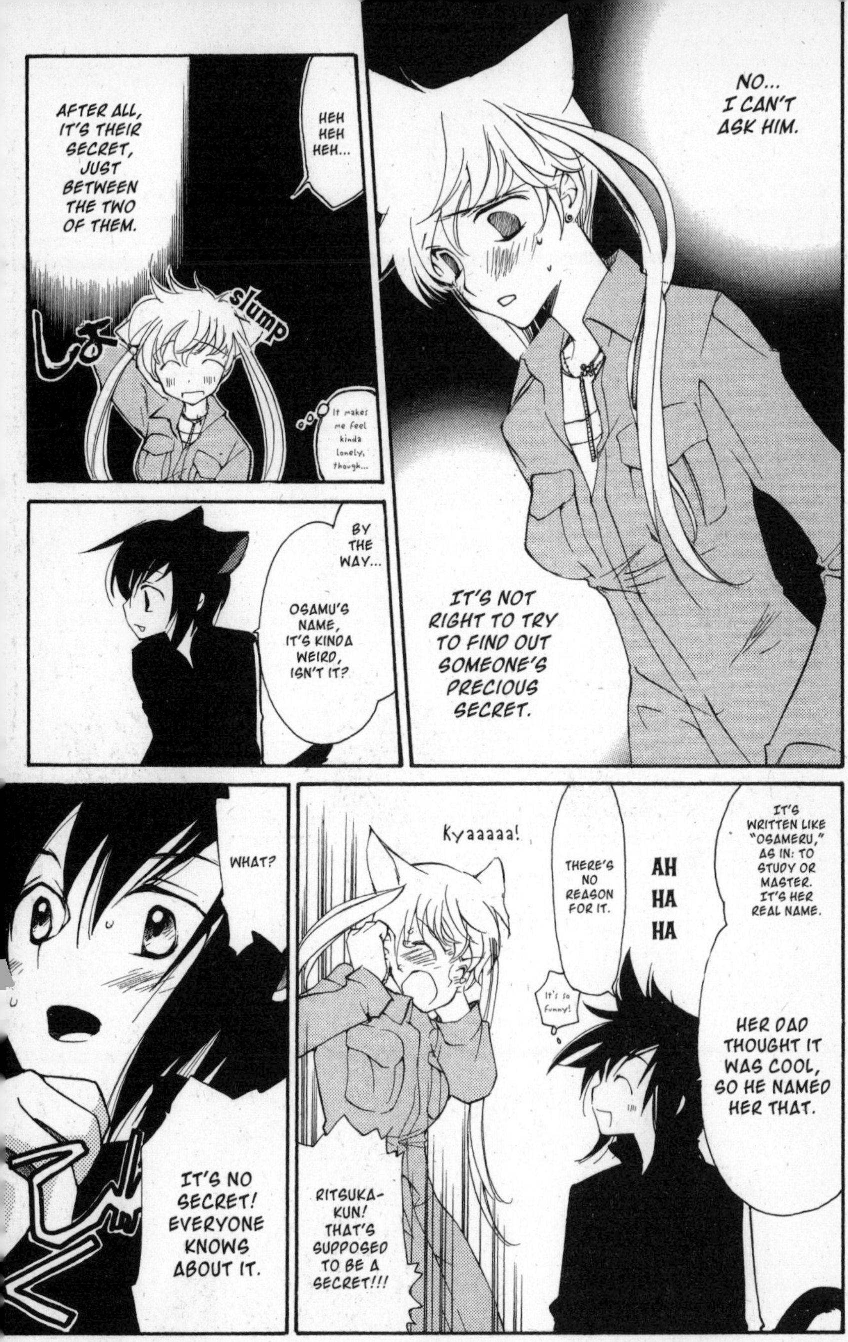
NO... I CAN'T ASK HIM.
IT'S NOT RIGHT TO TRY TO FIND OUT SOMEONE'S PRECIOUS SECRET.
HEH HEH HEH...
AFTER ALL, IT'S THEIR SECRET, JUST BETWEEN THE TWO OF THEM.
slump
It makes me feel kinda lonely, though...
BY THE WAY...
OSAMU'S NAME, IT'S KINDA WEIRD, ISN'T IT?
IT'S WRITTEN LIKE "OSAMERU," AS IN: TO STUDY OR MASTER. IT'S HER REAL NAME.
AH HA HA
THERE'S NO REASON FOR IT.
Kyaaaaa!
HER DAD THOUGHT IT WAS COOL, SO HE NAMED HER THAT.
It's so funny!
RITSUKA-KUN! THAT'S SUPPOSED TO BE A SECRET!!!
WHAT?
IT'S NO SECRET! EVERYONE KNOWS ABOUT IT.

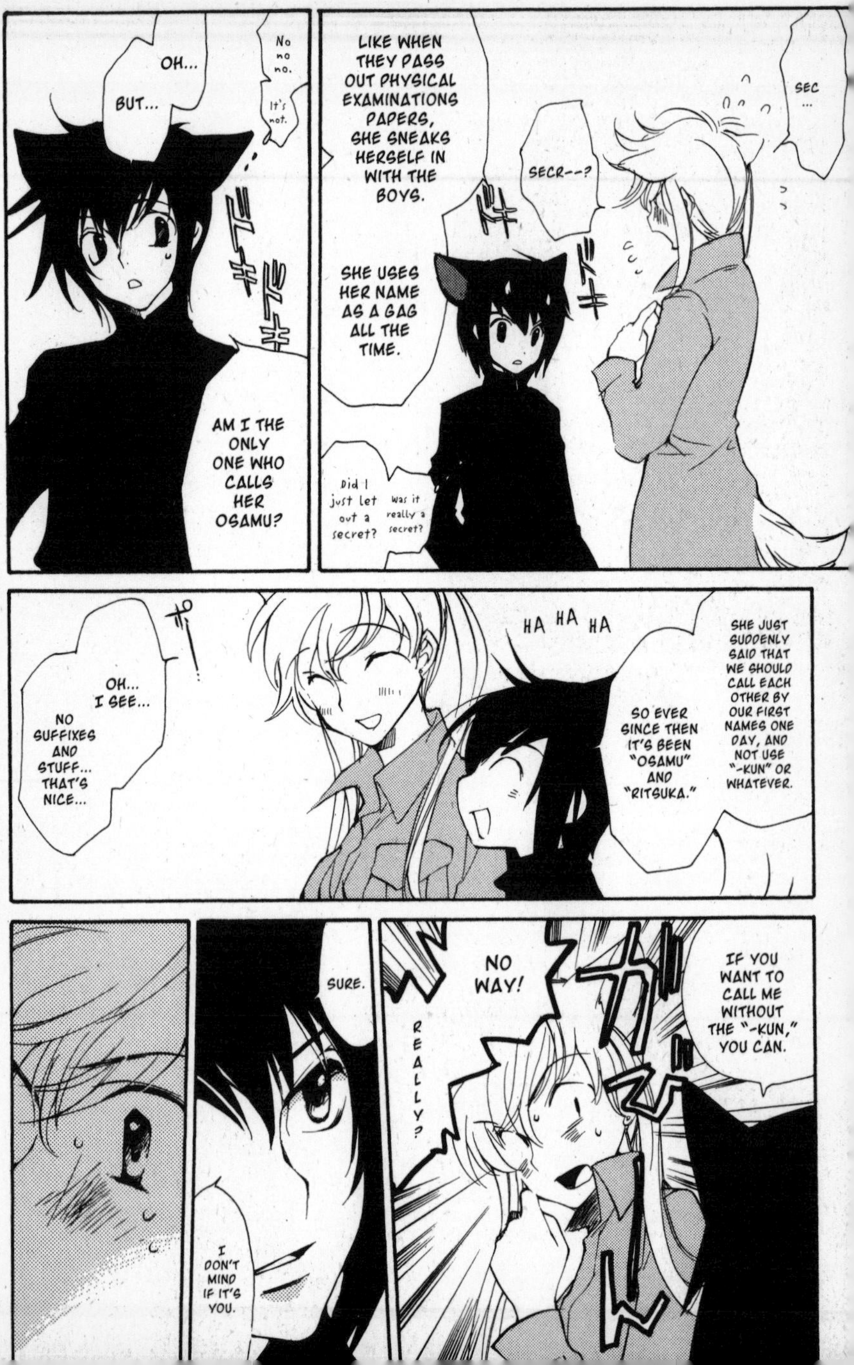
SEC...
SECR--?
LIKE WHEN THEY PASS OUT PHYSICAL EXAMINATIONS PAPERS, SHE SNEAKS HERSELF IN WITH THE BOYS.
SHE USES HER NAME AS A GAG ALL THE TIME.
Was it really a secret?
Did I just let out a secret?
No no no.
It's not.
OH... BUT...
AM I THE ONLY ONE WHO CALLS HER OSAMU?
SHE JUST SUDDENLY SAID THAT WE SHOULD CALL EACH OTHER BY OUR FIRST NAMES ONE DAY, AND NOT USE "-KUN" OR WHATEVER.
SO EVER SINCE THEN IT'S BEEN "OSAMU" AND "RITSUKA."
HA HA HA
OH... I SEE...
NO SUFFIXES AND STUFF... THAT'S NICE...
IF YOU WANT TO CALL ME WITHOUT THE "-KUN," YOU CAN.
NO WAY!
REALLY?
SURE.
I DON'T MIND IF IT'S YOU.

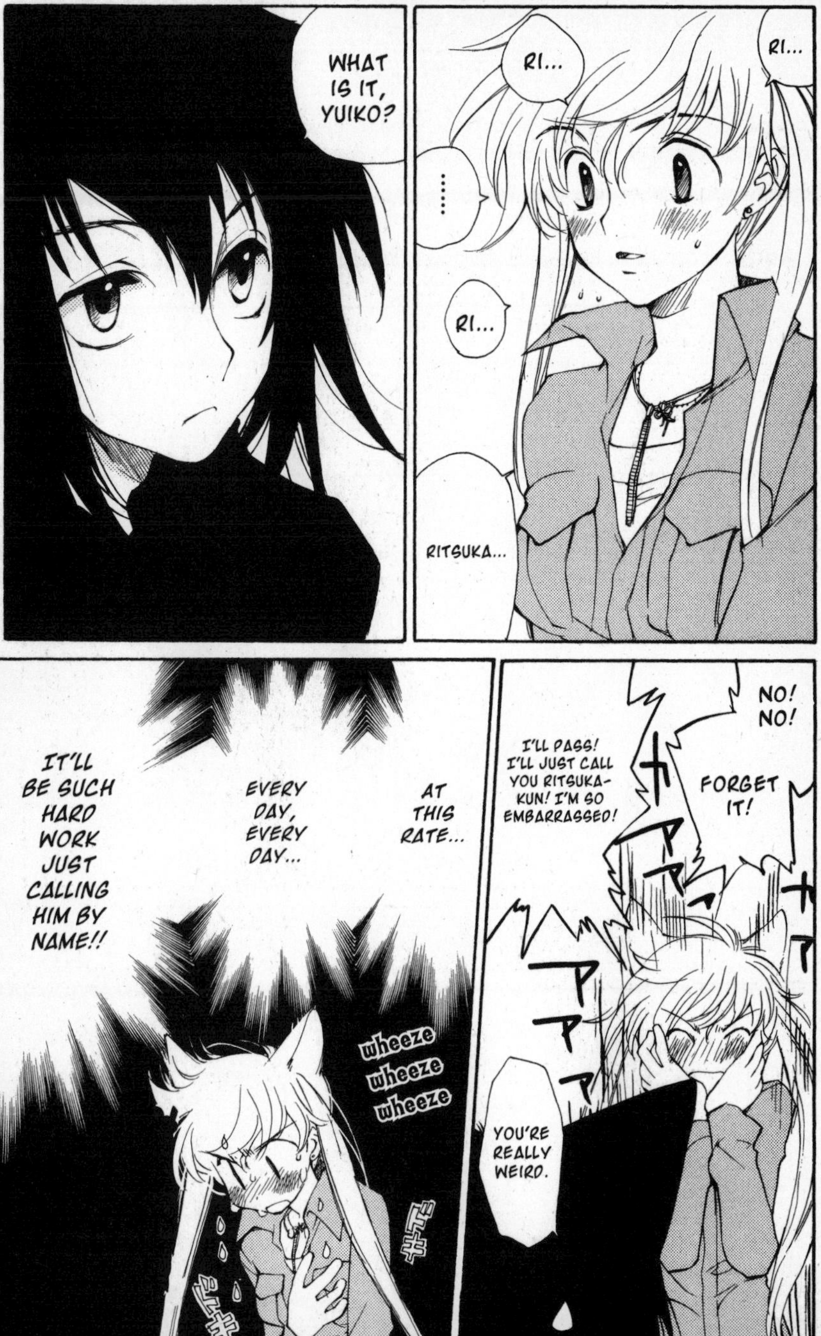
RI...
RI...
......
RI...
RITSUKA...
WHAT IS IT, YUIKO?
NO! NO!
FORGET IT!
I'LL PASS! I'LL JUST CALL YOU RITSUKA-KUN! I'M SO EMBARRASSED!
YOU'RE REALLY WEIRD.
AT THIS RATE...
EVERY DAY, EVERY DAY...
IT'LL BE SUCH HARD WORK JUST CALLING HIM BY NAME!!
wheeze wheeze wheeze

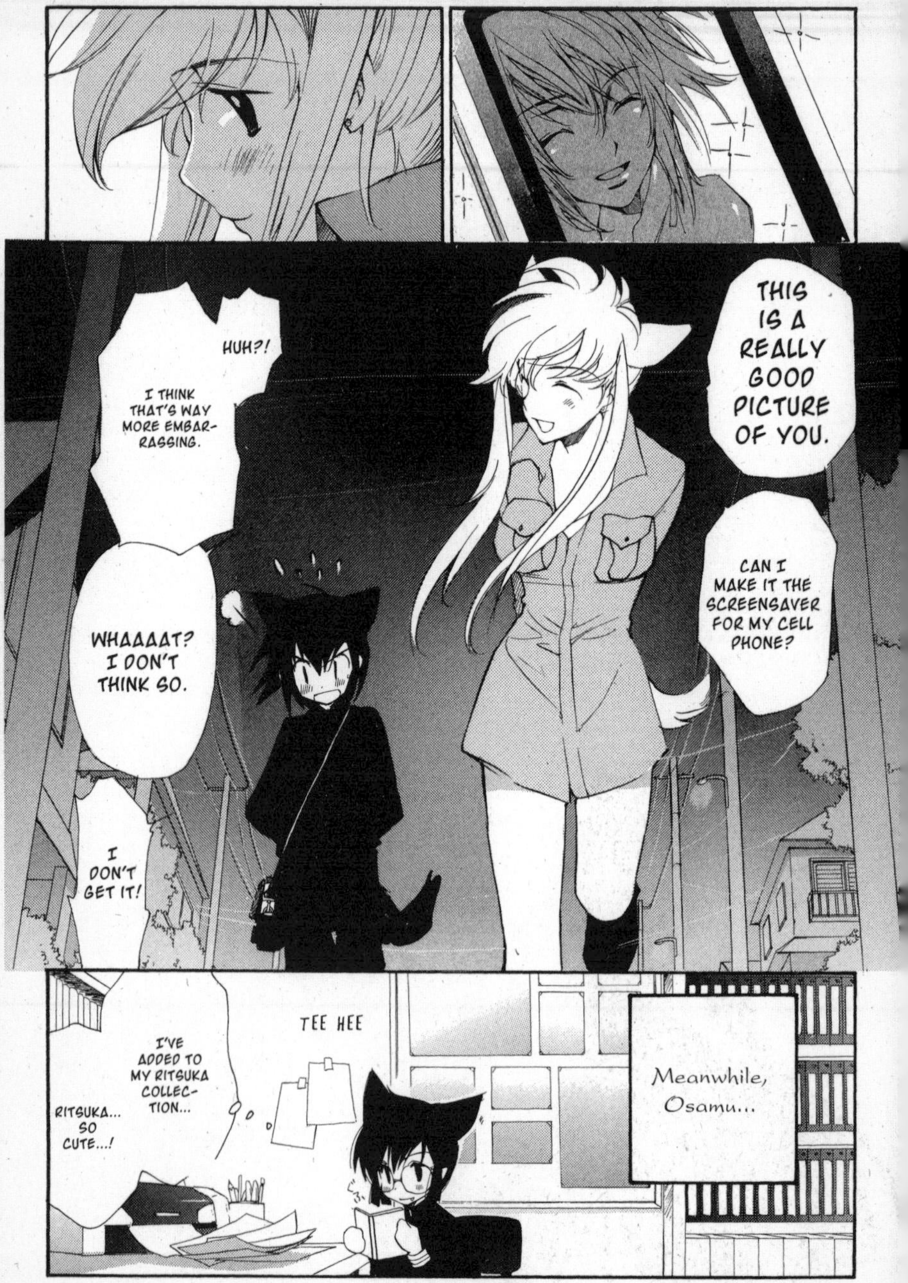
THIS IS A REALLY GOOD PICTURE OF YOU.
WHAAAAT? I DON'T THINK SO.
CAN I MAKE IT THE SCREENSAVER FOR MY CELL PHONE?
HUH?!
I THINK THAT'S WAY MORE EMBARRASSING.
I DON'T GET IT!
Meanwhile, Osamu...
TEE HEE
I'VE ADDED TO MY RITSUKA COLLECTION...
RITSUKA... SO CUTE...!

Loveless 4 The End

Postscript

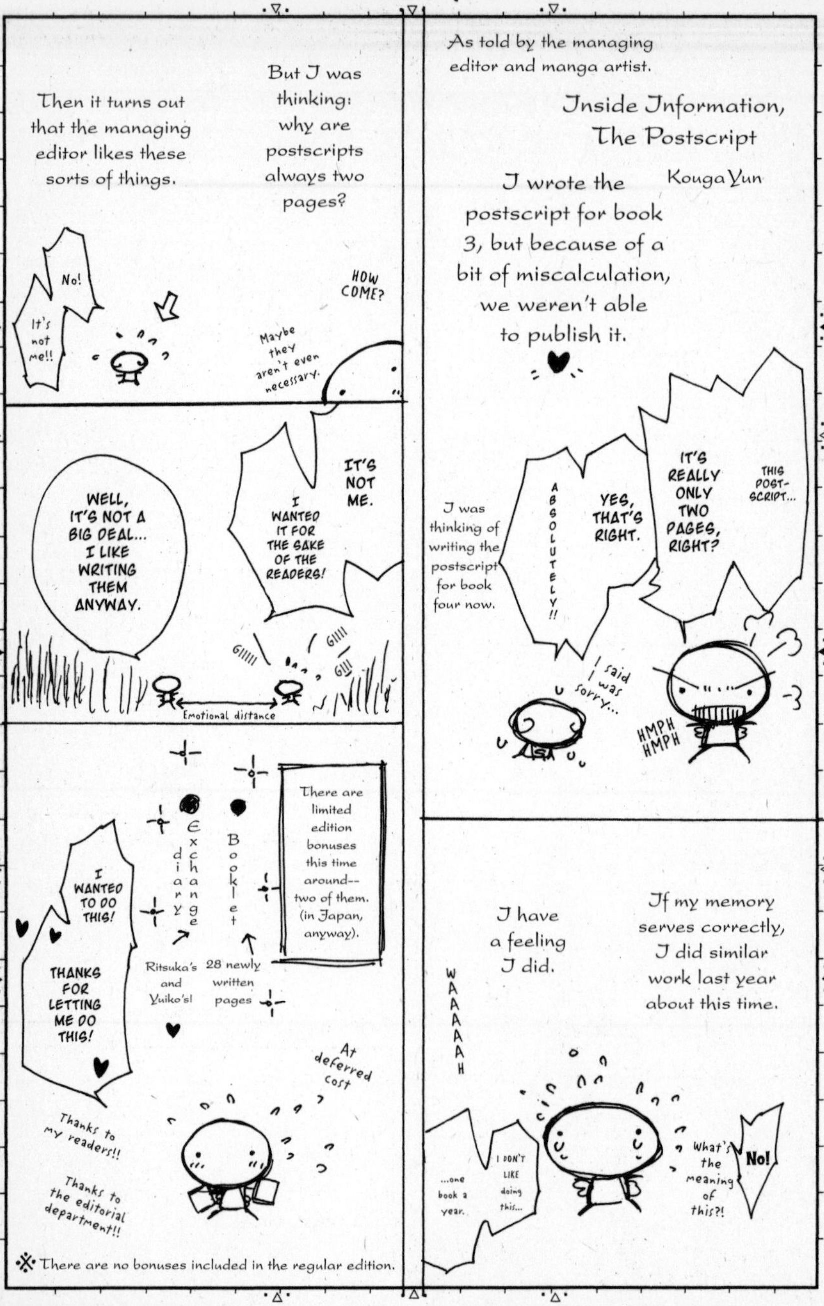
As told by the managing editor and manga artist.
Inside Information, The Postscript
Kouga Yun
I wrote the postscript for book 3, but because of a bit of miscalculation, we weren't able to publish it.
IT'S REALLY ONLY TWO PAGES, RIGHT?
THIS POST-SCRIPT...
YES, THAT'S RIGHT.
ABSOLUTELY!!
I was thinking of writing the postscript for book four now.
I said I was sorry...
HMPH HMPH
If my memory serves correctly, I did similar work last year about this time.
I have a feeling I did.
WAAAAAH
No!
What's the meaning of this?!
I DON'T LIKE doing this...
...one book a year.
But I was thinking: why are postscripts always two pages?
Then it turns out that the managing editor likes these sorts of things.
HOW COME?
Maybe they aren't even necessary.
No!
It's not me!!
IT'S NOT ME.
I WANTED IT FOR THE SAKE OF THE READERS!
WELL, IT'S NOT A BIG DEAL... I LIKE WRITING THEM ANYWAY.
GIIII
GIIII
GIIII
Emotional distance
There are limited edition bonuses this time around-- two of them. (in Japan, anyway).
Booklet
28 newly written pages
Exchange diary
Ritsuka's and Yuiko's!
I WANTED TO DO THIS!
THANKS FOR LETTING ME DO THIS!
At deferred cost
Thanks to my readers!!
Thanks to the editorial department!!
※ There are no bonuses included in the regular edition.

Postscript

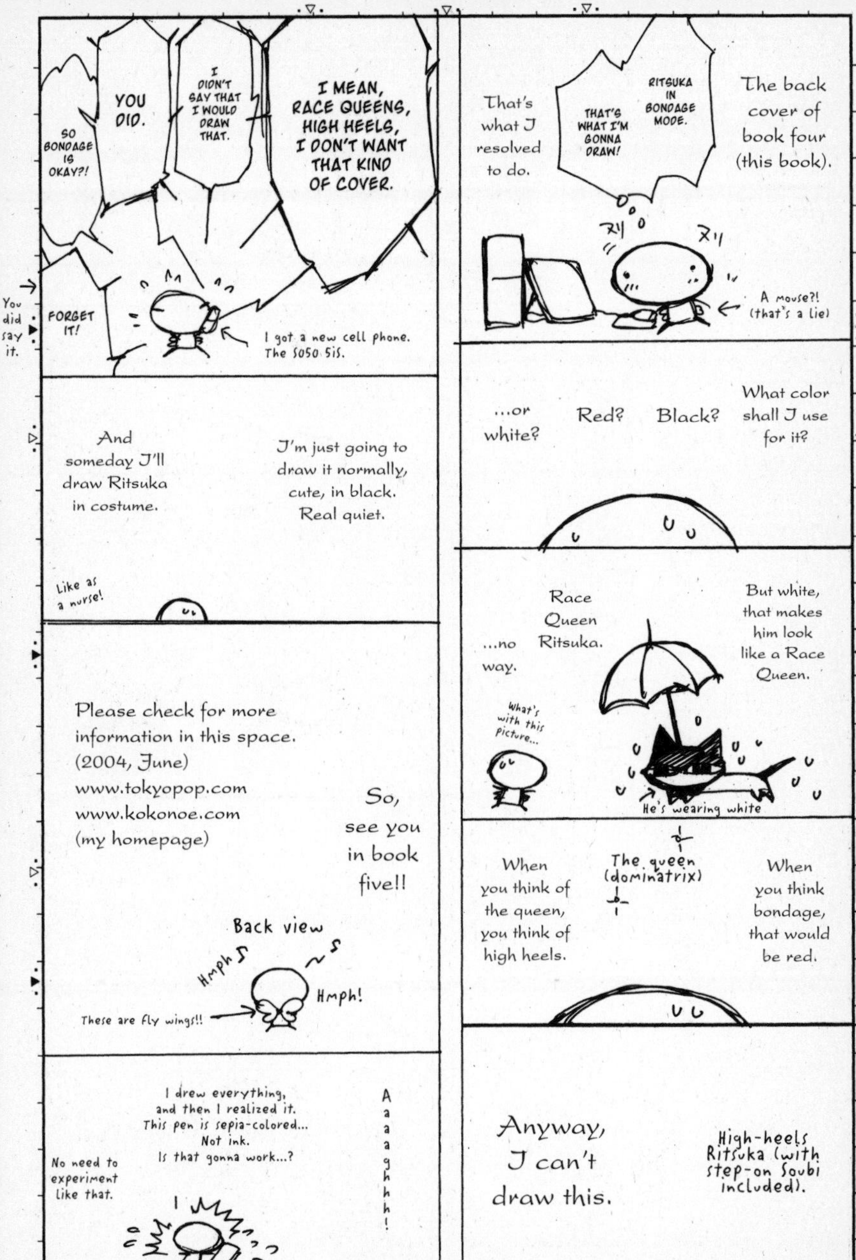

The back cover of book four (this book).
Ritsuka in bondage mode.
That's what I'm gonna draw!
That's what I resolved to do.
A mouse?! (that's a lie)
What color shall I use for it?
Black?
Red?
...or white?
But white, that makes him look like a Race Queen.
Race Queen Ritsuka.
...no way.
What's with this picture...
He's wearing white
When you think bondage, that would be red.
The queen (dominatrix)
When you think of the queen, you think of high heels.
High-heels Ritsuka (with step-on Soubi included).
Anyway, I can't draw this.
I mean, race queens, high heels, I don't want that kind of cover.
I didn't say that I would draw that.
You did.
So bondage is okay?!
Forget it!
You did say it.
I got a new cell phone. The 5050 5is.
I'm just going to draw it normally, cute, in black. Real quiet.
And someday I'll draw Ritsuka in costume.
Like as a nurse!
So, see you in book five!!
Please check for more information in this space.
(2004, June)
www.tokyopop.com
www.kokonoe.com
(my homepage)
Back view
Hmph!
Hmph
These are fly wings!!
Aaaaghhh!
I drew everything, and then I realized it. This pen is sepia-colored... Not ink. Is that gonna work...?
No need to experiment like that.
I

The End.

In The Next Volume of

LOVELESS

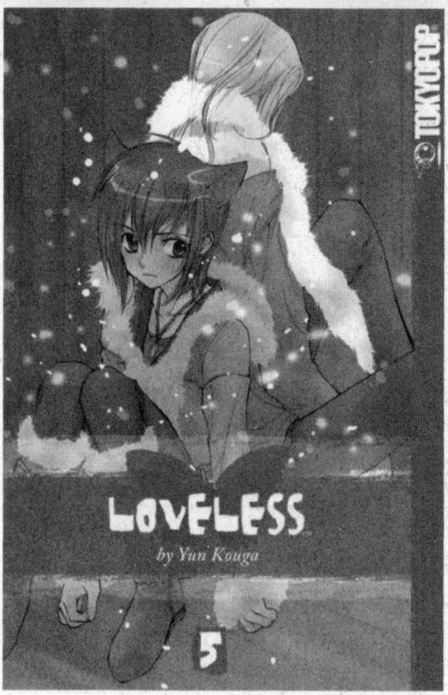
TOKYOPOP
LOVELESS
by Yun Kouga
5

Ritsuka skips school so he can rest up and stay up late talking to Seven through Wisdom Resurrection. Ritsu-sensei and Nagisa-sensei join the conversation as observers, and Soubi and the Zero boys watch from Ritsuka's side, as a shocking truth is revealed about Seimei. Ritsuka still has faith in his brother and his love for him, but evidence is building that Seimei's fate might not have been what Ritsuka believed it to be...

Loveless Vol. 5 Available May 2007

SPEAK LIKE A CHILD: THE INNER THOUGHTS OF CHILDREN IN LOVELESS.

It's surprisingly difficult for a writer to capture the inner mind a child. Characters either end up seeming younger than their years, or just like miniature adults, and kids are far more complex and varied than we grown-ups usually give them credit for. Anyone who has spent much time with children will have their own stories of how astute they can be, and one of my favorite aspects of Yun Kouga's writing is that she does an amazing job of describing and articulating the way children and young people see the world, both respecting their point of view and showing where it falls short.

Several characters point out that Ritsuka is surprisingly mature for his age. He's seen and experienced so much more than most 12-year-olds will ever go through, and while it has distanced him from his peers, it has also made him unexpectedly strong and well-grounded. He knows the avoidance techniques to keep from setting off his mother's fits of abuse, even if he doesn't understand the root cause of her madness (nor does the reader at this point, mind you). His internal monologues show that he's thoughtful, intelligent, aware of the world around him, and while he can come across as almost cynical at times (his ability to dodge Shinonome-sensei's good intentions is impressive), there's a rare and special kindness to him. His passionate advocacy of justice over something as trivial as Yuiko's strawberry jam rings very true. Sometimes Ritsuka has the sophistication to see shades of grey in the world around him, but in moments of high passion, his vision reverts to a childish black and white. Hurting someone's feelings is the worst possible crime for Ritsuka, and the reader can sense how betrayed he is when he begins to discover just how much his own beloved brother hurt Soubi.

However, for all the things he understands, part of his charm is the way he sometimes doesn't get the full implications of Soubi's many suggestive comments. He's (understandably) wary of Soubi's kisses even as he longs for human contact and companionship. He knows about sex and sexuality to some degree, but there are gaps in his awareness and bits of childish naivete. Soubi will make a joke that Ritsuka recognizes as off-color, but he'll miss the way in which Soubi relates that statement to their own relationship.

But one of my favorite scenes in the series is in the final chapter of this volume, dealing with Ritsuka's friend Osamu. I was unimpressed by it the first time I read it (yeah, yeah, everybody loves Ritsuka...), but upon further reflection, it's a great piece of storytelling and characterization. Both Osamu and Yuiko love Ritsuka for the child that he still is, in spite of all his sophistication, and the way they talk about him shows just how aware they are of the world they live in, and their place in it as children. Osamu comments that Ritsuka would never have thought to find Yuiko's favorite place along the river on his own, but he still likes playing in the water, now that it's been brought to his attention. Yuiko adds, in a bit of truly delightful childlike wisdom, that even though Ritsuka likes books, he's a really fast runner. In Yuiko's simple, clean-cut world, reading and running are contradictory activities, but her acceptance and appreciation for Ritsuka's ability to enjoy both hints at how much she understands him on a larger scale. It's an insightful comment on the boy who she is always watching from afar.

~Lillian Diaz-Przybyl

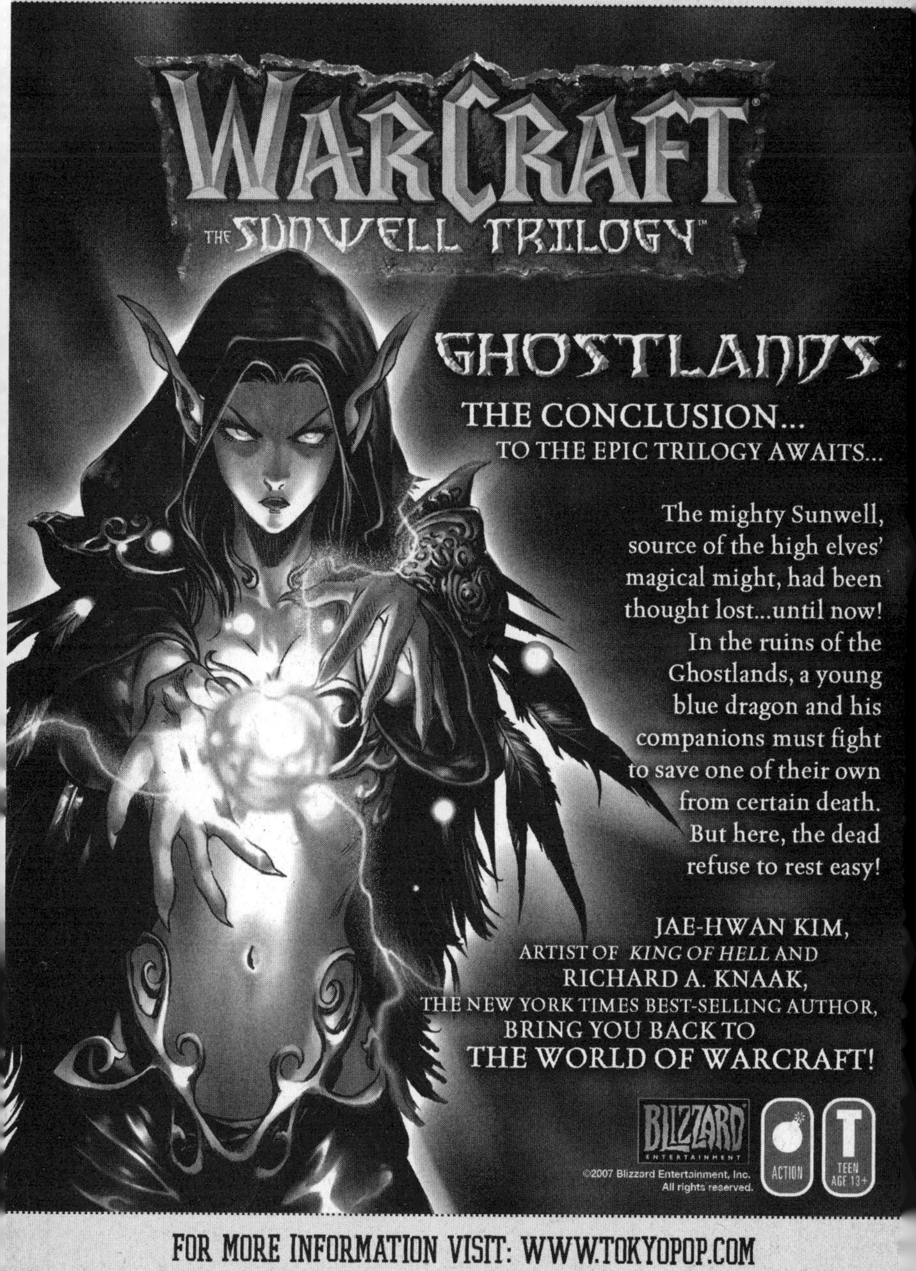
WARCRAFT
THE SUNWELL TRILOGY
GHOSTLANDS
THE CONCLUSION...
TO THE EPIC TRILOGY AWAITS...
The mighty Sunwell, source of the high elves' magical might, had been thought lost...until now! In the ruins of the Ghostlands, a young blue dragon and his companions must fight to save one of their own from certain death. But here, the dead refuse to rest easy!
JAE-HWAN KIM, ARTIST OF *KING OF HELL* AND RICHARD A. KNAAK, THE NEW YORK TIMES BEST-SELLING AUTHOR, BRING YOU BACK TO THE WORLD OF WARCRAFT!
BLIZZARD ENTERTAINMENT
©2007 Blizzard Entertainment, Inc. All rights reserved.
ACTION
T
TEEN AGE 13+

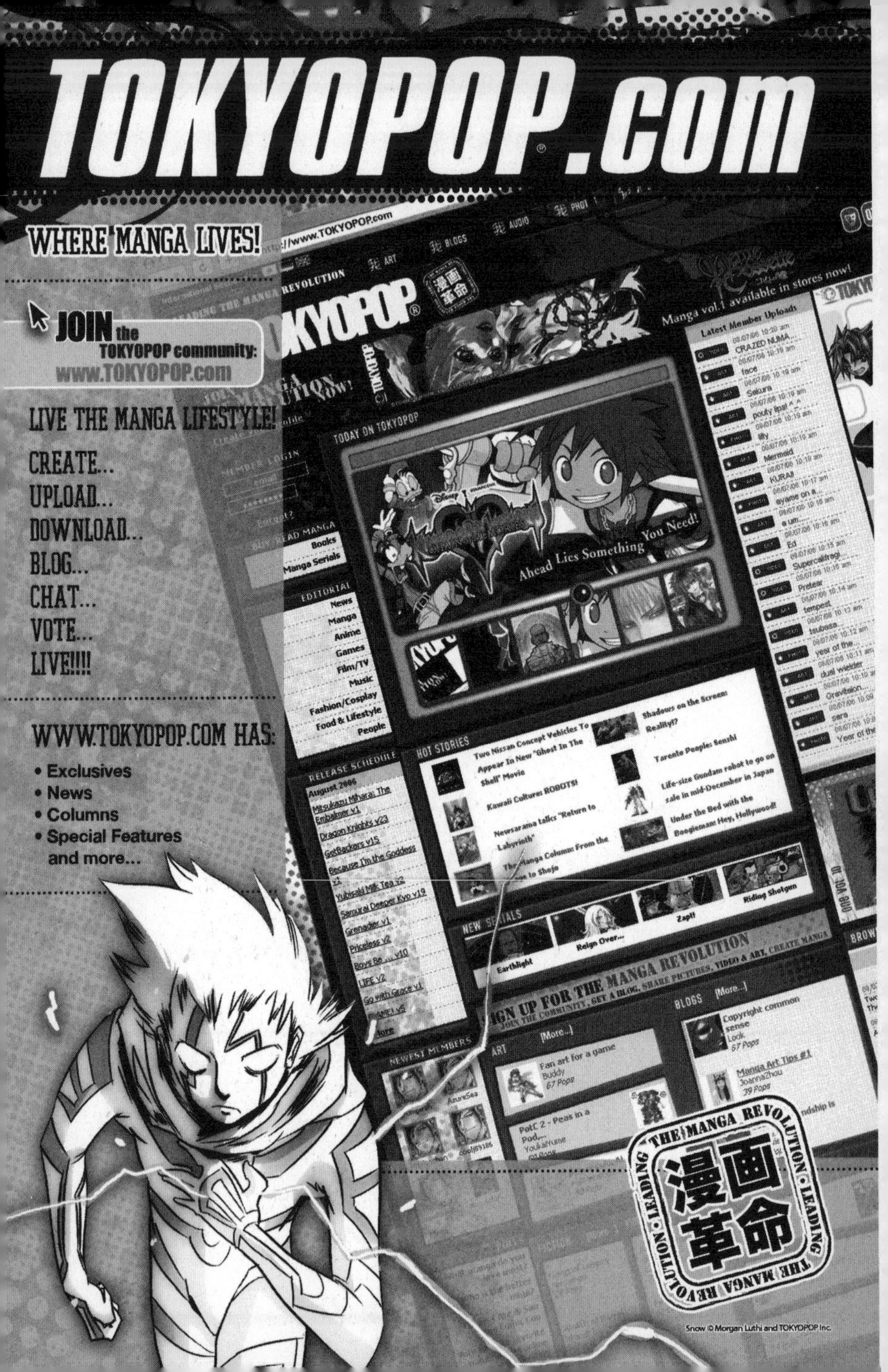
TOKYOPOP.com
WHERE MANGA LIVES!
JOIN the TOKYOPOP community:
www.TOKYOPOP.com
LIVE THE MANGA LIFESTYLE!
CREATE...
UPLOAD...
DOWNLOAD...
BLOG...
CHAT...
VOTE...
LIVE!!!!
WWW.TOKYOPOP.COM HAS:
• Exclusives
• News
• Columns
• Special Features
and more...
THE MANGA REVOLUTION • LEADING
漫画革命
Snow © Morgan Luthi and TOKYOPOP Inc.

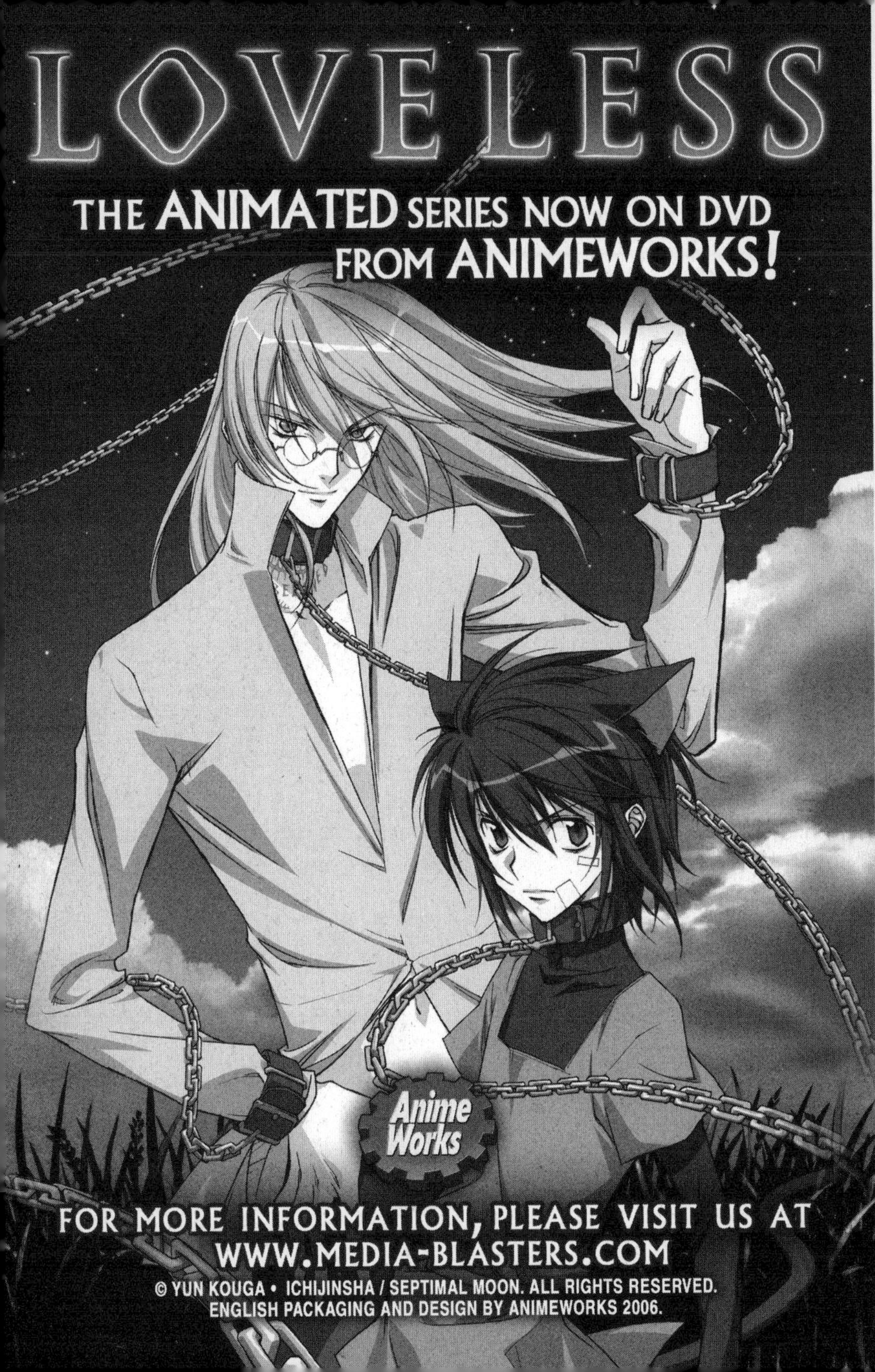
LOVELESS
THE ANIMATED SERIES NOW ON DVD
FROM ANIMEWORKS!
Anime Works
FOR MORE INFORMATION, PLEASE VISIT US AT
WWW.MEDIA-BLASTERS.COM
© YUN KOUGA • ICHIJINSHA / SEPTIMAL MOON. ALL RIGHTS RESERVED.
ENGLISH PACKAGING AND DESIGN BY ANIMEWORKS 2006.

STOP!

This is the back of the book.
You wouldn't want to spoil a great ending!

This book is printed "manga-style," in the authentic Japanese right-to-left format. Since none of the artwork has been flipped or altered, readers get to experience the story just as the creator intended. You've been asking for it, so TOKYOPOP® delivered: authentic, hot-off-the-press, and far more fun!

DIRECTIONS

If this is your first time reading manga-style, here's a quick guide to help you understand how it works.

It's easy... just start in the top right panel and follow the numbers. Have fun, and look for more 100% authentic manga from TOKYOPOP®!